GLOBAL JIHAD AND THE TACTIC OF TERROR ABDUCTION

GLOBAL JIHAD AND THE TACTIC OF TERROR ABDUCTION

A Comprehensive Review of
Islamic Terrorist Organizations

SHAUL SHAY

sussex
ACADEMIC
PRESS
Brighton • Chicago • Toronto

Copyright © Shaul Shay, 2014.

The right of Shaul Shay to be identified as Author of this work has been asserted in accordance with the Copyright, Designs and Patents Act 1988.

2 4 6 8 10 9 7 5 3 1

First published in 2014 by
SUSSEX ACADEMIC PRESS
PO Box 139
Eastbourne BN24 9BP

and in the United States of America by
SUSSEX ACADEMIC PRESS
Independent Publishers Group
814 N. Franklin Street, Chicago, IL 60610

and in Canada by
SUSSEX ACADEMIC PRESS (CANADA)
8000 Bathurst Street, Unit 1, PO Box 30010, Vaughan, Ontario L4J 0C6

All rights reserved. Except for the quotation of short passages for the purposes of criticism and review, no part of this publication may be reproduced, stored in a retrieval system or transmitted in any form or by any means, electronic, mechanical, photocopying, recording or otherwise, without the prior permission of the publisher.

British Library Cataloguing in Publication Data
A CIP catalogue record for this book is available from the British Library.

Library of Congress Cataloging-in-Publication Data
Shay, Shaul.
Global jihad and the tactic of terror abduction : a comprehensive review of Islamic terrorist organizations / Shaul Shay.
 pages   cm
Includes bibliographical references and index.
ISBN 978-1-84519-611-0 (hardback)
 1. Political kidnapping. 2. Qaida (Organization) 3. Islamic fundamentalism. 4. Jihad. I. Title.
HV6431.S4683 2013
363.325—dc23
                                                                    2013028379

Typeset and designed by Sussex Academic Press, Eastbourne.
Printed by TJ International, Padstow, Cornwall.
This book is printed on acid-free paper.

Contents

Preface	xii
1 Terror and Abductions – Theoretical Background	1
Defining Terror	1
Defining Abduction	7
The Goals of Abduction	9
The Modus Operandi	10
The Timing of Abduction	12
Abduction: An Act of War or a Criminal Act?	15
The Dilemma of Hostages, POWs, and Prisoners	17
State Intervention in Abductions	17
2 Al Qaeda and Terror Abductions	21
Al Qaeda and Abduction: The Financial Aspects	21
Al Qaeda Abduction Manual	22
Reasons for detaining one or more enemy individuals	22
Requirements needed to form a kidnapping group	23
Types of kidnapping	23
Stages of public abduction	24
Security measures for public abduction	26
Stages of secret kidnapping	26
Security measures for secret kidnapping	27
How to deal with hostages in both kidnapping types	27
Al Qaeda and the Use of Terror Abduction (2003–12)	28
Summary	31
3 Iran and Terror Abductions	33
Iran's Use of Terror	33
The Iranian Terror System	37
The Islamic Revolution in Iran	38
The Crisis at the American Embassy in Tehran	38
The attack on the embassy (November 1979)	39
Negotiations	40
The rescue (Operation Eagle Claw)	40
The end of the crisis	41
Iranian Involvement in Terror Abductions in Iraq	42

The abduction of five Britons in Baghdad (May 2007)	44
Iranian capture of three British ships and crews (June 2004)	46
Iranian capture of two British ships and sailors (March 2007)	47
Iran's abduction of three American hikers (July 2010)	48
Summary	53

4 Hizballah and Terror Abductions in Lebanon — 58

Hizballah Abductions Against Israel	58
The abduction of two IDF soldiers in Lebanon (February 1986)	59
The Ron Arad affair (October 1986)	60
"Operation Poplar's Whistle" (the Israeli SEALs' debacle) (September 1997)	62
The abduction of three IDF soldiers from Mount Dov (October 2000)	64
Hizballah abduction attempt at Rajar (November 2005)	65
The abduction of two IDF soldiers: The second Lebanon war (July 2006)	67
The Winograd Commission (April 2007)	70
Israel's Efforts to Obtain the Release of IDF Soldiers Held by Hizballah	71
The abduction of Sheikh Abd al Karim Obeid (July 1989)	72
Iranian and Hizballah attempts to release Sheikh Obeid	74
The abduction of Mustafa Dirani (May 1994)	76
The aftermath	76
Reciprocal Links Between Hamas and Hizballah Abductions	77
Israeli Policy Regarding POWs and Hostages	77
The Abduction of Foreign Nationals in Lebanon (1984–91)	80
Imad Muraniya and the attack mechanism	83
The United States	85
The abduction of William Buckley (March 1984)	86
The "Irangate" affair (September 1985)	86
The hijack to Lebanon of TWA flight 847 (June 1986)	89
The abduction of Colonel William Higgins (February 1988)	90
International response	91
The end of the western hostages' affair in Lebanon	95
Links between foreign hostage abductions and Israel	96
Summary	98

5 Terror Abductions in Afghanistan, Pakistan, and India — 102
Abductions in Afghanistan — 102
   Abduction of foreigners — 103
   The abduction of twenty-three South Korean missionaries (July 2007) — 104
   The first American soldier abducted in Afghanistan (June 2009) — 105
   The abduction of two American soldiers (July 2010) — 108
   Abductions in 2010 — 110
   French hostages in Afghanistan — 110
   Taliban prisoners escape from Afghan jails — 112
   Taliban abductions — 113
   Armed attacks on Afghan jails — 113
   Summary — 114
Abductions in Pakistan — 114
   The abduction of Tariq Azizuddin, Pakistani ambassador to Afghanistan (February 2008) — 114
   The abduction of John Solecki, head of Balochistan UNHCR (February 2009) — 115
   The abduction and murder of Daniel Pearl (January 2002) — 115
   The Pakistani Taliban abduct a Swiss couple (July 2011) — 117
   The Aafia Siddiqui affair (December 2002) — 119
   An American aid worker abducted in Pakistan (August 2011) — 123
   Summary — 125
India and the Islamic Terror Threat — 126
   The abduction of Rubaiya Sayeed (December 1989) — 128
   The hijack of Indian Airlines flight 814 (December 1999) — 128
   The Mumbai terror attacks (November 2008) — 129

6 Terror Abductions and Decapitations in Iraq — 142
Fallujah as a Hostage Center — 145
The Coalitions' Approach to the Hostage Issue in Iraq — 146
The Abduction of US Soldiers in Iraq — 148
Plots to Kidnap US Soldiers in Iraq — 149
Abduction and Massacre in a Baghdad Catholic Church (October 2010) — 150
   The rescue operation — 150
   An al Qaeda-affiliated group takes responsibility — 150
   Condemnation — 151
   New threats to the Iraqi and Egyptian Coptic churches — 151
   Summary — 152

	Abductions, Decapitations, and the Media	153
	The Tradition of Decapitation in Islam	154
	Abduction and Decapitation in Iraq from the Religious Aspect	155
7	**Terror Abductions in Saudi Arabia**	162
	The Siege of the Grand Mosque in Mecca	162
	Juhayman ibn Muhammad ibn Sayf al Otaibi	162
	Juhayman and the Mahdi	163
	The takeover of the Grand Mosque (November 1979)	164
	The siege	164
	The Shiite rebellion in east Saudi Arabia	166
	The American response	167
	The American embassy crisis in Pakistan (November 1979)	167
	The Iranian response	168
	The response from the Muslim world	168
	The Soviet invasion of Afghanistan (December 1979)	168
	The assassination of Anwar Sadat (October 1981)	169
	The assassination attempt on Pope John Paul II (May 1981)	169
	Juhayman's movement and al Qaeda in Iraq and Jordan	169
	The Abduction and Murder of Paul Marshall Johnson (June 2004)	170
	The response of Saudi Arabia	171
	The al Khobar Massacre (May 2004)	171
	The al Khobar petroleum center	172
	The Arab Petroleum Investments Corporation building	172
	The Oasis-3 compound	172
	The rescue operation	173
	Saudi Arabian Security Forces Free Two German Girls Kidnapped in Yemen (May 2010)	173
	Al Qaeda in Yemen Urge Kidnappings of Saudi Royals and Christians (June 2010)	174
	The US embassy in Saudi Arabia issues a kidnapping warning to its citizens	174
	A Saudi Diplomat Kidnapped in Yemen (March 2012)	175
8	**Terror Abductions in Yemen**	179
	Yemen and Islamic Terror	179
	The Abduction of Foreign Residents in Yemen	181
	The Arrest of the "British" Terror Network in Yemen (December 1998)	182

The Abduction of Foreign Tourists (December 1998)	182
Three French Aid Workers Abducted in Yemen (July 2011)	185
The French response	186
The release	186
Summary	186
Yemen and the "Arab Spring"	187

9 The "Arab Spring" and Terror Abductions in Syria and Lebanon — 191

The Abduction of Foreign Nationals in Syria	191
The abduction and release of Iranian pilgrims (August 2012)	192
The abduction of two Russians and an Italian (December 2012)	193
The abduction of a Ukrainian journalist (October 2012)	193
The abduction and release of UN peacekeepers (March 2013)	194
The abduction and release of US journalists (December 2012)	195
Abductions and Beheadings in Syria	195
The "Spillover" of Terror Abductions from Syria to Lebanon	196
The abduction of eleven Lebanese pilgrims (May 2012)	197
The abduction of Hassan Salim al Miqdad (August 2012)	197
The abduction of twenty Syrians in Lebanon (August 2012)	198
Summary	198

10 Terror Abductions in the Philippines — 201

The Abu Sayyaf Terror Organization	201
US Involvement in Counter-terror Operations in the Philippines	203
Examples of ASG Abductions	204
The Sipadan kidnapping (May 2000)	204
The abduction and release of American Jeffrey Schilling (August 2000)	205
The Dos Palmas abductions (May 2001)	205
The abduction of three aid workers (January 2009)	206
The abduction of Australian Warren Richard Rodwell (December 2012)	207
The abduction of Jordanian journalist Baker Atyani (June 2012)	208
List of ASG Terror Abductions	209

11 Al Qaeda and Terror Abductions in the Maghreb 214
GSPC and AQIM Abductions (2000–2008) 215
   The abductions of 2009 217
   The abductions of 2010–11 219
The In-Amenas Hostage Crisis in Algeria (January 2013) 222
   The target: In-Amenas gas field 223
   The militants: The "Masked Brigade" 223
   Mokhtar Belmokhtar 224
   The Algerian response 225
   The response of the United States 225
   France 226
   United Kingdom 226
Conclusions 227
Criminal and Terrorist Cooperation in Abductions 228
Summary 229
Recommendations 231

12 Terror Abductions in the Horn of Africa 235
Terror Abductions in Somalia 235
   French security advisors abducted in Somalia (July 2009) 235
The Abduction of Foreign Nationals from Kenya 239
   British woman abducted in Kenya (September 2011) 239
   The abduction of a British couple from their yacht (October 2009) 242
   Disabled French woman abducted in Kenya (October 2011) 243
   The abduction of two Spanish aid workers (October 2011) 245
   The Kenyan armed forces offensive into Somalia (October 2011) 246
   Summary 246
Piracy and Terror in the Gulf of Aden 247
   Piracy in the Gulf of Aden 247
   Al Qaeda and the maritime jihad 248
   Counter-piracy and counter-terrorism 250
Conclusions 250

13 Islamic Terror Abductions in the Russia–Chechnya Conflict 254
Background 254
The Budyonnovsk Hospital Hostage Crisis (June 1995) 257
   The hostage crisis 258
   Resolution of the crisis 258

Casualties	259
Aftermath	259
The Kizlyar–Pervomayskoye Hostage Crisis (January 1996)	259
The Kizlyar airbase raid	260
The Chechen terrorists' breakout	261
The hijack of a Turkish ferry	261
Casualties	261
The Moscow Theater Hostage Crisis (October 2002)	262
The rescue operation	262
Summary	263
The Beslan School Hostage Crisis (September 2004)	264
Day one	264
The beginning of the siege	265
Day two	266
Day three	267
The assault by Russian forces	268
Aftermath	269
The identity of the hostage-takers, motives, and responsibility	269
The hostage-takers	271
The captured terrorist's interrogation and trial	271
Soviet Union and Russian Counter-abduction Doctrine	272
14 Summary and Conclusions	**274**
Points of Emphasis and Lessons to be Drawn	274
Epilogue	**276**
Select Bibliography	285
Index	287

Preface

Occurring shortly before publication, the scope and scale of the September 2013 attacks in the Philippines and Kenya necessitated inclusion in a work of this nature. For discussion of these events, see the Epilogue.

The Mumbai terror assault of 26 November 2008 comprised eleven coordinated shooting, bombing, and hostage-taking attacks by members of the Pakistan-based Lashkar-e-Taiba militant Islamic organization; by its conclusion, 164 people (including foreign nationals) had been killed and at least 308 were wounded. "The hostages are of use only as long as you do not come under fire," a Lashkar-e-Taiba supervisor instructed the gunmen by phone from Pakistan, adding: "If you are still threatened, then don't saddle yourself with the burden of the hostages. Kill them immediately." A gunman replied: "Yes, we shall do so accordingly, God willing." This grim conversation was just one detail subsequently unearthed by Indian authorities investigating the horrific events in Mumbai.

On 16 January 2013, al Qaeda-linked terrorists affiliated with a brigade led by Mokhtar Belmokhtar took more than eight hundred hostages at the Tigantourine gas facility near In-Amenas, Algeria. After four days, Algerian commandos raided the site in a rescue effort: at least thirty-nine foreign hostages were killed (along with an Algerian security guard), while twenty-nine terrorists were killed and three were captured. Algerian Prime Minister Abdelmalek Sellal portrayed the military assault on the Islamist kidnappers as a matter of national character and pride: "The whole world has understood that the reaction was courageous," he said, calling the abductions "an attack on the stability of Algeria". "Algerians are not people who sell themselves out . . . when the security of the country is at stake, there is no possible discussion." Debate over Algerian handling of one of the worst hostage-taking episodes in recent memory reflected conflicting ideas of how to manage such mass abductions in a post-9/11 age of worldwide suicidal terrorist acts.

Algerians – and some western supporters – argue that the loss of innocent lives is unavoidable when confronting fanatics who would kill their captives anyway, while others claim that modern technology can provide means to minimize the death toll.

The two examples above represent a sad reality in today's world –

we coexist daily with many factors that threaten both our safety and security. Among these dangers, terrorism (and terror abduction) represents a major threat to the well-being of individuals, families, businesses, and even states.

Kidnapping constitutes a central component in the "attack repertoire" of terror organizations worldwide. Since the 1980s, in the wake of the Islamic revolution in Iran and the ascent of a terror-supporting regime in that country, Islamic terror entities such as the Lebanese Hizballah organization and the Palestinian Hamas movement have become preeminent in the Middle East (indeed, in the world) in all matters connected to terror in general, and kidnappings in particular.

The first annual report on the UK's strategy for counter-terrorism stated that kidnapping for ransom became an increasingly common terrorist tactic during 2008–12: over 150 foreign nationals had been kidnapped by Islamist groups since 2008, but the number abducted in 2012 (almost fifty) was more than double the total in 2010.[1] The director-general of the UK Office of Security and Counter-terrorism, Charles Farr, said that although Britain refuses to pay, other countries and companies do.[2]

This study addresses Islamic terror kidnappings in the following arenas:

- The Middle East: Israel (in the framework of the Israeli–Hizballah conflict), Lebanon, Syria, Iraq, Iran, Yemen, and Saudi Arabia.
- Asia: Afghanistan, Pakistan, India, and the Philippines.
- Africa: the Maghreb, the Sahel regions, and Somalia.
- Russia: as a part of the Russian–Chechen conflict.

Islamic terror organizations acted, and continue to act, in these arenas, using kidnapping as a means to promote the goals of their organizations and patrons. Kidnapping is a serious criminal business, worth an estimated US$500 million a year (in 2010) and involving a wide range of political, security, social, and economic implications. Furthermore, it is one area which continues to grow when measured by the numbers of victims, criminal profits, and the geographic spread of the problem. Kidnapping is still relatively under-reported and is treated as a series of individual tragedies, rather than a symptom of a wider problem.

The central role of Iran as a state that supports terror, and the use that country makes of kidnappings perpetrated by terror organizations operating under its patronage in order to promote Iranian interests, will be highlighted throughout the analysis to follow, while reciprocal links between Islamic terror organizations and terror-supporting states (in the context of kidnappings) will be examined in detail.

Islamic terror abductions can be categorized according to periods and influential factors:

- Abductions in Lebanon: the Hizballah organization (1983–2012).
- Abductions in Israel: the Hamas movement (1989–2012).
- Abductions in Syria: the "Arab Spring" (2011–12).
- Abductions in Yemen: under the influence of the global jihad (1998–2012).
- Abductions in Saudi Arabia.
- Abductions in Iraq: under the influence of the global jihad (2003–12) and in the aftermath of the invasion of Iraq by coalition forces in 2003.
- Abductions in Afghanistan and Pakistan: under the influence of the global jihad (2001–11) and in the aftermath of the invasion of Afghanistan by coalition forces in 2001.
- Abductions in the Philippines: the Abu Sayyaf organization (1984–2012).
- Abductions in Russia and Chechnya: as part of the Russian–Chechen conflict (1992–2012).
- Abductions in the African Maghreb and Sahel regions: the al Qaeda in the Maghreb organization (2004–12).
- Abductions and piracy in Somalia (2006–13).

Islamic terror organizations regard citizens of foreign countries (mainly western countries and Israeli nationals in the context of the Israeli–Arab conflict in the Lebanese and Palestinian arenas) as prime targets for kidnapping, although local residents constitute the most frequent target of these attacks. The theoretical aspects of the terror phenomenon in general, and kidnappings in particular, will be dealt with extensively.

Kidnappings can be categorized according to various criteria, which include:

- The method of perpetration: overt or covert.
- The kidnapping's purpose: bargaining, murder, or obtaining the means of combat.
- The kidnapper's demands: ransom, political concessions, or the release of prisoners, etc.
- The target of the attack: an individual, or group of individuals, in a building or a public place, airplane, boat, bus, etc.

The challenge issued by terror organizations to those countries whose citizens had been kidnapped, and the way those countries rose to that challenge, will be the central focus of the study that follows.

Notes

1 "CONTEST: The United Kingdom's Strategy for Countering Terrorism", *UK Home Office*, Annual Report, 2012.
2 Simon Israel, "$60m Paid Out in Terrorist Ransoms Since 2008", *News 4*, 26 March 2013.

1

Terror and Abductions
Theoretical Background

Defining Terror

The increasing intensity of international terror since the 1970s and the western democracies' need to understand and contend with this phenomenon led to the development of a research discipline that examines terror from legal, psychological, sociological, historical, and other aspects.[1]

The attacks on the United States of America (US) on 11 September 2001 (9/11) proved a watershed in the international community's approach to the global terror phenomenon, which was transformed overnight from a marginal nuisance to a central threat to world peace. President George W. Bush's "global war against terror", declared shortly after 9/11, defined the struggle against terrorists, terror organizations, and states that support terror as the top priority for the US and the coalition of countries that it heads. The 9/11 attacks exposed the vulnerability of the western world and found it unprepared to deal with the challenges posed by an unrestrained post-modern terrorism that knows no geographical limitations.

The phenomenon of modern terrorism is complex and problematic, and particularly difficult to define. This difficulty stems not from an inability to define terror, but rather that it appears impossible to arrive at a universally acceptable definition.

Various approaches have been adopted to distinguish between definitions, with varying degrees of success. A major differentiation exists between normative and analytical definitions.[2] The normative school bases its definitions on political values, from which it derives standards to judge political actions, and characterizes terrorism in terms of the political context in which it is created; therefore, it defines terror as "unjustified violence against a democratic country that permits effective forms of non-violent resistance".[3] Accordingly, a black man who detonated a bomb in a police station in South Africa during the apartheid period is not to be considered a terrorist, while a member of the Irish Republican Army (IRA) who attacked a British military base is included in the terrorist category. This example highlights the limitations of normative definitions that examine the phenomenon from a subjective point of view, according to which an ally or friend is defined in positive terms (a freedom fighter) while an opponent is defined negatively (a terrorist). Thus the normative definition makes it difficult to define the term "terror" in an unequivocal and universal manner.

Nevertheless, the importance and benefit of the normative definition lies in the standards used to judge the legitimacy of political violence. A key aspect of a state's handling of terrorism is legitimization of its own use of violence and legal nullification of the terrorist's violent challenge.[4] To a great extent, the objective of terrorism is to win legitimacy in the eyes of the population (or part of it) and to negate the legitimacy of the ruling government. Terrorism poses a challenge to a government's right to monopolize power in society and undermines its ability to maintain law and order.[5]

Other issues that stem from the normative approach address the moral aspects of terror. Martha Crenshaw argues that terrorism can best be judged by a moral examination of its consequences alongside a moral examination of its means. Regarding the consequences of terror activity, the criterion is whether the activity aims to establish a just, liberated, democratic government or serves the narrow and deplorable goal of establishing an authoritarian regime that will grant special privileges to a defined group and cause the diminishment of freedom *vis-à-vis* others. Discussion of the morality of means leads to examination of the terrorists' methods and the identities of terror victims in particular. Crenshaw defines two main groups of victims: The first group includes individuals that are vulnerable to terror due to the roles they fulfill within the state apparatus, and as a result are identified (to a certain extent) with the "unjust" policy that the terrorists are fighting. The second group includes citizens who do not play an official role in state operations and citizens of other countries who have no connection with, or direct influence upon, the policy of a "foreign" government. The "transgression" of these people (according to the terrorists) is that they obey the laws of an "unjust" government, thus becoming accomplices to its deeds.

The view of victims of terror constitutes another example of the problematic aspects of normative definitions: the observer's starting point is determined by that individual's moral approach to the case; thus it would appear impossible to develop objective moral judgment *vis-à-vis* the use of terror in various political circumstances. At the very most, one might state that the definition of a deed as an "act of terror" does not in itself constitute a moral or ethical determination regarding its substance.

While the normative school of thought strives to address terror by examining its ethics, the analytical school aims to define the phenomenon by constructing a neutral, theoretical definition general enough to cover the wide variety of terror attack types.

One of the most comprehensive analytical studies of this subject was conducted by Alex Schmid and Albert Jongman.[6] Their research assumed that, despite disagreement on the *definition* of terror, a common denominator existed in customary *views* of terror, and that such commonality could be clear enough to model a language for researchers investigating terrorism. Schmid and Jongman compiled 109 different definitions of terror and conducted a "content analysis" to highlight identical components among them. Their findings indicated the existence of twenty-five similar components: the most prominent of these being the use of violence or force (appearing in 83.5 percent of the definitions), a political goal (in 95 percent), spreading fear (51 percent), threats or psychological pressure (47 percent), addressing differences between the terror victims (37.5 percent), and methodical or planned activity (32 percent).[7]

Schmid and Jongman's compilation of parameters does not in itself suffice to provide an exact definition of the phenomenon of terror, but their list indicated terrorism's main components from which they attempted to construct a definition of terror.[8] The conclusion of their study found that terrorism is a method of assault in which coincidental or symbolic victims serve as instrumental targets for violence, selected according to group characteristics that constitute the terrorists' choice of victims. Previous usage of violence, or a proven threat to use violence, also victimizes other individuals in the target group, due to the state of "chronic fear" in which they are forced to subsist. This indirect method of attack aims to motivate victims to act in accordance with the terrorists' wishes or to induce secondary targets to change their behaviors to accord with the terrorists' goals.[9] Schmid and Jongman's comprehensive study contributed much to understanding terror and mapped the various components of different definitions, but was unable to produce a universal definition of the phenomenon of terror.

In his book, *The Labyrinth of Countering Terror*, Boaz Ganor offers the following definition of terror: "Terror is a type of violent struggle in whose framework intentional use is made of violence towards civilians in order to achieve political (national, social-economic, ideological, religious, and other) goals."[10]

Ganor's three-tier definition is based on the following:

- *The nature of the activity is a type of violent struggle.* According to this definition, any activity that does not involve violence. Demonstrations, protests, and strikes will not be defined as terror.
- *The goal at the basis of terror is always a political one.* From replacing a government by altering a regime or replacing powerful incumbents to revising economic, social, or other policies, terror is designed to achieve aims in the political arena. In the absence of a political goal, an action will not be defined as terror. Violent activity against civilians without a political agenda can only be considered criminal wrongdoing or an act of madness – it is unconnected to terror. The motive behind the political goal is irrelevant to the definition of terror, and can be ideological, religious, national, social, or economic.
- *The target of terror is civilians.* From this aspect, terror is to be differentiated from political violence such as guerilla warfare or popular uprising. The proposed definition emphasizes that terror is not the result of a coincidental attack against civilians who happen to be present in a volatile political arena: it is *primarily targeted* against civilians. Terrorism exploits the relative ease of striking the vulnerable civilian "underbelly" of society – and profits from the media exposure that comes in its wake.

The proposed definition of terror distinguishes between terror and guerilla warfare based on the perpetrators' target. Its most significant distinction is that terror necessitates "intentional use of violence against civilians in order to achieve political goals", while guerilla warfare consists of "a violent struggle in the framework of which use is made of violence targeted against military targets in order to achieve political goals."[11]

The actual goals that terror organizations strive to achieve are irrelevant to the proposed definition of terror (as long as a political goal exists). Both the terrorist and the guerilla fighter may aspire to achieve identical results, but each chooses a different method to realize them.[12] Thus a given organization may simultaneously be a terror organization (if its activities are intended to harm civilians) and a national liberation movement (if its goal is national liberation). The proposed definition of terror hopes to provide means to analyze specific incidents and assist in determining whether events are of a terrorist, or guerilla, nature.[13] Studies of terror's "by-products" such as international and state-supported terrorism exemplify the failure to find a universal definition for the phenomenon of terror.

In the 1970s, two American research institutes attempted to define international terror. The first study, by the RAND Corporation, defined international terror as "a single incident, or a series of incidents, that contravene prevalent law, diplomatic agreements, and the laws of war. The goal of international terror is to draw international attention to the existence of the problem being faced by the terrorists, and to stimulate fear. The aim of terror is to influence or effect a change according to the desires of its perpetrators, and the direct victim of terror is not necessarily identical to the entity that the terrorist factor is attempting to influence."[14] In the second study, researchers at the ITERATE project arrived at a different definition of international terrorism: "Use of, or a threat to use, violence for political purposes by an individual, or a group, acting in favor of, or against, an existing regime. The action is meant to influence a wider target audience than the attack's direct victims, and the victims, perpetrators, and their links know no boundaries."[15]

The various forms of state involvement in terror have been bound together within concepts of terrorist states and state-sponsored terrorism, but these terms over-generalize the varying levels of state involvement in terror. A more focused distinction is required to classify involvement of states in terror according to the following categories:

- *States supporting terrorism.* States that provide terror organizations with financial, ideological, military, or operational aid.
- *States directing terrorism.* States that initiate, direct, or perpetrate terror activities through sponsored organizations while refraining from direct involvement of their government entities in terror actions.
- *States perpetrating terrorism.* States that perpetrate terror through their intelligence and security agencies.

Paul Wilkinson indicates three conditions under which political terror becomes international terror:[16]

- When terror is directed against civilians or foreign targets.
- When terror is perpetrated by a government or an organization connected to more than one state.
- When terror is intended to affect the policy of another foreign state.

According to the above definition, when state-sponsored terror is instigated against one of the targets specified above, such action constitutes a specific case of international terror. Indeed, Wilkinson defines state-supported terror as "the direct or indirect involvement of a government, through formal or informal groups, in the generating of psychological and physical violence against political targets or another state in order to achieve desired tactical and strategic goals".[17]

State-supported terror is characterized by an ambivalent attitude towards international law and order.[18] States that utilize terror are willing to deviate from moral norms and international "rules of the game" in order to strike at their adversary, and hide their involvement to prevent retaliation by the victim.

Cooperation between a state and a terror organization is generally based on religious, ideological, or political solidarity, or on the basis of shared interests. The extent of the patron state's control over the terror organization varies according to the basis of cooperation and the degree that the sponsored organization depends upon its patron. A state's involvement in terror may be direct or indirect, and may be expressed in various levels of moral, political, economic, and operational aid or cooperation. In the majority of cases, links between the patron state and the terror organization are essentially clandestine.

Nationals of other countries are often recruited by a state to make it easier to deny involvement when terror activity is exposed, thus helping to prevent censure and international sanctions. Terror provides an alternative to the use of overt military force to achieve a state's objectives; while a state may support an act of terror against another state with which it is in conflict, terror recruitment may also be applied in situations where countries are not in a declared state of war. Terror is effective in achieving goals unlikely to be attained through direct military confrontation, such as undermining a state's political stability or damaging its diplomatic or economic ties with other countries.

A completely different approach is offered by Edward Luttwak, who maintains that *"terror is inevitably self-defeating"*:[19]

> "When trying to understand terror, the logic behind the strategy is completely futile. Unlike guerrilla warfare, a conventional war, a revolution, a coup – or any other use of force aimed at achieving a goal – terror is nothing but a violent form of self-expression or self-definition, a sort of graffiti etched in mutilation and blood, as rational as is propaganda through action. It may possibly provide emotional satisfaction to those bound to hatred; it can perhaps assuage those who seek vengeance or maybe even supply sensual pleasure to sadists, but it cannot achieve a victory of any kind: not the enemy's surrender, nor his physical conquest or even concessions wrung from him. On the contrary, terror is destined to strike at the target, which terrorists claim to be their goal. The only difference is the extent of the damage, from a severely flawed

public image to utter eradication. . . .[20] When the weak assault those who are strong, it is natural for them to avoid complicated targets, particularly military forces and their bases. They attack civilians and civilian targets indiscriminately. . . ."[21]

What distinguishes between terror and these aspects – which he condemns to futility and irrelevance – is the *source* of the violence. Luttwak continues:

"A handful of extremists can perpetrate terror acts of great magnitude, as was proven on 9/11."

However:

"It is impossible to carry out guerilla warfare with a handful of extremists. In the case of war or revolution or a coup – each according to its own configuration – the number of individuals involved must be significant."[22]

Luttwak then provides the ultimate reason why terror is sterile:

"There is no political or military victory that can be achieved by a handful of extremists who act in isolation – this can be likened to a similar number of Hitlers, without the backing of the Nazi Party."[23]

Defining Abduction

Abduction of individuals for use in bargaining for personal and political goals based on criminal, ideological, religious, or political motives has existed throughout the history of mankind. Kidnapping is a difficult term to define precisely, and legal variations exist in laws and conditions that may be specified or purposely remain general in scope. Standard English dictionaries define kidnapping as "to seize and hold or carry off (a person) against that person's will, by force or fraud, often for ransom".[24] One legal dictionary notes that "kidnapping occurs when a person, without lawful authority, physically moves another person without that other person's consent, with the intent to use the abduction in connection with some other nefarious objective",[25] while another describes kidnap as "an act that unlawfully seizes, confines, moves, decoys, or abducts any person, and detains that person or persons to extort ransom or reward, spotlight an agenda, or compel another involuntary concession".[26] A third definition describes kidnapping as "seizing an individual, or a group of individuals, and keeping them hostage against their will through the threat or actual use of violence, with the aim of achieving the abductors' goals in exchange for their release". Bearing this definition in mind, kidnapping may be perpetrated by abducting an individual or a group of individuals from an "open area", by taking over a building, or hijacking a means of land, marine, or aerial transportation.

Kidnapping is considered to be a complex type of terror attack that requires detailed planning and advanced operational skills, plus an ability to conduct negotiations under pressure, in order to reap the fruits of the action. Many Islamic organizations have made use of kidnapping, targeting both security personnel and civilians. There are differences between the modi operandi used by various terror groups; however, defining terms does not usually provide enough perspective to accurately assess information, conditions, or outcomes.

The three main categories of kidnapper are professional criminals, mentally-disturbed people, and terrorists, but such definitions may easily become blurred as the plans and actions of groups coincide – as when professional criminals work in conjunction with terrorist groups for monetary gain.[27] Kidnapping is a criminal act, yet a professional dialog can identify the purpose and intention of a kidnapping as a means to obtain ransom or revenge, to create social instability, to gain media coverage, or to spotlight an ideological or religious agenda for recognition.

The terrorism of recent decades expanded when abduction became a central modus operandi of worldwide terror organizations. For some Islamic terror organizations, such as Hizballah, abduction triggered discussion of the religious and moral justification for kidnapping civilians – these dilemmas, almost without exception, were resolved by religious decrees justifying the perpetration of abductions as an acceptable tool of the "Islamic struggle".

To a great extent, kidnapping matches the theoretical model that describes terror as a type of theater in which each participant plays a role designated to transmit the terrorists' message. Kidnapping is generally the most prolonged type of terror attack; therefore, it requires the best "script" and "actors" able to adapt to the shifting reality of the developing drama during the course of negotiations. In contrast to rapid, dramatic attacks such as drive-by shootings, throwing grenades, or exploding bombs, abductions are prolonged incidents with characteristic peaks, and involve a dialogue between the abductors, the hostages, the state in charge of the negotiations to release the captives, and additional entities involved in the incident such as mediators, representatives of international organizations, the media, or pressure groups.

In cases of shooting or explosion, governments cannot influence events in "real time" due to the speed of developments. The main activity of a government comes prior to an attack: taking steps to prevent and thwart attacks and, in the immediate aftermath, evacuating the victims or apprehending the assailants. In the case of an abduction, however, a government is forced to enter a complex process of crisis management under a tight schedule while facing moral, political, and military dilemmas and exposure to public and international censure, thus ensuring that kidnapping constitutes a particularly effective tool for terrorists to force their demands onto the agenda of decision-makers and impact their worldview upon local and international public opinion.

Kidnappings are particularly effective at arousing dilemma and necessitating decisions. A terror organization can generate crises in the country of its adversary and in the society of the victim's home country; indeed, kidnapping can sometimes trigger disputes between countries regarding the manner in which negotiations were handled. A terror organization may also constitute a constant threat to its adversary by declaring that similar abductions will follow a previous traumatic kidnapping incident.

This study does not address the entire spectrum of types of kidnapping throughout history, but concentrates instead on the use made of abduction by Islamic terror organizations to promote their goals in the modern age. It does not deal with hijack of means of transportation (airplanes, boats, or land vehicles) that are worthy of a separate, in-depth analysis of their own unique characteristics.

The sections that follow focus on the abduction of civilians and security personnel in different arenas.

The Goals of Abduction

As a rule, the goals of kidnapping are no different than those of other attacks that serve the interests of the terror organization; however, abduction offers certain benefits and "added value" compared with other types of terror attack.

Kidnapping attacks can be classified according to three main categories:

- The goal of the kidnappers.
- The identity of the hostage (the kidnapper's target).
- The modus operandi.

Common goals are:

- Altering reality in the confrontation arena, such as demanding the withdrawal of an adversary from a certain area, cessation of an invasion, or interruption of a process or negotiation.
- Freeing an organization's prisoners in exchange for the release of a hostage or hostages.
- Receipt of a ransom.
- A combination of several demands, including those above among others.

The Modus Operandi

Several main modi operandi used by terror organizations can be identified:

- *Clandestine abduction and bargaining.* The terror organization abducts hostages and the adversary learns of the abduction only after the kidnappers and hostages have been hidden in a "safe place". This method grants the terror organization a clear advantage because as long as the adversary does not know where the hostages are being held, it cannot carry out a direct military raid to release them. This type of attack is usually more prolonged than overt abduction and bargaining attacks.
- *Overt abduction and bargaining.* In this scenario, the terror organization takes hostages in a building or seizes a means of transportation (whether on land, air, or sea). A short time after taking the hostages, or sometimes even during that process, security entities become aware of and begin to contend with the terror activity and negotiations between the abductors and the authorities begin shortly after the actual attack. In this case, the duration of negotiations is shorter than in a covert abduction, and a rapid decision-making process is necessary, able to operate effectively under pressure and maximum media coverage.
- *Capture and negotiation attacks.* A terror cell seizes a private or public building and holds hostage the individuals within it. Negotiations are conducted with the authorities in order to achieve the terror group's goals in exchange for the hostages' release.
- *The seizure of transportation.* One of the most common modi operandi used by terror organizations is the hijack of means of transportation, which offers several obvious advantages:

- Hijacking transportation facilitates the capture of a large number of hostages.
- Hostages are held in a small area under crowded conditions, making rescue difficult.
- A means of transportation provides mobility to the terrorists. As long as the means of transportation is mobile, it is almost impossible to conduct a rescue mission. The drawback is that news of the kidnapping is quickly revealed to the authorities, who will locate the abduction site and prevent movement of the transport. From the moment that the means of transportation is located and immobilized, negotiations will begin between the abductors and the authorities and/or an attack will be launched to free the hostages.

Kidnappings can be classified according to the identity of the hostage (or hostages):

- Members of the security forces (soldiers, policemen, or intelligence agents).
- Civilians (a distinction must be made between government position-holders who are abducted because of their roles and civilians who are randomly abducted).
- Hostages as a chance target or a planned target:
  - A chance target (a civilian or a member of the security forces kidnapped as a random target).
  - A planned target (a civilian or a member of the security forces chosen as a specific target for various reasons). The kidnapping operation is aimed at the chosen target.

Kidnappings can be classed as minor if the number of hostages involved is small, but may also be extensive. This aspect can be depicted according to the following ranking:

1. A *mega-attack* that involves thousands of hostages and several dozen terrorists; for example, the Chechen takeover of a Moscow theater or the school at Beslan in North Ossetia.
2. A *multi-targeted attack* such as the simultaneous hijack of several passenger planes with the aim of kidnapping hundreds of hostages; for example, the attacks by the Popular Front for the Liberation of Palestine in 1968.
3. *The seizure of a public building and scores of hostages* by a terror cell; for example, the attack on the Israeli accommodation sector

at the 1972 Munich Olympic Games by the Palestinian group "Black September".
4. *The abduction of a single hostage* by a small terror cell, involving 2–3 kidnappers assisted by several collaborators.

The Timing of Abduction

Three main categories are indicated by the choice of timing for an abduction:

- *Random timing.* A terror organization will perpetrate a random kidnapping when it has adopted a policy of abducting hostages as part of the organization's struggle. Therefore, when an operational opportunity arises, the organization will abduct hostages, generally as a random target, and use them for negotiation purposes.
- *Planned timing.* A terror organization may plan a kidnapping at a specific time in order to promote the organization's goals and intensify the effect of the abduction. The timing may be chosen to undermine a political process such as the signing of a political agreement, a prime minister's visit, a significant state event such as the hosting of the Olympic Games, or an attempt to sway election results.
- *Timing based on operational constraints.* A terror organization may plan the abduction of a target that is of special importance to the organization. In these circumstances, the timing will stem primarily from the culmination of ideal operational conditions to enable the organization to carry out the abduction successfully.

Types of kidnappings may also be ranked according to the fate of the hostage:

- *Kidnapping for the purpose of bargaining over a live hostage* (with the intention of releasing the abducted individual if the negotiations succeed).
- *Kidnapping for the purpose of bargaining over a body* (negotiating over the body after the murder of the hostage – with or without the adversary's knowledge that the hostage is no longer alive).
- *Kidnapping that begins with negotiations over a live hostage and subsequently (after murder takes place) over the body.* This scenario can evolve if negotiations for the release of a live hostage fail and

the terror organization murders the hostage. The negotiation process continues in order to arrange return of the body.
- *Kidnapping and murder of the hostage without any negotiations.* This type of abduction is perpetrated mainly for the purpose of seizing a hostage's firearm or due to botched plans, etc.

Methods of negotiation can include:

- Negotiation with the actual abductors.
- Negotiation with the organization behind the abduction.
- Anonymous negotiation when the organization is unknown.
- Negotiation via the media.
- Negotiation via a direct intermediary.
- Indirect negotiation via a third party.

In order to achieve the abductors' goals and the release of the hostage(s), the timescale of negotiations can take the form of:

- Negotiations under a deadline and ultimatum.
- Prolonged negotiations that enable the abductors to obtain optimal media and psychological effects. The likelihood of this scenario becomes greater when it is clear to the abductors that their adversary will have a hard time gaining access to them.
- A "postponed" abduction: the announcement of an abduction after a significant delay. Another possible scenario is when an organization holding a hostage publicly denies the abduction but, despite the denial, it is clear that the hostage is in their hands and negotiations are conducted accordingly.

The kidnapping arena can include instances where:

- The site of the abduction or the venue where the hostage is being held is under the state's control.
- The abduction is perpetrated in an area under the state's control, but the hostage and his abductors leave this area in favor of a more secure, "friendly" location.
- The abduction is perpetrated in an area under the control of a third party and the hostage is held by abductors in that state, or alternatively is moved to a state that sympathizes with the terrorists.

A model for the conduct of a kidnapping[28]

	The Terror Organization	The State
1	Preparation for the kidnapping.	The state does not recognize preparations for the attack.
2	Perpetration of the kidnapping.	The family or other entity reports that the "abductee" is missing.
3	The organization that perpetrated the kidnapping claims responsibility.	Verification that the claim of responsibility is authentic.
4	The abductors present their demands for the hostage's release, and set a schedule or ultimatum.	A decision is taken whether to enter into negotiations or to refrain from doing so. Intense searches to find the hostage and the abductors. Pressure is placed on the organization that perpetrated the abduction.
5	Negotiations are conducted.	If such a decision is taken, negotiations are initiated with the organization or the abductors.
6	Thwarting a rescue operation. The abductors will strive to prevent military action by threatening to harm the hostage. During a rescue attempt, the abductors will try to shoot both the rescuers and the hostage. An attempt may be made by the abductors to escape during or after the rescue operation.	If the negotiations fail, or alternatively if a decision is taken to refrain from negotiations, then the state will initiate a military operation in an attempt to rescue the hostage.

The stages of a kidnapping will (most likely) include the following:

- *The planning stage.* Definition of the abduction's goal, the target, the modus operandi, the area where the abduction will be perpetrated, the hideaway where the hostage(s) and the abductors will stay, escape routes, and how to handle negotiations.
- *The preparation stage.* Recruitment of terror cell members, supply of weapons and equipment required for the abduction, preparation of the logistical infrastructure and the hideaway, renting or purchasing vehicles, patrols to become familiar with the area of the attack as well as learning approach and escape

routes, and establishing communications between the perpetrating cell and the organization's headquarters.
- *Perpetration of the kidnapping.* Abduction of the target and neutralization of the hostage(s), transporting them to the hideaway, and reporting successful completion of the operation to the organization's headquarters.
- *Conducting negotiations.* Supplying details identifying the hostage(s) to the entity conducting the negotiations, conduction of negotiations by senior members of the organization (sometimes by the abductors themselves), conducting psychological warfare via the media, and setting an ultimatum to meet the organization's demands. During negotiations, the hostage(s) may be injured, tortured, or even murdered.
- *Concluding the kidnapping incident.* There are several possibilities:
    ♦ Attainment of the abduction's goals, the hostage's release in exchange for the former, and the "disappearance" of the abductors.
    ♦ In the event of military action against the perpetrators, their elimination, and the hostage's release, the terror organization will strive to extract maximum media advantage despite the abduction's failure.
- *Drawing conclusions.* Learning details of the abduction process, examining points of success and failure, and implementing these lessons in the planning and perpetration of future abductions.

Abduction: An Act of War or a Criminal Act?

One of the dilemmas faced by terror researchers is the question of whether a terror attack is to be considered a "criminal act", an "act of war", or a "semi-act of war". In the latter two cases, handling of the event would stem from the norms and laws of warfare. Kidnapping is perhaps the most salient instance connected with this dilemma, particularly in cases where a terror organization demands ransom money in exchange for the release of hostages. In such an event, distinctions that may be made between a kidnapping for criminal reasons and a "terrorist" abduction become hazy.

There is disagreement among researchers as to whether terror should be considered as a criminal act or as deriving from an act of war. Both approaches have far-reaching implications regarding the ability to contend with the phenomenon of terror. On the one hand, the "criminal approach" entails routine police and legal procedures of compiling evidence, arresting the offender, and arraignment – that is, local processes deal with the transgressor. On the other hand, the "act of war" approach attributes less importance to individual guilt and identifies the terrorists, according to their grouping and organizational affiliation, as an enemy in a state of war. In such an event, it is legitimate for security entities to use any means available to protect the security of the state's citizens.

Each of these approaches has prominent advantages and disadvantages:

- *The "criminal approach"*, where the advantage lies in a state's adherence to stringent norms of equality in the eyes of the law and strict measures are established by law enforcement agencies regarding arrest and indictment of suspects. This approach effectively prevents authorities from manipulating the law and deters legal authorities from acting on the basis of political motives. The main drawback of this approach is that it impairs the effectiveness of security agencies attempting to respond to challenges posed by terror organizations.
- *The "national approach"*, which distinguishes between terror activity and criminal activity, attributes a completely different meaning to a terror attack even if there is no actual difference in the act itself or its consequences. Such an approach advocates granting considerable leeway to security agencies and enables such steps as the use of force – an unacceptable approach when dealing with criminals. The advantage of the "national approach" lies in the greater scope of effectiveness it affords to its security agencies. Its greatest drawback is a danger that authorities may employ draconian measures against not only an external foe, but may also take advantage of the situation to attain illicit domestic political goals. Either way, the clearest distinction between a criminal act and a terrorist attack lies in defining the goal that the deed is meant to achieve.

There is little dispute that, in contrast to criminal activity, terror is enacted to impose a political agenda – the motivation behind terror activity is not personal or group benefit that may be derived from the act. Nevertheless, terror poses a threat to personal and public safety as well as to the existing governmental order, thus constituting a substantially different threat to society than criminal offenses. Even if terror abductions are identical to criminal kidnappings from the aspect of their modus operandi, their context is different because they intervene on the political level via demands directly (or indirectly) connected to the overall struggle between the terror organization and the rival state. Thus each demand is examined not only from the point of view of its nominal significance, but also from the wider contexts of national security and international relations. In consequence, the decision-makers' approach to a terrorist abduction is inherently different from their reaction to a similar criminal incident, due to fears of political repercussions after the incident's ultimate resolution and how those factors may influence the future conflict between the opponents.

The Dilemma of Hostages, POWs, and Prisoners

The term "prisoner of war" (POW) suggests a state of armed conflict between states and thus the application of international rules related to such POWs. A prisoner of war is granted clear rights: he must be respected humanely and diplomatically, torture is illegal, and minimal information about prisoners is provided to the enemy. Chapter II of the annex to the Hague Convention (1907) covers the treatment of POWs, while Article 4 of the Third Geneva Convention (1949) defines the rights of captured military personnel, some guerrilla fighters, and certain civilians. This status, which is subject to international law, proposes a whole umbrella of negotiation strategies and diplomatic relations with the enemy.[29] However, a situation of a soldier abducted by a terrorist organization suggests a whole different configuration: it is an unlawful act that can be considered severe enough to legitimize the use of conventional forces against the kidnappers. According to the main dilemmas regarding a terror attack (whether it is to be considered as a "criminal act", an "act of war", or a "semi-act of war"), the "national approach" (as opposed to the criminal approach) advocates granting considerable leeway to security agencies and enabling such steps as the use of force.

State Intervention in Abductions

Previously we offered a detailed discussion of the definition of terror in general, and state terror in particular. This part of our study will address state involvement in abductions.

Each abduction or bargaining incident begins and ends in a sovereign state. This fact stands true even when the abduction is perpetrated in an international zone (such as when a ship or an airplane is hijacked), due to the fact that the perpetrators originated from a sovereign state and will ultimately find refuge in that state's territory. State involvement in abduction may be expressed in various ways:

- The "*state as a victim*". The abduction takes place in the territory of a state, against state targets, in order to force decision-makers to give in to the demands of the terror organization which the abductors represent.
- The "*state as the venue of the incident*". The abduction occurs in the state's territory, but the state is not the terrorists' target. This type of situation may exist with the state's blessing (for example, when a state is willing to allow a hijacked aircraft to land in its territory) or against its will, when it finds itself facing the fact that the abductors and hostage(s) are located in its sovereign territory.
- The "*state as initiator or supporter of a kidnapping*". This scenario relates to a state which supports terror and stands directly or indirectly behind the abduction. This scenario will be discussed extensively in the coming chapters.

A state may be involved in a kidnapping even without a territorial link to the incident, as when enemy state nationals fall victim to deliberate or random abduction. Another possibility is when the abductors are citizens of the state and, although they may not be acting on its behalf (and generally break its laws), their nationality involves their country in the incident.

As a rule, one can distinguish between two types of kidnappings:

- *A local incident* in which the abductors and hostages are nationals of the state where the incident occurs.
- *An international incident* in which citizens of various states are involved and/or the incident moves through the territories of several states before final resolution.

If an incident is sponsored by a state that supports terror or is perpetrated with a state's consent and knowledge, it can aid the terror organization behind the incident in various ways:

- As a departure base for the abductors.
- Collecting intelligence about the abduction target.
- Providing financial aid.
- Training the perpetrators.
- Supplying weapons.

- Providing documents to enable freedom of movement to the terrorists.
- Assistance in negotiating between the abductors and the target state.
- Guaranteeing refuge for the terrorists after the incident's conclusion.

States that support terror will generally aspire to conceal and downplay their involvement in terror incidents, thus most of the above-mentioned aid options will be provided covertly to refrain from leaving incriminating "fingerprints" pointing to a state's involvement.

During the course of an abduction or bargaining incident, the preferred position of a state that supports terror will be that of an "intermediary". In such cases, the state that supports terror declares that it is not involved in the terror attack, but is offering its "humanitarian" aid to help resolve the problem. In the event that its proposal to serve as "broker" is accepted, it can derive maximum benefit from the attack: the state does not take responsibility for the incident, but becomes partner to the negotiations and gains an ability to influence those results according to its own interests – thus profiting from an attack in which it served as an accomplice from the start. The state that has most frequently adopted this tactic is Iran, mainly in connection with the abduction of western hostages in Lebanon, but also during abductions perpetrated against Israel by its sponsored organizations.[30]

NOTES

1 This section is based on Shaul Shay, *Islamic Terror Abductions in the Middle East* (Eastbourne: Sussex Academic Press, 2008).
2 Martha Crenshaw, *Terrorism, Legitimacy and Power* (Middletown, CT: Wesleyan University, 1983), pp. 1–4.
3 Crenshaw, *Terrorism*, p. 3.
4 *Ibid.*, p. 1.
5 *Ibid.*, p. 2.
6 Alex Schmid and Albert Jongman, *Political Terrorism: A New Guide To Actors, Authors, Concepts, Data Bases, Theories, And Literature* (New Brunswick: Transaction Publishers, 2005).
7 *Ibid.*
8 *Ibid.*, p. 10.
9 *Ibid.*, p. 11.
10 Boaz Ganor, *The Labyrinth of Countering Terror: Tools for Decision Making* (Herzliya: Mifalot Publishing, IDC, 2005), p. 32.
11 *Ibid.*, pp. 32–33.
12 *Ibid.*, p. 35.

13 *Ibid.*
14 "The RAND Corporation Database of Worldwide Terrorism Incidents", *Chronology of International Terrorism*, http://www.rand.org/nsrd/projects/terrorism-incidents.html (n.d.).
15 "International Terrorism: Attributes of Terrorism Events", *ITERATE Project*, Duke University Libraries (n.d.).
16 Paul Wilkinson, *Terrorism and the Liberal State* (London: Macmillan Education Ltd., 1997), p. 182.
17 *Ibid.*
18 Ray S. Cline and Yonah Alexander, *Terrorism as a State-sponsored Covert Warfare* (Fairfax, VA: Hero Books, 1986), pp. 110–111.
19 Edward Luttwak, *Strategy: The Logic of War and Peace* (Cambridge, MA: Harvard University Press, 2001), pp. 11–13.
20 *Ibid.*
21 *Ibid.*
22 *Ibid.*
23 *Ibid.*
24 "Uniform Code of Military Justice, Article 134, Predefined Offenses – Kidnapping", *Library of Congress*, Military Legal Resources, http://usmilitary.about.com/od/punitivearticles/a/134_3.html;
and http://www.loc.gov/rr/frd/Military_Law/UCMJ_LHP.html. Accessed 17 April 2008.
25 "Kidnapping and Terror in the Contemporary Operational Environment", *US Army Training and Doctrine Command* (TRADOC) G-2 Handbook No. 16, 15 September 2008, pp. 1–9.
26 *Ibid.*
27 Norman Antokol and Mayer Nudell, *No One A Neutral: Political Hostage-Taking in the Modern World* (Medina, OH: Alpha Publications of Ohio, 1990), p. 24.
28 This is a relatively simple model that addresses a scenario in which a single hostage is abducted for negotiation purposes within the boundaries of a state with whose government the negotiations are conducted.
29 "Convention (III) Relative to the Treatment of Prisoners of War", *International Committee of the Red Cross* (ICRC), Geneva, 12 August 1949.
30 Shaul Shay, *The Axis of Evil: Iran, the Hizballah and Palestinian Terror* (New Brunswick: Transaction Publishers, 2005).

2
Al Qaeda and Terror Abductions

Osama bin Laden and al Qaeda's senior commanders understood the high potential of kidnapping as a strategic asset against their adversaries after suffering the consequences of their latest modus operandi developed for the 9/11 attacks: hijacking four airplanes and using them as "cruise missiles" to hit the strategic US targets of the World Trade Center and the Pentagon. Since the 9/11 attacks, al Qaeda has not repeated this type of hijacking, but has adopted kidnapping, mainly of western civilians and military staff, as a major tactic in its war of attrition against the "West".

Al Qaeda and Abduction: The Financial Aspects

After 9/11, al Qaeda was crippled by the US-led global squeeze on banks and financial institutions suspected of aiding the terrorist network. Since then, al Qaeda has financed itself mainly through private donors, large and small. The large donors are rich, sympathetic, private individuals in the Gulf states, while small donors are numerous throughout the Islamic world – Muslims inspired by bin Laden's anti-western rhetoric who fulfill their vow of *zakat* (charity) by giving alms to organizations loosely tied to al Qaeda.[1]

During the post-9/11 years in hiding, al Qaeda relied on cash couriers, most of whom were Pashtuns from the Afghan–Pakistan tribal areas. Scores of al Qaeda fighters married into these Pashtun clans. According to a tribal elder in South Waziristan, arrangements were made for these relatives to pick up suitcases filled with cash from sympathizers in the Gulf states during the annual *hajj* pilgrimage to Mecca in Saudi Arabia and pass them onto al Qaeda, but the amount transferred in this manner was a mere trickle compared with the millions of dollars received by al Qaeda before the international financial crackdown.[2]

In an August 2009 video, al Qaeda beseeched its supporters in Pakistan to "back the jihad and mujahideen with your persons, wealth, opinion, expertise, information, and prayers". In 2010, senior al Qaeda commander Mustafa Abu al Yazid appeared on a website pleading for cash: "If a holy fighter does not have the money to get weapons, food, drink, and the materials for jihad, he cannot fight jihad," he explained, while newspaper reports claimed that wannabe European jihadists were each charged US$1,200 by al Qaeda training camps in Pakistan.[3] The financial constraints suffered by al Qaeda since 9/11 certainly increased the significance of ransom money to the organization.

Al Qaeda Abduction Manual

Since 1996, several al Qaeda operational manuals have fallen into the hands of US and western security services – all state that kidnapping is a preferred modus operandi of the organization.

In 2004, al Qaeda published the tenth issue of its *al Battar* ("The Winner") online training manual. This terror road map included a simple, yet detailed, "Kidnapping for Dummies" guide,[4] written by Abdul Aziz al Muqrin, the commander of al Qaeda's offshoot in Saudi Arabia who was killed in June 2004.

The text from the section on abduction follows:

Reasons for detaining one or more enemy individuals

- Force the government or the enemy to succumb to some demands.
- Put the government in a difficult situation that will create political embarrassment between the government and the countries of the detainees.
- Obtaining important information from the detainees.
- Obtaining ransoms. Such was the case with the brothers in the Philippines, Chechnya, and Algiers. Our brothers from Muhammad's Army in Kashmir received a ransom of two million dollars that provided good financial support to the organization.
- Bringing a specific case to light. This happened at the beginning of the cases in Chechnya and Algeria, with the hijacking of the French plane, and in the kidnapping operations performed by the brothers in Chechnya and the Philippines.

Requirements needed to form a kidnapping group

- Capability to endure psychological pressure and difficult circumstances. In case of public kidnapping, the team will be under a lot of pressure.
- Intelligence and quick reflexes in order to deal with an emergency.
- Capability to take control over the adversary. The brother is required to possess fighting skills that will enable him to paralyze the adversary and seize control of him.
- Good physical fitness and fighting skills.
- Awareness of the security requirements, prior to, during, and after the operation.
- Ability to use all types of light weapons for kidnapping.

Types of kidnapping

Secret kidnapping. The target is kidnapped and taken to a safe location that is unknown to the authorities. Secret kidnapping is the least dangerous. Such was the case of the Jewish reporter, Daniel Pearl, who was kidnapped from a public place, then transferred to another location. It was also the case of our brothers in Chechnya who kidnap [*sic*] the Jews in Moscow, and the kidnapping operations in Yemen.

Public kidnapping. This is when hostages are publicly detained in a known location. The government surrounds the location and conducts negotiations. The authorities often attempt to create diversions and attack the kidnappers. That was the case of the theater in Moscow, and the Russian officers' detention by Shamil Basayev and the mujahideen brothers.

A counter-terrorism officer once said: "There never was a successful kidnapping operation in the world." This saying was intended to discourage the so-called terrorists. History is full of facts proving the opposite. Many operations by the Mafia and the mujahideen were successful. There are examples of many successful operations, such as those of Muhammad's Army, and Shamil in Moscow. Although not all the goals were met, some of them were. The operation of the leader, Shamil Basayev, was 100 percent successful because it brought the case back to the attention of the international media; therefore, the mujahideen got their reward, thanks to God.

Stages of public abduction

Determining the target. A target must be suitably chosen, to force the government to submit to your demands. Therefore, it is mandatory to make sure the kidnapped individuals are important and influential.

Gathering information about the location (kidnapping stage), and the people inside it. For example:

- *If the people are inside a building:* A thorough study must be made of the fences around the building, as well as the security teams and systems. A plan of the building with information on its partitions should be reviewed. The kidnappers could use cars that enter the building without inspection to smuggle their equipment. They should also identify individuals who are exempt from inspection when entering the building. When cars are parked outside the building, the driver could be kidnapped while parking, or the important people when entering with their cars. High places overlooking the building could be set for snipers, and to prevent the enemy from taking advantage of those strategic spots.
- *If the people are on a bus:* It is essential to know the nationalities of all the people on the bus, as these determine the effect of the operation. All information concerning the bus routing, stops for fuel or rest, protection procedures, the program set for the tourists, and other information should be obtained in order to determine the weak spots, and allow easy control of the group.
- *If the target is on a plane:* It is important to determine the destination of the plane. A connecting flight is a better option. Transit areas are more vulnerable where little inspection is provided. Our brothers in Nepal took advantage of such situation, put the weapons on the Indian plane, and hijacked it. Hijackers must be creative in bringing weapons or explosives onto a plane. They must also be familiar with the inspection process at airports.
- *If the target is in a convoy:* The same rules for assassination in a convoy apply for kidnapping.

Besides specifying the targets and gathering information on them, leaders must put together a suitable plan made at the level of the weakest team member. It has been said: "A chain is only as strong as its weakest link."

Execution of the abduction. The abductors' roles vary, based on the location of the kidnapping operation. They are grouped into three categories:

- The protection group, whose role is to protect the abductors.
- The guarding and control group, whose role is to seize control of the hostages, and dispose of them in case the operation fails.
- The negotiating group, whose role is extremely important and sensitive. The leader of this group is generally the negotiator; he conveys the mujahideen's demands, and must be intelligent, decisive, and determined.

Negotiations. The enemy uses the best negotiator he has, who is normally very sly and knowledgeable in human psychology. He is capable of planting fear in the abductors' hearts, in addition to discouraging them. Kidnappers must remain calm at all times, as the enemy negotiator will resort to stalling in order to give the security forces time to come up with a plan to storm the hostages' location. The duration of the detention should be minimized to reduce the tension on the abducting team. The longer the detention is, the weaker the willpower of the team is, and the more difficult control over the hostages is. One of the mistakes that the Red Army made in the Japanese Embassy in Lima, Peru – where they detained a large number of diplomats – was to allow the hostage situation to continue for over a month. In the meantime, the storm team excavated tunnels under the embassy, and was able to liberate the hostages and end the kidnapping. In case of any stalling, starting to execute hostages is necessary. The authorities must realize the seriousness of the kidnappers, and their dedicated resolve and credibility in future operations.

Hostage exchange process. This is a very delicate stage. If the enemy submits to the demands, and the purpose of the operation is to release our imprisoned brothers, it is essential to make sure that the brothers are in a good and healthy condition. If the purpose of the kidnapping is to obtain money, you have to ensure that all the money is there, that it is not fake, nor traceable. You must be sure there are no listening or homing devices planted with the money. The brothers must be constantly on alert for possible ambushes. In Bosnia, the UN set up an ambush for the brothers during the exchange; however, the brothers were prepared for it, and prepared a counter-ambush. When the enemy realized the brothers' readiness and high state of alert, they let the hostages go without interception. Our jihadi operations have proven that security forces are not capable of completely seizing control inside the cities; therefore, the brothers should find ways to transport their liberated brothers, even under tight security measures.

Hostage release. The brothers should be careful to not release any hostage until they have received their own people. It is essential for the brothers to abide by our religion and keep their word, as it is not allowed for them to kill any hostage after our demands and conditions have been met.

Withdrawal process. For the withdrawal, some hostages – preferably the most important – must be detained until the brothers have safely withdrawn.

Security measures for public abduction

- Detention must not be prolonged.
- In case of stalling, hostages must be gradually executed, so that the enemy knows we are serious.
- When releasing hostages such as women and children, be careful, as they may transfer information that might be helpful to the enemy.
- You must verify that the food transported to the hostages and kidnappers is safe. This is done by making the delivery person and the hostages taste the food before you. It is preferable that an elderly person or a child brings in the food, as food delivery could be done by a covert special forces' person.
- Beware of the negotiator.
- Stalling by the enemy indicates their intention to storm the location.
- Beware of sudden attacks, as they may be trying to create a diversion which could allow them to seize control of the situation.
- Combat teams will use two attacks: a secondary one just to attract attention, and a main attack elsewhere.

In case your demands have been met, releasing the hostages should be made only in a place that is safe for the hostage takers.

- Watch out for the ventilation or other openings as they could be used to plant surveillance devices through which the number of kidnappers could be counted, or gases could be used.
- Do not be emotionally affected by the distress of your captives.
- Abide by Muslim laws as your actions may become a *dawa* [a call to join Islam].
- Avoid looking at women captives.

Stages of secret kidnapping

They are very similar to the stages for public kidnapping:

- Specifying the target.

Al Qaeda and Terror Abductions   27

- Collecting enough information on the target.
- Setting the plan and providing appropriate training.
- The execution team must be formed of five groups: the watching group, which reports the movements of the target; the protection group, which protects the kidnappers from any external intervention; the kidnapping group, which kidnaps the target and delivers him to a shelter group; the sheltering group, whose role is to keep an eye on the hostage [*sic*] until it is time for exchange or to get rid of them; the pursuit deterring group, which will ensure the shelter group is not followed or watched.
- Transporting the target to a safe place.
- Getting rid of the target after the demands have been met by transporting him to a safe place from which he can be freely released. The hostage should not be able to identify the place of his detention.

Security measures for secret kidnapping

- The location where the hostage is transferred to must be safe.
- Beware of the police patrols.
- While the hostage is being transported, you must beware of police patrols by identifying their points of presence, to avoid sudden inspection.
- Look for listening or homing devices that VIPs often carry on their watches or with their money. A VIP could have an earpiece microphone that keeps him in touch with his protection detail.
- Everything you take from the enemy must be wrapped in a metal cover, and should only be unwrapped in a remote place far from the sheltering group.
- Never make contact from the location where the hostage is detained, and never mention him during phone calls.
- Use an appropriate cover to transport the hostage to and from the location. At some point in time the Hizballah were drugging the hostage and transporting him in an ambulance.
- It is imperative to not allow the hostage to know where he is. In this case, it is preferable to give him an anesthetizing shot or knock him unconscious.

How to deal with hostages in both kidnapping types

- You must search the hostages and take possession of any weapon or listening device.
- Separate the young people from the old, the women, and the

children; the young people have more strength, hence their ability to resist is high. The security forces must be killed instantly; this prevents others from showing resistance.
- Deal with the hostages in a lawful manner.
- Do not approach the hostages. In case you must, you need to have protection, and keep a minimum distance of one-and-a-half meters from them.
- Speak in a language or dialect other than your own, in order to prevent revealing your identity.
- Cover the hostage's eyes so that he cannot identify you or any other brothers.
- Wire the perimeter of the hostage location to deny access to the enemy.

[At the end of this section, *al Battar* provides information about the jihad and directions to those wishing to join the mujahideen.]

Al Qaeda and the Use of Terror Abductions (2003–12)

The terror manuals produced by al Qaeda were implemented by its branches and allies in a worldwide abduction campaign in Afghanistan and Pakistan, the Philippines, Iraq, Yemen, Saudi Arabia, North Africa, Somalia, and Nigeria. In recent years, Osama bin Laden and other senior al Qaeda commanders publicly threatened their enemies that the organization would kidnap citizens of western countries if the governments of those countries did not respond to al Qaeda's demands. Following are several examples:

The US Soldier in Afghanistan (September 2009): A senior al Qaeda official called on the Taliban to wage a campaign of kidnapping foreign civilians in Afghanistan in order to force US-led forces to negotiate prisoner exchanges.[5] The directive was issued by veteran al Qaeda advisor Mustafa Hamid (also known as Abu Walid al Masri) and stemmed from the US detentions in Guantanamo Bay, according to former counterterrorism analyst Leah Farrall, quoting an al Qaeda internet document written in late July 2009 that she uncovered while completing a doctorate on al Qaeda at Monash University in Australia.

The document, entitled "The US Soldier in Afghanistan: The First Step for the Release of All Prisoners of the War on Terror," argued that the capture of a US soldier in 2009 should be used as a precedent in a campaign of abducting western civilians to negotiate the release of Taliban and al Qaeda prisoners. Directing his article at the Taliban's leadership, al Masri said it was "time for them to start targeting foreign civilians as well as military personnel". He suggested that they, too, change the rules of the game as America had done and stated that it was now permissible to take foreign civilians from the street; this strategy, he advised, could result in the liberation of all prisoners held by the US in its war on terror. Al Masri argued that America's detention and torture of Muslims, and its failure to distinguish between civilians and the military, justified the use of this new strategy, saying the Taliban should "do as its enemy does".

A tape from al Qaeda leader Osama bin Laden (broadcast on 25 March 2010): The tape warned of stepped-up kidnapping and killing if the US executed Khalid Sheikh Mohammed, mastermind of the 9/11 attacks. If the US decided to execute Mohammed or other alleged al Qaeda members, "it will have taken a decision to execute whomever we capture", bin Laden said in the tape, broadcast by *al Jazeera*. He claimed that US President Obama was "following in the footsteps of his predecessor" George W. Bush with regard to escalation of the war in Afghanistan and the treatment of US prisoners: "The politicians in the White House were practicing injustice against us, and they still are, particularly in their support for Israel in its continued occupation of Palestine."[6] White House spokesman Robert Gibbs said that President Obama had already increased pressure on the al Qaeda network and "will continue to keep up the pressure to destroy it". "We see that al Qaeda has nothing to spread but hate," Gibbs said.[7]

A senior member of al Qaeda in Yemen released an audio message to sympathizers in Saudi Arabia (June 2010): In an audiotape distributed through the Dubai-based *al Arabiya* news channel, senior Yemeni al Qaeda commander Saeed al Shehri urged "major operations" against the Saudi kingdom after the arrest of Hayla al Qassir, widow of an al Qaeda operative who had been killed six years previously, who was accused of recruiting women for the militant group and responsibility for the group's finances. Al Shehri urged followers to kidnap members of the Saudi royal family and Christians: "Form cells to kidnap Christians and princes from the Saud family, and their top officials of ministers and officers. We tell our soldiers: 'You have to kidnap in order to release the prisoners,'" he said. "Stop knocking at the doors of the tyrants and their deviant *ulemas* [Muslim scholars]. If you want your relatives to be released from prison, they will only be out by the same way they were taken in."[8]

An audio recording attributed to bin Laden (released to *al Jazeera* on 27 October 2010): Bin Laden called on the people of France to stop "interven[ing] in the affairs of Muslims in North and West Africa". "The subject of my speech is the reason why your security is being threatened and your sons are being taken hostage," he said. "The taking of your experts in Niger as hostages, while they were being protected by your proxy [agent] there, is a reaction to the injustice you are practicing against our Muslim nation." He continued: "How could it be fair that you intervene in the affairs of Muslims, in North and West Africa in particular, support your proxies [agents] against us, and take a lot of our wealth in suspicious deals, while our people there suffer various forms of poverty and despair?" Bin Laden also used the latest recording to criticize France's plan to ban the wearing of full face veils in public (a law due to be implemented the following year): "If you unjustly thought that it is your right to prevent free Muslim women from wearing the face veil, is it not our right to expel your invading men and cut their necks?" He used the taped message to urge France to withdraw from Afghanistan, calling it an "unjust war", and pledged more kidnappings if his warnings were not heeded: "The equation is very clear and simple: as you kill, you will be killed; as you take others hostages, you will be taken hostages; as you waste our security, we will waste your security."[9] Al Qaeda's North African wing claimed responsibility for the September 2010 kidnappings of five French nationals, along with two others from Madagascar and Togo, and released photographs of the group in late September, showing the hostages sitting on the sand as several armed men dressed in Bedouin clothing stood behind them.[10]

An audio message (broadcast on *al Jazeera* on 21 January 2011): Osama bin Laden demanded that France withdraw its troops from Afghanistan in exchange for the release of French hostages held by al Qaeda affiliates:[11]

> "My message to you, today and in the past, is one and the same: the release of your prisoners held by our brothers is dependent upon the withdrawal of your troops from our countries. If you consider this a political dictate and 'despicable terrorism' while you consider the expulsion of Hitler's forces from your lands an act of heroism and 'blessed terrorism', then you are applying a double standard.
>
> "Oh, the French people, your president's refusal to withdraw from Afghanistan stems from his subordination to the US. By this refusal, [Sarkozy] has given the go-ahead for the immediate killing of your prisoners, so he could rid himself of the prisoners' case and its consequences. Nevertheless, we will not do it at the time determined by him. This position of his will cost both him and you dearly on several fronts, in France as well as abroad. You know full well that, given the extent of your debts and the weakness of your economy, you can do without opening new fronts."[12]

Summary

Since 2002, al Qaeda has adopted a new strategy of inflicting a war of attrition upon the US and her western allies. Due to the operational weakness of al Qaeda and its affiliated jihadi groups, they continue to fixate on attacking soft targets and kidnapping western citizens. Kidnapping may serve a purpose on several levels of conflict: al Qaeda in the Islamic Maghreb, al Qaeda of the Arabian Peninsula, al Qaeda in Iraq, and al Shabaab in Somalia openly target foreign nationals in their regional areas of operations. In selecting easy targets to kidnap, terrorists plan to exploit the media as an additional pressure on negotiators to agree to terrorist demands in exchange for release of kidnapped victims. Abduction of foreign nationals almost guarantees media attention, wherever the crime is committed.

The anxiety caused by the unknown condition of kidnap victims is a deliberate tactic, and extended timescales can increase the notoriety of a particular terrorist group and its agenda. After long periods of no information, terrorist techniques may include sending a videotape, or severed body parts of kidnapped victims, to their adversary. This grim technique was demonstrated in March 2008, when the severed fingers of several civilian contractors were sent to US military forces in Iraq.[13]

The abduction of contractors, tourists, and other foreign nationals can have a significant impact on foreign investment in a region. On a practical level, kidnapping can be a lucrative means to self-finance terrorism using ransom payments for the release of victims. Payment of large ransoms to kidnappers, reportedly of millions of euros or US dollars, are ever more frequent events.[14] Conversely, announcements by terror group leaders may proclaim loftier ideological goals that accord with their sense of theological righteousness or promulgate collective action in conjunction with other al Qaeda affiliates, in the belief that these acts will yield further recognition of their cause and enhance the negative psychological and physical effects that kidnapping creates upon ". . . our enemies . . . and apostates and crusaders".[15]

Al Qaeda is forcing its adversaries to increase expenditure to fund the escalating cost of the worldwide "war on terror". Such tactics keep security costs high and effectively threaten to bankrupt the west during this current period of economic austerity.

Groups associated with al Qaeda have become more transnational in their operational scope and targets. Associated groups such as al Shabaab, al Qaeda in the Arabian Peninsula, and al Qaeda in the Islamic Maghreb have extended their geographic reach from the regional level to the global. These groups are more than local franchises of al Qaeda; they operate independently, executing their own initiatives. It is likely that such regional groups associated with al Qaeda could reach out ever further to become more international, kidnapping western citizens and security servicemen, and perhaps even conducting attacks within the US and Europe.

Al Qaeda and its allies have found kidnapping to be one of the most "cost effective" assets against their adversaries; therefore, abduction will remain a strategy, tactic, technique, and procedure of al Qaeda and other jihadi terror organizations to intimidate and extort people, and to create anxiety, fear, and mayhem in support of their immediate, intermediate, and long-term objectives.

The charismatic figure of bin Laden was always the main source of inspiration for potential donors; his death will be followed by a reduction in donations, thus forcing the organization to find alternative financial sources and increasing the importance of ransom money raised by abductions.

Notes

1 "Al Qaeda's Big Post-Bin Laden Cash Crunch", *Time Magazine*, 3 May 2011.
2 *Ibid*.
3 *Ibid*.
4 "Al Qaeda's Online Training Manual", *al Battar*, Issue 10, 2004.
5 "Al Qaeda Calls For Foreign Kidnappings in Afghanistan", *Radio Liberty*, 16 September 2009.
6 "Bin Laden Vows Kidnappings, Killings for US Captive", *MC News*, 25 March 2010.
7 *Ibid*.
8 "Al Qaeda in Yemen Urge Kidnappings of Saudi Royals", *Digital Journal*, 3 June 2010.
9 "Bin Laden in Warning to France", *al Jazeera*, 27 October 2010.
10 *Ibid*.
11 "Al Qaeda Leader Osama bin Laden Threatens France", *Middle East Media Research Institute* (MEMRI), quoting a tape aired by *al Jazeera* on 21 January 2011.
12 *Ibid*.
13 "Kidnapping and Terror in the Contemporary Operational Environment", *US Army Training and Doctrine Command* (TRADOC) G-2 Handbook No. 16, 15 September 2008, pp. 1–9.
14 *Ibid*.
15 "An Interview with Abdelmalek Droukal", *The New York Times*, 1 July 2008.

3

Iran and Terror Abductions

Iran's Use of Terror

In the course of the thirty-two year reign of the Islamic regime from 1979 to 2012, the Islamic Republic of Iran has projected an image of a state with a radical foreign policy in which all means are fair, including terrorism, in order to export the Islamic revolution and to promote its political goals.[1] The use of terror as a tool to realize political interests is not unique to Iran, but there is no doubt that, during the period under discussion, Iran was among the most prominent nations that encouraged and utilized terror to realize political goals on the international level.[2]

In a speech delivered in February 2002, US President George Bush defined Iran as one of the "axis of evil" states that support terror and strive to create weapons of mass destruction. Since the early 1980s, Iran has appeared on the US State Department's list of states that support terror. Indeed, since the Islamic revolution in 1979, Iran has stood out among countries that used terror to promote their goals in the international arena.

Iranian terror activity is cunningly planned. Iran endeavors never to leave "fingerprints" that might implicate the country as the entity behind the terror; moreover, in its public statements, the Iranian leadership expresses reservations about terrorism and even condemns it. This stands true even regarding its own sponsored organizations such as Hizballah, which operates in Lebanon and lately prefers to define its terror activity as "legitimate resistance". The concealment of Iran's connection to the terror activity with which it is indeed involved enables optimal benefit: on the one hand, the terror victim's desire for revenge against Iran is neutralized, while on the other, Iran presents itself as an intermediary that ostensibly strives to mediate between the victim and the terror organization, and thus realizes its goals through active participation in the bargaining and negotiation process.

Most of the evidence exposing Iran's involvement in terror activity came to light when terror perpetrators were caught, questioned, and brought to trial, and was also apparent in the aftermath of terror attacks when the organizations claiming responsibility included declarations and/or demands that clearly reflected Iranian interests.[3] There is a close connection between terror activities and Iranian foreign policy, as evidenced by the consistent and methodical use of terror attacks in order to impose Iran's will on other countries after failure to achieve its goals through accepted diplomatic channels. Salient examples are Kuwait and France, both of which served as central targets for Iranian/Shiite terrorism during the 1980s due to the stance that those states adopted regarding the Iran–Iraq war and the aid they offered to Iraq.

In many instances, the terror weapon was activated to achieve a wide range of Iranian goals *vis-à-vis* the victim. For example, Iranian demands of France in the 1980s included the withdrawal of French forces from Lebanon, cessation of military aid to Iraq, revision of French foreign policy *vis-à-vis* the Israeli–Arab conflict, the return of Iranian funds frozen in France, the banishment of exiled Iranians and Iranian resistance organizations from French soil, and the release of Shiite terrorists arrested in France. One after the other, these goals were achieved by a series of different types of terror attacks (car bombs, abductions, sabotage, and more) that repeatedly led to French capitulation to most of the Iranian demands.

The timing of terror attacks was chosen carefully to affect political processes during negotiations with the victim, or sometimes to promote the launch of such negotiations. Although one might state that Iranian terror policy is ostensibly both rational and realistic with the aim of achieving Iran's goals, several additional phenomena are important factors in the formation of Iranian policy:

- The use of terror in the international arena is a central bone of contention within the leadership of the Iranian regime, between the circles that are called "moderate" and the "radical" circles that advocate an inexorable struggle against the regime's enemies. Thus, to a great extent, the scope and targets of the use of terror reflect internal Iranian power struggles.
- Iran often adopts an ambivalent policy, with "moderates" pulling towards negotiations and compromises while radical elements simultaneously continue to perpetrate terror actions (sometimes with the aim of undermining the moves of the "moderates").

- Iran's ambivalent policy has granted it flexibility in its political maneuvers, making it difficult for the country's adversaries to advocate stringent policies which might provide a suitable response to Iranian terror, assuming that it is important to encourage the "moderate" entities facing extremists within the Iranian regime because these must be considered "the lesser of two evils".

Iranian involvement in terror can be divided into two main periods:

- The "revolutionary" period: the period of Ayatollah Khomeini's reign (1979–89).
- The period of Khomeini's successors, which can be further divided into:
  - Rafsanjani's reign (1989–97)
  - Khatami's reign (1997–2005)
  - Ahmadinejad's reign (2005–12)

There was significant variation in the scope of Iranian terror activity over its full term from 1979 to 2012: the use of terror was most intensive during Khomeini's reign and diminished considerably during the terms of office of his successors. During Khatami's reign, Iranian involvement in terror decreased drastically, with the exception of the Israeli–Arab conflict in the Lebanese and Palestinian arenas.

Several examples can be noted that reflect Iranian willingness to sacrifice political interests in favor of ideological considerations. The most salient example is the Salman Rushdie affair: when sentencing the British writer to death, Khomeini also decreed conflict with western democracies as Islamic values and principles were contrasted with the democratic values advocated by western culture. The Rushdie affair shed light upon the nature of the Iranian leadership: first, there was across-the-board consent between extremists and moderates that Rushdie must die; secondly, even under the leadership of both Rafsanjani and Khatami after Khomeini's demise, it was made unequivocally clear that the decree was still in force and valid, although Iran itself would not enforce the death sentence. When it comes to issues of basic religious and ideological values, a consensus exists within the Iranian regime – while, at the same time, Iranian policies regarding matters of less paramount importance are generally pragmatic and motivated primarily by considerations of cost and benefit.

The dilemma regarding the nature of the Iranian leadership (moderates versus radicals) stems mainly from a viewpoint and judgment based on western norms and values. Close examination of the actions and statements of both moderate and radical Iranian leaders leads to the conclusion that, in reality, the more accurate distinction must be made between *radical* and *more radical* leaderships. As long as Khomeini's doctrine serves as the source of legitimacy and guides the Iranian leadership, differences between moderates and radicals will be expressed by different methods of achieving objectives, but the groups will not differ in their essential goals.

With regard to Iranian power over its Palestinian and Shiite sponsored organizations, Iran demonstrated both control and influence during the entire period under study. However, this statement must also be qualified, as control over such sponsored organizations is sometimes found in the hands of influential entities who are not necessarily those heading the official Iranian leadership. Thus it would be more correct to say that internal power struggles in Iran have a significant impact on the sponsored organizations operating under the authority of various factions within the Iranian regime.

One must also keep in mind that the sponsored organizations have their own goals and needs that are not always fully compatible with the needs of the "patron" state. In this context, most terrorist attacks perpetrated by Shiite and Palestinian organizations included both demands to release terrorists incarcerated in various countries and monetary ransom – demands that first and foremost serve the sponsored organizations themselves. The arrest of Shiite terrorists sometimes turned countries not originally earmarked as target states into terror attack targets (such as Switzerland and West Germany). Attacks against these countries did not serve Iranian interests at all – their sole aim was to liberate the terror groups' members. Iran's ally Syria is also deeply involved in this process, and both states finance and direct many of the Palestinian terror groups.

Khomeini's doctrine, which called for "Shiite activism" and "revolutionary violence", provides religious and ideological legitimacy for the use of terror – thus Iranian terror is inspired by a combination of religious and ideological motives as well as political needs.

Iran was the first entity to introduce the phenomenon of suicide bombers into the attack arsenal of the Middle Eastern arena – this suicidal tactic has continued from the 1980s until today. Iran encourages the Palestinians to use the weapons of terror and suicide attacks as tactical means in their strategic struggle against the State of Israel. Many years of experience contending with such Iranian policies has demonstrated that Iran's decision to use the instrument of terror is generally taken on the basis of a cost versus benefit, or profit versus risk, evaluation. From the Iranian viewpoint, a rational decision-making process is involved in terror, characterized by the following qualifications:

- When there is a conflict between political interests and a fundamental religious edict, such as the case of the *fatwa* (Islamic decree) in the Salman Rushdie affair, Iran usually favors the religious decree.
- Some international terror stems from internal power struggles between "moderate circles" and the radicals within Iran's supreme leadership. Through these activities, radicals strive to undermine the "conciliatory" policies of the "moderates" towards those entities they perceive as enemies of Islam.

The Iranian Terror System

Terror, subversion, and elimination of the regime's opponents abroad are activities subject to the approval of the top decision-makers in the Iranian regime,[4] who include the *Valiat Fakia*.[5] Ideas and initiatives in these areas are approved in principle within a small forum composed of the president and four ministers. Following their authorization, these proposals are transferred to the Supreme National Security Council that processes the recommendations and prepares them for approval by the *Valiat Fakia*, after which orders are transferred to the Supreme Council for Intelligence Matters (SCIM) that ensures their implementation, via the Ministry of Intelligence and Security (MIS), by the relevant ministries and the executive branches.

The 1997 trial of Iranian agents in Germany, who were tried and convicted of murdering four Kurdish émigrés in the Mikonos restaurant in Berlin, constitutes a prominent example of the Iranian decision-making chain. Indeed, a German court unequivocally indicated the responsibility of the Iranian government's top leaders in this terror attack. In his verdict, the judge pointed to the personal and direct involvement of the Iranian intelligence minister, Ali Fallahian, in planning and implementing the terror attack, and issued an arrest warrant against him in absentia.[6]

Since the early 1990s, both the SCIM and the MIS have played a central role in initiating, planning, and conducting terror activity abroad. The SCIM and its head are responsible for coordination between the relevant ministries in all matters related to planning and perpetration of operational activity.[7] As stated earlier, various Iranian agencies deal with the export of the revolution and international terror. The SCIM is responsible for recruiting terrorists, providing training in secret facilities in Iran or Lebanon, and their worldwide activation.[8] Hizballah acted as Iran's emissary in its power struggles in Lebanon and directed terror attacks against Israel, western and Arab state interests in

Lebanon, and in the international arena. Two main types of attack were characteristic of this organization: suicide attacks against western targets in Lebanon and Kuwait (and against Israeli targets in Lebanon) and the kidnapping of foreigners on Lebanese soil. Terror activity against foreign targets was perpetrated by the Hizballah's "Special Security Agency" (SSA) in Lebanon[9] and by various cells of Hizballah members abroad, supported by Iranian diplomatic infrastructure. Imad Muraniya headed the SSA and received his instructions directly from Iran.[10] The SSA was responsible for the hijacking of airplanes, the kidnapping of western hostages in Lebanon, and terror attacks worldwide.

The Islamic Revolution in Iran

Violent protests against Shah Reza Pehlavi's regime forced the shah and his family to flee from Iran in January 1979 and culminated in a revolution coordinated by Ayatollah Ruhollah Khomeini from his exile in France. Within weeks, Khomeini (who had been expelled from Iran by the shah in 1964) returned to Iran in February 1979, dismissed Prime Minister Shahpour Bahktiar, and installed Mehdi Bazargan as his replacement. In April, he declared an Islamic Republic of Iran, and since then has presided over a brutal and repressive regime.

The overthrow of the shah of Iran by an Islamic revolutionary movement led to a steady deterioration in Iran–US relations. The new ruler, Ayatollah Khomeini, railed against the American government, denouncing it as the "Great Satan" and the "Enemy of Islam". On 14 February 1979, about a month after the shah had fled, the American embassy in Tehran was attacked and briefly occupied; the American ambassador was held hostage for a few hours before members of Khomeini's retinue ordered him released. Between February and November 1979, attempts were made by the US to arrive at a modus vivendi with Iran's provisional government while the Iranian authorities sought to strengthen security around the embassy compound.

The Crisis at the American Embassy in Tehran (November 1979)

On 4 November 1979, an angry mob of Islamist "students" calling themselves "Imam's Disciples" laid siege to the American embassy in Tehran and held hostage sixty-six US citizens and diplomats. Although women and African-Americans were released a short time later, fifty-one hostages remained imprisoned for 444 days, while another individual was released midway through the ordeal because of illness.[11] The attack occurred months after the Islamic revolution that toppled the US-backed shah.[12] Since then, on every November 4th, Iran marks the annual anniversary of the 1979 capture of the US embassy in Tehran.

The attack on the embassy

When the shah was diagnosed with lymphoma (a malignant form of cancer), he requested to be treated by US doctors. His request was granted, and US authorities informed Iranian Prime Minister Mehdi Bazargan of the shah's impending arrival on American soil. Bazargan, in light of the February attack, guaranteed the safety of the US embassy and its staff.

The shah arrived in New York City on 22 October 1979.[13] The initial public response in Iran was moderate until, on 4 November 1979, the embassy was attacked by a mob of perhaps three thousand people, some of whom were armed. After a short siege, sixty-three American men and women were taken hostage (three additional members of the US diplomatic staff were seized at the Iranian foreign ministry). This time, however, Khomeini saw a chance to consolidate his power around a potent symbol and issued a statement in support of the action against the American "den of spies". Following Khomeini's message, the Revolutionary Guards and police did nothing to stop the takeover, while Iranian television indicated its support by broadcasting live pictures of the siege. The Iranian government denied responsibility for the incident, but its failure to take action against the hostage-takers belied its denial. Within the next few days, representatives of US President Jimmy Carter and Tehran-based diplomats from other countries attempted, but failed, to secure the release of the hostages. An American delegation, headed by former US Attorney-General Ramsey Clark – who had long-standing relations with many Iranian officials – was refused admission to Iran.

The storming of the embassy followed months of political and religious tension in Iran between Islamic radicals and the secular left, and between various personalities within the Islamic leadership surrounding Khomeini – the hostages were apparently caught in the stalemate resulting from this dispute. It soon became evident that no one within the virulently anti-American atmosphere of post-revolutionary Iran was willing, or able, to release the hostages. The hostage-takers themselves were most likely supporters of Khomeini, whose refusal to order the hostages' release led Prime Minister Bazargan to resign on 6 November 1979.[14]

Negotiations

US President Carter immediately imposed economic sanctions on Iran and applied diplomatic pressure to expedite negotiations for the release of the hostages. First he halted oil imports from Iran, then expelled a number of Iranians from the US before freezing about US$8 billion of Iranian assets. At the same time, he began several diplomatic initiatives to free the hostages – all of which proved fruitless.

On 12 November 1979, Iranian Foreign Minister Abolhassan Banisadr issued a list of demands for the hostages' release, including the return of the shah to Iran for trial, an apology for prior American involvement in Iran (including the coup of 1953), a promise to steer clear of Iranian affairs in the future, and a demand that the shah's US assets be returned to Iran.[15] From the US president's perspective, those demands could not be met.

On November 17th, Khomeini ordered the release of thirteen hostages (all women or African-Americans) on the grounds that they were unlikely to be spies. Another hostage, who became gravely ill, was released on 11 July 1980, reducing the final number of hostages to fifty-two. Throughout the crisis, Iran used the threat of putting the hostages on trial for various crimes, including espionage, as negotiating leverage.

The US bolstered its position by a campaign of international diplomacy against the Iranians. US diplomats twice obtained United Nations Security Council resolutions (on December 4 and 31) against Iran's actions and, on November 29th, the US filed suit against the Iranian government in the International Court of Justice, which ruled in favor of the US in May 1980. The consensus of the international community was against the seizure of the hostages, and diplomats from various countries sought to intervene on their behalf. One notable incident occurred on 28 January 1980, when Canadian diplomats helped six Americans who had managed to avoid capture to flee Iran – the Canadian embassy was subsequently closed.[16]

The rescue (Operation Eagle Claw)

Finally, with the Iranians showing no signs of releasing the hostages, President Carter decided to take a chance: on 11 April 1980, he approved a high-risk rescue operation called "Operation Eagle Claw", which had been planned for months. Tehran was surrounded on all sides by seven hundred miles of desert; the city itself was crammed with four million people, and the embassy was huge and well guarded. It was to have been a two-night process, requiring a minimum of six helicopters and a handful of C-130 cargo aircraft. To be on the safe side, eight helicopters were prepared for the mission.

On 24 April, the US attempted the rescue mission. After two of the eight helicopters were damaged, one helicopter had to turn back with operating problems, and a further helicopter was damaged in a dust storm, the mission was aborted. Upon attempting their retreat, a miscommunication caused one helicopter to lift off – the storm slammed the helicopter into a C-130, killing three in the chopper and five in the airplane. The following morning, Iranian media broadcast footage of the smoking remains of the rescue attempt's aftermath to the gleeful country. It was a total humiliation for the US and spurred an onslaught of investigations and congressional hearings. Cyrus Vance, the secretary of state who had objected to the plan, resigned in protest.

The end of the crisis

In September 1980, Khomeini's government decided it was time to end the matter.

After the death of the shah in Egypt in July 1980 (which neutralized one of the Iranian demands), the invasion of Iran by Iraq, and the ongoing sanctions there was little more advantage to be gained from the crisis. Despite rumors that Carter might pull out an "October Surprise" and get the hostages home before the election, negotiations dragged on for months, even after Ronald Reagan's November 1980 republican victory – a victory assisted by the Carter administration's failure to release the hostages. After the election, negotiations continued with the assistance of Algerian intermediaries.

On 20 January 1981, the day of Reagan's presidential inauguration, the US released almost US$8 billion in Iranian assets and the hostages were freed after 444 days in Iranian detention; the agreement also gave Iran immunity from lawsuits arising from the incident. On 21 January 1981, former-President Carter went to Germany to meet the freed hostages on behalf of the new US president.

In 2000, the former hostages sued Iran under the 1996 Antiterrorism Act that permitted US citizens to sue foreign governments in cases of state-sponsored terrorism. The following year, they won the lawsuit by default when Iran did not offer a defense.

Little has been changed in Tehran since 4 November 1979. The old American embassy compound seized is now under the control of the Revolutionary Guards, who have used several of its outbuildings as a recruiting depot, while the Chancery (the former American headquarters), vacant and stripped bare, is opened to the Iranian public as "a museum of American imperialism" on the anniversary of the attack.

In his memoir, *The Good Fight: A Life in Liberal Politics*, former-Vice-President Walter Mondale outlined the administration's efforts to get the hostages released. "Some days, we thought we were making progress and we would get our hopes up. But most days, we were trying everything and it was not happening," wrote Mondale.[17] "Trying everything" included a complex and risky military rescue operation on 24 April 1980, and the failure of the mission damaged both Carter's and Mondale's credibility with the American public. The incident occurred seven months before the 1980 presidential election and contributed to Jimmy Carter's defeat by the republican challenger, Ronald Reagan.

In November 2009, former-President Carter claimed he had no regrets about his handling of the Tehran hostage crisis more than 30 years previously, saying he didn't attack Iran as his advisors proposed because thousands of people would have died. Carter said one proposed option was a military strike on Iran, but he chose to stick with negotiations in order to prevent bloodshed and to bring the hostages home safely. "My main advisers insisted that I should attack Iran," he said. "I could have destroyed Iran with my weaponry. But I felt in the process it was likely the hostages' lives would be lost, and I didn't want to kill twenty thousand Iranians. So I didn't attack."[18] In his memoirs, Carter wrote: "I have said to many people, both religious and not religious, that that is the time when I prayed more than any time else in my life – during that time when the hostages were being held. My prayer was that I would protect the interests of my country, first of all, but that every hostage would come home safe and free."[19]

On 20 January 1981, Iran's revolutionary leader Ayatollah Khomeini waited for Ronald Reagan to be sworn into office before allowing the American hostages to leave Iranian airspace on their flight to freedom – a fact which upset Mondale. In their autobiographies, both the former president and vice-president wrote about the frustration and exhaustion of their final days in office, capped by humiliation on Inauguration Day. "It was a nasty thing that Khomeini did to insult us", writes Mondale. "But that is all right. We can take that. But it was playing cat and mouse with human beings there that had a right to be released."[20] Carter writes: "But I was so happy to know that the hostages were released that I was not worried then about who got credit for their release."[21]

Iranian Involvement in Terror Abductions in Iraq

The political and military struggle between the United States and Iran over influence of events in Iraq still continues today, eight years after the coalition invasion of Iraq, despite the American decision to halt operational involvement in Iraq and the subsequent withdrawal of US forces from that country.[22]

The Iranian *al Quds* ("Jerusalem") force, a special unit of the Iranian Revolutionary Guards, has two main objectives: to weaken and shape Iraq's nascent government, and to diminish the role and influence of the US in that country. Established by Khomeini after the 1979 Iranian revolution, the "Army of the Guardians of the Islamic Revolution" expanded its domestic influence under President Ahmadinejad (a former member of the corps); the Guards today play an important role in Iran's economy, politics, and internal security. The force, under the command of Brigadier-General Qasem Soleimani, has responsibility for foreign operations and often seeks to work though surrogates like Hizballah.

While the American government has long believed that al Quds has provided lethal assistance and training to Shiite militants in Iraq, field reports have provided new details about Iran's support for Iraqi militias and the American military's operations to counter them. After the 2003 invasion of Iraq during the administration of President George W. Bush, critics charged that the White House had exaggerated Iran's role to deflect criticism of its handling of the war to build support for a tough US policy towards Iran, including the possibility of military action. The field reports, never intended to be made public but disclosed by the WikiLeaks website, underscored the seriousness with which Iran's role in sponsoring terrorism is seen by the US military – concern that centers around Iran's role in arming and assisting Shiite militias. Citing (amongst other intelligence) the testimony of detainees, the diary of a captured militant, and numerous uncovered weapons caches, the field reports recount Iran's role in providing Iraqi militias with rockets, magnetic bombs that can be attached to the underside of vehicles, "explosively-formed penetrators" (EFPs), which are the most lethal type of roadside bomb in Iraq, and other weapons ranging from powerful ·50-caliber rifles to the Misagh-1 (an Iranian replica of a portable Chinese surface-to-air missile) that was fired at American helicopters and downed one in eastern Baghdad in July 2007, according to the reports.

Iraqi militants traveled to Iran to be trained as snipers and in the use of explosives, the field reports assert, and al Quds collaborated with Iraqi extremists to encourage the assassination of Iraqi officials. The US tried to kill or capture as many militiamen and al Quds operatives as they could, but interference by Iraqi officials meant that this effort could only go so far. The reports make it clear that the lethal contest between Iranian-backed militias and US forces continued even after US President Barack Obama sought to open a diplomatic dialogue with Iran's leaders and had reaffirmed the agreement between the US and Iraq to withdraw American troops from Iraq by the end of 2011.

The abduction of five Britons in Baghdad (May 2007)

Peter Moore, a 36-year-old IT consultant from Lincoln, was snatched from the Iraqi finance ministry building in Baghdad in May 2007, along with his four bodyguards. Between eighty and one hundred members of the pro-Iranian terror organization Asayib Ahl al Haq ("League of the Righteous") drove up to the ministry's buildings in Baghdad and kidnapped the five Britons in less than fifteen minutes. The hostages were taken to Baghdad's Sadr City and held there for one day before being transferred to Iran where they were incarcerated by the al Quds brigade of the Revolutionary Guards.[23] Moore was employed on a project to install new financial software to track money movements within the Iraqi finance ministry, and intelligence officials investigated allegations that the new systems would expose a practice in which coalition funds were routinely diverted by Shia officials to Iranian security forces in return for the arming and training of militias.[24]

Events surrounding the kidnapping were complicated, beginning with a series of American raids against Iranian operatives working within Iraq.[25] In 2006, US President Bush okayed the killing and capture of Iranians in Iraq who were supplying weapons and training to Shiite militias.[26] That policy led to the arrest of General Mohsen Chirazi in December 2006, a senior officer in the Iranian Revolutionary Guards al Quds Force who was in charge of Tehran's Iraq policy.[27] This event was followed by a speech by President Bush in January 2007, when he said that the US would stop Iran's interference in Iraqi affairs. Then, on January 11th, five Iranians were arrested in Irbil, Kurdistan.[28] The Americans actually missed their targets,[29] Mohammed Jafari (deputy-head of Iran's National Security Council) and General Minojahar Frouzanda (intelligence chief of the Revolutionary Guards), when Kurdish *peshmerga* (armed fighters; literally, "those who face death") stopped US forces at the Irbil airport.[30] In January of that year, Tehran retaliated by leading a raid on the Karbala Provincial Joint Coordination Center (PJCC), in conjunction with the League of the Righteous, that led to the deaths of five US soldiers.[31] US and UK forces detained the League's leaders, Qais and Laith Khazali, in Basra in March 2007.[32]

Qais Khazali was one of the leading figures in the Sadr movement,[33] created in the 1990s by Muqtada al Sadr's father, Ayatollah Mohammed Sadeq al Sadr. Qais helped keep the underground movement alive after

Saddam Hussein had the elder Sadr killed in February 1999. When Muqtada al Sadr emerged as one of Iraq's new leaders after the 2003 invasion, Qais was one of his top lieutenants. He then split with and rejoined Muqtada several times before creating his own group, the League of the Righteous, in 2006. That same year, he was also selected to lead the "Special Groups" that Iran was creating to achieve more direct control of Shiite gunmen in Iraq.[34]

Iran planned the May 2007 raid on the Iraqi finance ministry as part of its tit-for-tat exchange with the United States, while the League of the Righteous wanted hostages to facilitate the release of the Khazali brothers.[35] An unnamed former Revolutionary Guard told *The Guardian* newspaper: "It was an Iranian kidnap, led by the Revolutionary Guard, carried out by the al Quds brigade. My contact works for al Quds. He took part in the planning of the kidnap, and he watched the kidnapping as it was taking place. He told me that they spent two days at the Qasser Shiereen camp. They then took them deep inside Iran." A serving Iraqi government minister with links to Iran also told *The Telegraph*: "This was an IRG [Iranian Revolutionary Guard] operation. You don't think for a moment that those militia groups from Sadr City could have carried out a high-level kidnapping like this one."[36]

At a conference in Bahrain on 13 December 2009, the former US commander in Iraq, General David Petraeus (who was commander of the multinational forces in Iraq at the time of the kidnap and later headed US Central Command until his retirement in June 2010), said he was "90 percent certain" that the Britons were held in Iran for part of their period in captivity. "He didn't hesitate. He said 'I'm absolutely certain. I'm 90 percent certain,'" foreign correspondent Frank Gardner told BBC Radio 4's *Today* program. "I said: 'Is this a personal view or have you seen hard intelligence?' and he thought for a minute and he said: 'I am pretty sure I've seen hard intelligence on it . . . that they were held in Iran for some of the period of their captivity.'"[37]

The British foreign office was also accused of ignoring evidence of an Iranian link. A security consultant for the firm that employed Moore's security guards revealed he had submitted phone records demonstrating that one of the men's mobile phones had been used to text Iranian phones after the abduction, and claimed that the evidence amounted to intelligence that should have been used to track the group.[38] However, the British foreign office played down suggestions that the men had been held in Iran. A spokesman said: "We have no evidence that the British hostages, including Peter Moore, were held in Iran. We are not in a position to say with any certainty where they were held during each and every single day of their two-and-a-half-years in captivity."[39]

Iran dismissed reports of its involvement in the kidnapping as "baseless". Ramin Mehmanparast, an Iranian foreign ministry spokesman, claimed that the newspaper reports "emanate from the British anger towards the rallies in which millions of Iranians took part to condemn British interference in Iran's internal affairs", while Iran's Foreign Minister Manouchehr Mottaki said that Britain would "receive a slap in the mouth" if it did not "stop its nonsense".[40]

Almost two years later, Iraq, Britain, the US, Iran, and the League of the Righteous worked out a release plan, with Lebanon's Hizballah acting as a middleman. In March 2009, a deal was cut whereby the Americans would release all of the members of the League of the Righteous that they held, including Laith and Qais Khazali, in return for the British captives. In that same month, a video was released of Moore and was followed by the freeing of Laith Khazali. Subsequently, US prisons were emptied of some three hundred League followers (under the guise of an Iraqi reconciliation program)[41] along with the release of top al Quds force members who had been arrested in 2006–7,[42] in return for the bodies of the bodyguards: Jason Creswell, Jason Swindlehurst, and Alec MacLachlan.[43] The body of Alan McMenemy was later handed to the US embassy in Baghdad in 2012.[44] The process finally ended with the release of both Peter Moore and Qais Khazali. Some American military officers were against this deal, but the Status of Forces Agreement, signed between Washington and Baghdad at the very end of the Bush administration in December 2008,[45] required the US to release all detainees they held unless they had broken Iraqi law.[46]

Iranian capture of three British ships and crews (June 2004)

On 21 June 2004, Iran captured three British Royal Navy vessels in the Shatt al Arab waterway. The British servicemen, who were training Iraqi river patrol personnel, were seized after Iran claimed they had strayed into the Iranian side of the waterway,[47] the mouth of which divides southern Iran and Iraq close to the northern coast of the Persian Gulf. The weather was bad, causing negligible visibility that may have contributed to a possible crossing of the Iranian border by the Royal Navy.[48]

The UK claimed the men were "forcibly escorted" into Iranian territorial waters. During their detention, according to former detainee Scott Fallon, the hostages endured a mock execution in which they were marched into the desert and made to stand blindfolded in front of a ditch while their captors cocked their weapons. The British servicemen were later paraded blindfolded and made to apologize on Iranian TV before their release was agreed.[49] They were released unharmed three days later, on June 24th, after the British and Iranian governments agreed there had been a misunderstanding. After the crew were returned and events were analyzed, the British government affirmed its belief that the personnel were actually in Iraqi waters; however, they designated the incident as a misunderstanding and requested the return of their equipment.[50]

In 2005, one of the British boats captured by the Iranians was paraded through the streets of Tehran as the country celebrated the anniversary of the 1979 Islamic revolution. The vessel was manned by Iranian sailors as it weaved its way through crowds of thousands of Iranians. At the parade, Iranian President Mahmoud Ahmadinejad told a huge rally that his country would not back down "one iota" in its nuclear dispute with the United States. The Iranian FARS news agency said that the boat paraded was that "of British violators seized in the Persian Gulf" and was put on display in front of the Cultural Heritage Organization, without giving any further details.

Iranian capture of two British ships and sailors (March 2007)

On 23 March 2007, Iranian naval vessels seized fifteen British servicemen who had boarded a merchant ship in Iraqi waters of the Persian Gulf.[51] The team of eight sailors and seven marines, in two boats from the frigate HMS *Cornwall*, had been searching a merchant dhow for smuggled cars when they were detained at gunpoint by the crews of eight small Iranian vessels. The British servicemen and women were subsequently taken to an Iranian Revolutionary Guards base in Tehran for questioning.[52]

Britain immediately protested the detentions, and Foreign Secretary Margaret Beckett demanded the immediate and safe return of the HMS *Cornwall* servicemen.[53] The incident came at a time of renewed tensions with Iran over its nuclear program and followed claims that most of the violence against UK forces in Basra was engineered by Iranian elements. Colonel Justin Maciejewski, based in Iraq, said Iran was providing "sophisticated weaponry" to insurgents and "Iranian agents" were paying local men to attack British troops.

In conversations with foreign ministry officials in Brunei, US diplomats heard what their counterparts believed was behind the capture of the fifteen British servicemen and women by Iran earlier in the month: Brunei officials claimed the move was carried out to distract attention within Iran from the passage of UN Security Council resolution 1747 that stepped up sanctions on Iran in response to its continuing nuclear program.[54]

In London, the British government summoned the Iranian ambassador to the foreign office. "He was left in no doubt that we want them back," Foreign Secretary Beckett said after the meeting. Iranian officials claimed that they arrested the sailors and marines because they were operating inside Iranian territorial waters, while information provided by Britain initially and consistently placed the boats in Iraqi waters. Intense diplomatic efforts ensued to secure the release of the detainees.

On 28 March 2007, television channels around the world showed footage released by the Iranian government of some of the fifteen British sailors and included a statement by a captured sailor, Faye Turney, along with a letter she wrote under compulsion in which she apologized for "British intrusions into Iranian waters".[55] Two days later, a further video was aired on Iranian television showing three of the detained Britons, and two further letters (again attributed to Turney) were released – once again claiming the British boats were in Iranian waters.[56] Iran stated that an apology from British officials would "facilitate" the release of the personnel.[57]

On April 4th, Iranian President Ahmadinejad held a news conference in Tehran to announce the release of the sailors as a "gift" to Britain, stating: "On the occasion of the birthday of the great prophet, and for the occasion of the passing of Christ, I say the Islamic Republic government and the Iranian people – with all powers and legal right to put the soldiers on trial – forgave those fifteen. This pardon is a gift to the British people."[58]

Once returned to the UK, the group claimed to have been put under constant psychological pressure from the Iranian authorities.[59] In addition, British equipment, including secure voice communication kits and navigational hardware, was reported as not having been returned. However, the subsequent report by the House of Commons' Foreign Affairs Select Committee confirmed that the UK Ministry of Defense (MoD) map presented to the worldwide media was "inaccurate" as it presented a boundary line where no maritime boundary between the two countries had been agreed upon, and so determined that "the government was fortunate that it was not in Iran's interests to contest the accuracy of the map."[60]

Reports in April 2008, citing documents from the MoD inquiry, stated that the British sailors were in disputed waters, that the US-led coalition had drawn a boundary line between Iran and Iraq without informing the Iranians, and that Iranian coastal protection vessels regularly crossed this coalition-defined boundary.[61]

Iran's abduction of three American hikers (July 2010)

The episode began when four American tourists traveled from Syria to northern Iraq, planning to hike in the Ahmed Awa, a mountainous area with a dramatic waterfall. One American, Shon Meckfessel, became ill and stayed behind when his friends set out on 31 July 2010. Sarah Shourd, Joshua Fattal, and Shane Bauer were arrested by Iranian soldiers as they were hiking near the Iran–Iraq border.[62]

The kidnap and arrest of the hikers

A classified American military report, made public by WikiLeaks, describes the chaotic day when the hikers were detained and asserts that the hikers were on the Iraqi side of the border when they were seized.[63] A field report, dated 31 July 2010, stated that Meckfessel learned of the arrests when a "female called him saying they were being surrounded by armed men". At first, the US military did not know who was holding the Americans. The report noted that an unnamed intelligence officer, based at the American army division in northern Iraq, initially described the event as a "kidnapping" and said the three American tourists "were being taken to the Iranian border". The report also listed a number of military grids where the Americans were believed to have been hiking or had been detained – all were on the Iraqi side of the border.

As documented in the report, frenetic efforts to locate the hikers and to interview Meckfessel appear to support the claim that the captives were tourists, not American intelligence operatives as was alleged by Iran. An unmanned drone aircraft was sent to look for the missing hikers and two F-16 jet fighters were put on alert, while US special operations forces were sent to pick up Meckfessel so he could be taken to Baghdad for questioning. As the day wore on, the Americans received a report from an officer of the *peshmerga* (the Kurdish military force in northern Iraq) that the Iranians had detained three American citizens "for being too close to the border". The July report reflected some frustration with the hikers for their "lack of coordination" in venturing to northern Iraq, and offered some thoughts on the episode's broader implications: "The leadership in Iran benefits as it focuses the Iranian population on a perceived external threat, rather than internal dissension."

The trial

In August 2011, an Iranian court began closed-door proceedings in the espionage trial of the three Americans, two of whom were still in custody while one had been freed on bail.[64] The trial of Bauer, Fattal, and Shourd (who had been released on bail in September 2010) came eighteen months after they had been arrested on suspicion of spying near Iran's border with Iraq – a crime which could carry the death penalty. The Iranian prosecutors said they had evidence the three were connected to US intelligence agencies. The two Americans pleaded not guilty at the start of the trial, which had been due to take place in November 2010 but was postponed because Ms Shourd had not been summoned to attend.

The men's lawyer, Masoud Shafii, said he had been unable to see his clients before the trial to prepare their defense. "I should have met with Shane and Josh to prepare the defense, but I was not allowed . . . I have been told I might see them one or two hours before the trial," he stated.[65]

Ms Shourd had been freed on health grounds in September 2010, following mediation by Oman and a US$500,000 bail payment, and returned to the US. Iran said she would forfeit the bail money if she did not return to stand trial.[66] President Obama met Shourd on her return to the United States, an event he called "bittersweet" due to the continued detention of the other two, one of whom was Shourd's fiancé. The US repeatedly said there was no basis for the trial and called on Iran to release Bauer and Fattal. As the trial was held behind closed doors, observers such as Swiss Ambassador Livia Leu Agosti, who represented US interests in Iran, were barred from attending.[67] Washington had had no diplomatic ties with Iran since the 1979 Islamic revolution and the subsequent storming of the US embassy by revolutionary students.

On 20 August 2011, Iranian state television reported that Bauer and Fattal had each been sentenced to three years' imprisonment for illegal entry into Iran, and five years each for spying for the United States. Iranian authorities did not immediately confirm the report and made no further comment – although it was carried on Iran's highly-controlled state media, which was frequently used to make high-profile announcements.[68] Earlier, in August 2011, Foreign Minister Ali Akbar Salehi had said he hoped "the trial of the two American defendants who were detained for the crime of illegally entering Iran will finally lead to their freedom". Their lawyer also had expressed hope that the hikers might receive a pardon for the Islamic holy month of Ramadan. The announcement seemed to send a hard-line message from Iran's judiciary – which answered directly to the ruling clerics – weeks after the country's foreign minister had suggested that the trial of Bauer and Fattal could clear the way for their freedom. The last direct contact that family members had had with the prisoners was in May 2010, when their mothers were permitted a short visit to Tehran.

The mediators

Mediators from Switzerland, Iraq, and Oman were involved in the negotiations to free the two men on humanitarian grounds. Swiss officials were involved as representatives of US Iranian interests, which had no diplomatic ties with Tehran.[69] Iraq also sent envoys to neighboring Iran during negotiations over the release.

Oman had close ties with both Tehran and Washington, held a strategic position in the region, and played a key role in the release of the hikers from the jail in Iran, even dispatching at least two of its sultan's close advisors to Tehran on board a plane reportedly designated to carry the hostages out of Iran when a deal was reached.[70] IRNA (Iran's official news agency) reported that Oman's Foreign Minister Yusuf bin Alawi discussed "issues of mutual interest" with Iran's top diplomat in the week prior the release of the Americans,[71] and the government of Oman paid the US$1 million bail set for the two men; it had also previously paid the bail for the earlier release of Ms Shourd.[72] Both the Swiss ambassador to Tehran and a delegation from Oman were present when the two American prisoners were freed.

A delegation of Muslim American and Christian leaders had traveled to Iran for a six-day visit on 13–19 September 2011, at the invitation of President Ahmadinejad. Their visit included meetings with Iranian religious scholars and leaders in the holy city of Qom, and a meeting with Ahmadinejad where top government and clerical officials indicated that the two American hikers would be released. The delegation also met with family members of Iranian citizens held in the US, and emphasized that government officials there needed to work more effectively at "securing the freedom of Iranians in American jails".[73]

The release

In February 2011, Ahmadinejad suggested that the Americans might be released as part of a prisoner swap for Iranians he said were abducted or tricked into going to the US and jailed there without due legal process. In June 2011, Iran called for an "unconditional and swift release" of its national Shahrzad Mir-Gholikhan, who had been in US captivity since 2007, in a letter sent by Iran's foreign ministry to the Swiss embassy (that represented US interests) in Tehran. Mir-Gholikhan had been arrested by US agents while she was on a tour of Cyprus, on the charge that her ex-husband Mahmoud Seif had allegedly tried to export night-vision goggles from Austria to Iran. However, in the absence of her ex-husband, she was sentenced to five years in prison by a Florida federal court.[74]

On 11 September 2011, Ahmadinejad announced that he would release and unconditionally pardon[75] Bauer and Fattal, describing the release as a "humanitarian gesture", while an Iranian court set bail for each man at US$500,000.[76] Ahmadinejad told *The Washington Post*: "I am helping to arrange for their release in a couple of days so they will be able to return home. This is of course going to be a unilateral humanitarian gesture . . . It is a unilateral pardon." Asked how the pair would return to the US, Ahmadinejad said that "they are free to choose".[77] In a separate interview with NBC, he said Bauer and Fattal would be released "in two days", but their lawyer said they would be freed only when the bail had been paid. In the NBC interview, Ahmadinejad highlighted what he said was the way Iranians suffer in American jails: "Do you know how many Iranians are now in American jails? It's not only about two people in Iran. These two people are having very good conditions here in prison. It's like staying in a hotel," he claimed.[78] US Secretary of State Hillary Clinton said in reaction to the news: "We have followed this very closely and we are encouraged by what the Iranian government has said. We obviously hope that we will see a positive outcome from what appears to be a decision by the government."[79]

There was confusion over the men's release after an Iranian judiciary official denied reports of their imminent freedom, a day after Ahmadinejad had told *The Washington Post* that he was "helping to arrange for their release". A statement from Iran's judiciary said: "Information about this case will be provided by the judiciary. Any information supplied by individuals about this is not authoritative."[80] After the subsequent delay in their release, Clinton said that her country "continues to hope the Americans will be released" and added that Washington had received word through a number of sources that the two would be returned to their families.[81] The release of Bauer and Fattal could be perceived not only as a humanitarian gesture by the Iranian president, but also as a US$1 million "bail-for-freedom" deal.

The men's lawyer said he could not complete the paperwork to secure his client's liberty because a second judge, who was needed sign the documents, was on holiday; the first judge had already signed the papers.[82] The second Iranian judge returned to work on 21 September 2011 and signed an order paving the way for the release of the hikers.[83] The same day, Iran released the Americans and they left Tehran's Evin prison shortly after their lawyer had completed the paperwork. Immediately after their release, Bauer and Fattal left for Mehrabad airport and later flew to the Gulf state of Oman.[84]

News of the release came moments before the US president was set to address the United Nations General Assembly in New York City. President Obama hailed the release of Bauer and Fattal in a written statement: "I welcome the release of Shane Bauer and Josh Fattal from detention in Iran, and am very pleased that they are being reunited with their loved ones. The tireless advocacy of their families over these two years has won my admiration, and is now coming to an end with Josh and Shane back in their arms. All Americans join their families and friends in celebrating their long-awaited return home."[85] President Obama also voiced his excitement about the hikers' release to a CNN camera as he left the UN: "Wonderful, wonderful news about the hikers," he said. "We are thrilled. And I could not feel better for the families and those moms we've been in close contact with. A wonderful day for them, and for us."[86]

Summary

The affair heightened tensions between Tehran and Washington, which had severed diplomatic ties after the storming of the US embassy in 1979. Tensions were already high over other issues, including Iranian support for the insurgency in Iraq and Afghanistan, and Tehran's disputed nuclear program. The US government appealed for the two men to be released, insisting that they had done nothing wrong, and claimed that the arrest of innocent foreign citizens formed part of an Iranian strategy to use them as bargaining chips to promote Iranian political interests. Famously, Iran waited until just moments after Ronald Reagan's presidential inauguration in January 1981 to free the fifty-two American hostages held for 444 days at the former US embassy after it was stormed by militants backing Iran's Islamic revolution. The timing was seen as a way to embarrass ex-President Jimmy Carter for his backing of the shah, Iran's former monarch. But, although the release eased one point of tension between Iran and the US, major conflicts still persist to this day.[87]

The case of the American hikers most closely paralleled that of freelance journalist Roxana Saberi, an Iranian-American who was convicted of spying in Iran and sentenced to eight years imprisonment before being released in May 2009, after an appeals court reduced that verdict to a two-year suspended sentence and allowed her to return to the US. A spokesman for the Iranian judiciary said at the time that the court ordered the reduction as a gesture of "Islamic mercy" because Saberi had cooperated with authorities and expressed regret.[88]

In May 2009, a French academic named Clotilde Reiss was also freed after her ten-year sentence on espionage-related charges was commuted. In 2010, Iran freed Iranian-American businessman Reza Taghavi, who had been held for twenty-nine months for alleged links to a bombing in the southern city of Shiraz that killed fourteen people. Taghavi denied any role in the attack.[89]

Iran insisted that its judiciary was independent from political currents, but the fate of the foreign prisoners was used by Iran to support its political maneuvers. The sentences of Bauer and Fattal came just two days after President Obama made his most direct call for the resignation of Syrian President Bashar al Assad, who remained among Iran's closest Middle East allies. Iranian officials used the detained Americans to draw attention to alleged mistreatment of Iranians in US prisons and others who were held by US forces in Iraq. The announcement of the release of the two hikers came on the eve of Ahmadinejad's visit to New York for the annual General Assembly at the United Nations, and Iran may have timed the hikers' release, just minutes before President Obama addressed the UN, as a strategic public-relations move ahead of that visit.[90] There was no direct evidence that Iran timed the release of the Americans to overshadow Obama's speech, but Iran had conducted similar international political stagecraft in the past.[91] The delay in the release of the Americans and the mixed signals from Iran were thought to be an attempt by Ahmadinejad's political rivals to prevent him from gaining traction on the world stage, and may have been a reflection of a political power struggle inside Iran between President Ahmadinejad and the supreme Shiite leader Ayatollah Sayyid Ali Khamenei, who controlled the Iranian justice system. Iran's judiciary swiftly reminded the public that only their courts had the power to control the timing of the release.[92]

Notes

1 This chapter is based on the book by Shaul Shay, *The Axis of Evil: Iran, Hizballah and Palestinian Terror* (New Brunswick: Transaction Publishers, 2005).
2 "Patterns of Global Terrorism", *US Department of State*, 1993–2004.
3 The most prominent instances were the "Mikonos Affair" in Germany and testimony given by Iranian defectors.
4 *Ma'ariv*, 28 June 1996.
5 "*Valiat Fakia*" refers to the supreme Shiite spiritual and political leader that all believers are obligated to obey.
6 *Der Spiegel*, 9 April 1997.
7 *Ma'ariv*, 28 June 1996.
8 Marvin Zonis and Daniel Brumberg, "Khomeini, The Islamic Republic of Iran and the Arab World", in *Harvard Middle East Papers* Issue 5 (Cambridge, MS: Harvard University Press, 1987), p. 34.
9 A. Fishman, *Hadashot*, 18 February 1992.
10 *Ma'ariv*, 2 February 1987.
11 John Skow, "The Long Ordeal of Hostages", *Time Magazine*, 26 January 1981.
12 "US Embassy Seizure Milestone for Iran", *Press TV*, 4 November 2010.
13 Mark Bowden, *Guests of the Ayatollah: The First Battle in America's War*

    with Militant Islam (New York: Atlantic Monthly Press, 2006), p. 19.
14 Shaul Bakhash, *The Reign of the Ayatollahs: Iran and the Islamic Revolution* (New York: Basic Books, 1986), p. 115.
15 Bowden, *Guests of the Ayatollah*, pp. 548–551.
16 Norman Hillmer, "Kenneth Douglas Taylor", in *The Canadian Caper: The Canadian Encyclopedia*, http://www.thecanadianencyclopedia.com/articles/kenneth-douglas-taylor (n.d.).
17 Walter Mondale, *The Good Fight: A Life in Liberal Politics* (New York: Simon and Schuster, 2010).
18 Kane Farabaugh, "Carter on Iranian Hostage Crisis: I Prayed More than Any Other Time in My Life", *Voice of America*, 1 November 2010.
19 *Ibid.*
20 Mondale, *The Good Fight*.
21 Farabaugh, "Carter on Iranian Hostage Crisis", *Voice of America*, 1 November 2010.
22 Michael R. Gordon and Andrew W. Lehren, "Leaked Reports Detail Iranian Aid for Iraqi Militants", *The New York Times*, 22 October 2010.
23 David Williams, "Evidence Grows that British Hostage Peter Moore was Held by Iranians", *The Mail*, 1 January 2010.
24 *Ibid.*
25 "British Hostages in Baghdad", *The Guardian*, 31 December 2009, http://www.guardian.co.uk/world/2009/dec/31/british-hostages-baghdad-iraq-iran.
26 "Iranians Planned Kidnapping and Held British Captives Taken in Iraq", *Education for Peace in Iraq* (EPIC), 4 January 2010.
27 "US Troops Raid 2 Iranian Targets in Iraq, Detain 5 People", *The Washington Post*, 12 January 2007, http://www.washingtonpost.com/wp-dyn/content/article/2007/01/11/AR2007011100427.html.
28 "US Raid on Iranian Consulate Angers Kurds", *CNN*, 12 January 2007, http://www.campaigniran.org/casmii/index.php?q=node/1092.
29 "GIs Raid Iranian Building in Irbil", *The New York Sun*, 12 January 2007, http://www.nysun.com/foreign/gis-raid-iranian-building-in-irbil/46598/.
30 "The Botched US Raid that Led To the Hostage Crisis", *The Independent*, 25 September 2009, http://www.independent.co.uk/news/world/middle-east/the-botched-us-raid-that-led-to-the-hostage-crisis-443102.html.
31 "US Releases 'Dangerous' Iranian Proxy behind the Murder of US Troops", *The Long War Journal*, 31 December 2009, http://www.longwarjournal.org/archives/2009/12/us_releases_dangerou.php.
32 "Iranians Planned Kidnapping", *EPIC*, 4 January 2010.
33 "The Fragmentation of the Sadrist Movement", *Institute for the Study of War*, Report 12, 2009, http://www.understandingwar.org/report/fragmentation-sadrist-movement.

34 "Iranians Planned Kidnapping", *EPIC*, 4 January 2010.
35 *Ibid.*
36 *Ibid.*
37 *Ibid.*
38 *Ibid.*
39 Peter Moore was released in Baghdad by his abductors on 30 December 2009, after two-and-a-half-years of captivity.
40 Williams, "Evidence Grows", *Mail*, 1 January 2010.
41 "5 Revolutionary Guards Members Let Go By US", *Musings on Iraq*, 16 July 2009, http:/musingsoniraq.blogspot.com/2009/07/5-revolutionary-guards-members-let-go.html.
42 *The Times*, http://www.timesonline.co.uk/tol/news/world/iraq/article6971841.ece (n.d.).
43 "Iranians Planned Kidnapping", *EPIC*, 4 January 2010.
44 *The Guardian*, 20 January 2012.
45 "Iranians Planned Kidnapping", *EPIC*, 4 January 2010.
46 *Ibid.*
47 "Timeline: UK-Iran Relations", *BBC News*, 23 March 2007.
48 "Iran Holds British Sailors as West Set to Tighten Sanctions", *AFP*, 3 March 2007.
49 David Williams, "Iran Seeks to Humiliate Britain by Parading Captured Naval Boat on Streets of Tehran", *The Mail*, 11 February 2008.
50 "Iran Releases British Servicemen", *BBC News*, 24 June 2004.
51 "UK Says 15 Sailors Detained by Iranian Navy", *AP*, 23 March 2008.
52 "Seized Sailors 'Held in Tehran'", *BBC News*, 3 March 2007.
53 "UK Says 15 Sailors Detained by Iranian Navy", *AP*, 23 March 2008.
54 "US Embassy Cables: Ahmadinejad Ordered Capture of British Servicemen for Domestic Reasons", *The Guardian*, 10 December 2010.
55 "Iran Shows Held Sailors on Television", *Reuters*, 28 March 2007, http://investing.reuters.co.uk/news/articlenews.aspx?type=UKNews1&storyID=2007-03-28T201514Z_01_L28126061_RTRUKOC_0_UK-IRAN.xml&WTmodLoc=HP-C1-TopStories-5.
56 "Iran Airs Second Sailor 'Apology'", *BBC News*, 30 March 2007, http://news.bbc.co.uk/1/hi/uk/6509813.stm.
57 "Apology From UK Gov't Will Aid Release of British Sailors: Diplomat", *Islamic Republic News Agency* (IRNA), 31 March 2007, http://www2.irna.ir/en/news/view/menu-236/0703316242100934.htm.
58 "Iran to Free 15 Captive British Sailors and Marines", *Breaking Legal News*, 4 April 2007, http://www.breakinglegalnews.com/entry/Iran-to-free-15-captive-British-sailors-and-marines.
59 "Royal Navy Captives: Key Quotes", *BBC News*, 6 April 2007, http://news.bbc.co.uk/1/hi/uk/6533287.stm.
60 Sophie Walker, "British Map in Iran Crisis 'Inaccurate'", *Herald Sun*, 22 July 2007, http://www.casmii.org/CASMII /index.php?q=node/2631.

61 "British Sailors Captured by Iran Were in Disputed Waters: Report", *AFP*, 16 April 2008, http://news.yahoo.com/s/afp /20080417/wl_mideast_afp/britainiranmilitarysailors_080417033507.
62 Michael Gordon and Andrew W. Lehren, "Iran Seized US Hikers in Iraq, US Report Asserts", *The New York Times*, 22 October 2010.
63 *Ibid*.
64 "Iran Opens Trial of US Hikers", *al Jazeera*, 6 February 2011.
65 "Three US Hikers Accused of Iran Spying Go on Trial", *BBC News*, 6 February 2011.
66 *Ibid*.
67 *Ibid*.
68 "US Hikers in Iran Sentenced to 8 Years in Prison", *The Huffington Post*, 20 August 2011.
69 "'Holiday' Delays Release of US Men in Iran", *al Jazeera*, 18 September 2011.
70 *Ibid*.
71 *Ibid*.
72 "Shane Bauer and Joshua Fattal, Hikers Freed from Jail in Iran Arrive Oman", *ABC News*, 21 September 2011.
73 Stan Wilson, "US Christian, Muslim Leaders to Return from Seeking Hikers' Release", *CNN*, 19 September 2011.
74 "Iran Calls For Unconditional Release of National Held in US", *Payvand Iran News*, 14 June 2011.
75 "Why Iran is Releasing the Jailed American Hikers: Three Theories", *The Week*, 13 September 2011.
76 *Ibid*.
77 "Iran 'To Release' Two US Men Jailed as Spies", *al Jazeera*, 14 September 2011.
78 *Ibid*.
79 *Ibid*.
80 "'Holiday' Delays Release", *al Jazeera*, 18 September 2011.
81 *Ibid*.
82 *Ibid*.
83 "Iran 'Set to Free' Two US Hikers", *al Jazeera*, 21 September 2011.
84 "Iran Releases US Men Jailed as Spies", *al Jazeera*, 21 September 2011.
85 "Shane Bauer and Joshua Fattal", *ABC News*, 21 September 2011.
86 *Ibid*.
87 "Iran Releases US Men", *al Jazeera*, 21 September 2011.
88 "Iran 'To Release' Two US Men", *al Jazeera*, 14 September 2011.
89 *Ibid*.
90 "Why Iran is Releasing the Jailed American Hikers", *The Week*, 13 September 2011.
91 "Iran Releases US Men", *al Jazeera*, 21 September 2011.
92 "Hikers Freed from Jail Arrive Oman", *ABC News*, 21 September 2011.

4

Hizballah and Terror Abductions in Lebanon

Hizballah Abductions Against Israel

A central bone of contention in the prolonged conflict between Hizballah ("Party of God") and the State of Israel is the issue of captives.[1] Hizballah grasps the sensitivity of Israeli society and its decision-makers *vis-à-vis* its civilians and soldiers. Therefore, the targeted abduction of Israel Defense Force (IDF) soldiers has become a central tactic within the organization's modi operandi: the hostage becomes a "strategic asset" that Hizballah exploits to promote its goals in its conflict with Israel, and to strengthen its position in the Lebanese Republic and the Arab world.

During the years 1986–2006, Israelis were captured by organizations under Iranian sponsorship (Hizballah and the "Faithful Resistance") in six incidents:

- *17 February 1986*: In the course of a Hizballah ambush, two IDF soldiers – Yosef Fink and Rahamim Alsheikh – fell captive.
- *16 October 1986*: An Israeli Air Force (IAF) plane crashed in Lebanon. The plane's navigator, Ron Arad, was taken captive by the Amal organization. Later, he was held hostage by Mustafa Dirani, head of the "Faithful Resistance", and apparently was subsequently handed over to the Iranians.
- *4 September 1997*: On the night of 4–5 September 1997, an IDF patrol was ambushed by Hizballah in the Antsaria area of south Lebanon – eleven soldiers were killed in the attack and four were wounded. One body and the body parts of two soldiers were left at the site after the evacuation.
- *2 October 2000*: Three IDF soldiers – Binyamin Avraham, Adi Avitan, and Omar Sued – were abducted by Hizballah from the Mount Dov sector of northern Israel.

- *October 2000*: Israeli civilian Elhanan Tannenbaum was lured to Dubai, abducted by Hizballah, and transferred to Lebanon.
- *July 2006*: Two Israeli soldiers – Ehud Goldwasser and Eldad Regev – were abducted by Hizballah from the Zarit sector of northern Israel.

Israel left no stone unturned to free the captives: diplomatic channels, direct and indirect pressure on Hizballah, and military operations were all utilized. During the years 1986–91, Hizballah consistently refused to divulge any reliable information regarding either the number of soldiers that it was holding or their physical and mental condition, and was unwilling to enter negotiations regarding their return to Israel – Hizballah leaders rejected negotiations, claiming that they did not recognize Israel's existence. Political and strategic changes in the region, and the new approach adopted by Hizballah's patrons, Iran and Syria, eventually forced the organization to change its position regarding the issue of Israeli prisoners of war.

At the end of 1990 – for the first time – Hizballah leaders issued statements that appeared to prepare its supporters for a change of policy regarding the Israeli hostages. Their spiritual leader, Sheikh Muhammad Fadlallah, called for the mutual release of Arab and western hostages on a "humanitarian basis". In 1991, following the appointment of Sheikh Abbas al Musawi as Hizballah's secretary-general, the organization agreed to enter into negotiations with Israel for a prisoner exchange, parallel to negotiations that were being conducted at that time for the release of western hostages being held by the organization.

The abduction of two IDF soldiers in Lebanon (February 1986)

On the morning of 17 February 1986, an IDF force set out on a military operation into Lebanon, departing from Beit Jabil towards a roadblock at Beit Yahun in a convoy comprising of three vehicles. Shortly after noon, when the convoy reached a curve on the northern road at Kfar Kunin, it encountered a Hizballah ambush.

The ambush had been well planned, and consisted of a group that shot at the convoy and carried out the abduction, while two other cells positioned to the north opened diversionary mortar fire at a nearby South Lebanon Army (SLA) stronghold. The Hizballah ambushers opened fire at the two rear vehicles after the first had taken the curve; the driver of the second vehicle was killed and crashed into a ditch at the side of the road. An officer and soldier jumped out into the ditch and immediately opened fire at a nearby house from where they thought the shooting had originated; however, they were unable to clearly identify the source of the gunfire. A few minutes later, the officer got into the vehicle and attempted to make radio contact, but was unsuccessful. Subsequently, the officer attempted to see what had happened to the third car, but could not approach it due to gunfire.

At about 12:45 p.m., an IDF force arrived at the site, but the Hizballah ambushers had already withdrawn. A search of the area revealed that two Israeli soldiers – Rahamim Alsheikh and Yosef Fink – had been abducted from the third vehicle.

An investigation of the incident indicated that the abductors had fled via Wadi Alka east to Barashit and then traveled down a dirt path parallel to the road before entering an ambulance in the vicinity of the Shakra petrol station and continuing towards the Jamijama intersection. The ambulance's destination was never verified, nor is it known to where the hostages were taken.

Immediately after news of the soldiers' abduction had been reported to IDF headquarters, steps were taken to close roads in the area to prevent the abductors' flight from the security zone. The IDF performed an extensive search over several days to try to locate the abducted soldiers (the "Electric Pipe" campaign), carried out by combat helicopters and troops from the IDF's Ninety-First Division together with SLA soldiers. At the same time, the Israeli navy took action to prevent the removal of the soldiers from Lebanon via the sea. But the soldiers were never found.

During the "Electric Pipe" campaign, two IDF soldiers were killed along with eighteen terrorists. Some 184 men suspected of membership of terrorist organizations were arrested, and a large number of weapons were confiscated, including land mines, fifty rocket-propelled grenade (RPG) launchers, 147 Kalashnikov rifles, several 122-millimeter artillery shells, fifty 107-millimeter rockets, and two SA-7 shoulder-launched antiaircraft missiles.

After prolonged negotiations with Hizballah through intermediaries, the bodies of Rahamim Alsheikh and Yosef Fink were finally returned. In 1991, Hizballah had verified that the captives were dead in exchange for the release of ninety-one Lebanese prisoners and the bodies of nine Hizballah members who had been killed during attempted terrorist attacks. Five years later, on 21 July 1996, the remains of the two abducted soldiers were returned to Israel in exchange for the liberation of forty-five Lebanese prisoners and the return of the remains of 123 Hizballah combatants.

The Ron Arad affair

On 16 October 1986, IAF navigator Ron Arad bailed out of his plane due to a technical problem during a flight mission over Lebanon and was taken captive by the Amal organization. At the time of the incident, Nabih Berri stood at the head of Amal. Berri claimed responsibility for Arad's capture on various occasions (as will be elaborated subsequently), and even declared: "Not even a hair on Ron Arad's head will be touched" as long as he (Berri) headed the organization. At the time when Arad was taken into captivity, Mustafa Dirani served as head of Amal's security agency. Berri had appointed Dirani as security director in 1985. In the framework of this role, Dirani was also responsible for Maadushiya, the village near the site where Arad had landed after parachuting out of his Phantom aircraft.

After falling captive, Arad was handed over to Dirani as Amal's representative. At first, Dirani held him in his headquarters in western Beirut, but subsequently moved him frequently from one safe house to another so that Israel would not be able to track him down. During the transfers, Arad was bound and placed in the trunk of a car, and left without food or water for several days. During this period, Dirani abused and humiliated his prisoner, while preventing any contact with his family. A short time after Arad's capture, Berri left his headquarters in Beirut and moved to Damascus; the move was initiated by Berri's cohorts, the Syrians, to ensure his personal security and to protect him from the long arm of the State of Israel due to his involvement in the affair. After Berri's departure, Arad remained under Dirani's complete control. On 18 October 1986, Israel officially announced, for the first time, that it regarded Amal as solely responsible for Ron Arad's well-being.

During the first two months of his captivity, Amal enabled Syrian interrogators, and possibly the Russians as well, to question Arad. At the beginning of 1987, tension escalated between Amal and Hizballah against the background of a dispute between the Shiite organizations regarding control over south Lebanon. At the same time that fighting broke out between Amal and Hizballah, the Israeli navy imposed a naval blockade on Sidon and al Uzai (cities that were under Amal's control) on 8 February 1987, in order to impress upon Arad's captors that they were responsible for his safety due to fears that he might be hurt in skirmishes with Hizballah. In response to the blockade, Berri announced that, if it were not lifted, he would not be responsible for Arad's life. His response served as additional confirmation that Ron Arad was being held by Amal under Dirani's control.

In a press conference held in April 1987, Berri proposed that the Red Cross serve as an intermediary in an exchange deal: Ron Arad in exchange for Shiite prisoners incarcerated in Israel and Israel's withdrawal from south Lebanon. During the negotiations, Amal members several times disclosed information about Arad and the state of his health. In September 1987, as part of the negotiation process between Israel and Amal, letters and two pictures of Arad were handed over to his family – these letters and pictures were the last signs of life received from Ron Arad.

At that time, Dirani founded an independent radical Islamic organization called the "Faithful Resistance", headed by himself. Soon afterwards, Dirani and his men left Amal in favor of the new organization, which cooperated with Hizballah and the Iranians. On 20 October 1987, Dirani "abducted" Ron Arad from Amal, where he had previously served as its security director, and resumed full control over him in the framework of his new organization. Over a period of eighteen months following his abduction from Amal, Arad was again moved from place to place, deprived of the basic rights granted to a POW by the Geneva Convention, and the Red Cross was not allowed to visit him.

Dirani's ties with Iran, and his organization's affiliation with the Revolutionary Guards, led him to search for an opportunity to hand Arad to the Iranians as a "deposit". Immediately after his "abduction" of Arad, Dirani initiated negotiations with Iran regarding terms for holding the "deposit". Towards the end of 1987, Arad was held in Dirani's house while the latter was negotiating with the Iranians regarding the transfer. In early 1988, Berri informed Israel that Arad was in Dirani's hands and claimed that Dirani had announced his intention to transfer the captive to Iran or to Hizballah. Israel contacted Dirani, who demanded the release of hundreds of prisoners incarcerated in Israel. But despite Israel's agreement in principle to release the prisoners, its efforts to progress with the discussions ended in naught – on 4 May 1988, Dirani "sold" Arad to Iranian entities (apparently the Revolutionary Guards), and the captive disappeared without a trace.

On 21 May 1994, Dirani was captured at his home in Lebanon by Israeli forces, brought to Israel, and incarcerated in a prison facility of the Israeli security service.

"Operation Poplar's Whistle" (the Israeli SEALs' debacle)

"Operation Poplar's Whistle" took place on the night of 4–5 September 1997, and was carried out by a total of sixteen soldiers from Israel's navy SEAL Force 13. While making its way towards the target, the force encountered an ambush – in the first moments of the encounter, two explosions detonated nearby. Some three minutes after the beginning of the skirmish, an explosive device carried by Sergeant-Major Itamar Iliya detonated as a result of the initial explosions. With the exception of one soldier, all members of the force were injured as a result of the shooting and explosions: eleven were killed, including the force's commander, Lieutenant-Colonel Yosef Kuarkin, and four were wounded. An air rescue force was summoned to extricate the survivors and exchanged fire with the ambushers, during which the rescue force's doctor was killed. The injured and dead were evacuated from the site but, following a detailed account from the evacuees at the Nahariya hospital, it became clear that Sergeant-Major Iliya's body had been seized, and body parts belonging to Sergeant-Major Tubi Raz and Staff-Sergeant Golan Guy were also missing.

The initial contact for the return of the bodies was launched on 5 September 1997, the day after the debacle. Yaakov Peri, a former head of Israel's General Security Service (GSS), was Israel's representative in the negotiations and transferred an appeal to the Lebanese government through the Red Cross. Initially, it was unclear who was holding Iliya's body but, three days later, it was decided that negotiations would be conducted via the Lebanese government. The initial Lebanese demand was to release all prisoners from Israel's al Hiyam prison and the return of all bodies of Lebanese terrorists buried in Israel. Israel rejected this demand and stated that it would only return the terrorists' bodies. When it became clear that the deal did not stand a chance of success if live terrorists were not returned, Israel agreed to a gesture that would include the release of some terrorist prisoners. Lebanon was not satisfied with Israel's promise to carry this out and demanded a third-party guarantee that the deal would take place – the subsequent letter of commitment signed by Israeli Prime Minister Netanyahu was accompanied by a guarantee from the French president, Jacques Chirac.

On 29 May 1998, Chirac visited Lebanon. Israel decided to take advantage of his trip to break the deadlock in negotiations, and Israel's President Ezer Weizmann sent a personal letter to the French president stipulating Israel's final offer: the bodies of forty terrorists, and sixty prisoners – ten from Israeli prisons and fifty from al Hiyam. Several days later, Lebanon announced that the proposal had been accepted. A short time later, Sheikh Hassan Nasrallah announced that Israel and Lebanon had reached an agreement regarding the exchange, adding that his son's body would be included in the deal. On 5 June 1998, the Lebanese government officially approved the deal and requested another letter of guarantee of all matters related to the exchange arrangements and the schedule. On 25 June 1998, after prolonged negotiations, the body of Itamar Iliya was returned together with the body parts of Tubi Raz and Golan Guy. As noted earlier, it had been agreed to transfer sixty prisoners and the bodies of forty terrorists interred in northern Israel (including the body of Nasrallah's son, who was killed during IDF activity in Lebanon); on June 26th, fifty-nine prisoners were returned to Lebanon (one of the prisoners refused to leave the Israeli prison, claiming that his life would be endangered if he returned to Lebanon). Nasrallah defined the deal as "a great achievement for the Hizballah and the Lebanese people".

The abduction of three IDF soldiers from Mount Dov (October 2000)

On Saturday morning, 7 October 2000, a motorized patrol set off to inspect the northern border security fence in the Mount Dov sector. The patrol comprised of three soldiers – the commander, Binyamin Avraham, and scouts Adi Avitan and Omar Sued. When the vehicle arrived at a gate in the border fence that enabled access into Lebanon, two explosive charges were detonated, causing injuries to the soldiers. The gate itself was damaged by another explosive device. A vehicle containing Hizballah members then entered Israeli territory and abducted the three wounded soldiers.

The subsequent investigation indicated that the operations room of the IDF's Hermon brigade received an electronic warning regarding the intrusion through the security fence, but the abduction was only discovered fifteen minutes later, when the squadron's commander was unable to reach the soldiers on the two-way radio and went out to see what was happening. Due to a large-scale bombardment of artillery fire and antitank missiles along the sector that took place simultaneously as cover for the abduction, precious time passed before the commander could approach the burning patrol vehicle and declare the incident an abduction. Once verified, IDF forces pursued the abductors inside Lebanon, while IDF helicopters strafed roads and bridges in order to prevent the abductors from fleeing deep into Lebanese territory, but the kidnappers got away.

Hizballah planned the abduction meticulously: In the morning, their civilian supporters gathered near Zarit to demonstrate and throw stones at IDF soldiers, thus distracting the attention of the Mount Dov sector command where the abduction was to take place. At about noon, Hizballah began an extensive bombardment of Mount Dov and IDF strongholds on Mount Hermon with hundreds of mortar shells and dozens of missiles, which prevented the rescue force from responding immediately.

The Israeli response was limited to bombing a few Hizballah positions and a Syrian radar station in Lebanon. Regional and local concerns at that time played a significant role in the decision of Israeli Prime Minister Ehud Barak to refuse to order a large-scale retaliation against Hizballah. The Palestinian *al Aksa* intifada had broken out just a few days before the kidnapping, and Israel preferred at that time to avoid another armed confrontation on its northern border. Another internal political reason not to escalate the situation in the north of Israel was Barak's unwillingness to reopen the internal political debate regarding his previous decision to withdraw from south Lebanon.

This first cross-border operation after the Israeli withdrawal was considered by Lebanon and the Arab world as a significant achievement for Hizballah, and reflected badly on Israel. The lack of a strong Israeli military response and the high price that Israel was eventually forced to pay encouraged Hizballah to continue with abduction as an effective tactical tool.

Hizballah abduction attempt at Rajar (November 2005)

On 21 November 2005, Hizballah carried out a number of attacks against IDF posts in the Rajar and Mount Dov sectors in an attempt to kidnap IDF soldiers. IDF units were successful in repulsing these attacks, although eleven soldiers were wounded and at least four Hizballah terrorists were killed.[2] This was the second attempt by Hizballah to kidnap Israeli soldiers following the withdrawal of IDF forces from Lebanon in 2000.

The attacks

On the afternoon of 21 November 2005, Hizballah initiated a terror attack against Israeli civilian and military targets – an attack which included rocket fire, mortar shelling, and gunfire in the areas of Metulla, Rajar, and Mount Dov. Both an officer and a soldier situated in IDF positions were severely wounded.

The abduction attempt

At the same time, Hizballah carried out an abduction attempt against IDF posts in the Rajar area. Dozens of Hizballah militants crossed into Israel on foot, on motorcycles, and in all-terrain vehicles (ATVs) to attack an IDF position in Rajar; but, relying only on a general intelligence warning, the force there had recently changed location, and Hizballah stormed an empty post and were themselves ambushed. A young IDF sharpshooter, Corporal David Markowitz, killed three Hizballah terrorists in this encounter.

The Israeli response

In response to these attacks, the IAF bombed a Hizballah command post and several access routes to the area. Early on 22 November 2005, an IDF engineering squad demolished an outpost used by Hizballah in the Rajar attacks, located approximately twenty meters north of the village. The bunker was built by Hizballah following the departure of the IDF from southern Lebanon and was used by the terrorist organization to collect intelligence on IDF activity necessary to carry out attacks against the entire sector in general, and Rajar in particular.

The following statement was issued by the head of the northern Israeli Ground Operations Command (GOC), Major-General Udi Adam:[3]

> "The incident began when the Hizballah terrorist organization fired mortar shells and rockets, initially aiming them at IDF posts in the Mount Dov and Rajar regions, and later on targeting the entire border area. Hizballah used its full arsenal against us – mortar shells, Katyusha rockets, anti-tank missiles, and sniper fire. No IDF activity was carried out in the area prior to this attack. This attack had been in the planning for a long time, and we haven't seen such a wide-scale coordinated attack by Hizballah in a long time.
>
> "IDF units responded very well to this threat. Hizballah underestimated our capabilities for a quick and effective response. Forces implemented pinpointed attacks at the sources of fire and at Hizballah posts in southern Lebanon. We believe that Hizballah intended to kidnap IDF soldiers through the border village of Rajar. However, their attempts were thwarted by IDF units. Overall, eleven IDF soldiers were wounded in this attack. We know of four terrorists who were killed.
>
> "Mortar shells and rockets have also landed in populated areas. A house in the city of Metulla was damaged. So far, we know of no casualties, although structural damage was caused. It's been a long time since we last had to direct the civilian population in northern Israel to enter their bomb shelters.
>
> "Hizballah is attempting to recreate its image as a defender of southern Lebanon. The UN has decided that this terrorist organization must disarm itself, and so Hizballah is searching constantly for justification to continue its activities. Israel is free to respond to such attacks in any way it deems appropriate.
>
> "We see the Lebanese government as responsible for any activity carried out from its territory, and hope it will be able to prove itself as a responsible and capable body in dealing with this issue."

Summary

Kidnapping Israeli soldiers has long been at the top of the Hizballah agenda. This attack was a repeat of previous failed attempts, only more severe and intense in scope. Hizballah's two-prong attack on the village of Rajar and an IDF outpost involved sophisticated planning, tactics, and resources (ATVs and motorcycles), and clearly demonstrated that, rather than being deterred from continuing such activities, they were only further encouraged.

The abduction of two IDF soldiers: The second Lebanon war (July 2006)

On 12 July 2006, eight IDF soldiers were killed and two were abducted in an attack by Hizballah near Zarit in northern Israel. Five civilians were injured, in addition to five soldiers. The incident began in the morning, when two armored vehicles on a routine patrol alongside the border were ambushed between Zarit and Shtula. A group of terrorists had cut the border fence and penetrated into Israel undetected, taking advantage of a blind spot noted in the IDF border surveillance. The attackers stalked the IDF soldiers and surprised the patrol with a lethal spray of gunfire some two hundred meters inside Israeli territory. Three soldiers were killed in this initial attack, one was severely hurt, and another was lightly injured. The terrorists abducted two wounded IDF soldiers – Eldad Regev and Ehud Goldwasser – and took them into Lebanese territory.

As soon as the IDF became aware of the abduction, it began to pursue the terrorists inside Lebanon. In the course of the chase, a Merkava tank was hit by an explosive device and four of its crew members were killed; during attempts to extricate the crew, a soldier from the Nahal brigade was killed and two others were lightly injured.

Hizballah's demands and Nasrallah's speech

The stated goals of Hizballah's "Operation Truthful Promise" (previously named "Operation Freedom for Samir al Quntar") were:[4]

- To take IDF soldiers hostage in order to pressure Israel to release Lebanese prisoners held in Israeli prisons – in particular, the terrorist Samir al Quntar, who was convicted by an Israeli court in 1980 of the murder of five civilians and sentenced to five life sentences, plus an additional forty-seven years in prison for injuries he inflicted on the victims.
- To seek return of the disputed Israeli-occupied Shebaa Farms area to Lebanese control.

Shortly after the abduction, Hizballah claimed responsibility and demanded indirect negotiations for a prisoner exchange deal, indicating that it might include Gilad Shalit, who was kidnapped in Gaza on 25 June 2006. Hizballah's General-Secretary Hassan Nasrallah demanded the release of convicted terrorists Samir al Quntar, Nassim Nasser, and

Yehye Sahhaf, and promised that he would demand the release of still more prisoners. On 12 July 2006, Nasrallah held a press conference in Beirut, declaring: "The kidnapped soldiers are far, far away." He addressed Israeli Prime Minister Olmert as follows: "I strongly recommend that you act responsibly. Any military action to release the abducted soldiers on the Israeli side, and any military escalation will be met by Hizballah surprises . . . we will respond with force to any action. The two soldiers will only be released through negotiations." Nasrallah also mocked the lack of experience of the Israeli prime minister, defense minister, and chief of staff, and advised them to consult with the people they had replaced.

Israel's response to the attack

At the end of an emergency session held around midnight, the Israeli government decided to declare all-out war against Hizballah until the thousands of missiles that the organization had sited along Israel's northern border were completely annihilated, unanimously approving "Operation Fair Pay" – a series of military actions against Hizballah and the Lebanese government. Amongst other tactics, the massive bombardment of Lebanese infrastructure and elimination of Hizballah officials were discussed. No time limit was to be placed on the military operation, which was to include air raids, massive artillery and naval barrages, and ground operations. Israel's strategic goals were to reestablish its deterrent capabilities in Lebanon, to set new ground rules, and to push Hizballah back from its northern border.

"We will not allow ourselves to be held hostage to the threat of rockets," declared Prime Minister Ehud Olmert in response to security agencies' assessments that Hizballah might launch dozens or hundreds of rockets towards Israel. "We will act because the current reality forces us to respond to this threat once and for all." Olmert told cabinet members that the incidents on the northern border could not be perceived merely as a single event in a series of incidents *vis-à-vis* Hizballah, but rather as the crossing of a red line that no other country would tolerate. Sources close to the prime minister defined the emergency meeting and its resolutions as "a declaration of war".[5]

Defense Minister Amir Peretz met late that night with the Home Front commander and briefed him about impending events, noting that Hizballah had built up a massive missile arsenal in recent years and stating that the time had now come for the inevitable confrontation. Peretz informed the cabinet that "we intend to act with all the force at our disposal so that when the conflict ends, the Lebanese government and Hizballah will rue the moment they initiated the conflict." At the end of the meeting, the cabinet members agreed that operative decisions would be approved by a special team that would include the prime minister, Foreign Minister Tzipi Livni, Deputy Prime Minister Shimon Peres, Defense Minister Amir Peretz, and ministers Shaul Mofaz and Avi Dichter.[6] Given the cabinet's green light, the IDF launched "Operation Fair Pay" (later renamed "Operation Change Direction") on the night of 12–13 July 2006, with the goals of exacting both a fitting price and the restoration of Israel's deterrent effect in the region.

Lebanese and international responses

Lebanese Prime Minister Fouad Siniora called for urgent talks with Hussein Khalil, Nasrallah's closest advisor. Siniora was pessimistic and furious as he foresaw the IDF response, recalling the day after Gilad Shalit's abduction, when Gaza was ravaged. As an answer, Hizballah leaders claimed that "everything will quiet down in twenty-four to forty-eight hours".[7] Amine Gemayel, the country's former president, stated: "Hizballah was responsible for dragging all of Lebanon into a military struggle far larger than it could handle."[8]

The International Red Cross approached Hizballah in order to be able to examine the two abducted soldiers. Their demand was rejected – a decision that was criticized by the Human Rights Watch.[9] The leaders of the world's eight most powerful industrial states supported Israel's right to self-defense at the G-8 Conference on 16 July 2006; their concluding statement was the most significant declaration of support that Israel had received since the onset of the fighting, four days earlier, and cast full responsibility upon Hamas and Hizballah for the regional crisis.[10] While Iran, Syria, and Yemen supported Hizballah, the Arab League was divided: Egypt and Jordan criticized Hizballah and supported Lebanon. This response was best interpreted in the joint statement of King Abdullah II of Jordan and Egyptian President Hosni Mubarak: "We condemn the irresponsible escalatory act that has the potential of leading the region into a dangerous situation." In addition, the declaration of Saudi Foreign Minister Saud al Faisal was unequivocal, defining Hizballah's acts as "unexpected, dishonorable, and irresponsible. They will put the region back years and are utterly unacceptable".[11]

UN resolution 1701

On 11 August 2006, the United Nations Security Council unanimously approved UN resolution 1701 that ended the hostilities. The resolution, backed by the Israeli government, and later by the Lebanese government, called for the disarmament of Hizballah, the return of the hostage IDF soldiers, Israel's withdrawal from Lebanon, and the deployment of both Lebanese soldiers and an enlarged United Nations

Interim Force In Lebanon (UNIFIL) presence in southern Lebanon.[12] However, the Lebanese government stated that it would not disarm Hizballah, while UNIFIL claimed that it was not within its mandate to do so. Meanwhile, the Lebanese army began deploying in southern Lebanon on 17 August 2006. As for Regev and Goldwasser, the Red Cross was not permitted to visit them – a violation of international law.

On 1 October 2006, all Israeli troops withdrew from Lebanon. Later intelligence reports indicated that large quantities of arms had continued to flow unhindered from Syria to Hizballah during the course of the conflict.

Summary

The scale of the Israeli response was a total shock for Hizballah. Not only did the organization misjudge the Israeli response, it also underestimated the implications that the abduction of Israeli soldiers held for the Lebanese political arena.[13] During the war, Hizballah fired about four thousand rockets into Israel, killing forty-four Israeli civilians and injuring nearly 1,500 – the Hizballah rockets fell on Israeli Arabs and Jews alike. On the Lebanese side, 1,109 people died (the vast majority were civilians) and more than four thousand were injured.[14] Israeli civilian casualties were relatively low thanks to well-organized civil defense preparations.

On Wednesday, 16 July 2008, after two years of negotiations, Hizballah finally transferred the remains of Eldad Regev and Ehud Goldwasser to Israel, in exchange for imprisoned Palestinian Liberation Front (PLF) terrorist Samir al Quntar, four other imprisoned Hizballah members, and the bodies of about two hundred Lebanese and Palestinian terrorists.

The Winograd Commission (April 2007)

The purpose of the Winograd Commission, appointed in September 2006 in response to the Israeli public's disappointment with the results of the second Lebanon war and the way it was managed by the political and military echelons, was to investigate and report on the events that occurred during the military engagement in Lebanon in 2006.

According to the commission's preliminary report, published on 30 April 2007, the second Lebanon war was a "missed opportunity", and "Israel initiated a long war, which ended without a defined military victory." The report continued: "A semi-military organization of a few thousand men resisted, for a few weeks, the strongest army in the Middle East, which enjoyed full air superiority and size and technology advantages." Furthermore, Hizballah's rocket attacks continued throughout the war and the IDF did not provide an effective response to the threat. Following a long period of standoff firepower and limited ground activities, the IDF finally launched a large-scale ground offensive shortly before the UN Security Council's resolution imposed a cease-fire; the offensive did not result in military gains and was halted prematurely before attaining its goals, the report stated.

The commission further stated that "[A] decision [was] made in the night of 12 July to react [to the abductions] with immediate and substantive military action and to set . . . ambitious goals." This decision had immediate repercussions that limited subsequent decisions to a choice between "a short, painful, and unexpected blow on Hizballah" or "to bring about a significant change of the reality in the south of Lebanon with a large ground operation, [occupying] . . . the south of Lebanon and 'cleaning' it of Hizballah". The fact that Israel went to war before it had decided which option to select, and without an exit strategy, constituted a serious failure of the decision-making process.

As for achievements, the commission concluded that "Security Council Resolution 1701, and the fact that it was adopted unanimously, were an achievement for Israel."[15] The final report was submitted to the Israeli government on 30 January 2008.

Israel's Efforts to Obtain the Release of IDF Soldiers Held by Hizballah

After the abduction of IDF soldiers Yosef Fink and Rahamim Alsheikh, followed by the capture of IAF navigator Ron Arad, Israel made tremendous efforts to rescue its soldiers and return them home, alive or dead. However, Hizballah refused to divulge any information about the fates of Fink and Alsheikh, while in Arad's case there was some limited information supplied before he was transferred by his captors to Iran.

Due to the fact that all efforts to force Hizballah to release prisoners before 1989 had proved to be futile, it was decided to try to promote their release by obtaining "bargaining chips" that would serve as an incentive for Hizballah to enter into negotiations. The first step of the attempt to secure a "bargaining chip" *vis-à-vis* Hizballah was carried out in September 1989, when an IDF force abducted Sheikh Karim Obeid from his home in Lebanon and brought him to Israel.

Obeid was one of the senior Hizballah members in southern Lebanon. After his abduction had failed to bring about the desired results, Israel initiated another operation in May 1994, and caught

Mustafa Dirani, leader of the "Faithful Resistance", who had held Arad hostage and later turned him over to Hizballah and the Iranians.

Dirani's abduction to Israel had three goals:

- An attempt to acquire information about Arad.
- The use of Dirani as an additional "bargaining chip" for Arad's release.
- Punishing Dirani for his cruel and humiliating treatment of Arad while he was being held hostage by him, and for turning the prisoner over to the Iranians.

Dirani's subsequent interrogation in Israel clarified certain issues regarding Arad's fate, but did not provide up-to-date information about his location, while Dirani's incarceration in an Israeli prison did nothing to contribute to Iran's or Hizballah's willingness to enter into negotiations for Arad's release.

The abduction of Sheikh Abdel Karim Obeid

In July 1989, Israeli security authorities decided to try to force the hand of Iran and Hizballah to obtain the return of Ron Arad. The goal was to obtain another high-value "bargaining chip" by abducting one of Hizballah's leaders – the security authorities decided that the prime candidate was Sheikh Abdel Karim Obeid, a key Hizballah figure in south Lebanon since 1983.

Obeid was born in the village of Jibsheet in southern Lebanon, and was a follower of Hizballah's spiritual leader, Sheikh Muhammad Hussein Fadlallah. In 1980, in the aftermath of the Islamic revolution, Obeid departed for the city of Qom in Iran (where Ayatollah Khomeini resided) to continue his Islamic studies in a religious seminary. While there, he also underwent firearms and explosives training, and was taught various terrorist attack methods. In 1982, after the first Lebanon war, he returned to his village and was appointed an *imam* (Islamic prayer leader).

Obeid maintained his close ties with Iran, and even compared the relationship between Muslims in Lebanon and Iran to the relationship between Christians worldwide and the pope's Holy See at the Vatican.[16] During the period that he served as one of Hizballah's leaders in south Lebanon, Obeid received funds from Iran and even hosted the Iranian ambassador to Damascus at that time, Ali Akbar Mohtashami-Pour, who was one of the founders of Hizballah and was in charge of Iran's ties with the organization.

Obeid's interrogation in Israel indicated that he had been involved in the planning, management, and support of many terror events, including:[17]

- The abduction of IDF soldiers Yosef Fink and Rahamim Alsheikh in February 1996.
- Multiple attacks against IDF forces in south Lebanon.
- The abduction of Lieutenant-Colonel William Higgins and his transfer to Beirut, in addition to providing the abductors with a safe haven (his home in Jibsheet).

Obeid stated that the plan for Higgins' abduction took shape in his house, and that the Mercedes in which the victim had been abducted was kept hidden near his home for about a month. He claimed that two additional cars were used during the abduction, a Mercedes and a Volvo, and divulged that he had turned Higgins over to Hizballah members in south Beirut.

The plan to abduct Obeid was prepared by the IDF and approved by the security cabinet. On Friday 28 July 1989, at about 2:00 a.m., helicopters carrying members of the general-headquarters' elite reconnaissance unit landed near Obeid's village, seven kilometers from the border of the security zone. The force members made their way stealthily towards his home at the village's eastern end; Obeid was taken from the house, together with four Shiites who were in his company, and transported to Israel by helicopter. The next day, Israel admitted responsibility for the sheikh's abduction.

Obeid's interrogation in Israel indicated that he lacked concrete information about Ron Arad. He believed that Arad was still alive and was being transferred from place to place by his captors, who maintained strict compartmentalization even *vis-à-vis* the organization's leaders. In the aftermath of Obeid's abduction by the IDF, Defense Minister Yitzhak Rabin proposed an exchange of prisoners: "Israel once again calls for the release of the Israeli POWs and the other hostages being held by Shiite organizations in Lebanon. Israel proposes an exchange of prisoners, detainees, and hostages. According to this proposal, the Israelis and the foreign hostages being held by the Shiite organizations will be exchanged for all of the Shiite prisoners being held in Israel, including Sheikh Abdel Karim Obeid, Juad Katsfi, and others."[18]

The Israelis hoped that this offer would elicit a positive response from Hizballah regarding the prisoner swap. Instead, Hizballah declared: "We will not negotiate with Israel. He who was abducted forcefully will be returned by force."

Iranian and Hizballah attempts to release Sheikh Obeid

In the aftermath of Obeid's abduction, Iran and its sponsored organizations in Lebanon took various steps to try to release him. Among their political and propaganda moves was a statement made by Iranian Foreign Minister Ali Akbar Velayati: "We condemn the abduction of Sheikh Obeid and ask the international community to exert pressure on the Zionist regime to release him." Iran also appealed to the UN, holding Israel responsible for Obeid's well-being and safety.[19]

Iran and Hizballah also threatened to attack Israeli and American targets in Lebanon and to execute hostages if Obeid was not released. In 1989, when Obeid was abducted, his friend Ali Akbar Mohtashami-Pour was Iran's minister of the interior. It came as no surprise, therefore, when Pour immediately placed himself at the head of the list of those demanding Obeid's immediate release and appealed to Islamic militia fighters in Lebanon to increase their attacks against Israeli and American targets in that country. Pour also accused the US of playing a role in Obeid's abduction. In the Hebrew newspaper *al Hamishmar* ("The Guard"), he stated: "The American and Israeli criminals must be held responsible for any reaction of faithful Muslims," and added: "As long as the regime that conquered Jerusalem is in control of Palestine, it is forbidden for Muslims to strip off their combat uniforms, and they must exact revenge from the United States and the Israeli criminals."[20]

Hizballah also threatened to execute Lieutenant-Colonel William Higgins if Obeid was not released. The related declaration, entitled "In the Future it will be Even Worse,"[21] was published by the "Organization of the Oppressed on Earth" and distributed by the Associated Press representative in Beirut.

This is the full text of Hizballah's declaration regarding the hanging of Lieutenant-Colonel Higgins:

"In the name of merciful Allah!
"As criminal America and the Zionist enemy did not take our decision seriously to execute the American spy Higgins, and due to the fact that Sheikh Obeid and his two brothers were not released on the designated date, out of disdain for our ultimatum, Higgins' life and everything that we hold holy, and out of a desire to carry out Allah's righteous will, the American spy Higgins was executed by hanging today, Monday afternoon. He will serve as an example and model for those who fear Judgment Day.

"We renew our demand that the virtuous Sheikh [Abdel Karim Obeid] and his two brothers be released immediately, otherwise it may be even worse in the future, and American and Israel will take full responsibility for this. Death for America and Israel, for those who are arrogant and their agents.

> *Glory and immortality for our nation's heroes and righteous martyrs. We vow that we will continue our struggle along the path they outlined with their weapons and blood to uproot the Israeli cancer and to cut off the hands of the arrogant people who play in our land, particularly America, in order to magnify and glorify the Muslim faith and Muhammad's nation, until the banner of Muslim unity will wave proudly over the entire world.*
> "The Organization of the Oppressed on Earth"

Hizballah also threatened to execute the hostage Joseph Cicippio.[22] A leader of Hizballah in Lebanon, Hussein Musawi, threatened: "We will execute one of the Israeli soldiers being held captive if it serves Islamic interests." And he added: "Even if all of the Hizballah leaders, including myself, are abducted, we will not negotiate with Israel." In actual fact, Iran and Hizballah did not carry out their threats. The pictures showing Higgins' hanging were fake – Higgins had been executed by his captors much earlier – and hostage Joseph Cicippio was not murdered by his captors.

In contrast to the threatening and hostile tone adopted by most Hizballah leaders, the organization's spiritual leader, Sheikh Muhammad Hussein Fadlallah, stated the following in an interview with the Islamic radio station, The Nation's Voice:[23]

> "Let us agree and search together, each of us with his own means and influence, for the way to put an end to the crisis of the hostages, all of the hostages, and the ways to put an end to the question of Arab prisoners inside and out. The issue will move toward a realistic solution, something that will take a good deal of time. But it will not be possible to push the issue forward due to the American activity. The military activity will only exacerbate the danger to the hostages' well-being and increase the possibility that something that the Americans define as terror will happen. The deployment of the American navy constitutes preparations for a coordinated military operation between the United States and Israel."

Nevertheless, Iran and Hizballah refused to participate in negotiations with Israel for the release of Arad and the other POWs that the organization was holding (Fink and Alsheikh). During Nachshon Wachsman's abduction five years later in 1994, another attempt was made by Hizballah and Iran to bring about Obeid's release – this time by an abduction perpetrated by the Palestinian terror organization, Hamas.

The abduction of Mustafa Dirani

Mustafa Dirani had long been marked as a candidate for abduction as Israel believed that Dirani could fill in the intelligence blanks regarding Ron Arad's fate.[24]

Dirani was a Shiite Muslim who served as Amal's security officer from the mid-1980s. In the framework of this role, he was responsible for the capture of Arad in October 1986. Following a process of religious radicalization, Dirani and several of his associates left Amal at the beginning of 1988 and established a new organization called the "Faithful Resistance" that was affiliated with Iran and Hizballah. For eighteen months, Dirani held Arad hostage and controlled his life until handing him over to Iranian factions in May 1988, when he disappeared without a trace.

Both in his role as Amal's security officer and as the leader of the "Faithful Resistance", Dirani was responsible for attacks against IDF forces in Lebanon. He was captured on 21 May 1994, during an intricate military operation carried out by an IDF force that raided his home in the village of Kfar Kaser, from whence he was transferred to Israel. Documents confiscated in Dirani's home were also brought to Israel; among these was a letter written by Dirani to Hizballah Secretary-General Sheikh Abbas al Musawi, in which he protested the fact that Arad had been abducted from his possession without any kind of compensation. During his interrogation in Israel, Dirani claimed that Arad had been kidnapped from him by the Iranians and that he had not willingly handed the POW over or "sold" him.

The Israeli authorities believed that the letter was an "insurance document" that Dirani had prepared for a rainy day in order to shirk any responsibility for Arad's fate. In any event, Dirani was interrogated thoroughly in Israel and divulged everything he knew up until the day that he handed Arad over to Hizballah and the Iranians. The Israelis assumed that Dirani would provide up-to-date information about Arad that would help (together with their other "bargaining chip", Sheikh Obeid) to convince Hizballah and Iran to enter into negotiations for the release of Arad and the other IDF prisoners; but, as in the case of Obeid, the abduction failed to bring about the desired breakthrough.

The aftermath

On 29 January 2004, after conducting negotiations through a German intermediary, Hizballah returned to Israel the bodies of the three kidnapped soldiers and an Israeli hostage, businessman Elhanan Tannenbaum. In exchange, Israel released four hundred Palestinian prisoners, twenty-nine prisoners from Arab countries, and the bodies of sixty Hizballah terrorists. *Among the terrorists who were returned to Lebanon were Sheikh Obeid and Mustafa Dirani.*

Reciprocal Links Between Hamas and Hizballah Abductions

During the 1980s, Israel fought a violent struggle on two fronts simultaneously: the Lebanese and the Palestinian. In spite of fighting in these two arenas, Israel's security agencies thwarted multiple terror attacks and incarcerated hundreds, at times even thousands, of Lebanese and Palestinian prisoners involved in terror activities. The release of these prisoners, particularly senior Hamas cleric Sheikh Ahmad Yassin, constituted a main goal for the terror organizations.

The strategic Iranian concept that regarded struggle against Israel as a joint battle of the entire Muslim world – Shiite and Sunni alike – was also adopted by Hizballah and the Palestinian organizations, which regarded the merging of their forces as a vital component in their struggle against Israel. As a result of the adoption of this approach, operational cooperation developed between terror entities in both the Lebanese and Palestinian arenas, and was reflected by similar abduction-bargaining attacks perpetrated in both areas. In exchange for the release of Israeli hostages, Hizballah consistently demanded the release of prisoners from other Palestinian terror organizations in addition to the release of their own imprisoned members, particularly those belonging to Islamic Jihad and Hamas.

A similar phenomenon was identifiable in the Palestinian organizations. For example, Hamas demanded the release of Obeid, Dirani, and twenty additional prisoners from Hizballah during the abduction of Nachshon Wachsman.

Israeli Policy Regarding POWs and Hostages

The release of Israeli POWs and the return of remains of its soldiers killed in action are some of the most sensitive issues faced by Israeli society and its leadership. The extreme sensitivity of these subjects stems from several reasons: the value of human life and personal freedom in the eyes of Israeli society; the traditional Jewish obligation to redeem prisoners; the religious and moral importance attributed to the return of bodies of civilians and soldiers to Israel for burial; Israel's moral obligation to preserve the life and safety of its citizens; and the obligation of the Jewish state to protect those members of its security forces who fall into enemy hands while acting on its behalf.

In contrast to Jewish law, the commandment to redeem captives or bodies of the fallen is not an obligation in Islam. A study of the Koran and the *Hadith* ("Islamic Tradition") reveals that the only issue discussed is that of the fate of an *infidel* (non-believer) who falls into Muslim hands, not the redemption of a Muslim captive. There is a dispute in the *Hadith* regarding how a captive should be treated, and two alternatives are raised: either accept *fidaa* (ransom money) or execute the prisoner. As to the bodies of fallen Muslims in the enemy's hands, there is no religious obligation to bring them home.

Several times, Nasrallah addressed the issue of the bodies of Lebanese nationals in Israel's hands (which included the body of his son, Hadi), stating that there was no obligation to return them to their families because they were buried in the holy earth of Palestine.[25] Thus the interest of Islamic terrorist organizations in captives and prisoners does not stem from Islamic religious doctrine, but rather from practical (political, social, or humanitarian) considerations. The difference between the religious and normative approaches held by Jewish/Israeli society when compared to Muslim values imparts the Islamic terror organizations with significant bargaining power – power which they fully exploit. Over the years, Israel's policy regarding negotiations *vis-à-vis* terror organizations has reflected two polarized approaches: an adamant refusal to succumb to terror, and a flexible policy of clandestine negotiation.

As a rule, when Israel had the opportunity to release hostages or captives through a military operation without succumbing to the terrorists' demands, the decision-makers preferred this alternative. In other cases, when a military operation was not an option, Israel generally demonstrated flexibility and endeavored to bring about the hostages' release via negotiations, meeting the terror organizations' demands either partially or fully. By its very definition, Israel's "flexible policy" characterized negotiations over the price it was willing to pay to mollify its (political, defense, and social) communities, the type of terror organization that was partner to the negotiations, and the quality of the "bargaining chips" in Israeli hands. Yitzhak Rabin, who served as Israel's minister of defense in 1989, shed light on Israeli policy *vis-à-vis* the handling of hostages in an interview following the abduction of Obeid, in which he stated: "In the framework of the war on terror, and regarding the issue of Israeli hostages, Israel has chosen two courses of action. When there is the possibility of rescuing the prisoners through a military operation, we prefer this course. That is what we did in the Entebbe operation. We have a special responsibility to IDF soldiers who were sent to war in Lebanon and are missing or fell into the hands of Shiite organizations. We are willing to negotiate for their return and exchange them for Shiites who were abducted for this purpose and are being held by us."[26]

Former (and now current) Israeli Prime Minister Binyamin Netanyahu describes his worldview on the subject of handling terror in general, and abductions in particular, in his book, *Terrorism: How Can the West Win?*

> "The taking of hostages forces the government in charge of their welfare to face a difficult dilemma: If it prefers the use of force to release the hostages over capitulation there is the possibility that the number of casualties will rise. On the other hand, if you cave in to the terrorists' demands, they will emerge victorious."[27]

Sometimes the terrorists themselves resolve this dilemma when they execute some hostages and threaten to kill the rest if their demands are not met. In some cases, these demands are simply unacceptable; at other times, it is unclear whether or not capitulation to these demands will cause additional casualties. In this event, the government may argue that, as the terrorists will undoubtedly kill additional hostages, it must take immediate action. But how should the government act if the terrorists have not yet begun to execute hostages? In such circumstances, has the need for military action diminished? The answer is: no. Terrorists need to be under no illusion that a government is willing to take determined action against the abductors, regardless of the fact that hostages have not been executed. The very act of hostage abduction justifies this policy. It is a grave error to allow terrorists to believe that they are immune to military operations in certain situations. The terrorists' fear of military action serves as a significant deterrent and causes a decrease in the number of abductions. This is clearly reflected in Israel's case – there is no other country in the world that has suffered more from this type of attack.

In the 1970s, Israel experienced a series of abductions, including hijackings, the taking over of schools, apartment buildings, hotels, and even buses. In all of these cases, the government refused to give in to the terrorists' demands, and the IDF stormed the locations and freed the hostages. It was not an easy approach to adopt. But what were the consequences of this determined refusal to give in to terrorist demands? The incidence of abductions inside Israeli territory decreased, even became rare. But what steps should be taken in situations where the chances of extricating hostages are remote or even non-existent? And what should be done, for example, if the terrorists not only grab hostages, but also keep them hidden? Whether or not this type of rescue mission is possible, future Israeli governments need to persevere in their refusal to concede. First and foremost, it is their moral duty to the Israeli public, because only by adamantly refusing to capitulate can they significantly decrease such incidents in which additional civilians will fall victim to future abductions. Furthermore, this is the only policy that can effectively contend with an ongoing series of abductions. Once governments accept this principle, they can effectively handle other grave kidnapping incidents.

The most complex situation occurs when terrorists hold hostages in a hostile country. There are no options – what can be done aside from declaring war? Despite the difficulties involved, a limited military operation to rescue the hostages should not be ruled out; in any event, the principle of standing firm and issuing the threat of intervention or reprisal must be staunchly upheld. Reprisal can take various forms, whether against the terrorists themselves or the countries that offer them shelter. What concerns the terrorists and the governments supporting them is the belief that they will be punished, sooner or later. This method of exerting pressure may not always lead to immediate retribution against the terrorists, but will always improve, at least to some extent, the chances of the rescue of hostages without capitulation to the terrorists' demands.

The Abduction of Foreign Nationals in Lebanon (1984–91)

Hizballah has made extensive use of (sometimes with Iranian guidance, at other times on the organization's sole initiative) the tactic of abducting foreign citizens (as well as locals) and holding them hostage.[28] Between 1984 and 1989, ninety-six foreign citizens were kidnapped in Lebanon, most of who were Americans and Frenchmen.[29] At the heart of the attacks stood ideological hostility towards the US and Israel (indeed, towards any foreign presence in Lebanon), but there were also other motives – perhaps even stronger ones:[30]

- Obtaining a bargaining chip for the release of Shiites imprisoned abroad. The most prominent targets of terror attacks for this purpose were the US, Kuwait, France, Britain, and Germany. Among the leading activists in this type of terror attack were relatives of imprisoned Shiites.
- Implementation of the Iranian terror policy that advocated activating terror to achieve political goals and as a means to place

pressure on countries that supported Iraq during the Iran–Iraq war.

The first western hostage to be abducted in Lebanon was the president of the American University in Beirut, David Dodge, who was abducted in July 1984. From that initial event, hostage-taking continued until 1989. Some hostages were executed by their captors, others died from lack of medical care and miserable conditions, others were released in exchange for the liberation of Hizballah prisoners, the supply of weapons to Iran, or ransom money, while some simply "disappeared" and their fates remain unknown. The abduction of foreign nationals in Lebanon stopped in 1989, apparently against the backdrop of the conclusion of the Iran–Iraq war and Iran's desire to improve its relations with the US and other western countries. The last of the western hostages were released in 1991–92, thanks to the intervention of a special UN envoy.

The abduction of foreign hostages in Lebanon as a political bargaining tool characterized the Shiite organizations in that country, although Palestinian organizations (such as Abu Nidal's group) also made successful use of this tactic. Between 1982 and 1988, there were sixty-seven kidnapping incidents in Lebanon; Hizballah was responsible for fifty-five of those kidnappings, Amal for eight, and the remainder was perpetrated by various organizations, some of which were Palestinian.[31] Hizballah, much like other terror organizations worldwide, justified its use of terror by claiming it constituted a self-protection measure against the greater power of western imperialism. As an organization with a religious orientation, Hizballah needed moral arguments to justify the abduction of innocent civilians and to accord with Muslim religious law; from the moral aspect, there is a difference between terror attacks against Israeli, American, or French military targets that are defined as part of the struggle against foreign forces, and the abduction of civilians. The basic justification made for abduction was generally an accusation that the hostages had been spying for a western country.[32] In any event, the issue of religious justification for the abduction of hostages remained controversial: radical leaders like Hussein Musawi supported the abductions, while Hizballah's spiritual leader, Sheikh Fadlallah, publicly condemned them, claiming that they contradicted the spirit of Islam and were detrimental to the Muslim image. Nevertheless, Fadlallah himself never took any steps to prevent abductions, probably due to fear of a confrontation with Ayatollah Khomeini and radical circles within Hizballah.[33]

Hizballah turned the abduction of hostages (mainly of western origins) into a central bargaining tool to achieve political and military goals set by the organization and its patrons in Iran. The organization's leaders knew how to exploit western sensitivities regarding the welfare of its citizens and the backlash produced by the fanfare of the media and public opinion, in order to apply pressure on decision-makers in those states.

An example of shrewd exploitation by Hizballah and Iran in an attempt to influence the political system of a western country in order to promote their interests is discernible during the French presidential election campaign of 1987. President François Mitterand declared that he was opposed to negotiation with the abductors of hostages and that France would continue supplying weapons to Iraq despite the terror threats.[34] The response from the abductors was dispatched to Jacques Chirac, who had been a resistance leader during World War II: Hizballah demanded that Chirac publish an announcement within forty-eight hours expressing his concern regarding the French president's declaration. Additionally, the message stated, if Chirac failed to do so, a French hostage would be executed. By preferring Chirac over Mitterand and by fanning the internal political struggle in France, the Hizballah kidnappers served Iranian interests as the latter preferred to negotiate with Chirac rather than Mitterand.[35]

Hizballah consistently denied any connection with the abduction of hostages, instead placing the blame for perpetuating the problem and its complications upon the US and the west, while calling for the release of all of Lebanese, Palestinian, and Iranian prisoners incarcerated in Israeli jails. On 3 May 1990, in response to an announcement made by the US administration, Hizballah claimed:

> "The American attempt to blame the Hizballah in the matter of the foreign hostages and to conceal the real reasons for this problem will not prevail . . . It is the United States that supports the method of holding civilians in captivity by covering for the crimes perpetrated by the Zionists against the Palestinian people and supporting them . . . the Zionist entity was founded on the basis of kidnapping innocent civilians and massacring them, and it still adheres to this method. The kidnapping of Sheikh Obeid from his home is the most prominent example of this Zionist method; a method which is protected, supported, and covered up by the American administration."[36]

These examples, among others, indicate that Hizballah is motivated by practical and rational considerations as well as ideological-religious motives, and is equipped with a detailed knowledge of the weaknesses and vulnerabilities of western democracies. Recognition of the sensitivity of these regimes to the media and public opinion, familiarity with the various political entities in these countries, and awareness of the crucial timing within the internal political frameworks of various countries (elections, political crises, and more) – all of these factors were shrewdly manipulated by the organization to increase its bargaining leverage and to derive propaganda-related benefits by maneuvering the "bargaining chips" of the hostages that it held.

The differing approaches of various countries to the hostage issue, and how these states contended with the Shiite/Iranian entities in this matter, are detailed below.

Imad Muraniya and the attack mechanism

Imad Fayez Muraniya was born on 12 July 1962, in the village of Tir Daba in south Lebanon, some fifteen kilometers from Tyre.[37] He was the eldest of three sons and a daughter; his father, a religious Shiite, died in 1979. He spent most of his childhood in Bir al Abed, one of the more disadvantaged sections of Beirut. His family was poor, but the Muraniya clan was considered to be a respected lineage in Shiite society; one of its leaders, Sheikh Muhammad Muraniya, was considered a *marja taklid* (a respected religious figure in the Shiite community).

After dropping out of high school in the late 1970s, Muraniya joined the Palestinian Fatah movement and underwent training in guerrilla warfare. He subsequently joined Force 17 – Fatah's security unit – and was one of the bodyguards for Abu Iyad (the deputy chief and head of intelligence for the Palestine Liberation Organization [PLO] and the second-most senior Fatah official after Yasser Arafat). In 1982, when Fatah was about to evacuate Beirut during the first Lebanon war, Muraniya decided to stay in Lebanon and joined the Islamic al Dawa organization, thus consequently becoming a member of its successor, Hizballah.

In 1983, Muraniya married his cousin, Saada Badr al Din, and the couple had two children – Fatima (August 1984) and Mustafa (January 1987). In contrast to other young leaders of Hizballah such as Abbas Musawi, Subhi Tufeili, and Hassan Nasrallah, Muraniya had no religious or political authority – his activities focused on the operational area. Muraniya's first role in Hizballah was to serve as the bodyguard of Sheikh Fadlallah, Hizballah's spiritual leader. Shortly afterwards, he transferred to another job, but his brother, Jihad, inherited his position and Imad Muraniya continued to be responsible for Fadlallah's security by "remote control".

In 1983, a decision was made by Iran and Hizballah to take action to remove the American and French presence in Lebanon through the perpetration of terrorist attacks. Muraniya volunteered to execute these attacks, aspiring to boost his status within Hizballah and in the eyes of their patrons in Tehran. Muraniya did indeed orchestrate the series of terror attacks against the US embassy in Beirut, the headquarters of the US marines, and French forces in Beirut. Due to these "successes" he was appointed head of Hizballah's "Special Security Agency" (SSA) – otherwise known as "Islamic Jihad".

The SSA under Muraniya's command was responsible for a series of attacks in Kuwait against US and Kuwaiti targets. On 12 December 1983, his men blew up the US embassy in Kuwait City and attacked other targets, including a shopping center in Shueiba and the control tower at Kuwait airport. Five people were killed in these attacks, and eighty-six were injured. The Kuwaiti authorities arrested seventeen suspects and sentenced seven of them to death. One of the condemned men was Mustafa Badr al Din, Muraniya's brother-in-law and friend; another was Hassan Musawi, cousin of Hizballah Secretary-General Abbas Musawi who was killed in a targeted attack by Israeli helicopters in 1992.

Muraniya regarded the liberation of the convicted terrorists as a central goal and used every means at his disposal to achieve their release. After the Kuwaiti royal family refused to release them, Muraniya initiated an assassination attempt against Emir Jaber al Sabah, using a Shiite suicide attacker who detonated his car bomb near a convoy in which the emir was traveling in Kuwait City on 25 May 1985. Both of the emir's bodyguards were killed, but al Sabah emerged unscathed. Subsequently, Muraniya's followers hijacked a Kuwaiti passenger plane (flight 211 from Dubai to Karachi), forced it to land in Tehran, and killed two American government employees before turning themselves in to the Iranian authorities in exchange for political asylum.

Starting in the mid-1980s, Muraniya's agency was involved in the abduction of western nationals in Beirut in order to apply pressure on Kuwait through those countries to release the condemned men and to achieve additional objectives *vis-à-vis* western countries according to the interests of Hizballah and its patrons in Tehran. In June 1985, Muraniya was responsible for the hijacking of TWA flight 847 from Athens to Rome; the aircraft landed in Beirut and an American soldier onboard was killed in the course of the hijacking. On 5 April 1987, Muraniya's henchmen hijacked a Kuwaiti airplane on a flight from Bangkok to Kuwait and forced it to land at Mashhad in northern Iran. From there, the hijackers flew with their hostages to Larnaca, Cyprus. The incident finally ended in Algeria, where the hijackers reached agreement with the authorities, released the aircraft and its passengers, and "disappeared".

As stated earlier, Muraniya was behind most of Hizballah's terror attacks against western targets inside and outside of Lebanon since the 1980s. To this day, there is no clear picture of the hierarchical structure or subordinate relationship of Muraniya, and the agency that he heads, to the parent organizations of Hizballah and Iran. Within Hizballah, there is a group called "Shurat al Jihad" to coordinate attacks, comprised of two agencies: one is responsible for gathering information, while the second, "Islamic Jihad", perpetrates the attacks. The agency headed by Imad Muraniya is part of Hizballah's attack mechanism but, due to Muraniya's status and importance, a certain vagueness surrounds the group's direct links with Iran.

Muraniya constituted an important target for intelligence services worldwide, particularly those of Israel and the US (which placed him on its list of the twenty-two most wanted terrorists, alongside Osama bin Laden). Although several opportunities arose over the years to arrest him during his travels around the world under false identities, he was not caught and continued to direct the terror activities of Hizballah and Iran. In 1988, he was almost arrested at Charles de Gaulle airport in Paris; previously, he had nearly been caught during a stopover at Riyadh, Saudi Arabia, in April 1995.

Muraniya was killed on 12 February 2008 by a car bomb in the Kfar Suseh neighborhood of Damascus, Syria.[38] His assassination took Hizballah completely by surprise. At Muraniya's funeral, Hassan Nasrallah appeared via a video link; in a lengthy eulogy delivered for his fallen comrade, he declared: "You crossed the borders. Zionists, if you want an open war, let it be an open war anywhere."[39] Iran condemned the killing as "yet another brazen example of organized state terrorism by the Zionist regime".[40] Israel officially denied being behind the assassination.

The United States

Since the mid-1980s, Iran has promoted its interests by abducting western hostages in Lebanon through its proxy, Hizballah. Four examples of the US handling of incidents in which American hostages were held by Hizballah are listed below:

- The abduction of William Buckley.
- The "Irangate" affair.
- The hijacking of TWA flight 847.
- The abduction of Colonel Higgins.

The basic approach of the US to the hostage issue avers that under no circumstances should there be any surrender to the abductors' demands.[41] In actual practice, however, the US administration was often forced to take the influence of various powers into account, such as the families of hostages who generated public pressure for their release and the extensive influence of the media, which made it difficult to implement its declared policy. At times, public pressure was directed into political channels by opposition groups that criticized the administration's policies. For example, in June 1986, in contrast to the declared policy of the administration at that time, 247 congressmen sent a letter to the Syrian president in which they prevailed upon al Assad to use his influence to liberate the American hostages.

In fact, during most of the hostage situations, the US conducted secret negotiations with the kidnappers through Syrian, Iranian, or Algerian mediators; public pressure was harmful to these delicate contacts and made it difficult for the administration to take effective action.

The abduction of William Buckley (March 1984)

On 16 March 1984, William Buckley, head of the US Central Intelligence Agency (CIA) branch in Beirut, was abducted by Islamic Jihad.[42] Buckley was held under dreadful conditions, tortured, and denied medical treatment for 444 days. He died in captivity, apparently on 3 June 1985, due to the lack of medical treatment for his illness. During his captivity, Buckley was interrogated by Iranian intelligence entities. According to the testimony of David Jacobsen, a hostage who was held together with Buckley and was subsequently released, the person in charge of the guards was an Iranian called "Ali". The US spared no effort to bring about Buckley's release (see also the "Irangate" affair, below), but to no avail.

The "Irangate" affair (September 1985)

The "Irangate" affair was a prominent example of American willingness to conduct covert negotiations for the release of hostages. The central issue was the sale of American arms to Iran through Israeli intermediaries in exchange for the release of hostages.

There were two main reasons for America's participation in shipping weapons to Iran: First, the US wanted to liberate seven US nationals who had been abducted in Beirut between 7 March 1984 and 9 June 1985. As stated earlier, one of the seven was William Buckley, head of the CIA branch in Beirut, who was abducted on 16 March 1984. Information discovered by US intelligence indicated that most, or even all, of the captive Americans were being held by Hizballah, which had acted in cooperation with Iran.[43] Secondly, the US had an undeclared interest in renewing relations with Iran, due to its strategic importance and fears of Soviet intervention during "successor struggles" after Khomeini's death (in actual fact, Khomeini died only in 1989, and his successor was appointed without any crisis). In secret talks between the US and Iran via intermediaries, an agreement was reached regarding the provision of combat means to Iran (which was in dire straits due to the Iraq–Iran war) in exchange for the release of American hostages being held by Hizballah in Lebanon.

According to the agreement, at the end of August and the beginning of September 1985, Iran received shipments of American-made BGM-71 tube-launched, optically-tracked, wire-guided (TOW) antitank missiles, and in exchange Hizballah released American hostage Benjamin Weir on 14 September 1985. The US anxiously awaited the release of additional hostages according to the bargain, but this failed to take place.

On 26 July 1986, an additional hostage was freed in Lebanon: Father Lawrence Martin Jenco. Hizballah's security service, Islamic Jihad, published an announcement stating that the release was an act of goodwill, but it is known that Iran received an additional shipment of TOW weapons on 3–4 June 1986, a short time before the captive's release. According to some sources – and this information was never verified – the release of the two hostages also involved payment of an unknown amount of ransom money.

The final shipment of combat weapons reached Iran in October 1986, after which American hostage David Jacobsen was released on 2 November 1986. He was the third and final hostage to be released in the framework of the "Irangate" weapons-for-hostages agreement. The US concealed the details of the deal until its exposure at the end of 1986.

While the deal with the Iranians was still being closed, a British Church of England envoy named Terry Waite acted as an intermediary in Lebanon for the release of western hostages. Initially, it was thought that the hostages were released thanks to Waite's efforts; only later did it become clear that they had been released within the framework of the arms deals between the US and Iran.[44]

The deals with Iran that had brought about the release of the hostages were ostensibly successful, but the findings of the committees of inquiry into the matter (such as the Tower Committee) described this approach as an utter failure *vis-à-vis* basic policy and long-term American interests in the war on terror and international relations. The Tower Committee pointed out that only three hostages were actually released, although the basic purpose of the arrangement was to liberate all of the foreign hostages. It turned out that William Buckley, who constituted a central reason for American consent to the deals, had been murdered a long time before negotiations began for his release. Moreover, during September and October 1986, in the course of the negotiations between Iran and the US, Hizballah abducted three additional American nationals in Beirut: Frank Reed, Joseph Cicippio, and Edward Tracey. These additional abductions ultimately demonstrated that submission to blackmail and a willingness to supply Iran with weaponry in exchange for the release of hostages was not the right way to handle this issue, even in the short-term, and that this approach had a grave negative impact on the campaign formulated by western states against terror and states that support terror. The report of the Tower Committee stated:

"The Iranian initiative contravened the American administration's policy regarding terror, the Iran–Iraq war, and military aid for Iran. The committee believes that the inability to face these contradictions was the basis for the erroneous decisions that were made. No acceptable ongoing examination of the initiative was made, nor was it studied properly by the sub-cabinet levels. No proper use was made of intelligence sources. Legal restrictions were not taken into account. The entire issue was discussed too informally, without leaving records regarding discussions and decisions.

"Although the initiative was under the jurisdiction of the CIA, the State Department, and the Defense Department, these entities did not intervene. The initiative depended on a private network of operators and intermediaries. The operation was not subjected to a serious discussion at any stage, nor was there a periodical assessment of the initiative's process. The consequences were an unprofessional operation, lacking in satisfactory results."

The report continued:

"The Iranian initiative was a covert operation which contradicted declared policy. But the initiative itself was made up of contradictions. Two goals were clear from the start – opening a strategic dialogue with Iran and freeing the hostages in Lebanon. It would appear that the sale of weapons to Iran provided a means to achieve these goals. The concept played into the hands of others who were motivated by different considerations, including profitable gain.

"In actual fact, the selling of arms was not the appropriate means to achieve any one of these goals. Iran needed arms. The United States wanted to free the hostages. Thus, the arms deal in exchange for the hostages was the best way to achieve the goals of both sides. But if the US goal was more extensive, then the arms sale should have been postponed until after establishing strategic relations. The arms deal in exchange for hostages would have interfered with the achievement of this goal.

"In addition, the release of the hostages necessitated contact with elements in Iran that influence the Hizballah, which are the more radical elements in Iran. The opening of a strategic dialogue, as the United States desired, could only have been achieved with entities that appeared to be more moderate.

"American officials that handled the affair had three different outlooks. For some, the main goal was to initiate a strategic dialogue with the Iranians. For others, the strategic dialogue was an excuse for the arms sale in order to release the hostages. There were still others that clearly viewed the affair as an arms deal in exchange for hostages."[45]

The hijack to Lebanon of TWA flight 847 (June 1986)

On 17 June 1986, four Shiite members of Hizballah's Islamic Jihad hijacked TWA flight 847 on a flight from Athens to Rome. Imad Muraniya stood at the head of the hijackers.[46]

The members of the cell that hijacked the plane belonged to a unit that dubbed itself the "Sadr Brigades", after Imam Mousa al Sadr, a Shiite leader from south Lebanon who disappeared during a visit to Libya. There were 152 passengers and crew members on the plane, 139 of whom were American. On 18 June 1986, the hijackers released most of the passengers in order to make it easier to control the hostages, but continued to hold thirty-six passengers and crew members. The hijackers demanded the release of 766 Shiites imprisoned in Israel in exchange for the passengers' release. In order to prove their determination, they murdered an American passenger and dumped his body on the runway. But Israel refused to meet the hijackers' demands, and the US did not press the Israelis to give in. The hijacking was meant to test US President Reagan's declarations regarding the war on terror. During the months prior to the hijacking, Reagan had made several references to the US intention to activate a policy of "determent, prevention, and reprisal" against Iran. Now the time had come to "settle the debt". While constantly conferring with Amiram Nir, the Israeli prime minister's advisor on the war against terrorism, US Colonel Oliver North planned a rescue operation for the airplane's passengers.

A unit of the counter-terrorism Delta Force was sent to Europe and the aircraft carrier *Nimitz* was stationed off the coast of Lebanon. However, due to fear of an American military rescue operation, the hijackers had dispersed the hostages to private homes in west Beirut and its suburbs, thus thwarting the mission. The timing of the hijacking had the power to disrupt Iranian efforts to obtain American weapons, either directly or through Israel (see the "Irangate" affair, above). Therefore, Iran apparently had decided that it was preferable to resolve the situation; on 24 June 1986, in the middle of the crisis, the chairman of the Iranian parliament, Hashemi Rafsanjani, arrived in Damascus. At a press conference held in the Syrian capital, Rafsanjani denied his country's involvement in the hijacking, and said: "If we had known the identity of the hijackers, we would have thwarted the hijacking." Rafsanjani met with Hizballah leaders in Damascus and "mediated" for the release of the passengers and crew.

The day after Rafsanjani's visit, on 25 June 1986, Syrian President Hafez al Assad raised the solution that eventually brought about the release of the TWA passengers: he proposed that Israel release Shiite prisoners from its Atlit prison but, in order to prevent it from looking like capitulation to terror, the prisoners would not be released at the same time as the passengers – they would be released at a later date. Assad asked the US if this concept was acceptable, and Israel replied that, as it was about to release some of the Shiite detainees in any case, it did not object to helping the US in this matter. Iran accepted Assad's formula and ordered Islamic Jihad to accept it too. On 29 June 1986, the hostages were taken by bus to Damascus, from where they were flown to Europe on a special flight. On 3 July 1986, Israel released three hundred Shiite terrorists, thus meeting its obligation to the United States.

Iran's involvement in the hijacking of the TWA aircraft confirmed assessments that the Iranian government stood behind terrorist acts in Lebanon and Europe. It would be reasonable to say that a very important by-product of the deal to release the TWA passengers was the exposure of evidence regarding Iran's involvement in terror abductions and its ability to control its sponsored organizations.

The abduction of Colonel William Higgins (February 1988)

Lieutenant-Colonel William Higgins served with the United Nations Forces In Lebanon (UNIFIL) force in southern Lebanon. On 17 February 1988, Higgins met with one of the commanders of the Shiite Amal organization in the city of Tyre. Quite ironically, the agenda of the meeting was to coordinate activities of UNIFIL and the south Lebanese militias during a hostage situation.[47]

After finishing the meeting, Higgins called UNIFIL headquarters and noted that his return journey would pass through areas where armed Hizballah members were located; he asked that headquarters keep track of his movements and maintain contact with him until his return. Higgins and his escorts traveled in a two-car convoy; Higgins was alone in the second car. After passing through one of the turns in the road, the driver of the first car noticed that the colonel's car was missing; he stopped, reversed, and discovered Higgins' jeep standing empty at the side of the road.

Higgins' escort in the first car notified UNIFIL headquarters about his disappearance and an abduction alert was immediately declared. Roadblocks were set up and searches were conducted, but the efforts were futile. Five days later, a group identifying itself as the "Oppressed on Earth" (a name Hizballah had used in previous abductions) claimed responsibility for the abduction and released a video in which Colonel Higgins appeared with his abductors.

On 21 April 1988, the group released a photograph of Higgins in captivity – this was the last communication received by his family. From that time on, his fate remained a mystery. During the ensuing months, the abductors occasionally released announcements in which it threatened to bring him to trial for espionage or to execute him. In 1988, the UN's peacekeeping forces in Lebanon were awarded the Nobel Prize for Peace and the UN general-secretary took advantage of the opportunity to call for the colonel's release, but to no avail. In July 1989, when Higgins had already been held in captivity for eighteen months, IDF forces abducted Sheikh Obeid. Two days after the abduction, Hizballah demanded Obeid's immediate release and threatened that if its demand was not met, it would hang the colonel. On 31 July 1989, when its demand had not been met, Hizballah released another video in which Higgins was seen hanging by his neck. The video was transferred to CNN and broadcast all over the world. The US was outraged by the execution and started preparations for a military operation in Lebanon in order to prevent the execution of other hostages.

Two years later, in 1991, Higgins' body was returned and flown to the US. A postmortem examination clearly indicated that he had been killed by his captors before the production of the video in which they had ostensibly hanged him.

International response

France

France dealt with the hostage problem via two parallel channels: firstly, through direct talks with Hizballah's patron, Iran; and secondly, with Hizballah itself, with the help of Syrian, Algerian, and Saudi Arabian mediation.

One of the mediators who acted in the service of France was Dr Razah Raad, a French doctor of Lebanese origin who had maintained close contact with the Shiite community in Lebanon. In the course of 1985, Raad made two trips to Lebanon and Syria in an attempt to liberate four French hostages who had been kidnapped in March and November 1985, but his efforts were unsuccessful.[48] In 1986, following the abduction of four members of a French TV crew in Lebanon, another mediator was sent to Damascus – a Syrian businessman named Amran Adham – in order to deal with their release. At the same time, French Prime Minister Jacques Chirac, who had recently been elected, began to contend with the issue of the hostages through other emissaries, including Dr Raad.

In June 1986, two of the kidnapped French TV crewmembers were released. The French prime minister thanked Syria, Algeria, and, ironically, Iran, for their assistance in freeing the hostages.[49] Two weeks after the release of the hostages, France expelled several hundred activists from the anti-Iranian underground Mujahideen-e-Khalq ("People's Mujahideen of Iran"), including the organization's leader, Massoud Rajavi – this was France's form of payment to Iran for its release of the hostages.[50]

In November 1986, another French hostage was released in Lebanon, and this time too, the French prime minister thanked Syria, Algeria, and Saudi Arabia for his release. A short time later, France announced its intention to return part of the Iranian loan given to France during the shah's reign (a total sum of around US$1 billion). In fact, France actually paid Iran a sum of approximately three hundred and thirty million dollars. A short time after the transfer of the money to Iran, another hostage was released.[51] Through these actions, Iran not only succeeded in causing Iranian resistance members to be deported from France, but also regained some of the Iranian funds frozen in France since Khomeini's revolution.

The release of the two remaining TV reporters on 27 November 1987 was also the result of French capitulation to Iranian demands: France agreed to withdraw all of its charges against Wahid Gordji, an Iranian terrorist involved in a terror network that had perpetrated a series of attacks in France in the course of 1986. Gordji had found asylum in the Iranian embassy in Paris, which the French authorities subsequently surrounded and demanded that he be turned over to them. The Iranians took similar action in Tehran: they accused Paul Toure, the French consul, of espionage, and besieged the French embassy. The eventual French surrender in the matter of Gordji put an end to the "Embassy War" between the two countries. France repeated its declaration regarding its intention to continue repaying its debts to Iran, while the third French gesture towards Iran was the further deportation of Iranian opposition members from France. Some sources also claimed that France had agreed to supply Iran with military spare parts, but the French authorities emphatically denied this accusation.[52]

On 4 May 1988, the last French hostages were released, and the two countries renewed diplomatic ties on 16 June 1988. France undertook to act for the release of Anis Nakash (one of the terrorists who had assassinated the shah's exiled former president, Shapour Bakhtiar, in August 1991) and agreed to pay Hizballah a ransom of about US$30 million. There were several reports regarding further intentions to reduce the scope of arms consignments to Iraq and to renew weapon supplies to Iran via Syria. The release of Muhammad Mukhajar, a Hizballah activist arrested in France a year earlier, was apparently also connected to the deal regarding the hostages in Lebanon.

Regarding the deal between Iran, Hizballah, and France, it is interesting to quote Sheikh Fadlallah, who stated in March 1986 that "their release was the outcome of the deal between France and Iran" and "only a similar deal between Iran and the United States may bring about the release of the US hostages".[53] The meaning to be derived from his declaration is that Iran was the entity that stood behind Hizballah's activities, and it was Iran that could bring about the release of the hostages in exchange for achievement of its political objectives.

In summary, it is obvious that France's repeated acquiescence to Iranian demands encouraged Iran and Hizballah to activate further terror against France until most of Iran's political, economic, and military demands had been satisfied by the French.

Britain

For the most part, the British approach was characterized by Britain's refusal to submit to kidnappers' demands or even to enter into negotiations with terror organizations for the purpose of liberating hostages.[54]

Hizballah was involved in a relatively small number of abductions of British citizens in Lebanon, and most were released within a relatively short time. An exception was the abduction of Church of England envoy Terry Waite, who was visiting Lebanon in an attempt to mediate to release hostages and was himself kidnapped in 1986. Britain refused to meet the ransom demands posed by the kidnappers, and condemned France and Germany for their surrender to the kidnappers' demands in order to free their hostage nationals. According to information that was never officially verified, Britain conducted talks with Iran in order to achieve Waite's release in late 1987, but the discussions were discontinued when Britain refused to pay a ransom. Waite was finally released, together with other western hostages, in 1991.

Switzerland

Eric Werley, who was kidnapped by Hizballah on 3 January 1985, was freed in exchange for the release of a Hizballah member, Hussein Talaat, who had been arrested at Zurich airport on 18 November 1984, in possession of explosives designated for an attack against the US embassy in Rome.[55] Additional abductions were perpetrated in order to free the hijacker of the Air Africa plane, Ali Muhammad Hariri, also imprisoned in Switzerland, but to no avail. The kidnapped Swiss citizens were subsequently released during the years 1991 and 1992, in the framework of Iran and Hizballah's resolution to release all western hostages.

Germany

The first kidnappings of German citizens in Lebanon occurred in 1987, and were connected to the arrest of two Shiite terrorists – the Hamadi brothers – in Germany. A few days after their arrest, a German citizen was abducted in Lebanon and, several days later, a second abduction occurred. Shortly after the kidnappings, Germany appealed to Syria and Iran to help obtain the release of the German hostages. The German ambassador in Beirut even met with Hizballah's spiritual leader, Sheikh Fadlallah, in the knowledge that the latter had consistently opposed the kidnapping of foreign hostages. The dilemma faced by the German government was that, on the one hand, the Americans were demanding the extradition of Muhammad Ali Hamadi on the charge of hijacking a TWA plane in 1985 and murdering an American passenger, while, on the other hand, the abductors had declared that if Hamadi were extradited to the US, the hostages would be executed. The German resolution was that Hamadi would not be extradited to the US, but would be brought to trial in Germany charged with hijacking and murder. On 7 September 1987, Hizballah freed one of the hostages – Alfred Schmidt – and announced that his release was in exchange for the release of the Hamadi brothers held in Germany.

Germany thanked Syria and Iran for their assistance in liberating the hostage, but denied any kind of deal with the abductors. British sources claimed that Schmidt's release had been part of a deal according to which Muhammad Ali Hamadi would be sentenced to a short prison term, after which he would be deported to Lebanon, while his brother would be liberated after serving an even shorter sentence.[56]

The second German hostage, Rudolph Cordes, was released shortly afterwards. There were reports in the press claiming that Germany had paid Hizballah US$3 million through the mediator Rashid Makrum, a German businessman of Lebanese origin. The German Siemens company, which employed Cordes, was also involved in the deal, and it appears that the company closed the deal in Damascus with Syrian arbitration.[57]

On 16 May 1989, two German citizens were abducted in Lebanon: Heinrich Sturbig and Tomas Kamptner. No organization claimed responsibility for the kidnapping. On 30 May 1989, Hussein Musawi, one of the leaders of Hizballah, was interviewed by the German DPI news agency in Baalbek, Lebanon.[58] In the interview, Musawi stated: "Germany has no conflict with anyone in Lebanon, not even with the Hamadi family. The government in Bonn agreed to release Hamadi in exchange for the two hostages, Alfred Schmidt and Rudolph Cordes." However, when this promise was rescinded and Hamadi was sentenced to life imprisonment, the Hamadi family apparently carried out the abduction in a renewed attempt to achieve his release. In the early 1990s, the German hostages were released along with the rest of the western hostages.

Kuwait

Many abductions of foreign hostages were perpetrated in Lebanon in order to apply pressure on Kuwait to release seventeen Shiite terrorists who were incarcerated there, some of whom had been sentenced to death. Kuwait's unyielding policy not to give in to the abductors' demands under any circumstances stood firm during the entire period, despite the considerable pressures under which it was placed, probably due to the Kuwaitis' understanding that the abduction of hostages in Lebanon was only a single component of an overall and broader Iranian threat against Kuwaiti interests.[59] Fifteen terrorists were released by Iraq when it invaded Kuwait in August 1990, and were transferred to Iran.

The End of the Western Hostages Affair in Lebanon

During the series of abductions in Lebanon, at least eight hostages were executed by their captors, but most were released years later following negotiations conducted with Lebanese Shiite terror organizations and Iran. The hostage abduction affair finally ended with the release of the last of the western hostages in December 1991, apparently due to Iran's desire to improve its ties with the west. As Iran was the one to create the problem, it also had the key to its resolution.[60]

Binyamin Netanyahu eloquently summarized the principles connected to this phenomenon:

"The roots of the problem of international terror lie in the involvement of hostile governments. Similarly, the roots of the solution lie in the counter-actions of the governments under attack. Terror countries are influenced by a sober calculation of profit and loss, no less than the terrorists. They rely on the terrorists to attack their opponents without having to take the risks involved in overt warfare. As long as they succeed in denying their involvement, they find it easy to evade punishment. But when their support of terror is exposed to everyone, in a way that the victims can no longer pretend to believe their denials, the rules of the game will change dramatically."[61]

Over the years, Hizballah attempted to apply enormous pressure on Israel through western states, mainly the US, by indicating that Israel possessed the key to the liberation of the western hostages. They presented Israel's refusal to release hundreds of Lebanese detainees that it and its SLA allies held as the main reason for the prolonged suffering of the foreign hostages.

Links between foreign hostage abductions and Israel

Incident	Demands of Israel	Result
The hijacking of a TWA airplane by Hizballah (14 June 1985).	A demand to release Shiite prisoners in Israel.	Hostages released on 19 June 1986.
		Israel responded positively to an American request to release Shiite prisoners in exchange for the western hostages on 3 July 1986.
The abduction of seven Americans, including the head of the CIA Beirut branch, William Buckley, and their captivity by Hizballah, 1984–5.	The supply of combat means to Iran in exchange for the release of western hostages.	Between August 1985 and November 1986, three western hostages were released.
		Several arms shipments were delivered from Israel to Iran.
		Contacts were severed, and the US arrangement was sharply criticized by the Tower Committee.

The abduction of Sheikh Karim Obeid by Israel, 28 July 1989.	Hizballah demanded the release of Sheikh Obeid and threatened that if he is not released, Colonel Higgins will be executed.	Sheikh Obeid was not released.
		Hizballah staged the "execution" of Colonel Higgins; in fact, he had been killed much earlier by his captors.

A study of the examples presented above indicates that, at least on several occasions, Iran and Hizballah succeeded in achieving their goals *vis-à-vis* Israel by leveraging pressure against the west. Processes took place on global and regional levels (the collapse of the Soviet Union and the Gulf war of 1991) along with adjustments in the Lebanese power balance, and triggered changes in the priorities of each of the three parties involved in the issue of hostages and captives: Iran, Syria, and Hizballah. Recognition that prolonging the matter would turn it into a burden, rather than an asset, is what finally triggered a breakthrough and the beginning of negotiations for the release of the western hostages through the intercession of the UN general-secretary in August 1991.[62]

From the Iranian aspect, the end of the Iran–Iraq war in the summer of 1988 and Khomeini's death in June 1989 paved the way towards greater openness regarding the west, with the aim of rehabilitating the country's economy. In the new reality of international dialogue with Iran, the hostages in Lebanon became an obstacle in the new Iranian strategy of renewed economic links and full diplomatic ties with some western countries. Iranian President Rafsanjani took vigorous action to promote Iranian ties with Europe and America, and aspired to resolve the hostage crisis within this framework. Iranian willingness to end the hostage crisis grew in the wake of the Iraqi invasion of Kuwait on 2 August 1990, and was based on the claim that the hostages had "lost their value".[63] At the same time, Damascus expressed a growing interest in ending the affair. For years, Syria had played a central role in the matter of the western hostages. As part of its political and military influence in Lebanon, Syria indirectly encouraged the continued existence and activities of Hizballah, the organization responsible for the abductions, but, for the purposes of world public opinion, Syria presented itself as the entity that brought about the release of the hostages. From the Syrian point of view, the liberation of the hostages also served as a means to prove that country's ability to control Lebanon.[64]

The Iraqi invasion of Kuwait in August 1990 cancelled out an additional reason for holding the hostages: it brought about the release of fifteen Shiite terrorists incarcerated in Kuwaiti prisons for perpetrating terror attacks against western and local targets in December 1983. Since their arrest, Hizballah had acted to liberate them in various ways, including the abduction of western hostages. After the invasion, the fifteen terrorists were transferred to Iran as part of Saddam's efforts to obtain Iranian support against the western coalition and no longer constituted a stumbling block on the path to releasing the captives.[65]

During the negotiation process, talks began for the release under UN auspices of the IDF prisoners of war. Western governments called on Israel to accelerate the process by making the gesture of releasing Lebanese prisoners even before a reciprocal release of IDF prisoners; but, by spring 1993, the bodies of Yosef Fink and Rahamim Alsheikh still had not been returned. In addition, there was no new information regarding either Ron Arad or the three IDF soldiers missing in action from the first war in Lebanon: Zecharia Baumel, Yehuda Katz, and Zvi Feldman. Israeli hopes were dashed that the end of the western hostages' affair would also trigger a resolution of the issue of IDF prisoners. The problem was only partially resolved later, following negotiations between Hizballah and Israel.

Summary

The United States' declared policy regarding the handling of terror in general, and the abduction of US citizens in particular, was not to give in to terrorist blackmail. The US activated its covert agencies and special units in order to apprehend terrorists wanted by the US authorities, even those located outside US territory, with the aim of bringing them to justice in America.

In this framework, efforts were made to apprehend Imad Muraniya, whose name surfaced as the individual responsible for many abductions in Lebanon, but these efforts met with no success. On the other hand, US intelligence agencies succeeded in apprehending another Shiite terrorist, Awaz Yunis, who had been involved in several abductions, and in bringing him to trial in the United States. In practice, the US – much like other countries that fell victim to abduction of their citizens – was forced to negotiate with the abductors, usually through a third-party mediator, and to meet the abductors' demands either directly or indirectly.

Notes

1. This section is based on documents from court hearings in the matter of the petitions of Obeid and Dirani, as well as Ran Edelist and Ilan Kfir, *Ron Arad: the Riddle* (Tel Aviv: Yediot Aharonot, 2000).
2. "IDF Responds to Hizballah Attack on Northern Border", *Embassy of Israel*, Washington, DC, 23 November 2005.
3. *Ibid*.
4. *Yediot Aharonot, Ma'ariv, Ha'aretz* newspapers, 13 July 2006.
5. *Ibid*.
6. *Ibid*.
7. A. Harel and A. Issacharoff, *34 Days: Israel, Hizballah, and the War in Lebanon* (New York: Palgrave MacMillan, 2008), p. 75.
8. *Ibid*., p. 82.
9. "Why they Died: Civilian Casualties in Lebanon during the 2006 War", *Human Rights Watch* (HRW), 6 September 2007, p. 40.
10. *Ibid*., p. 106.
11. *Ibid*., p. 103.
12. "Security Council Calls for End to Hostilities Between Hizbollah, Israel", *UN Security Council Resolution 1701*, 11 August 2006.
13. Maria Alvanou, *Hamas and Hizbullah Kidnappings: The Political and Strategic Implications* (Milan: Italian Team for Security, Terroristic Issues and Managing Emergencies (ITSTIME), July 2006), p. 1.
14. "Why they Died", *Human Rights Watch*, p. 64.
15. "Preliminary Report", *Winograd Commission*, 30 April 2007.
16. *Yediot Aharonot*, 1 August 1989.
17. The French weekly *Paris Match*, as quoted in *Yediot Aharonot*, 13 August 1989.
18. *Yediot Aharonot*, 1 August 1989.
19. *Ibid*.
20. *Al Hamishmar*, 30 July 1989.
21. Its translation was published in *Yediot Aharonot*, 1 August 1989.
22. *Yediot Aharonot*, 4 August 1989.
23. Quoted in *Yediot Aharonot*, 13 August 1989.
24. The information in this section is based on material from the legal discussions regarding Dirani's incarceration in an Israeli prison. For example, *Sheikh Obeid and Mustafa Dirani v. the Minister of Defense*, Israel High Court, 26 December 2000.
25. *Alrai Alam*, 16 November 2001.
26. *Yediot Aharonot*, 1 August 1989.
27. Binyamin Netanyahu, *Terrorism: How Can the West Win?* (Tel Aviv: Sifriat Ma'ariv, 1987).
28. This section is based on Shaul Shay, *The Axis of Evil: Iran, Hizballah and Palestinian Terror* (New Brunswick: Transaction Publishers, 2005).
29. Maskit Burgin, Ariel Merari, and Anat Kurz, *Foreign Hostages in Lebanon*,

Issue 25 of JCSS Memorandum (Tel Aviv: Jaffee Center for Strategic Studies, Tel Aviv University, 1988).
30 Magnus Ranstorp, *Hizballah in Lebanon: The Politics of the Western Hostage Crisis* (New York: St. Martin's Press, 1997), pp. 86–88.
31 Burgin, Merari, and Kurtz, *Foreign Hostages in Lebanon*, 1988.
32 Martin S. Kramer, *The Moral Logic of Hizballah*, Volume 1 of Occasional Papers (Tel Aviv: The Dayan Center for Middle Eastern and African Studies, The Shiloah Institute, Tel Aviv University, 1987), p. 13.
33 Ranstorp, *Hizballah in Lebanon*, pp. 41–49.
34 *International Herald Tribune*, 12 March 1987 (quoting *AFP*).
35 In one of its declarations, Hizballah condemned the Socialist Party for its ties with Zionism. In March 1986, the organization's periodical *al Ahad* wrote that the safety of French citizens worldwide depends upon the defeat of the Socialist Party in the upcoming elections. See *Le Monde*, 6 May 1988.
36 The declaration made by Sheikh Yizbakh of Hizballah, as it appeared in *al Anwar*, 12 July 1990.
37 This section is based on Ronen Bergman, "The Terrorist with Nine Lives", in *Yediot Aharonot*, 27 October 2009; and "Hizballah: A Special Collection of Information", *Center for Intelligence Heritage*, March 2003, pp. 36–39.
38 Kevin Peraino, "The Fox is Hunted Down", *Newsweek*, 25 February 2008, http://www.newsweek.com/id/112771?from=rss.
39 "Hizbollah Threatens 'Open War' on Israel", *ADL*, 31 March 2008.
40 "Bomb Kills Top Hizballah Leader", *BBC News*, 13 February 2008, http://news.bbc.co.uk/1/hi/world/middle_east/7242383.stm.
41 R. K. Ramazani, "Iran's Foreign Policy Contending Orientations", *The Middle East Journal*, Vol. 43, No. 2 (Spring 1989), pp. 204–206.
42 This section is based on documents included in the claim which William Buckley's partner made against Iran.
43 Ilan Kfir (ed), "The 'Irangate' Affair", in the *Tower Committee Report* (Tel Aviv: Modan Publishing, 1988), p. 8.
44 Burgin, Merari, and Kurtz, *Foreign Hostages in Lebanon*, August 1988.
45 Kfir, "The 'Irangate' Affair", *Tower Committee Report*, p. 17.
46 The hijacking of aircraft is not a topic of this study, but I consider it appropriate to include the hijacking of TWA flight 847 for two main reasons: first, it sheds light on the complexity of the situation when there is state involvement in an abduction, and second, from the moment that the hostages on the aircraft were spread out in different hideaways in Beirut, the incident took on the character of a terror abduction.
47 This section is based on documents from a trial in the United States in which Higgins' family sued Iran as the party responsible for his abduction and murder. *Robin L. Higgins v. The Islamic Republic of Iran*, United States District Court for the District of Columbia, 21 September 2000.
48 *Le Monde*, 6 May 1988.

49 *The Jerusalem Post*, 27 March 1986 (quoting *Reuters*).
50 *Newsweek*, 23 June 1986.
51 *International Herald Tribune*, 26 December 1986 (quoting *Reuters*).
52 *Ma'ariv*, 12 November 1986.
53 *al Nahar*, 24 March 1986.
54 *The Times*, 23 June 1990, quoting an interview with British Prime Minister Margaret Thatcher.
55 *Yediot Aharonot*, 20 June 1986 (quoting *The Daily Express*).
56 *Ha'aretz*, 11 September 1987 (quoting *The Times*).
57 *Ma'ariv*, 20 September 1987 (quoting *The Times*).
58 *The Times*, 30 May 1989 (quoting *DPI*, the German news agency).
59 Shahram Chubin, *Iran and Its Neighbors: The Impact of the Gulf War* (London: Centre for Security and Conflict Studies, 1987).
60 Anat Kurz, Maskit Burgin, and David Tal, *Islamic Terror and Israel* (Tel Aviv: Papyrus Press, 1993).
61 Netanyahu, *Terror: How Can the West Win?*, p. 237.
62 Kurtz, Burgin, and Tal, *Islamic Terror*, pp. 94–97.
63 *Ibid.*
64 *Ibid.*
65 *Ibid.*

5

Terror Abductions in Afghanistan, Pakistan, and India

Abductions in Afghanistan

There is a burgeoning kidnapping industry in the Islamic Republic of Afghanistan, part of the conflict economy fed by the tens of billions of dollars the international forces and community have pumped into the country since 2001.[1] Much of the industry is simply criminal, and the kidnapping gangs often have links with those in positions of power. As security deteriorates in Afghanistan, even the capital Kabul is no longer safe.[2] Amrullah Saleh, chief of Afghanistan's National Directorate of Security (NDS), warned that kidnapping had matured into "a sort of business for some elements of society". Saleh's comments are among the few that have emanated from the Afghan government regarding these types of crimes.[3]

Most kidnappings end either in the payment of a ransom or the death of the hostage and, although wealthy Afghans are the usual victims of abduction for ransom, ransoms for foreigners can approach US$500,000. Many business leaders blame kidnappings on organized crime groups operating inside Afghanistan, but with strong links to criminals in Asia, and even Europe.[4] According to the Afghanistan International Chamber of Commerce (AICC), 173 businessmen were kidnapped across the country in the years 2007–9, and a number of them were killed. As the insurgency appears to spread, exacerbated by the general sense of lawlessness that accompanies any security vacuum, Afghan business leaders fear the kidnapping phenomenon could worsen and hasten the rate of entrepreneurs fleeing the country.

In 2010, the targeting of affluent Afghans became increasingly common. A number of engineers, de-miners, and road construction workers were abducted, with varying degrees of success regarding their eventual release. In most cases, their drivers were also kidnapped.[5] Former Afghan consul-general in Peshawar, Abdul Khaliq Farahi, was abducted in September 2008 and released on 13 November 2010 as a result of negotiations.[6] On the eve of the 2010 elections, violence and kidnapping spread from west to east across Afghanistan. Noor Mohammad Noor, a spokesperson for Afghanistan's Independent Election Commission (IEC), said that two candidates, eight IEC officials, and ten campaign workers were kidnapped despite increased security preparations across the country before the voting.[7]

Abduction of foreigners

The risk to foreigners of abduction in Afghanistan is high. Some kidnappings are conducted by the Taliban and other insurgent groups, but most are carried out by criminal gangs. Holding hostage an abducted foreigner can be quite difficult as, unlike the case with Afghan locals, significant military and political pressure will be brought to bear by the International Security Assistance Force (ISAF) and the Afghan government to find and free the foreign captive. Petty criminals will therefore sell a kidnap victim "up the chain" to groups with the power to control and exploit them – a practice that often causes western hostages to be transferred across the border to Pakistan, and into the hands of the Taliban.[8]

Another cause of the rising threat of kidnapping was growing fragmentation of the Afghan insurgency, partly caused by the expansion of the Taliban that incorporated all sorts of diverse groups, some little more than bandits who used the name "Taliban" as a cover for their money-making activities.[9]

In September 2007, Afghanistan's Taliban vowed to continue abducting foreign nationals, saying the kidnapping of twenty-three South Koreans[10] had proved that the tactic was an effective tool against the government. "We found this a very effective tactic against the Kabul administration and the invading forces . . . We'll continue kidnapping foreigners," Taliban spokesman Yousef Ahmadi said by telephone from an undisclosed location. "Through the kidnapping of the Koreans we gained worldwide media coverage, the Kabul administration was saying that we do not exist and we are a group based outside Afghanistan. When we held face-to-face talks with the Koreans, we showed that we're here and have control over ground inside the country."[11]

The abduction of twenty-three South Korean missionaries (July 2007)

On 19 July 2007, twenty-three South Korean missionaries were captured and held hostage by the Afghan Taliban. Two male hostages were executed before a deal was reached between the Taliban and the South Korean government.

The kidnapping

The group, composed of sixteen women and seven men, was captured while traveling by bus from Kandahar to Kabul on a mission sponsored by the Saemmul Presbyterian Church.[12] The crisis began when two local men, who the driver had allowed to board, started shooting to bring the bus to a halt. Over the next month, the hostages were kept in cellars and farmhouses, and regularly moved in groups of three to four to new locations.[13]

The negotiations

The Taliban's initial demand was that South Korea withdraw its two hundred troops from Afghanistan, but later also sought the release from prison of twenty-three Taliban militants. The Taliban issued and extended several deadlines for the release of the prisoners, after which they threatened to begin killing the hostages. Of the twenty-three hostages, two men – Bae Hyung-kyu, a forty-two-year-old South Korean pastor of the Saemmul Church, and Shim Seong-min, a twenty-nine-year-old South Korean man – were executed on July 25th and July 30th, respectively.

Face-to-face meetings between the Taliban and South Korea began on 10th August, resulting in the release of two female hostages – Kim Ji-na and Kim Gyeong-ja – on August 13th.[14] However, on August 18th, a Taliban spokesman said that the talks had failed and the fates of the remaining hostages were being considered.[15]

The release

The freedom of the remaining nineteen hostages (fourteen women and five men)[16] was secured on August 28th,[17] with the participation of Indonesia as a neutral Muslim mediator. The release of the hostages was secured by a South Korean promise to withdraw its two hundred troops from Afghanistan by the end of 2007. Although the South Korean government offered no statement, a Taliban spokesman claimed that the militant group had also received some US$20 million in exchange for the captured missionaries. All nineteen were eventually released on August 29th and August 30th.

The first American soldier abducted in Afghanistan (June 2009)

On 30 June 2009, Private Bowe Robert Bergdahl disappeared from a small combat outpost in southeastern Afghanistan, and is the only known American serviceman in captivity. Bergdahl was a paratrooper with the First Battalion, 501st Parachute Infantry Regiment, Fourth Brigade Combat Team, Twenty-Fifth Infantry Division, based at Fort Richardson, Alaska. His unit deployed to Afghanistan in March 2009, and he served at a base in Paktika province near the border with Pakistan in an area known to be a Taliban stronghold. US military officials said that low-level militants in the province nabbed the soldier and reportedly "sold" him to members of the Haqqani network, a hard-line terror group with ties to the Taliban and Osama bin Laden. It was the first time that a US soldier had been captured in Afghanistan since the war began in 2001.[18]

The Taliban claims responsibility

Two days after his disappearance, a Taliban network led by veteran jihadist Jalaluddin Haqqani claimed to be holding the soldier. A man describing himself as a Taliban commander told the Agence France-Presse (AFP) news agency that Private Bergdahl had been taken across the border to Pakistan. "Our leaders have not decided on the fate of this soldier, they will decide on his fate, and soon we will present video tapes of the coalition soldier and our demand to media," he stated.[19]

The American response

US troops scoured eastern Afghanistan and tried to seal off the area to prevent the captured American soldier from being taken to Pakistan. "We are using all of our resources to find him and provide for his safe return," said US spokeswoman Captain Elizabeth Mathias. US troops blanketed the area with two flyers: one of them asked the Afghan people for information on the missing soldier and offered a US$25,000 reward for his return; the other was aimed at insurgents and showed two US soldiers knocking down a door, with the message: "Please return our soldier safely [or] we will hunt you."

Videos released by the Taliban

Bergdahl appeared in four videos released by the Taliban: on 19 July 2009, 25 December 2009, 7 April 2010, and 9 December 2010.

The first video: On 19 July 2009, the Taliban released the first video, in which Bergdahl talked about his love for his family, his friends, motorcycles, and sailing. "I'm a prisoner. I want to go home," he said in the video, made available by the Washington-based Site Intelligence Group that monitors militant websites. "This war isn't worth the waste of human life that it has cost both Afghanistan and the US. It's not worth the amount of lives that have been wasted in prisons, Guantanamo Bay, Bagram, all those places where we are keeping prisoners," he said. At times speaking haltingly, Bergdahl (clad in what appeared to be an army shirt and fatigues) clasped his hands together and pleaded: "The pain in my heart to see my family again doesn't get any smaller. Release me. Please, I'm begging you, bring me home." He added that he was strong, and was given the freedom to exercise and to be a human being, even though he was a prisoner. At the end of the video, a speaker, reportedly Afghan Taliban spokesman Zabihullah Mujahid, demanded the release of a limited number of prisoners in exchange for the American soldier. US military officials condemned the video as propaganda and vowed to find Bergdahl. "We strongly condemn this public exploitation and humiliation of a prisoner. It's a violation of the international law of war and we will continue to use all resources available to us to return this soldier to safety," stated US military spokesman Colonel Gregory Julian in Kabul.

The second video: The Taliban released a video on Christmas Day, 2009, showing Bergdahl seated, facing the camera, wearing sunglasses and what appeared to be a US military helmet and uniform. On one side of the image was written: "An American soldier imprisoned by the Mujahideen of the Islamic Emirate of Afghanistan."[20] The man identified himself as Bergdahl, born in Sun Valley, Idaho, and gave his rank, unit, birth date, blood type, and his mother's maiden name before beginning a lengthy verbal attack on the US conduct of the war in Afghanistan and its relations with Muslims. "I'm afraid to tell you that this war has slipped from our fingers and it's just going to be our next Vietnam unless the American people stand up and stop all this nonsense," he said.[21] Bergdahl told his fellow soldiers they were facing a well-organized and patient enemy – perhaps a reference to a statement made by the White House the previous month, predicting that the US would not be in Afghanistan in nine years time. "To all you soldiers out there who are getting ready to come over here for the first time because of the stupidity of our country and leaders . . . you are fighting very smart people who know exactly how to kill us and are extremely patient," he concluded.

The video, which had an English-language narration in parts, also showed images of prisoners being abused in US custody. Bergdahl said he did not suffer such ill treatment.[22] A statement read by

Taliban spokesman Zabihullah Mujahid appeared at the end of the video and renewed demands for a "limited number of prisoners" to be exchanged for Bergdahl, stating that more American troops could be captured and claiming that US officials kept leading America "into the same holes", citing examples including Vietnam, Japan, Germany, Somalia, Lebanon, and Iraq.[23] "This is just going to be the next Vietnam unless the American people stand up and stop all this nonsense," he proclaimed.[24]

The video of 7 April 2010: The Taliban released a video of Bergdahl in which he said he wanted to go home and claimed the war in Afghanistan was not worth the number of lives that had been lost or wasted. The seven-minute video of Bergdahl showed him sporting a beard and doing a few push-ups to demonstrate he was in good physical condition. There was no way to verify when the footage was taken. At the end of the video, a speaker again demanded the release of a limited number of prisoners in exchange for the American.[25]

The video of 9 December 2010: A video, released by the Taliban on 9 December 2010, contained footage of a man believed to be Bergdahl. Appearing thin and with a wound on his left cheek, he was seen standing next to Taliban commander Mullah Sangreen Zadran, who had claimed responsibility for the kidnapping and had threatened to execute the hostage. The video, which also showed footage of militant attacks in Afghanistan, was released by Manba al Jihad, a video production group affiliated with the Taliban. The man believed to be Bergdahl appeared only briefly in the video and was not the main focus of the release.[26] NATO spokesman Brigadier-General Josef Blotz said the coalition was not sure whether the footage was old or new.[27]

A commander of the Haqqani terror organization, who spoke by telephone from an undisclosed location, denied that his organization held Sergeant Bergdahl (he had been promoted in absentia) as the US believed. He did say, however, that Bergdahl was a captive of another branch of the Taliban and denied earlier reports that the twenty-six-year-old soldier was in danger. "I deny the remarks . . . that this will endanger the life of the American soldier," the commander said, speaking on condition he not be identified, as Taliban field commanders feared being targeted if their identities became known. "We are not cowards, and we consider it as cowardly to harm prisoners," he said. The US claimed that Bergdahl had been held by the Pakistan-based Haqqani group since 2009. However, the commander suggested that the hostage was with militants on the other side of the Afghan–Pakistan border: "The American soldier is with the Emirate center [a reference to Taliban based inside Afghanistan] . . . The Americans also know it." He also revealed that the Taliban leadership council had previously issued instructions to its commanders, including those belonging to the Haqqani network, not to harm prisoners.[28]

In June 2013, a spokesman for the Taliban stated that they were ready to free Bergdahl in exchange for five senior operatives imprisoned at Guantanamo Bay. The offer came amid planned peace talks in Qatar involving three key players: the US, the Afghan government, and the Taliban.[29]

The abduction of two American soldiers in Afghanistan (July 2010)

At around 8:00 p.m. on 23 July 2010, two US-navy sailors, Petty Officer Jarod Newlove and his companion, Petty Officer Justin McNeley, went missing in an area of Logar province to the south of Kabul, known to be dominated by the Taliban. The two left Camp Julien base on the outskirts of Kabul that housed NATO's counter-insurgency academy and might have taken a wrong turn that sent them toward Logar province.[30]

The abduction

NATO officials offered no clear explanation why the sailors were in Logar. "The two left their compound in the Afghan capital, Kabul, but never returned," claimed a NATO statement. Samer Gul, chief of Logar's Charkh district, said a four-wheel-drive armored sports utility vehicle was seen that Friday night by a guard working for his office. The guard tried to flag down the vehicle, carrying a driver and a passenger, but it kept going. "They stopped in the main bazaar of Charkh district. The Taliban saw them in the bazaar," Gul said. "They didn't touch them in the bazaar, but notified other Taliban that a four-wheel [*sic*] vehicle was coming their way. The second group of Taliban tried to stop the vehicle but, when it refused to halt, the insurgents opened fire and the occupants in the vehicle shot back," he said, explaining that there was a well-paved road that led into the Taliban area and suggesting the Americans may have mistaken that for the main highway, which was much older and more dilapidated.[31]

The Taliban did not claim responsibility for the missing sailors until more than forty-eight hours after the ambush. That fact suggested that the attack was unplanned and the militants were trying to figure out how to best handle the opportunity.

The Taliban demands

Taliban spokesman Zabihullah Mujahid said the soldiers drove into an area of Logar province that was under insurgent control. He claimed that during a brief gunfight, one American was killed and the other was captured; both were taken to a safe area and "are in the hands of the Taliban".[32] Mujahid did not mention the condition of the hostages in any detail, stating only that the Taliban leaders were waiting to decide what to do with them.

A local Afghan official claimed the Taliban sent a message through intermediaries offering to hand over the body of a US sailor in exchange for jailed insurgents. Later, the Taliban posted a message in English and Arabic on their website that claimed one American service member had been kidnapped in Logar and said another was killed in a shootout. The message included a picture of one of the sailors, but did not say whether he was alive or dead.

The NATO response

US and NATO officials confirmed that two American navy personnel went missing in the eastern province of Logar after an armored sports vehicle was seen driving into a Taliban-held area. Admiral Mike Mullen, chairman of the US Joint Chiefs of Staff, said that NATO launched a widespread search to find the two US sailors. The manhunt involved both helicopters and vehicles, and targeted a number of compounds suspected of harboring Taliban fighters or bomb-makers. At least two Logar radio stations broadcast descriptions of the men and offered rewards of US$10,000 for the safe return of each of them. Hundreds of posters with photographs of the two missing sailors were hung at checkpoints throughout Logar province, while NATO troops stopped vehicles, searched people, peered inside windows, and checked trunks. The posters stated: "This American trooper is missing. He was last seen in a white Land Cruiser vehicle. If you have any information about this soldier, kindly contact the Logar Joint Coordination Center" (which was run by coalition and Afghan forces). A phone number was listed along with information about a US$20,000 reward offered for information leading to their location.[33]

The recovery of the two bodies

The body of McNeley was recovered on Sunday. According to local Afghan authorities, he was believed to have been wounded during a firefight when militants abducted the two sailors, and later died from his wounds. The Taliban also said the sailor had died from wounds sustained during the abduction.[34]

Newlove's body was found on Wednesday afternoon in Yousuf

Khiel, a village in the Baraki Barak district. This area of southwestern Logar Province is adjacent to Charkh district where the two sailors were abducted. Ghulam Mustafa Muhsini, the Logar provincial police chief, said that a villager reported finding a body to the Afghan police at about noon on Wednesday. A team of NATO and Afghan forces then recovered the corpse, which was still clad in a uniform. It was not immediately known whether Newlove had died of wounds suffered in the firefight or was killed by insurgents while in captivity.[35]

Summary

Kidnappings of foreign soldiers are rare in Afghanistan, where a ten-year insurgency has been escalating, particularly in the southern provinces of Helmand and Kandahar. In 2010, the Taliban warned that they would target foreign military and government installations and staff, as well as Afghans working for them or for the Kabul government. After the abduction and killing of the sailors, NATO tightened its security. US military personnel were prohibited from driving alone, and traveled in convoys of at least two vehicles.[36]

A *New York Times* reporter, David Rohde, was also kidnapped in Logar province while trying to make contact with a Taliban commander. He and an Afghan colleague escaped in June 2009 after seven months in captivity, most of it spent in Taliban sanctuaries in Pakistan.

Abductions in 2010[37]

- Two kidnapping attempts saw victims meet violent deaths in the northeast of the country.
- An aid worker working for DAI, a USAID-affiliated charity, was killed in an armed raid by International Security Assistance Force (ISAF) troops.
- In September 2010, gunmen abducted and killed six Americans, two Afghans, one Briton, and one German working for an optical charity in Badakhshan.
- A Dutch national, on the road between the northern Taluqan and Kunduz provinces, was kidnapped for a short time.
- Two French journalists were abducted in Kapisa province at the end of 2009.

French hostages in Afghanistan

In December 2009, cameraman Stéphane Taponier and reporter Hervé Ghesquière, who worked for France-3 public television, were seized along with three Afghan colleagues in the mountainous and unstable Kapisa province east of Kabul. Taliban militants threatened to kill the two French journalists unless their demands were met, which included the release of some detainees held by France.[38]

In a video posted on the Taliban's "alemarah" website on 12 April 2010, the journalists were shown in separate clips. Speaking in English and French, one read a lengthy statement saying that if the full video was not aired on French television, the journalists would be killed along with their translator and driver. "The French president, Mr Nicolas Sarkozy, must understand that we are now in danger of death. I repeat: the French president must negotiate very quickly, otherwise we will be executed soon," he said.[39] In a written statement, the Taliban said they had submitted a list of detainees to the government of France "for release as an exchange for the two Frenchmen and their Algerian colleague". It added: "There is no other option for the release of the said detainees except the option of detainees' exchange." The statement described the detainees as "miserable" and "living a life under torture and brutalities".

Later that month, France-3 revealed that another video had been made by the kidnappers a month earlier and was released to French authorities, although not made public. French officials authenticated the video, in which the hostages appeared to be in good health. France-3 then announced that the journalists had recorded video messages to their families. Taponier's parents were shown the film at the foreign ministry in Paris, and said afterwards that the two hostages appeared in the video to their government for help and looked thin, but in good shape.[40] The French government said that securing the release of the journalists was an "absolute priority".

Taponier and Ghesquière were released on 29 June 2011, along with an Afghan interpreter; the other two Afghans had been freed months before. The journalists had been held for eighteen months by the Taliban – their detention was the longest hostage saga involving French journalists since the 1980s Lebanon hostage crisis. The exact circumstances of the men's release after 547 days were not clear. The Elysée denied paying a ransom, while *Le Monde* reported that conditions for the release were met months ago, but had been delayed because of differences between the local Taliban and their senior hierarchy. President Sarkozy publicly thanked "everyone who took part in freeing the hostages," and praised Afghan President Hamid Karzai for his handling of the situation.[41]

Taliban prisoners escape from Afghan jails (2008–10)

About fifteen thousand suspected Taliban insurgents were incarcerated in Afghan jails, in addition to around one thousand prisoners held at foreign military detention centers in Afghanistan, with more than eight hundred of those at Bagram, north of Kabul.[42] In the years 2008–10, Taliban inmates escaped from Afghan prisons on three occasions:

> *On 18 June 2010*, a smuggled bomb exploded at a prison in Farah province, just as Taliban fighters staged coordinated diversionary attacks on four police checkpoints in the city, allowing twenty-three inmates – including suspected insurgents – to escape.[43] A guard died in the explosion and one police officer was wounded. One prisoner died and three were wounded when guards opened fire on the fleeing prisoners, and eight other inmates were recaptured. The prison blast came shortly after 2:00 a.m., destroying a gate and allowing the prisoners to run out of the building.[44] About four hundred prisoners were being held in a building meant for only eighty-six, and were a mix of suspected insurgents and common criminals because the province had no funds to build separate detention facilities.[45] Taliban spokesman Qari Yousef Ahmadi sent a message to reporters, taking responsibility for the jailbreak and saying "all of our mujahideen" were freed, while claiming that fifteen prison guards were killed.
>
> *On 24 November 2009*, twelve prisoners escaped from the Farah prison via a tunnel. A thirteenth prisoner, arrested during his attempted escape, said the tunnel took ten days to dig and the plan was to slowly empty the prison overnight.[46]
>
> *On 14 June 2008*, the Taliban staged a sophisticated jailbreak that freed nearly 1,150 prisoners from the Sarposa prison in the southern city of Kandahar. At least 750 criminals and around four hundred Taliban inmates escaped after a suicide bomber detonated a water tanker full of explosives at the compound's main entrance, wrecking the gate and a police post and killing the officers inside. A short time later, a second suicide bomber detonated a device against the wall at the rear of the prison, opening a second escape route, while gunmen stormed into the ruins to attack the guards.[47]

Taliban spokesman Qari Yousef Ahmadi said that thirty insurgents on motorbikes and two suicide bombers had attacked the prison, and claimed militants had been planning the assault for two months. "People are rejoicing and sacrificing sheep. They are welcoming our people into their homes," he added.[48] At least nine guards were killed and twelve more were injured as militants bombarded the prison buildings with rocket-propelled grenades and heavy machine-gun fire. NATO troops and police launched house-to-house searches in a desperate effort to round up the fugitives, but not one was captured. Kandahar is less than two hours' drive from the Pakistan border where the Taliban had safe havens beyond the reach of NATO operations. Most of the four hundred militants who escaped were battle-hardened veterans of the seven-year struggle with international and Afghan forces.

Taliban abductions

The Taliban conducted a series of high-profile abductions in order to force the Afghan government to release Taliban prisoners in exchange for the hostages. In most cases, the Afghan government denied reports of a prisoner swap, but Taliban hostages were released:

> *10 October 2007*: Taliban kidnappers freed German engineer Rudolf Blechschmidt and four of his Afghan colleagues in exchange for the release of five Taliban prisoners held by the government in Kabul.[49] Blechschmidt was one of two German engineers abducted along with six Afghan colleagues in July 2007 when visiting a construction site. One of the Afghan captives apparently escaped, while the other German hostage, a forty-four-year-old man, was reportedly shot dead by his abductors a few days after being kidnapped.
>
> *19 July 2007*: the Taliban kidnapped twenty-three South Korean aid workers. Two of the hostages were murdered, and the rest were released in August 2007 after negotiations between the South Korean and Afghan governments.
>
> *March 2007*: five imprisoned Taliban were freed in exchange for a kidnapped Italian journalist, Daniele Mastrogiacomo.

Armed attacks on Afghan jails

In Taliban attacks on the Afghan jails at Sarposa prison in 2008, and Farah prison in 2009 and 2010, about 1,200 prisoners were released – several hundred of whom were Taliban commanders and combatants. The successful attacks on the jails were considered to be significant blows to the prestige of the regime of Afghan President Hamid Karzai. The Taliban conducted a series of high-profile abductions, mainly of foreign citizens, in order to force the Afghan government to release Taliban prisoners in exchange for the hostages. The release of their members will remain a high-priority goal on the Taliban agenda and will be a significant component in any negotiation on national reconciliation between the Karzai regime and the Taliban. It must be taken into consideration that the Taliban will not halt their campaign of abductions as long as the violent insurgency continues.

Summary

The Taliban made great efforts to release its prisoners, using two main methods:

- Kidnapping foreign civilians, military staff, and Afghan government workers.
- Armed attacks on Afghan jails.

Abductions in Pakistan

Kidnapping for ransom is one of the most profitable and widespread criminal enterprises in the Islamic Republic of Pakistan; it is a flourishing business and an easy source of money for criminals, the Taliban, and al Qaeda terrorists. The abduction of government officials, key leaders, and members of international organizations provides bargaining power to terrorists. The problem inherent in high-profile abductions is that the state can no longer adhere to its stance of "not negotiating" with the terrorists when it comes under pressure to pay a ransom to get the abducted person back. Additionally, when the hostage is an important person, the terrorists will also demand the release of its followers held by the state. Although kidnapping was not an entirely new tactic by the network's core leadership, material retrieved from bin Laden's residence in Pakistan confirmed that it was "discussed further as a way of dealing with funding woes"; al Qaeda in Pakistan has resorted in recent years to kidnapping for ransom payments as one more way to raise funds for its terrorist operations, due to a cash shortage resulting from international monetary regulations designed to halt the flow of money to terrorist groups.

The abduction of Tariq Azizuddin, Pakistani ambassador to Afghanistan (February 2008)

In March 2008, Tariq Azizuddin, the Pakistani ambassador to Afghanistan, was kidnapped while transiting the Khyber Pass area.[50] Once abducted along with his bodyguard and driver, his captors traveled for ten hours to a temporary location, and Azizuddin was later moved three times during his captivity. He was released in May 2008, after being held for three months by his Taliban kidnappers. In exchange, the Pakistan government released more than forty militants and paid a US$2.5 million ransom, according to the daily newspaper *Dawn*.

The abduction of John Solecki, head of Balochistan UNHCR (February 2009)

On 2 February 2009, John Solecki, the Balochistan head of the United Nations High Commission for Refugees (UNHCR), was kidnapped when he was going unguarded in his car to his office in the Chaman neighborhood of Quetta, Balochistan. Solecki was a "valuable" victim because of his status as a UN official and his US nationality. Therefore, the reaction from the UN was most inconvenient for Pakistan as the UNHCR was crucial to Pakistan's efforts to take care of war-displaced refugees – the UN had the option of terminating its mission if its personnel were not minimally secure.

Solecki's abduction was claimed by a previously unknown group, the Balochistan Liberation United Front. After two months in captivity, he was released on 4 April 2009, for "humanitarian reasons", without any of the group's demands being met.[51] He was discovered in the city of Khadkhutcha, some fifty kilometers south of Quetta, and later flown home to the US.

The abduction and murder of Daniel Pearl (January 2002)

Daniel Pearl was an American-Jewish journalist who was kidnapped, tortured, and murdered in Karachi by al Qaeda terrorists. At the time of his kidnapping, Pearl served as the South Asia bureau chief of the *Wall Street Journal* and was based in Mumbai in the Indian Maharashtra state. He had traveled to Pakistan as part of an investigation into alleged links between Richard Reid (the "shoe bomber"), al Qaeda, and Pakistan's Inter-Services Intelligence agency (ISI). He was subsequently beheaded by his captors.

Pearl had been researching a radical Islamic leader, Sheikh Mubarak Ali Gilani, head of the Jamaat-ul-Fuqra ("Community of the Impoverished") group. Gilani had been linked to the so-called "shoe bomber", Richard Reid, who tried to blow up an American Airlines flight from Paris to Miami in December 2001. To find his way to Gilani, Pearl reached out to new contacts and made himself accessible. He had traveled to Pakistan at a particularly tense time, soon after the fall of the Taliban regime in neighboring Afghanistan when many radical Islamists had entered Pakistan, which was something of a haven due to long-standing relations with existing militant Islamist groups in that country. At a hotel in Islamabad, he was introduced to a man who called himself Bashir. Pearl thought he was meeting a potential source who could help him get access to Gilani; in fact, his real name was Ahmed Omar Saeed Sheikh, a British-born Pakistani militant with a record of kidnapping westerners. The meeting with Saeed, instead of helping Pearl to land a scoop, set events in motion that led to his entrapment, abduction, and murder.

On 23 January 2002, after exchanging e-mails with Saeed for nine days, Pearl was lured to a restaurant in Karachi. He got into a car he thought would take him to interview Gilani – instead, he was kidnapped by a militant group calling itself "The National Movement for the Restoration of Pakistani Sovereignty" that demanded the release of Pakistani detainees from the US naval base at Guantanamo Bay, Cuba. The kidnappers accused Pearl of being a spy – an accusation strongly denied by both the CIA and his newspaper – and vowed to kill him if their demands were not met. Photos were attached of Pearl handcuffed, with a gun at his head and holding up a newspaper.

There was no response to pleas for mercy from Pearl's editor and from his wife. Nine days later, Pearl was beheaded. His body was found on 16 May 2002, cut into ten pieces and buried in a shallow grave on the outskirts of Karachi. Pearl's body was returned to the US and interred in the Mount Sinai Memorial Park Cemetery in Los Angeles, California.

Three suspects were caught, including Saeed, the mastermind of the kidnapping:

Ahmed Omar Saeed Sheikh was a member of the militant Islamic group Jaish-e-Mohammed ("The Army of Muhammad"), whose goal was to unite Indian-administered Kashmir with Pakistan. He told police that he plotted to seize Pearl because he wanted to strike at the US and embarrass Pakistani President General Pervez Musharraf on the eve of his visit to Washington. President Musharraf expressed his profound grief over the tragic death of Daniel Pearl, and offered his heartfelt condolences to Pearl's wife, his family, and the editors and journalists of the *Wall Street Journal*. Musharraf said that such acts of terror were painful experiences for society, but would not deter him, his government, or the people of Pakistan from acting with all their strength against terrorists and in fighting the menace together with the international community. The president also said that Pakistan would stay the course to ensure that his country, and indeed the world, is free of terror.

Saeed had been held in an Indian prison in connection with the abduction of western tourists in India in 1994, and had been freed by the Indian government in December 1999 in exchange for passengers on board the hijacked Indian Airlines flight 814. Saeed turned himself in to police on 12 February 2002, but told a court in Karachi that he had first surrendered to the Pakistani ISI one week earlier in Lahore. What took place during his time with the ISI is not known.

Fazal Karim was a militant member of Lashkar-e-Jhangvi ("Army of Jhangvi"), a Sunni Muslim group with ties to the Taliban. He claimed that he witnessed Pearl's execution by three Arabic-speaking men who showed up without warning.

Mohammad Hashim Qadeer was a member of the Kashmiri separatist group Harkat-ul-Mujahideen, who first introduced Pearl to Saeed. He was detained in July 2005.

On 10 March 2007, Khalid Sheikh Mohammed (al Qaeda's third-ranking operative, who was snared in March 2003 near Islamabad) claimed at a closed military hearing in Guantanamo Bay that he had personally beheaded Pearl. This confession repeated phrasing leaked from his interrogation at a clandestine CIA "black site" in 2002. On 19 March 2007, Saeed's lawyers cited Mohammed's confession in defense of their client. They said they acknowledged that their client had played a role in Pearl's murder, but had always argued that Khalid Sheikh Mohammed was the actual murderer and planned for Mohammed's confession to play a central role in the appeal of their client's death sentence.[52] However, on 21 March 2002, Ahmed Omar Saeed Sheikh and two other suspects were charged for their part in the abduction and murder of Daniel Pearl. In July 2002, a court sentenced Saeed to death by hanging. The three others convicted of the kidnapping received twenty-five-year jail sentences.

The Pakistani Taliban abduct a Swiss couple (July 2011)

Two Swiss tourists were kidnapped in Pakistan by the Tehrik-i-Taliban Pakistan (TTP; literally, "Student Movement of Pakistan") on 2 July 2011. Olivier David Och, aged thirty-one, and Daniela Widmer, aged twenty-eight, had arrived in Pakistan from India on 28 June 2011. The tourists were driving a blue Volkswagen van from Punjab and may have been heading for Quetta, possibly en route to Iran. When they reached Loralai City, about 150 kilometers from Quetta, they were given a police escort. However, once they reached its outskirts beyond the area under police jurisdiction, the police turned back and they were left without security guards.[53] They were kidnapped by five gunmen as they dined at a hotel. The gunmen spoke Pashto, and drove off with the pair in a green car across the Zhob area of Balochistan to South Waziristan.[54]

The TTP claim responsibility

The Pakistani Taliban claimed that they were holding the Swiss couple. Wali-ur-Rehman, deputy head of the TTP, said that he ordered the kidnapping in order to gain freedom for Aafia Siddiqui, a Pakistani scientist jailed in the US. However, he did not provide proof that his group held the pair, but said they were in good health. "The Swiss couple are with the TTP. They are at a very safe place," he said by telephone. "They are completely in good health, they are getting reasonable food, and they have not fallen ill since they landed in our custody."[55]

Rehman said the Taliban would release the couple if the US freed Aafia Siddiqui, a female neuroscientist sentenced in 2010 for the attempted murder of US government agents in Afghanistan. "We call upon the western world to put pressure on America for the release of Aafia Siddiqui," he said. "If America does not agree to her release then our *shura* (council) will take a decision about the Swiss hostages."[56] Other Taliban sources later confirmed TTP's claim and added that the hostages were being held in the lawless border district of South Waziristan, a notorious haven for the Taliban and al Qaeda. Previous kidnappings in Pakistan had also been followed by demands for Siddiqui's release, without effect. Rehman said the group had not issued a ransom demand.

The Swiss response

The kidnapping was the first such incident involving Swiss citizens in Pakistan, and the Swiss authorities set up a task force combining police and intelligence services to work on the case.[57] The task force "is pressing for everything necessary to be done to allow the hostages' liberation in good health", a Swiss statement said, adding that the embassy in Islamabad was in constant contact with local authorities and police searching for the pair. The Swiss embassy sent one of its Pakistani employees, a former army officer, to collect information about the matter, and Swiss diplomats were also in touch with the Loralai commissioner. Since 2008, Switzerland had advised its citizens against non-essential travel to Pakistan, citing risks including the threat of kidnapping.

The release

The couple were released under mysterious circumstances in March 2012, when they presented themselves at around 3:00 a.m. at a military checkpoint in North Waziristan (a Taliban and al Qaeda stronghold) claiming that they had escaped from their captors. However, the Taliban claimed that they had been released after the decision of a *shura* (council), fuelling suspicions that a ransom had been paid. Unconfirmed reports stated that up to one hundred Taliban prisoners had been freed in exchange for the couple's release.[58]

The Aafia Siddiqui affair

Aafia Siddiqui, dubbed "Lady al Qaeda" by the press, was one of the world's most wanted women. She was a Pakistani neuroscientist who once studied at the Massachusetts Institute of Technology (MIT). Her parents were Pakistani strivers – middle-class folk with strong faith in Islam and education. Her father Muhammad was an English-trained doctor; her mother Ismet befriended the dictator General Zia-ul-Haq. Aafia was a smart teenager and in 1990 followed her older brother to the US. Impressive grades won her admission to the prestigious MIT and, later, Brandeis University, where she graduated in cognitive neuroscience. In 1995, she married a young Karachi doctor, Amjad Mohammed Khan; a year later, their first child, Muhammad Ahmed, was born.[59]

Siddiqui was also an impassioned Muslim activist. In Boston, she campaigned for Afghanistan, Bosnia, and Chechnya; she was particularly affected by graphic videos of pregnant Bosnian women being killed. She wrote e-mails, held fundraisers, and made forceful speeches at her local mosque. But the charities she worked with had sharp edges: the Nairobi branch of one, Mercy International Relief Agency, was linked to the 1998 US embassy bombings in East Africa; three other charities were later banned in the US for their links to al Qaeda.[60]

The 11 September 2001 attacks marked a turning point in Siddiqui's life. In May 2002, the FBI questioned her and her husband about some unusual internet purchases they had made: about US$10,000 worth of night-vision goggles, body armor, and forty-five military-style books, including "The Anarchist's Arsenal". Mr Khan claimed he had bought the equipment for hunting and camping expeditions.[61] Their marriage started to crumble. A few months later, the couple returned to Pakistan and divorced that August, two weeks before the birth of their third child, Suleman.[62]

On Christmas Day, 2002, Siddiqui left her three children with her mother in Pakistan and returned to the US, ostensibly to apply for academic jobs. The FBI claimed that, during her ten-day trip, she opened a post box in the name of Majid Khan, an alleged al Qaeda operative accused of plotting to blow up gas stations in the Baltimore area.

The post box, prosecutors later said, was to facilitate his entry into the US.

Six months after her divorce, she married Ammar al Baluchi, a nephew of the 9/11 mastermind, Khalid Sheikh Mohammed, at a small ceremony near Karachi. During interrogations by CIA officials in March 2003, Mohammed named her as one of his accomplices. According to US intelligence and military officials, Siddiqui was involved in Mohammed's post-9/11 plotting against the US homeland. She had been tasked, among other assignments, with helping an al Qaeda operative sneak into the US to attack gas stations on the east coast. The FBI issued a "Seeking Information Alert" for Siddiqui in 2003, and added her to its most-wanted list in May 2004.

When the FBI issued a global alert for her and her first husband in March 2003, she disappeared from her family home in Karachi, Pakistan. From 2003 to 2008, Siddiqui dropped out of sight. The whereabouts during that period of her and her three children have remained a mystery to this day.

She was arrested in July 2008 in Ghazni, Afghanistan, with her eldest child, Ahmed, then aged 12. Ahmed was later sent to be with his aunt, Dr Fauzia Siddiqui, a neurologist who studied and taught at Johns Hopkins University, and who later accused the Pakistani intelligence agencies of handing her sister over to American officials. She claimed that Siddiqui was transferred to the US airbase at Bagram, Afghanistan, and was tortured there. Her accusation was widely accepted in Pakistan, while strenuously denied by American officials. Fauzia's second husband, Mr Baluchi, was arrested and jailed at Guantanamo, accused of a role in financing the 9/11 attack.

The Bagram myth

One of the most enduring myths concerning Siddiqui is that she was secretly imprisoned and tortured for years at the American-run detention facility in Bagram.[63] She was called the "Grey Lady of Bagram" by her supporters, alluding to her alleged time there. There is no evidence to back up this claim, yet it is widely believed in Pakistan and elsewhere. According to a recently leaked State Department cable made available on the website of the British newspaper *The Guardian*,[64] Bagram officials denied ever holding Siddiqui. In addition to the aforementioned officials at Bagram, US authorities have repeatedly denied that she was ever held there prior to 2008.

Al Qaeda operatives, however, have taken to making up stories about seeing Siddiqui there. Senior al Qaeda commander Abu Yahya al Libi, who himself was held at Bagram before he escaped in 2005, claimed that during his time there, Siddiqui was "there before us and her [internment] number was 650", which was "one of the older numbers in the prison". He continued: "How we used to hear her scream and yell in her solitary cell. In order to save honor, blood has to be shed."[65] The Bagram myth was used by al Qaeda, and even by the broader Pakistani public, to explain Siddiqui's supposedly "missing" years between 2003 and 2008. She was most likely on the run until she was captured in July 2008. Still, the fiction that Siddiqui and her children were kidnapped by American officials has endured.

In 2010, Siddiqui was jailed for eighty-six years after being found guilty of grabbing a rifle at an Afghan police station where she was being interrogated and opening fire on servicemen and FBI agents. She missed, and in a struggle was herself shot by one of the US soldiers.

Calls for the release of Siddiqui

Afghan and Pakistani Taliban Islamic movements, and al Qaeda: Siddiqui was a cause célèbre in Pakistan for Islamist terror groups, Islamist and secular political parties, and the Pakistani government:

- In February 2010, the Afghan Taliban demanded the release of Siddiqui, and threatened to execute an American soldier, Bowe Robert Bergdahl, whom they were holding. They claimed Siddiqui's family had approached the Taliban network through a *jirga* (assembly of tribal elders), seeking their assistance to put pressure on the US to provide her with justice.[66]
- In September 2010, Muttahida Qaumi Mahaz ("Muttahida Qaumi Movement") leader Altaf Hussain held a rally in Karachi that called for the release of Siddiqui, and said the charges against her "are false".[67] The rally drew over 300,000 people.
- A British aid worker, Linda Norgrove, aged thirty-six, was kidnapped by Afghan Taliban fighters in Afghanistan on 26 September 2010, and was killed during a rescue attempt, along with six insurgents, after US forces stormed a compound in eastern Kunar province where she had been held for two weeks. A local Taliban commander named Mohammad Osman said he had kidnapped the woman and her Afghan colleagues in Kunar province. He told Afghan Islamic Press (AIP), which had close ties to the Taliban, that he was demanding an exchange for Siddiqui.[68]
- In November 2010, al Qaeda number two Ayman al Zawahiri released a tape entitled "Who Will Avenge the Scientist Aafia Siddiqui?" Zawahiri called on Pakistanis to "take the only available path, that of jihad . . . which will liberate Aafia Siddiqui".
- In December 2010, top al Qaeda ideologue Abu Yahya al Libi

released a propaganda tape calling on Muslims to wage jihad to avenge Siddiqui.

In Pakistan, Siddiqui became a national symbol of honor and victimization, and an emblem of Pakistani womanhood that represented the kind of female rebel acceptable in a rapidly Islamizing Pakistani society. In a rare display of unity, Prime Minister Yousaf Raza Gilani, who described Siddiqui as a "daughter of the nation", and opposition leader Nawaz Sharif promised to push for her release.

State Department cables released by Wikileaks revealed that Pakistani government officials repeatedly and persistently lobbied the US government to transfer Siddiqui. The cables reveal, however, that such lobbying was most likely carried out to assuage popular discontent with Siddiqui's imprisonment. The same cables note that the Pakistani public's support for Siddiqui was based on widespread misinformation.[69] A cable of 29 October 2008 states that acting Pakistani Foreign Secretary Khalid Babar "reiterated . . . requests to repatriate" Siddiqui in a meeting with US Ambassador Anne Patterson. The cable notes that, although press reports in Pakistan said Babar had made a "strong protest" in this vein, as well as his objections to US air strikes on Pakistani soil, his discussion was really "pro forma".[70] "We have told the [Ministry of Foreign Affairs] repeatedly that there currently is no legal basis to repatriate Siddiqui," the cable reads, "and we have no idea on the location of her other two children."

Another cable of 11 November 2008 said that Prime Minister Gilani asked a US congressional delegation to pursue Siddiqui's release to Pakistani custody.[71] "Gilani argued that the needs of her family and reports of her being ill provided humanitarian grounds for such a transfer," the cable reads. Gilani "also argued that her case whipped up mass popular support, diverting his government's attention from the counter-terrorism mission".

Another cable, dated 12 February 2010, notes the strong negative reaction to the guilty verdict handed down in Siddiqui's case.[72] The State Department noted that the Afghan Taliban had threatened to kill a US soldier they had kidnapped if Siddiqui wasn't released. In addition, Jamaat-e-Islami (JI; literally, "Islamic Party") women activists demonstrated outside the party's headquarters in Mansoora. According to the US embassy's analysis, widespread criticism of the US as "anti-Muslim", as well as criticism of the Pakistani government for supposedly not doing enough to secure Siddiqui's release, was being fanned by the Pakistani press. "Many Pakistanis were undoubtedly taken by surprise by the verdict, as one-sided media coverage of the case reported only her defense, and not the prosecution's case, leading local observers to conclude her acquital [*sic*] was a near certainty," the cable reads. "We expect this issue to persist for some time as a nationalistic cause with the active involvement of the JI, who never tire of anti-American agitation."

Still another cable, dated 19 February 2010, recounts a meeting between high-level Pakistani officials and Senator John Kerry.[73] The cable says that Prime Minister Gilani "asked the [US government] to consider repatriating Dr Aafia Siddiqui on humanitarian grounds". Gilani said that "this was a very contentious issue in Pakistan", and that by returning Siddiqui, "the US would be in the Pakistani people's good graces". Gilani and Interior Minister Rehman Malik "assured Kerry that the [Government of Pakistan] would honor the terms of Dr Siddiqui's jail sentence, and suggested that she complete her jail time under house arrest". The cable concluded: "Kerry agreed to look into the prisoner transfer issue."

In February 2011, the Pakistani government attempted to work a deal with the US to exchange CIA contractor Raymond Davis for Siddiqui. The Pakistani government ultimately freed Davis after a month of intense US diplomatic pressure. Siddiqui remains in jail.

An American aid worker abducted in Pakistan (August 2011)

American aid expert Warren Weinstein, aged sixty-three, was kidnapped at gunpoint in the Pakistani city of Lahore after gunmen stormed his residence and overpowered security guards.[74] Weinstein was working as the Pakistan national director of Virginia-based development company J. E. Austin Associates. He described his work as supervising a four-year, US$11 million "competitiveness project", funded by the American government, that was involved in dairy, horticulture, furniture, and medical equipment projects in the country's tribal areas, where Pakistani troops had been battling militants for years.[75]

The abduction

Weinstein was snatched at dawn in the upmarket neighborhood of Model Town. According to a police official, six to eight people broke into his house at around 3:30 a.m. local time, when security guards on duty were making preparation for *sehri* (the Ramadan fast observed by Muslims).[76] Somebody knocked on the main door. One of the guards said that when he opened the door, he saw three men standing there. They offered meals to the guards, who refused, and five more men entered the house using the back door, overpowered the guards, and tied their hands behind their back.[77] They asked Weinstein's driver, Muhammad Israr, to knock on Weinstein's bedroom door and, when the US citizen opened the door, they snatched him.[78] Israr informed investigators that his employer had received a severe head injury when one of the kidnappers hit him with his pistol, leaving the victim bleeding and unconscious. Given his age, investigators said his head injury might have caused his death, since his abductors would not risk taking him to a hospital for fear of arrest.[79] The head injury account was corroborated by investigators who visited the crime scene and said there was a trail of blood from his living room on the upper floor to the stairs leading to the ground floor of the house. Weinstein had traveled widely within Pakistan and had returned to Lahore from Islamabad on 11 August 2011.[80] Pakistani police claimed that the manner in which the kidnapping was carried out was extremely well-planned and meticulously executed. Investigators added that the kidnappers searched Weinstein's body to ensure there were no embedded chips that could help investigators track him.[81]

In May 2012, al Qaeda released a "proof of life" video of Weinstein,[82] and later, in September 2012, released a second video.[83] Weinstein remains in captivity until this day.

American-Pakistani relations

The kidnap of Weinstein came at a time of uneasy relations between the two countries. Pakistan's seven-week detention of CIA contractor Raymond Davis, who killed two men in Lahore in January 2011, and the covert American raid that killed Osama bin Laden in May 2011, had heightened tensions while, in the same month, a US consulate vehicle was attacked in the northwestern city of Peshawar, killing one person and injuring a dozen, including two US employees of the mission.

The abduction came as US Senator John McCain met with top Pakistani officials, including Prime Minister Gilani, in Islamabad on 13 August 2011. In a statement made after the meeting, Gilani said he told the Republican lawmaker that Pakistan desired an enduring partnership with the US and said he would welcome a visit by Secretary of State Hillary Clinton, adding that Pakistan looked forward to a deeper level of engagement with the US in all areas, including energy, the social sector, and economic cooperation. Gilani said he appreciated McCain's continued support for Pakistan in the US Congress, and gave reassurances that the Pakistani government was doing all it could to find Weinstein. Husain Haqqani, Pakistan's ambassador to the US, said on Twitter: "Pakistani and US law enforcement authorities will work together to find Warren Weinstein and apprehend his abductors."

Summary

Foreigners have frequently been targeted by militants in Pakistan in recent years, although it is rare for the assailants to stage such a raid on a victim's home. Kidnappings for ransom are also common in Pakistan, though most of the victims are Pakistani; these abductions are usually carried out by criminal gangs, but ransoms are also believed to help fund militant groups. Americans in Pakistan are considered especially at risk from militant attacks because the insurgents oppose both Islamabad's alliance with Washington and the US-led war in Afghanistan. US diplomats, aid workers, and other foreign nationals were urged to take strong security precautions.[84] Anti-US sentiment runs high in Pakistan, and already-prickly ties between Islamabad and Washington hit a low point after the May 2nd killing of al Qaeda chief Osama bin Laden in an attack that Pakistan termed a breach of its sovereignty.[85]

The kidnapping of the Swiss couple underscored the deep security crisis in Pakistan, where abductions have been on the rise. Abductions for ransom have become a lucrative business in Pakistan: in June 2011, Pakistan Interior Minister Rehman Malik told parliament that 15,365 incidents of kidnapping had taken place in the country in 2010. Out of the total, 13,497 took place in Punjab, 1,293 in Sindh, 273 in Khyber Pakhtunkhwa, 250 in Balochistan, and 52 in Islamabad.[86] Most kidnapping victims in the country were Pakistani, but foreign aid workers, diplomats, and other foreigners were also targeted. Foreign hostages included a Chinese engineer, a Polish oil worker, and an American, John Solecki, who worked for the UNHCR and was released after two months in captivity.[87] A French tourist was held hostage for three months in Balochistan, from May to August 2009, while traveling from Quetta to Iran with two other Frenchmen, a woman, and two children in a camper van.[88]

Pakistani officials said that the security forces had to deal with a new phenomenon of so-called "quicknappings": middle-class Pakistanis were abducted and their families were forced to rapidly find ransom money, ranging from US$2,000–5,000, in order to prevent the killing of their relative.[89] Balochistan is a particularly dangerous region in Pakistan: it is the scene of a low-level separatist insurgency and criminal gangs involved in the kidnapping-for-ransom trade are common. Hundreds of people have died since 2004, when rebel movements demanded political autonomy and a greater share of profits from the region's natural oil, gas, and mineral resources.

By focusing on Aafia Siddiqui's case, the Pakistani Taliban clearly tried to tap into deep anti-American sentiment as well as widespread discontent with the Pakistani government. Siddiqui became the subject of popular mythology: in the imagination of the Pakistani public, she was not an al Qaeda operative who evaded American authorities for years, but instead a victim of the American-led "war on terror". The Pakistani government attempted to placate this resentment by lobbying for Siddiqui's release, but failed, while the Taliban attempted to take advantage of the situation to win more support for its jihadist agenda by highlighting the ineffectiveness of the Pakistani government's attempts to secure Siddiqui's release. The Taliban also sought to play on the widely-held misconception in Pakistan that the US is "anti-Muslim" for imprisoning Siddiqui.

India and the Islamic Terror Threat

On the terrorist front, the Republic of India is living in an unenviable neighborhood. Terrorism in India, according to the Indian Home Ministry, poses a significant threat to the state. Basically, there are two types of terror threat faced by India: external and internal. External terrorism emerges from neighboring countries, while internal terrorism emanates from religious or communal violence and Naxalite-Maoist insurgency. Terror activities involve both natives and foreign citizens. Islamic terrorism in India is essentially of an imported (external) variety: the manpower, weapons, finances, ideological motivation, and plans involved in terrorist actions originate largely from its neighborhood. Except in Kashmir, where some youths, motivated by various forms of temptation, went to Pakistan for training and weapons, only a minuscule proportion of Indian Muslims joined the terrorist ranks. However, subversive propaganda and the cascading effect of global radicalization have increased the threat of terror abductions from Islamic terrorist organizations in the area.[90]

The insurgency in Kashmir has existed in various forms. Thousands of lives have been lost since 1989 due to intensification of both the insurgency and the fight against it. The widespread insurgency started with the disputed 1987 Kashmir elections, when some elements from the state's national assembly formed militant wings that acted as a catalyst for the emergence of armed insurgency in the region.[91] The Pakistan ISI has been accused by India of supporting and training mujahideen to fight in Jammu and Kashmir provinces.[92] According to official figures released by the Jammu and Kashmir assemblies, there were 3,400 cases of disappearance, and the conflict left more than 47,000 people dead, as of July 2009.[93] However, the number of insurgency-related deaths in those states has fallen sharply since the start of a slow-moving peace process between India and Pakistan.[94]

The Indian strategic response to terrorism has been a delicate blending of the hard and soft power of the state; a policy that, at times, invites snide comments like "a democracy that has room even for violence". Besides safeguarding national security interests, India's response has been conditioned by its democratic polity, the need to accommodate communal sensitivities, and the safety of its citizens. The global and regional settings, the complexity of relations with neighboring countries, and international obligations on the terrorist front have also influenced their response.[95] Moreover, India's long historical experience of grappling with civilizational conflicts has conditioned the mind-set, both of the rulers and the ruled. India has traditionally avoided head-on collisions with civilizational adversaries, preferring tactics of conflict avoidance and conflict resolution to try to contain physical confrontation at a low level. The high tolerance of Indian civil society, and its ability to take losses in its stride, is also a great national strength whose strategic import may not be obvious to a western analyst.[96]

One of the cornerstones of India's counter-terrorist strategy has been to "de-link" Islam from terror and to treat terrorists as a class devoid of any religious identity. India seeks to defeat terrorists' efforts to project themselves as soldiers of Islam and to seize control of Muslim society through coercion and persuasion. In achieving this goal, communal polarization of the civil society on religious fault lines is prevented. Muslims are seen as victims of the phenomenon rather than its perpetrator. This policy was duly reflected in the enactment and enforcement of laws, affirmative actions to redress genuine grievances, support of liberal and pluralistic Islamic thought, and the political engagement of Muslims.

The elected governments had a political interest in maintaining law and order, and democracy was used as an effective tool to fight terrorists. In Jammu and Kashmir, even at the height of terrorist violence when the number of killings was as high as three thousand a year, elections to state assemblies were held in 1996 and 2002 (the state assemblies having a six-year term) with an impressive turnout. Even parliamentary elections for the central government were held regularly along with rest of the country. Terrorist resistance to the elections by unleashing violence against the party leaders, candidates, and voters was resolutely countered. The successful completion of free and fair elections proved to be a silent, but most effective, display of the rejection of terrorists by civil society – in terms of both means and ends.[97]

This study now presents a few examples of how India has responded to terror abductions:

The abduction of Rubaiya Sayeed (December 1989)

The kidnapping of Rubaiya Sayeed was carried out by members of the Jammu Kashmir Liberation Front,[98] a Kashmiri Muslim militant organization, on 8 December 1989.[99] Rubaiya was the daughter of Mufti Mohammad Sayeed, then the Home Minister of India in the V. P. Singh government. Rubaiya was kidnapped within five days of her father becoming the first Muslim Minister for Home Affairs in India.[100]

The kidnappers demanded the release of five of their comrades in exchange for Rubaiya's release – the government accepted their demands and freed the jailed terrorists on 13 December 1989. Rubaiya was freed two hours later.

The hijack of Indian Airlines flight 814 (December 1999)

Indian Airlines flight 814 Airbus A300 was en route from Tribhuvan airport (KTM) in Kathmandu, Nepal, to Indira Gandhi airport (DEL) in Delhi on 24 December 1999, when it was hijacked. Harkat-ul-Mujahideen, a Pakistan-based group, was accused of the hijacking.[101]

About thirty minutes after takeoff, a passenger armed with a pistol stood up and announced that the plane was being hijacked. Four other men wearing red masks then stood up and took positions throughout the aircraft. The hijackers demanded to be flown to Lahore (LHE), Pakistan. Authorities there, however, refused to allow the plane to land. With the plane low on fuel, the crew was forced to fly to Raja Sansi airport (ATQ) at Amritsar, India. The Indian authorities refused to allow the plane to land and dispatched a fuel tanker to block the runway. As the tanker sped towards the aircraft, air traffic control radioed the pilot to slow down and the tanker immediately came to a stop. This aroused the hijackers' suspicion and they forced the aircraft to take off immediately, without clearance from air traffic control. The aircraft missed the tanker by only a few feet.[102]

The plane was then again flown to Lahore (LHE) in Pakistan, but authorities closed the airport to keep the plane from landing. The pilot told the control tower, however, that the plane would crash if not given permission to land, and made an emergency landing. The hijackers demanded food, water, and fuel – all of which were provided.

The aircraft departed Lahore and was flown to Kabul airport (KBL) in Afghanistan, but was unable to land because there were no night-landing facilities. The plane flew on to Seeb airport (MCT) in Muscat, Oman, where authorities also refused permission to land. The plane was then taken to Dubai airport (DXB) in the United Arab Emirates, where permission to land was again refused. The pilot, however, was directed to al Minhad airbase (NHD), located in a remote area of Dubai, and landed there on December 25th. Twenty-seven passengers were subsequently released in exchange for food and fuel, along with the body of a passenger who had been executed earlier by the hijackers. The aircraft was then finally flown to Kandahar airport (KDH) in Afghanistan, arriving on December 26th, and stayed there for the remainder of the hijacking. Once in Kandahar, the hijackers issued their demands and the Taliban positioned well-armed fighters around the hijacked aircraft in an attempt to prevent Indian forces from storming the plane.

India's lack of recognition of the Taliban regime in Afghanistan complicated negotiations between Indian authorities and the hijackers.

The demands of the hijackers:
The hijackers demanded that India release Maulana Masood Azhar, a Pakistani leader of the Kashmiri separatist group Harkat-ul-Mujahideen, who was imprisoned in India. The hijackers also demanded the release of thirty-five other jailed guerrillas, a payment of US$200 million, and the body of a slain Kashmiri separatist.

On December 26th, a UN official arrived to mediate between the hijackers and Indian authorities, following a request by the ruling Taliban authorities. On December 27th, the hijackers announced a deadline and threatened to kill passengers if their demands were not met. Negotiations between the hijackers and Indian diplomats continued through December 29th. The hijackers eventually dropped their demands for the ransom payment and for the release of the prisoners. In return, India agreed to exchange three prisoners for the safe return of the aircraft and passengers. The hijacking lasted for seven days and ended after India released three militants: Mushtaq Ahmed Zargar, Ahmed Omar Saeed Sheikh, and Maulana Masood Azhar. After the three militants landed in Kandahar, the remaining hostages aboard the flight were freed on the afternoon of December 31st, and flown to Delhi. Meanwhile, the Taliban had given the hijackers ten hours to leave Afghanistan. The hijackers were later escorted by the Taliban across the Pakistani border. Pakistan denied that any of the militants remained in Pakistan, but it was later discovered that all three terrorists, Azhar (living in Muzaffarabad, Pakistan), Sheikh (from Lahore, Pakistan), and Zargar (also living in Muzaffarabad, Pakistan) were indeed living in that country.

The Mumbai terror attacks (November 2008)

The Mumbai terror attacks of 2008 took place on November 26th of that year, and have been described as "India's 9/11".

The attacks, carried out simultaneously in several locations, comprised of eleven coordinated shooting, bombing, and hostage-taking attacks across India's financial capital, carried out by members of Lashkar-e-Taiba (LeT), a banned Pakistan-based Islamic militant organization. The attackers allegedly received reconnaissance and intelligence assistance before the attacks and were trained in Pakistan and backed by the ISI, Pakistan's intelligence agency.

According to the subsequent investigation into the attack, ten gunmen boarded a small boat in Karachi at 8:00 a.m. on November 22nd, and sailed a short distance before boarding a bigger carrier, believed to be owned by an important operative of the LeT. The next day, the men took over an Indian fishing trawler, killed four crew members, and sailed 550 nautical miles along the Arabian Sea. Each man carried a weapons pack containing a Kalashnikov assault rifle, a 9-millimeter pistol, ammunition, hand grenades, and a bomb consisting of a military-grade explosive, steel ball-bearings, and a timer with instructions inscribed in Urdu.

By 4:00 p.m. on November 26th, the trawler approached the shores of Mumbai. The leader of the crew, identified by Indian investigators as Ismail Khan, aged twenty-five, from a Pakistani town in the Northwest-Frontier province, contacted his handlers. When darkness set in, the men killed the trawler's captain and boarded a dinghy with an engine that investigators said bore marks from a Lahore-based import company.

The attacks

The attacks began on Wednesday, 26 November 2008, and lasted until Saturday, 29 November 2008, killing 164 people, including foreign nationals, and wounding at least 308.

Eight of the attacks occurred in southern Mumbai: at the Chatrapati Shivaji rail terminus, the Oberoi Trident hotel, the Taj Mahal Palace & Tower hotel, the Leopold cafe, the Cama hospital, the Nariman House Jewish community center, the Metro cinema, and in a lane behind a building housing a leading newspaper and Saint Xavier's college. An explosion also took place at Mazgaon, in Mumbai's port area, and in a taxi in the Vile Parle neighborhood.

The first target was in the main hall of Mumbai's Chatrapati Shivaji Terminus railway station, where the gunmen fired indiscriminately into the crowd of passengers. The gunmen then ran out of the station and into neighboring buildings, including the Cama hospital.

The Taj Mahal Palace & Tower and Oberoi Trident hotels

Two hotels, the Taj Mahal Palace & Tower and the Oberoi Trident, were among the locations targeted. During the first night, firefighters rescued two hundred hostages from the Taj Mahal Palace via windows using ladders.

Harrowing audio recordings that recorded the attacks on the two luxury hotels and Nariman House in downtown Mumbai are what gave "Terror in Mumbai" its historic importance – it was the first time ever that we were able to see the inner workings of a major terrorist operation and to hear the terrorists' every word, indeed, every breath, until the moment they achieved their final goal: death. For, as the controller reminds one of the gunmen: "For your mission to succeed, you must be killed."

Taj Mahal Hotel – *Transcripts of communications between the terrorists and their HQ in Pakistan:*
0108 hours:
Pakistan caller: "How many hostages do you have?"
Mumbai terrorist: "We have one from Belgium. We have killed him. There was one chap from Bangalore. He could be controlled only with a lot of effort."
Pakistan caller: "I hope there is no Muslim amongst them?"
Mumbai terrorist: "No, none."
0126 hours:
Pakistan caller: "Are you setting the fire or not?"
Mumbai terrorist: "Not yet. I am getting a mattress ready for burning."
Pakistan caller: "What did you do with the dead body [on the boat]?"
Mumbai terrorist: "Left it behind."
Pakistan caller: "Did you not open the locks for the water below?" [Thought to be a prearranged plan to sink the vessel.]
Mumbai terrorist: "No, they did not open the locks. We left it like that because of being in a hurry. We made a big mistake."
Pakistan caller: "What big mistake?"
Mumbai terrorist: "When we were getting into the boat, the waves were quite high. Another boat came. Everyone raised an alarm that the Navy had come. Everyone jumped quickly. In this confusion, the satellite phone of Ismail got left behind."
0137 hours:
Pakistan caller: "The ATS [Anti-Terrorist Squad] chief has been killed. Your work is very important. Allah is helping you. The *vazir* [minister] should not escape. Try to set the place on fire."
Mumbai terrorist: "We have set fire in four rooms."
Pakistan caller: "People shall run helter-skelter when they see the

flames. Keep throwing a grenade every fifteen minutes or so. It will terrorize."
0310 hours:
Mumbai terrorist: "Greetings!"
Pakistan caller: "Greetings! There are three ministers and one secretary of the cabinet in your hotel. We don't know in which room."
Mumbai terrorist: "Oh! That is good news! It is the icing on the cake."
Pakistan caller: "Find those three, four persons and then get whatever you want from India."
Mumbai terrorist: "Pray that we find them."
Pakistan caller: "Do one thing. Throw one or two grenades on the navy and police teams, which are outside."
Mumbai terrorist: "Sorry. I simply can't make out where they are."

During the attacks, both hotels were surrounded by Rapid Action Force personnel and Marine commandos (MARCOS) and National Security Guard (NSG) troops.[103] Security forces stormed both hotels, and all nine attackers were killed by the morning of 29 November. Thirty-two hostages were killed at the Oberoi Trident hotel. A number of delegates to the European Parliament Committee on International Trade were staying in the Taj Mahal hotel when it was attacked, but none of them were injured.

Oberoi Trident Hotel – *Transcripts of communications between the terrorists and their HQ in Pakistan:*
0353 hours:
Pakistan caller 1: "Brother Abdul. The media is comparing your action to 9/11. One senior police official has been killed."
Mumbai terrorist 1: "We are on the 10th/11th floor. We have five hostages."
Pakistan caller 2: "Everything is being recorded by the media. Inflict the maximum damage. Keep fighting. Don't be taken alive."
Pakistan caller 1: "Kill all hostages, except the two Muslims. Keep your phone switched on so that we can hear the gunfire."
Mumbai terrorist 2: "We have three foreigners, including women, from Singapore and China."
Pakistan caller 1: "Kill them."
[Voices of gunmen can be heard directing hostages to stand in a line, and telling the two Muslims to stand aside. Sound of gunfire. Sound of cheering voices.]

Nariman House

On November 26th, between 9:20 and 10:00 p.m., two gunmen seized control of the Nariman House complex. Police surrounded the buildings that housed the Jewish Chabad Lubavitch Jewish center in Colaba, known as the Mumbai Chabad House. Police evacuated adjacent buildings and exchanged fire with the attackers, wounding one. NSG commandos arrived from Delhi and a helicopter took an aerial survey. During the first day, nine hostages were rescued from the first floor.

Nariman House – Transcripts of communications between the terrorists and their HQ in Pakistan:
1945 hours:
Mumbai terrorist: "Greetings! What did the Major-General say?"
Pakistan caller: "Greetings. The Major-General directed us to do what we like. We should not worry. The operation has to be concluded tomorrow morning. Pray to God. Keep two magazines and three grenades aside, and expend the rest of your ammunition."
Pakistan caller: "Keep in mind that the hostages are of use only as long as you do not come under fire because of their safety. If you are still threatened, then don't saddle yourself with the burden of the hostages. Immediately kill them."
Mumbai terrorist: "Yes, we shall do accordingly, God willing."
Pakistan caller: "The army claims to have done the work without any hostage being harmed. Another thing: Israel has made a request through diplomatic channels to save the hostages. If the hostages are killed, it will spoil relations between India and Israel."
Mumbai terrorist: "So be it, God willing."
Pakistan caller: "Stay alert."
2226 hours:
Pakistan caller: "Brother, you have to fight. This is a matter of prestige of Islam. Fight so that your fight becomes a shining example. Be strong in the name of Allah. You may feel tired or sleepy, but the Commandos of Islam have left everything behind: their mothers, their fathers, their homes. Brother, you have to fight for the victory of Islam. Be strong."
Mumbai terrorist: "Amen!"

The following day, at 7:30 a.m., commandos were dropped from helicopters on to Nariman House and began a sweep through the building. After a long battle, one commando and both attackers were killed. Rabbi Gavriel Holtzberg and his wife Rivka, who was six months pregnant, had been murdered by the attackers along with four other hostages inside the complex. On the morning of November 27th, the commandos had secured the Jewish center. By the morning of November 28th, all locations, except for the Taj Mahal Palace, were secured by Mumbai Police and security guards. On November 29th, India's NSG conducted "Operation Black Tornado" to drive out the remaining assailants.

The single captured terrorist, Mohammed Ajmal Kasab, said later that the attackers were members of the Pakistan-based terror outfit, Lashkar-e-Taiba. On 7 January 2009, Pakistan officially accepted Kasab's Pakistani nationality.

Lashkar-e-Taiba

Since the beginning of the conflict with India over control of Kashmir in the aftermath of the hasty breakup of the British Raj after World War II, Pakistan had relied on militant organizations to carry out attacks across its border with India. Lashkar-e-Taiba ("Army of the Pure") was founded in 1989 – with Pakistani state support – to fight Indians in Kashmir. While the primary area of operations of LeT's militant activities is the Kashmir valley, the group's professed goal was not limited only to challenging India's sovereignty over Jammu and Kashmir: LeT sees the issue of Kashmir as part of a wider global struggle.[104] The group has repeatedly claimed through its journals and websites that its main aim is to destroy the Indian republic, and to annihilate Hinduism and Judaism. The LeT has declared Hindus and Jews to be the "enemies of Islam" and India and Israel to be the "enemies of Pakistan".[105]

The LeT believes that violent jihad is the duty of all Muslims and must be waged until eight objectives are met: ending persecution against Muslims, establishing Islam as the dominant way of life in the world, forcing infidels to pay *jizya* (Islamic tax levied on non-Muslim residents), fighting for the weak and feeble against oppressors, exacting revenge for killed Muslims, punishing enemies for violating oaths and treaties, defending all Muslim states, and recapturing occupied Muslim territories.[106] It is one of the most feared groups fighting for control of Kashmir and has launched multiple strikes against India, including the 2001 attack on the Indian parliament in New Delhi.

After Pakistan joined America in its "war on terror" following the 9/11 attacks, LeT was added to a list of banned organizations in 2002 by President Pervez Musharraf, under pressure from Washington. LeT acted quickly to establish a political arm, the Jamaat-ud-Dawa (JuD), as a front organization to serve as its public face while it continued to operate much as it had before the ban, with offices in most Pakistani cities and support from members of the army. LeT also gained footholds in communities by investing in charity projects – after the 2005 Kashmir earthquake, JuD relief workers reacted more quickly and successfully than the government.

India blamed the LeT for orchestrating the Mumbai attacks that inflamed relations between the two nuclear-armed neighbors. The masterminds of the Mumbai terrorist attacks displayed sophisticated thinking in their choice of targets and their efforts to achieve multiple objectives. The attack was carried out by ten men, armed with easily-obtained assault weapons, semi-automatic pistols, hand grenades, simple improvised explosive devices, mobile phones, Blackberries, and GPS locators, and reflected a rise in the influence and effectiveness of Lashkar-e-Taiba.

Pakistan's ISI agency has been a longtime supporter of LeT. For over three decades now – and continuing to this day – the ISI has maintained strong institutional, albeit subterranean, links with LeT, and has supported its operations through generous financing and combat training.

The captured terrorist, Mohammed Ajmal Kasab

The sole terrorist survivor, Mohammed Ajmal Kasab, a Pakistani citizen, was one of the ten gunmen who conducted the terror attacks in Mumbai after entering India by boat on 26 November 2008. Captured by a photographer striding through Mumbai's main train station, an assault rifle in hand, the baby-faced Kasab quickly became the iconic image of the siege. His interrogation by Indian police unearthed one of the most frightening details: he was part of a cadre of thirty-two would-be suicide bombers, later joined by three more men. Ten went to Mumbai, while six went to Indian-administered Kashmir, Kasab told his interrogators.

An Indian judge sentenced Kasab to death on 6 May 2010, after he was found guilty of all eighty-six counts with which he was charged, including waging war against India, murder, and terrorism. Kasab cried that day as he heard the sentence. In his appeal against this verdict, both the Mumbai High Court (21 February 2011) and the Supreme Court of India (29 August 2012) upheld his death sentence. Kasab was hanged in secrecy at a jail in Pune, near Mumbai, after Indian President Pranab Mukherjee rejected his plea for mercy. "This is a tribute to all innocent people and police officers who lost their lives in this heinous attack on our nation," said R. R. Patil, the home minister for the state of Maharashtra where Mumbai is located. Indian authorities faced public pressure to quickly execute Kasab, so the government fast-tracked the appeal and execution process, which often can take years or, in some cases, decades.

The American-Pakistani terrorist, David Headley

Headley was one of the leading planners of the 2008 Mumbai terrorist attacks. The son of a Pakistani father and an American mother, Headley had been chosen for the mission because he looked like a western non-Muslim. He used those looks and his US passport to plan logistics for several of the attacked locations.

Soon after his birth in the United States, Headley and his parents moved to Pakistan. He was born Daood Sayed Gilani, the son of a prominent Pakistani broadcaster, but in 2006 changed his name to David Headley. After his parents divorced, Headley's mother moved back to the US while Headley remained in Pakistan with his father, who sent him to elite military schools. However, after getting into some trouble, Headley was sent to live with his mother. As a young man, he slid into drug addiction and drug trafficking.

Headley and Lashkar-e-Taiba

Headley became involved with the Islamic militant group Lashkar-e-Taiba. He started taking unauthorized trips to Pakistan in 2000 and 2001, and started showing all the signs of Islamic radicalization. Headley continued to travel back and forth between the US and Pakistan. During this time, several phone calls were made to the FBI about Headley's possible ties with terrorism, but Headley was never interviewed. He was later sent by the LeT to collect information about potential targets in Mumbai.

The arrest of Headley

Headley was arrested in Chicago in 2009, and charged with planning terrorist attacks in India and in Denmark, where he was involved in a plot to attack a Danish newspaper that had published satirical political cartoons of the Prophet Muhammad. A year later, Headley pleaded guilty in a deal that let him avoid the death penalty, but obligated him to testify against a friend, Tahawwur Rana, who was also charged with helping to plot the attacks in Mumbai. Headley described the training, funding, coordinated decision-making, and detailed planning of the attacks.

In a federal courtroom in Chicago, he was sentenced to thirty-five years in prison for his role in the 2008 Mumbai attacks that killed 164 people, including six US citizens. Headley gave specific evidence about the close alliance between the ISI, Pakistan's intelligence force, and the LeT terrorist group. He described meeting with both ISI and LeT officials before the Mumbai operation. He also described meeting a Pakistani military official at LeT headquarters: the officer gave LeT advice on how to carry out a maritime attack. Because of this evidence, the US attorney's office in Chicago indicted Major Iqbal, a Pakistani intelligence official – the first time that a serving Pakistani intelligence officer had been charged in relation to the murder of Americans.

NOTES

1. Matthieu Aikins, "The Big Business of Kidnapping in Afghanistan", *AFPAK*, 20 October 2010.
2. Soraya Shaddi, "Afghan Kidnappings Increasingly Common", *NPR*, 11 March 2011.
3. "Abduction Fears take Heavy Toll on Afghanistan Society", *Thaindian News*, 12 March 2009.
4. Martin Patience, "Afghanistan's Kidnapping Industry", *BBC News*, 16 September 2011.
5. "Kidnap Report: Q4 2010 Hotspots", *AKE Group*, 3 November 2011.
6. *Ibid*.
7. "Afghanistan Hit by Kidnappings on Eve of Votes", *Reuters*, 17 September 2010.
8. Aikins, "The Big Business of Kidnapping", *AFPAK*, 20 October 2010.
9. *Ibid*.
10. The Taliban released nineteen of the South Koreans after holding them for six weeks. It killed two in July and set free two others in mid-August, when it began direct talks with the South Korean government.
11. "Taliban Vow More Abductions in Afghanistan", *International News Safety*, 3 September 2007.
12. "Korean Missionaries under Fire", *Time Magazine*, 27 July 2007, http://www.time.com/time/world/article/0,8599,1647646,00.html.
13. "South Korean Hostage Apologizes for Being Captured", *CBC News*, 31 August 2007.
14. Amir Shah, "Taliban to Free 19 S. Korean Hostages", *AP*, 29 April 2007.
15. "Taliban say Korean Hostage Talks Fail", *China Daily*, 18 August 2007 (via *Reuters*).
16. Taimoor Shah, "Taliban Release 2 Korean Hostages", *The New York Times*, 13 August 2008.
17. "Taliban 'Agree to Free' Hostages", *BBC News*, 28 August 2008.
18. Stephen Gaskell, "US Soldier Was Sold to Local Insurgent Group, Terrorists Say they Will Release Video Soon", *NY Daily News*, 2 July 2009.
19. *Ibid*.
20. "Taliban Release Video of Captured US Soldier", *The Guardian*, 25 December 2009.
21. "Taliban Issue Video of Captive US Soldier", *Reuters*, 25 December 2009.
22. "Taliban Release Video", *Guardian*, 25 December 2009.
23. "Taliban Issue Video", *Reuters*, 25 December 2009.
24. "Taliban Release Video", *Guardian*, 25 December 2009.
25. "Taliban Releases New Video of Captured Soldier", *Komo News*, 7 April 2010.

26 "Taliban Video May Show Soldier Held in Afghanistan", *The China Post*, 9 December 2010.
27 "Taliban Video Shows US Soldier Held in Afghanistan", *Tehran Times*, 9 December 2010.
28 Kathy Gannon, "Captive Soldier Safe, says Haqqani Commander", *AP*, 8 September 2012.
29 Nate Rawlings, "The Return of Bowe Bergdahl? Taliban Suggest Prisoners Swap of Last Remaining US POW", *Time*, 21 June 2013.
30 "Two Missing Soldiers in Afghanistan Took Wrong Turn, NATO Says", *The Washington Post*, 27 July 2010.
31 Rahim Faiez, "Taliban: One Missing US Sailor Dead, Other Captured", *AP*, 27 July 2010.
32 "Taliban: One Missing US Sailor Dead, Other Captured", *The Jerusalem Post*, 3 August 2010.
33 "Afghan Manhunt for Missing US Servicemen", *BBC News*, 25 July 2010.
34 Richard Oppel and Abdul Waheed Wafa, "Body of Second Missing US Sailor Found", *The New York Times*, 29 July 2010.
35 *Ibid*.
36 "Two Missing Soldiers in Afghanistan Took Wrong Turn", *Washington Post*, 27 July 2010.
37 "Kidnap Report: Q4 2010 Hotspots", *AKE Group*, 3 November 2011.
38 "Bin Laden Vows to Kill Hostages if France Stays, France to Stay in Afghanistan Despite Bin Laden's Threat", *al Arabiya*, 21 January 2011.
39 "Taliban Militants Threaten to Kill Kidnapped Journalists", *CNN*, 12 April 2010.
40 "Bin Laden Vows to Kill Hostages if France Stays", *al Arabiya*, 21 January 2011.
41 Angelique Chrisafis, "French Journalists Freed in Afghanistan", *The Guardian*, 29 June 2011.
42 Suleman Shah Durani, "Taliban Hit Afghan Posts, Frees 23 Prisoners", *Surghar Daily*, 18 July 2010.
43 *Ibid*.
44 Muhammad Yusuf, "Taliban Blew the Door of a Prison and Freed 23 Prisoners who were Members of the Group", *Allvoices*, 18 July 2010.
45 "Taliban Staged Daring Prison Escape in Afghan City", *Yahoo News*, 18 July 2010.
46 "Twelve Inmates Escape from Western Afghan Prison", *China Daily News*, 25 November 2009.
47 James Sturcke, "Afghan Forces Hunt Fugitives after Taliban Jailbreak", *The Guardian*, 14 June 2008.
48 Bill Sandler and Stephen Khan, "Kandahar Locked Down after Taliban's Dramatic Prison Raid", *The Independent*, 15 June 2008.
49 Ron Sinovitz, "Afghanistan's Government Refused the Exchange of Taliban Prisoners", *Turkish Weekly*, 11 October 2007.
50 "Taliban Kidnap Pakistani Ambassador to Afghanistan, Demand Release

of Mansoor Dadullah", *The Long War Journal*, 12 February 2008.
51 "Pakistani Group Frees US Hostage", *BBC News*, 4 April 2009.
52 Mark Tran, "Confession Triggers Appeal in Daniel Pearl Case", *The Guardian*, 19 March 2007.
53 Simon Bradley, "Abducted Swiss May be in Pakistan Tribal Belt", *Swiss Info*, 4 July 2011.
54 "Swiss Confirms 2 Nationals Kidnapped in SW Pakistan", *Arab Times*, 2 July 2011.
55 "Taliban Offers Exchange for Swiss Hostages", *Swiss Info*, 29 July 2011.
56 *Ibid.*
57 "Taliban Admits Kidnapping Swiss Couple", *Swiss Info*, 5 July 2011.
58 Rob Crilly, "Kidnapped Swiss Tourists 'Escape' Clutches of Pakistani Taliban", *The Telegraph*, 15 March 2012.
59 Declan Walsh, "The Mystery of Dr Aafia Siddiqui", *The Guardian*, 24 November 2009.
60 *Ibid.*
61 *Ibid.*
62 Thomas Joscelyn, "'Lady al Qaeda' in Propaganda", *The Long War Journal*, 16 December 2010.
63 *Ibid.*
64 "US Embassy Cables", *The Guardian*, July 2008, http://www.guardian.co.uk/world/us-embassy-cables-documents/164310.
65 "Senior al Qaeda Commander in Afghanistan Killed in US Airstrike", *The Long War Journal*, 31 July 2008, http://www.longwarjournal.org/archives/2008/07/senior_al_qaeda_comm.php.
66 "The Taliban to Execute US Soldier if Sister Aafia Siddiqui is Not Released", *Pure Islam*, 5 February 2010.
67 "MQM Slams US for Dr Aafia Siddiqui's Sentence", *The Express Tribune*, 29 September 2010.
68 Richard James, "Kidnapped British Aid Worker Killed in Afghanistan in Failed Rescue Mission by US Special Forces", *The Daily Mail*, 9 October 2010.
69 Joscelyn, "'Lady al Qaeda'", *The Long War Journal*, 16 December 2010.
70 "US Embassy Cables", *The Guardian*, July 2008, http://www.guardian.co.uk/world/us-embassy-cables-documents/175741.
71 "US Embassy Cables", *The Guardian*, July 2008, http://www.guardian.co.uk/world/us-embassy-cables-documents/178104.
72 "US Embassy Cables", *The Guardian*, July 2008, http://www.guardian.co.uk/world/us-embassy-cables-documents/248613.
73 "US Embassy Cables", *The Guardian*, July 2008, http://www.guardian.co.uk/world/us-embassy-cables-documents/249587.
74 Harriet Alexander, "American Aid Worker Warren Weinstein Kidnapped in Pakistan", *The Telegraph*, 13 August 2011.
75 Rameez Khan, "Pre-dawn Abduction: American 'Aid Expert' Kidnapped in Lahore", *The Express Tribune*, 14 August 2011.

76 Alexander, "American Aid Worker Kidnapped", *Telegraph*, 13 August 2011.
77 "Gunmen Kidnap US Aid Worker in Pakistan", *Reuters*, 13 August 2011.
78 Khan, "Pre-dawn Abduction", *Express Tribune*, 14 August 2011.
79 Asad Kharal, "No Headway: Investigators Fear the Worst for Abducted American", *The Express Tribune*, 16 August 2011.
80 *Ibid.*
81 *Ibid.*
82 "US Hostage Warren Weinstein Makes Plea to Obama in Al Qaeda Video", *Christian Science Monitor*, 7 May 2012, http://www.csmonitor.com/World/terrorism-security/2012/0507/US-hostage-Warren-Weinstein-makes-plea-to-Obama-in-Al-Qaeda-video-video.
83 "SNS RT US Pakistan Hostage", *The Chicago Tribune*, 12 September 2012, http://www.chicagotribune.com/news/sns-rt-us-pakistan-hostage-netanyahubre88b155-20120912,0,106794.story.
84 *Ibid.*
85 "Gunmen Kidnap US Aid Worker in Pakistan", *Reuters*, 13 August 2011.
86 Bradley, "Abducted Swiss May Be in Pakistan", *Swiss Info*, 4 July 2011.
87 *Ibid.*
88 *Ibid.*
89 *Ibid.*
90 Ajit Doval, "Islamic Terrorism in South Asia and India's Strategic Response", in *Oxford Papers: Policing*, Volume 1, Issue 1 (Oxford: Oxford University Press, 2007), pp. 63–69.
91 "Kashmir Insurgency", *BBC News*. Retrieved 1 November 2010.
92 Mahmud Ali, "Pakistan's Shadowy Secret Service", *BBC News*, 9 October 2006.
93 "India Revises Kashmir Death Toll to 47,000", *Reuters*, 21 November 2008.
94 "Indian Officials Say 3,400 Missing in Held Kashmir", *AFP*, 18 August 2009.
95 Doval, "Islamic Terrorism in South Asia", *Oxford Papers*, 2007.
96 *Ibid.*
97 *Ibid.*
98 "Years Down, JKLF Admits Rubaiya Kidnap", *The Times of India*, 2 August 2004.
99 "Kashmir Muslims Kidnap Indian Aide's Daughter", *The New York Times*, 12 October 1989.
100 Praveen Swami, "A Man of Many Parts – and Parties", *Frontline Magazine*, Volume 19, Issue 23 (The Hindu), 11 October 2002.
101 Aviation Safety Network Database, *Flight Safety Foundation*.
102 "Cover Story: Hijacking: In Amritsar, a Speeding Tanker Causes Panic", *India Today*, 10 January 2000.
103 Pasricha, Anjana, "Commandos Launch Operations to Clear Luxury

Hotels Seized by Gunmen in Mumbai", *Voice of America*, 27 November 2008, http://voanews.com/english/archive/2008-11/2008-11-27-voa9.cfm. Archived from the original on 17 July 2011.

104 Angel Rabasa, Robert D. Blackwill, Peter Chalk, Kim Cragin, C. Christine Fair, Brian A. Jackson, Brian Michael Jenkins, Seth G. Jones, Nathaniel Shestak, and Ashley J. Tellis, *The Lessons of Mumbai* (Santa Monica, CA: The RAND Corporation, 2009).

105 Husain Haqqani, "The Ideologies of South Asian Jihadi Groups", in *Current Trends in Islamist Ideology* (Indianapolis, IN: Hudson Institute, 2005), pp. 12–26.

106 Stephen Tankel, "Lashkar-e-Taiba: Past Operations and Future Prospects", in *National Security Studies Program Policy Paper* (Washington, DC: New America Foundation, April 2011), pp. 1–4.

6

Terror Abductions and Decapitations in Iraq

In the framework of the ongoing conflict between coalition forces and terror/guerilla organizations in the Republic of Iraq, the phenomenon of the abduction of local and foreign hostages has become prominent, and kidnapping for ransom or for political ends has become a key component of Iraq's resistance movement. While terrorist kidnappers have long been able to attract publicity, create crises, and occasionally obtain political concessions, insurgents in Iraq have transformed kidnapping into a strategic weapon. Iraq presents ideal conditions for kidnappings: the country is mired in conflict, government authority is weak, and the police are largely ineffectual. Besides these factors, the country is filled with guns, explosives, and large numbers of unemployed veterans skilled in violence.

It would appear that the abduction of hostages, negotiations for their release, and an occasional execution if the captors' demands are not met do not constitute a new phenomenon – the current innovation lies in the continuous media coverage that broadcasts the "drama" to the homes of millions of viewers, right up to the horrendous climax, thus intensifying the psychological effect that the terrorists strive to achieve. Some of these abductions end with the decapitation of hostages in front of a video camera – the footage is subsequently distributed to the worldwide media.

Between three hundred and four hundred foreign nationals have been abducted in Iraq since its invasion by the US-led coalition. Although over fifty-seven foreign national hostages were executed, the majority were eventually released by their captors.[1] Due to the unstable security situation, many of the foreign nationals working or serving in Iraq live in the "Green Zone": a complex of residential buildings and offices secured by the US military on the bank of the Euphrates River in Baghdad. Shiite and Sunni Islamic terror groups, as well as criminal gangs, have turned abductions in Iraq into a "thriving industry" – an estimated seven thousand Iraqis were kidnapped in the years 2003–10. Taking advantage of the breakdown in national authority after the overthrow of Saddam Hussein, criminal gangs began kidnapping Iraqis, at first mainly targeting Christians, who had no protection within Iraq's tribal structure. Dr Mustafa Alani, on the staff of a Dubai research center, claims that some ten Iraqi citizens are abducted daily for criminal reasons. Most of the victims are middle-class professionals whose families are forced to pay a ransom for their release. Dr Alani also points out that children from middle-class homes constitute relatively easy prey for abductors.[2]

Most victims are held for only a few days and, while some are freed in police operations, many are released after their families have paid a ransom. Current settlement figures stand at around US$50,000 per person. Most victims are Iraqi citizens, but foreign nationals have also become a "popular item" in the Iraqi "abduction industry". There are strong links between local criminal elements and terror organizations in the Iraqi arena: when criminal elements succeed in abducting foreign nationals, they often "sell" them to Islamic terror organizations.

While local criminal gangs deal in the abduction of local and foreign residents in order to extort as much ransom money as possible, the Islamic terror organizations in the Iraqi arena make political stipulations in addition to demanding ransom payments. For example:

- The removal of military forces, humanitarian, or economic organizations of the country whose citizens are being held captive.
- The release of terrorist prisoners.
- Political statements condemning the invasion and the coalition's presence in Iraq.
- The rebuilding of houses destroyed by coalition operations.
- A combination of several of the above demands.

Kidnappers have portrayed the abductions and executions as just retribution for the mistreatment of Muslim prisoners and humiliations suffered by the Arab world, visibly demonstrating affirmative action at a time when no government or group appeared to do more than denounce such insults. In many cases, hostages are tortured by their captors or even executed during a horrifying and well-documented decapitation ceremony.

Local terror organizations, as well as entities affiliated with the global jihad and al Qaeda, are active in Iraq. More than twenty resistance groups have carried out kidnappings in the country – some are linked with one another or use different *noms de guerre* for individual operations, while others are little more than criminal gangs who kidnap on spec, then sell their hostages to the highest bidder.

The Islamist group Tanzim Qa'idat al Jihad fi Bilad al Rafidayn ("al Qaeda of Jihad in the Land of the Two Rivers"), led by Abu Musab al Zarqawi, is the most active and lethal insurgent group inside Iraq, and the most prominent terror organization *vis-à-vis* the abduction and decapitation of foreign nationals. Zarqawi's men previously operated under the "brand name" al Tawhid wal Jihad ("Group of Monotheism and Jihad"), until their leader was promoted to al Qaeda commander in Iraq.

Other organizations that have claimed responsibility for the abductions of foreign nationals are:

- The Jamaat Ansar al Sunna ("Assembly of the Helpers of Sunna") organization.
- The Jaish al Mahdi ("Mahdi Army"), a Shiite militia under the command of Muqtada al Sadr.
- The Islamic Army and the Khalid ibn al Walid Brigades.
- The National Movement for the Land of the Two Rivers.
- The Islamic Army of Iraq.
- The Abu Bakr al Siddiq Brigade.
- The Green Brigades.
- The Black Flags.

As a rule, it is accurate to state that a Muslim hostage has a better chance than a foreign national of surviving an abduction and being released, but this statement must be qualified: citizens of Muslim states that are identified with the coalition are often no less vulnerable to harm than the nationals of western countries. Turkish, Egyptian, and Jordanians were among the nationals of Muslim states murdered by their abductors in Iraq.

Sometimes, the targets of abduction/decapitation attacks are specific individual foreigners, but occasionally groups of victims are kidnapped. On 31 August 2004, a group of twelve workers from Nepal was abducted – the largest abduction of a group of foreign nationals by a terror organization in Iraq. A video later distributed by the kidnappers showed the decapitation of one of the hostages and the bodies of the remaining eleven captives, each executed by a gunshot to the head.[3]

The largest abduction/decapitation attack took place in Iraq's western al Anbar province, on 9 March 2005; the bodies of twenty-six people (one of them a woman) were found in al Qa'im, a town some five hundred kilometers west of Baghdad, close to the Syrian border. A hospital to which the bodies were taken announced that the victims had been shot two days earlier. Another fifteen bodies, some riddled with bullets, others decapitated, were found in the "death triangle" south of Baghdad, in an area under Sunni control. This massacre of forty-one people carried the "signature of the rebels": decapitation or a gunshot in the neck – a modus operandi characteristic of the groups headed by al Zarqawi.[4]

Fallujah as a Hostage Center

The Iraqi city of Fallujah served as a central hub for al Zarqawi's activity. Following the takeover of the city by coalition forces, a search of the environs and surrounding area revealed an infrastructure that serviced the holding of hostages in captivity.[5] US officers stated that almost twenty sites were discovered where atrocities had been committed against hostages, including several buildings adapted as prisons. At one house, reporters were shown a black banner bearing a yellow sun and the words "Tawahid and the Jihad" (a group headed by al Zarqawi). This banner became infamous when it appeared in the background of many videos of hostage decapitations in Iraq. In another house, the press was shown a wire cage for holding hostages. Both houses were opened to the media after objects belonging to the terrorists were removed – photos of these items were later presented in a detailed catalog and included handcuffs, propaganda material, and bloody javelins and knives.

According to coalition sources, Fallujah was one of the main bases where hostages were held by rebel forces. One Iraqi informer, who helped the US forces to find the houses, claimed that he himself had been held captive and that during his incarceration he heard the voices of at least three other hostages held in nearby rooms. He believed that one of them was the British engineer, Kenneth Bigley, who was later decapitated.

The two buildings displayed to the media provided the most detailed picture to date of the lives of the abducted hostages. Officers noted that hostages had been imprisoned in two rooms in one of these houses; leg-cuffs and handcuffs used to shackle the captives were discovered in both locations, while in one of the rooms there were manacles attached to metal rods, which apparently served as neck shackles. A small room was discovered in the basement where the hostages were apparently interrogated and tortured, and black masks and black tennis shoes, of a type generally worn by the rebels, were found at the site. The cage found in the second house, made out of metal and barbed wire, could barely accommodate a human being: it was 2.1 meters high, two meters wide, and about one meter deep, leaving the captive very little space for movement.

The Coalitions' Approach to the Hostage Issue in Iraq

The citizens of twenty-five different countries became victims of abductions in Iraq; some of those states were part of the US-led coalition, a number of others maintained military forces in Iraq, while certain states merely contributed to Iraq's rehabilitation. Those countries did not advocate a uniform policy when their citizens were abducted in Iraq – and their differing responses can be depicted on a scale: at one end of the spectrum were the US and Britain that refused to negotiate with the abductors; in the middle were countries that negotiated with the terrorists, generally through an intermediary; while at the other extreme were the countries that capitulated almost immediately to the terrorists' demands. The different states' responses to abductions were significantly influenced by the nature of the demands – when the terrorists demanded a ransom payment that could be paid secretly without any damage to a country's image, the response was more expedient than when demands stipulated that a state's military forces must be withdrawn or the country's nationals removed from Iraq.

Examples of abductions and the responses of various countries are detailed below:

- On 16 September 2004, two American citizens were abducted by al Zarqawi's men: Eugene Armstrong and Jack Hensley, along with a British national named Kenneth Bigley. The US and Britain adhered to their policy of not negotiating with the terrorists, as was expressed by the spokesman of the US Administration in Iraq, Dan Snor: "The United States will not negotiate with terrorists holding the hostages. The FBI and CIA, as well as the coalition forces and Iraqi security agencies, are acting to locate the captors and their captives in Iraq." The two Americans and the British hostage were executed in a gruesome decapitation "ceremony" documented on video.
- On 20 July 2004, a Filipino truck driver named Angelo de Cruz was abducted by a terror organization in Iraq, which demanded that the Philippine military force (comprising of fifty-one soldiers) withdraw from Iraq. As these troops were due to complete their tour of duty in August 2004, the Philippine government agreed to the abductors' demands and brought

forward the departure of their soldiers to 16 July 2004. The captive was released.

- On 20 August 2004, two French journalists were abducted on their way to the city of Najaf in Iraq. France was not a member of the coalition and opposed the war in Iraq. Following negotiations conducted by France through various intermediaries, the two journalists were released on 22 December 2004. The French government denied that it had paid a ransom for their release.

- On the night of 2 July 2005, Ihab al Sharif, who was serving as Egypt's acting ambassador to Iraq,[6] was abducted near his home in Baghdad. Previously, from September 2000, al Sharif had served as the Egyptian ambassador to Israel. He was abducted shortly after an announcement that Egypt was planning to upgrade his status to official ambassador. If al Sharif had been appointed to the post, he would have been the first Arab ambassador to Iraq since the toppling of Saddam's regime. Al Sharif was abducted when he went out to buy a newspaper. According to eyewitnesses, as he started back towards his home, armed men grabbed him and pushed him into a vehicle. The abduction was part of the opposition's struggle against the Iraqi government to prevent the granting of international, and particularly Arab, legitimacy for Ibrahim al Jaafari's government. The rebels had already declared that they would take determined action against the presence of Arab diplomats in Iraq, claiming that such activity by Arab governments bestowed legitimacy upon an Iraqi government that was sponsored by the US and obeyed American orders. Several days after the emissary's abduction, al Zarqawi's organization claimed responsibility for al Sharif's abduction and execution.

Another "complex" affair attesting to the considerable sensitivity prevailing among the coalition countries *vis-à-vis* the issue of abductions and the liberation of hostages in Iraq is reflected in the abduction and release of Italian journalist Giuliana Sgrena, who was kidnapped in Baghdad on 4 February 2005.[7] In a video distributed by the abductors, they demanded the withdrawal of Italian forces from Iraq (some three thousand Italian soldiers were serving in Iraq at that time) and threatened to execute the journalist if their demands were not met. The Italian daily newspaper *La Repubblica* reported several weeks after the abduction that coalition forces in Iraq believed they had located the place where Sgrena was being held, and proposed to Rome that an attempt be made to liberate her in a military operation by elite units with a "75 percent chance that no harm would come to the hostage".

The Italian authorities felt that the risks were too great, and the operation was shelved.

At this point, so the newspaper claimed, negotiations for a ransom payment were entering the final stage. On 4 March 2005, an Italian intelligence agent, Nicola Calipari, agreed to meet the terrorists, unaccompanied and without a GPS tracker, in a rented car at a predetermined site. He also promised to refrain from contact with the Americans. Once the ransom money had been handed over, the hostage was released and Calipari rushed Sgrena to the Baghdad airport in an attempt to evade the authorities and prevent the ex-hostage's interrogation by both the US and the Iraqis.

While the agent was driving the released captive to the airport, he attempted to circumvent a coalition roadblock that opened fire, killing Calipari and wounding Sgrena. In an editorial, the newspaper claimed that the Italian government had not informed the Iraqi authorities of Calipari's arrival in Baghdad to release the journalist. This conclusion was based on a statement made on 8 March 2005 by Italian Foreign Minister Gianfranco Fini: "We announced Calipari's presence in order to facilitate the activity, but did not divulge the reason for his presence." According to the newspaper, Fini did not deny that a ransom was paid for the journalist's release. In a reply to a question on this matter, he stated: "We adopted diplomatic and political directions as well as the aid of the secret services."

The American military headquarters in Baghdad announced that it had invited high-ranking Italian entities to join an official investigation of the incident. *La Repubblica* called for a public debate in Italy to discuss whether ransoms should be paid to terrorists or if such a policy would expose its citizens to further abductions, and whether the Italian state should undertake the financial burden of paying ransoms, which the editorial claimed could total US$15 million.

The Abduction of US Soldiers in Iraq

In March 2008, the remains of Staff-Sergeant Keith "Matt" Maupin were identified after a long period of uncertainty as to the outcome of his kidnapping in Iraq during an attack on a convoy near Baghdad in 2004. About a week after the attack, terrorists released a video of him as a captive. Around two months later, terrorists released a second videotape that claimed to show his murder. At the time, US officials were not convinced of the authenticity of the video and continued to list Maupin as "missing in action" until the March 2008 announcement.[8]

Plots to Kidnap US Soldiers in Iraq

The internet site Wikileaks published documents relating to a plot to kidnap American soldiers in Baghdad. According to the 22 December 2006 report, a militia commander named Hasan Salim devised a plan to capture US soldiers from their Humvees (High Mobility Multipurpose Wheeled Vehicles) and hold them hostage in the Sadr City area of Baghdad in order to deter American raids on that neighborhood.[9] To carry out the plan, Salim turned to Azhar al Dulaimi, a Sunni who had converted to the Shiite branch of the faith while studying in the holy Shiite city of Najaf in 1995, who was chosen for the operation because he "allegedly trained in Iran on how to conduct precision, military-style kidnappings". Those kidnappings were never carried out but, the following month, militants conducted a raid to kidnap US soldiers from the Iraqi security headquarters in Karbala, known as the Provincial Joint Coordination Center (PJCC).

The documents made public by WikiLeaks didn't include an intelligence assessment as to who carried out the Karbala operation, but US military officials said after the attack that al Dulaimi was the tactical commander of the operation and that his fingerprints were found on the getaway car, and claimed that he had collaborated with Qais and Laith al Khazali, two Shiite militant leaders who were captured after the raid along with a Hizballah operative. The Khazali brothers were later released as part of an effort at political reconciliation and are believed to have fled to Iran.

The documents, however, do provide a vivid account of the Karbala attack as it unfolded:

At 7:10 p.m., several sport utility vehicles (SUVs), of the type typically used by the American-led coalition forces, blocked the entrance to the headquarters' compound. Twenty minutes later, an "unknown number of personnel, wearing American uniforms and carrying American weapons, attacked the PJCC", the report said. The attackers managed to kidnap four US soldiers, dragging them into an SUV that was then pursued by police officers from an Iraqi SWAT unit. Calculating that they were trapped, the militants shot the handcuffed hostages and fled. Three of the abducted US soldiers died at the scene. The fourth later died of his wounds, the report said, while a fifth soldier was killed in the initial attack on the compound.

Summing up the episode, the US commander of a police training team noted that that the adversary appeared to be particularly well trained. "PTT leader on ground stated insurgents were professionals and appeared to have a well-planned operation," he stated in the report.

Abduction and Massacre in a Baghdad Catholic Church (October 2010)

On 31 October 2010, during the Sunday evening Mass, armed attackers stormed the Church of Our Lady of Salvation in the Karrada neighborhood of central Baghdad.

The events began with an initial attack on the stock exchange building. After a battle with security forces in which the assailants killed two guards, the nine armed men, with suicide bombs attached to their belts, fled to the nearby church, took about one hundred people hostage, and demanded the release of al Qaeda prisoners from Iraqi and Egyptian jails, including the widow of Hamid Dawud Mohamed Khalil al Zawi (also known as Abu Omar al Qurashi al Baghdadi), the purported head of Dawlat al Iraq al Islamiyyah ("Islamic State of Iraq") who was killed in April 2010.[10]

The rescue operation

A US army spokesman said that about one hundred people had been in the church when the attackers came in, but some nineteen of them managed to escape. "They [Iraqi Special Forces] went into the church and rescued the hostages," he said, also stating that US forces provided air support, but did not provide ground troops.[11] The Iraqi security forces killed eight of the terrorists during the operation to free the hostages, while the ninth died when he activated a suicide bomb.[12] Major-General Qassim al Moussawi, a Baghdad security spokesman, told news agencies that the operation had "finished successfully".[13] Iraqi Defense Minister Abdul Qader al Obeidi said: "Right from the very beginning [the terrorists'] phone calls were fully intercepted, and we strongly believe there were non-Iraqi people among the group. We will investigate their nationalities."[14]

At least fifty-five people were killed in the attack and seventy were injured.[15] All three priests leading the service died: Father Wasim Sabieh and Father Thaier Saad Abdal were killed during the attack, while the third priest, Father Raphael Qatin, was wounded and died later in hospital.[16]

An al Qaeda-affiliated group takes responsibility

The *al Baghdadia* television station said that during the attack it had received a phone call from someone claiming to be one of the attackers, who demanded the release of all al Qaeda prisoners in Iraq and Egypt. The "Islamic State of Iraq", a group linked to al Qaeda, later claimed responsibility for the attack in a statement posted online after the incident.[17]

Condemnation

Pope Benedict XVI condemned the attack in his speech to pilgrims gathered to hear his prayer in Saint Peter's Square on 1 November 2010 for the Catholic All Saints' Day holiday: "I pray for the victims of this senseless violence, made even more ferocious because it struck defenseless people who were gathered in the house of God, which is a house of love and reconciliation."[18]

Italy's foreign ministry expressed "strong condemnation" of the terrorist assault and also took note of "the 'timeliness' of the Iraqi security forces for the liberation of the hostages".[19] Iraqi Prime Minister Nouri al Maliki also condemned the siege, saying it was an attempt to drive more Christians out of the country. "The cowardly, terrorist crime at Our Lady of Salvation Church in Baghdad last night shook us and all honorable Iraqis around the world," he said. "Those with deviant thoughts from al Qaeda and their allies belonging to the followers of the ousted regime targeted our Christian brothers in a terrorist crime that aims at undermining security and stability, inciting strife and chaos, and sending Iraqis away from their home."[20]

New threats to the Iraqi and Egyptian Coptic churches

Just days after the attack on the Catholic church in Baghdad, the "Islamic State of Iraq" declared in an internet statement that all Christians and their churches had become "legitimate targets" of the terrorist group and therefore were in danger, labeling all Christians as "idolaters" and dubbing the pope a "hallucinating tyrant". The group called for the release of two Egyptian women: Camilia Cheh and Wafa Constantine, the wives of Coptic priests, who were detained against their will in a convent after converting to Islam, according to the terrorists. The statement concluded: "the killing sword will not be lifted from the necks of Christians" until its demands were met.[21]

The statement from al Qaeda also made explicit reference to the Vatican. While confirming its desire to attack Christians, the group said they wanted to give "one more chance to the Catholics of the Church of Rome", claiming that "The war office of the Islamic State of Iraq announced that, starting today, all the churches and Christian organizations and their leaders are a legitimate target for mujahideen," but added: "These politicians and their bosses in the Vatican should know that the sword will not fall on the heads of their followers if they proclaim their innocence, and distance themselves from what has been done by the Egyptian Church." Al Qaeda called on Catholics to "send a clear signal to the mujahideen of their effort to put pressure on the Egyptian Church in order to obtain the release of two women, their prisoners".[22]

Summary

Iraq's Interior Minister Jawad al Bulani said that by the end of November, Iraqi police had arrested seventeen members of the al Qaeda-affiliated "Islamic State of Iraq" terror organization that were involved in the attack on the church. The suspects were arrested in raids in the upscale west Baghdad neighborhood of Mansour, and on Palestine Street in the capital's east, and were said to include Huthaifa al Batawi, the Baghdad chief of the "Islamic State of Iraq", and Abu Ammar al Najadi, a senior leader of the group.[23]

Christianity in Iraq dates back to near the beginning of the religion. In the first century CE, the Christian Church of the East came into being in Assyria, Babylonia, and Persia – an area which today consists of Iraq, southeast Turkey, and western Iran. The Christian faith was spread east of the Roman–Byzantine empire by Saint Thomas, one of the twelve apostles of Jesus. Most Iraqi Christians are Chaldeans, eastern-rite Catholics whose hierarchy operates somewhat autonomously from the Vatican, but still recognizes the authority of the pope. In many of the Chaldean churches in Iraq, services are recited in ancient Aramaic, the language of Jesus. Assyrians, the descendants of the ancient empires of Assyria and Babylonia, adopted Christianity in the first century CE (the Assyrian kingdom was centered on the upper Tigris River). Other ancient churches in Iraq include Syrian Catholics, Armenian Orthodox, and Armenian Catholic Christians, along with Greek Orthodox, Greek Catholic, and Anglican churches.

The four-hour ordeal on 31 October 2010 at Our Lady of Salvation was only the bloodiest of numerous terrorist attacks targeting Iraq's Christian communities in the past years: five other Christian places of worship had been targeted by terrorists in coordinated attacks on 1 August 2004. The Human Rights Watch (HRW) organization said the number of Christians in Iraq had fallen to about 675,000 in 2008, down from approximately one million at the time of the US-led invasion in 2003.[24] Most Christians abandoned their homes and fled to Syria, Jordan, or Egypt, while many of those who remained in the country moved to safer areas, such as the Kurdish-held north.[25] While they made up less than 5 percent of Iraq's population when the war began (about one million), Christians now constitute an estimated 10 percent of internally-displaced Iraqis and 20 percent of Iraqi refugees in neighboring nations, according to a 2009 report.[26] Their displacement not only threatens to end Christianity's two-thousand-year history in Iraq, but also deprives the country of a huge swath of middle-class professionals at a critical time. Since no Christian was able to hold a government job under Saddam Hussein's regime, university graduates became lawyers, doctors, and engineers. Crucial to Iraq's recovery, they are now scattered, afraid to return.[27]

Abductions, Decapitations, and the Media

Terror organizations in Iraq make extensive use of the media, television, and internet to intensify the impact of the abduction, and occasional decapitation, of their victims. Most abductions perpetrated by Islamic terror organizations are accompanied by video footage that is dispatched to the media and distributed worldwide.

Three "scenario" stages are discernible in the majority of abductions:

- The distribution of a video of the hostage in the hands of the captors, who present their demands for the hostage's release.
- If the captors' demands are not met, an additional video is distributed of the hostage pleading for his life and appealing to his country to act on his behalf.
- If the captors' demands are still not met, the abduction may draw to a tragic close with the hostage's execution at the hands of his captors, at times by decapitation.

Most state media refrain from airing horrific images of executions or else choose to broadcast censored sections of the incident, but the internet enables uncontrolled distribution of these images. Jihadi websites serve as the main channel for the distribution of such content, but western websites also make use of these tapes. According to an article published in the Baghdad newspaper *Asharq al Awsat*, research indicates that the internet is one of the most influential factors in the recruitment of young men for the jihad movement.[28]

In an article in the Israeli daily *Ha'aretz*, Shahar Samoha describes the problematic handling by western websites of the issue of abductions: "South Korean citizen Kim Sum-il was abducted in Iraq. The kidnappers delivered an ultimatum to the South Korean government to withdraw its forces from Iraq, or else Kim Sum-il would be executed. The ultimatum appeared on several western websites. The South

Korean government refused to respond to the kidnappers' demands, and Kim Sum-il was executed. His decapitation was documented on a home video."[29]

The horrific video clip was uploaded onto several websites identified with the al Qaeda terror network. Shortly afterwards, two versions of the video also appeared on various western websites, one of which was the "Ogrish" site that presented both versions: the first of Kim's heartrending pleas, and the second featuring the brutal murder. Thus, courtesy of Ogrish and other internet sites, al Qaeda's psychological assault was accomplished and the clip's real target audience – western citizens who could not access it on the Arabic websites – joined the terror "theater". Obviously, Ogrish was not the only western website to provide its visitors with uncensored information regarding the atrocities perpetrated by terrorists in Iraq and elsewhere; it is clear that the internet provides terror organizations like al Zarqawi's with a free, safe, and significant platform, thus intensifying the psychological impact of the struggle that Islamic terror organizations are fighting against the coalition states.

The Tradition of Decapitation in Islam

Decapitation is not a new phenomenon in Islam – it has been a part of Islamic culture since the spread of that religion across the Arabian peninsula, throughout its "Golden Age" marked by the conquest of Spain (711–1492 CE), and continues today.

Amputation – including decapitation as a death sentence – is part of the Islamic penal arsenal, and the punishment of limb amputation is still applied in some Muslim states. Over the twenty-year period before 2003, around 1,100 people were executed by decapitation in Saudi Arabia, according to Amnesty International. In 2003 alone, fifty-two people were beheaded (based on the verdicts of Saudi courts).[30] The Koran specifically refers to decapitation, and al Qaeda and its supporters exploit that fact to justify the decapitation of Jews, "infidels", and other people who have "betrayed" Islam. The Koran describes an incident in which a tribe of Jews who had signed a pact with the Prophet Muhammad reneged on the agreement and joined Muhammad's enemies: when the Jewish tribe had been routed, Muhammad instructed his followers to decapitate all of the six hundred male members of the tribe and to sell the women and children into slavery. More recently, radical Islamic entities decapitated their captives during conflicts in Afghanistan, the Balkans, Chechnya, Algeria, and elsewhere. In Bosnia, for example, a video documenting the decapitation of Serb captives was distributed in the thousands among the Balkan Muslim population and to Islamic radicals worldwide.[31]

The purpose of terrorism is to strike fear into the hearts of opponents in order to win political concessions. As the shock value wears off and the western world becomes immunized to any particular horror, terrorists develop new tactics to maximize the media reactions upon which they thrive.[32]

The first foreign victim of abduction and decapitation was the journalist Daniel Pearl, who was abducted in Pakistan by a radical Islamic organization and later decapitated by his captors. In Iraq, terrorists filmed the beheadings of Americans Nicholas Berg, Jack Hensley, and Eugene Armstrong, while other victims included Turks, an Egyptian, a Korean, Bulgarians, a British businessman, and a Nepalese national. Scores of Iraqis, both Kurds and Arabs, also fell victim to the Islamist terrorists' knives. The new fad in terrorist brutality extended to Saudi Arabia, where Islamist terrorists murdered American businessman Paul Johnson, whose head was later discovered in a freezer in an al Qaeda hideout.[33]

Islamic civilization is not a historical anomaly in its sanction of decapitation – the Roman empire beheaded citizens (such as the Christian Saint Paul), while they crucified non-citizens (such as Jesus Christ), and French revolutionaries later employed the guillotine to decapitate opponents. Nevertheless, *Islam is the only major world religion today that is cited by both state and non-state actors as legitimizing beheadings.*[34]

Abduction and Decapitation in Iraq from the Religious Aspect

On 18 November 2004, a two-day conference of the Trustee Council of the International Federation of the Muslim *ulema* (religious scholars), established in London in July 2004, was held in Beirut.[35] At the end of the conference, a manifest was published bearing the signatures of the federation's director, Sheikh Doctor Yusuf al Qaradawi, and its secretary-general, Sheikh Doctor Muhammad Salim al Awa. The declaration, which appeared on a website related to al Qaradawi, stated that the resistance in Iraq against the coalition forces was the personal obligation of anyone able to undertake it, whether or not they were Iraqi residents.

The declaration opened with a theological introduction regarding the behavior of Muslims during war, which stated:

"The International Federation of the Muslim *ulema* [believes] that in light of the situation prevailing in the world in general, and among Muslims in particular, it must bind the [believers] of the monotheistic religion [Islam] to several moral and religious principles regarding how Muslims should behave, and to clarify to people the rules of behavior among Muslims and between Muslims and those who are not Muslim . . . It is forbidden to attack those who are not fighting, even if they are part of the aggressive countries. The human soul is holy, and an attack against it can be likened to an assault against all of humanity. [As it says in the Koran 5:32] 'He who kills one soul which is not weighed against another, or not due to the dissemination of corruption in the land, it is as if he killed all of the people.' The Prophet Muhammad banned the killing of women and children, stating 'do not kill a child', and added 'do not kill progeny and workers with ease', meaning all those hired to carry out services who are not connected to the fighting. Also, Islam forbids the murder of hostages and monks that dedicate themselves to God. It does not permit the taking into captivity of those who are not involved in the combat. If those who are not involved in combat are taken prisoner, Allah instructed Muhammad, his emissary, to treat them well [as stated in the Koran 76:8] 'Out of their love [for Allah] they feed the poor, orphans, and prisoners.' [So says Muhammad] 'treat prisoners compassionately.'

"It is forbidden to hold hostages and threaten the lives of those who are not in combat due to actions that others took or did not take. The hostages are not responsible for this action and could not prevent it. Allah said 'One soul will not carry the burden of another soul,' [Koran 6:164] and the Prophet [Muhammad] says 'a criminal will be punished only for his own deeds.'"

Following the theological introduction regarding the proper religious behavior of Muslims during wartime, the manifest moved on to discuss developments in the world in general, and the fighting in Iraq in particular. As noted earlier, the statement declared that the resistance in Iraq was a personal religious obligation and constituted a jihad of self-defense. The statement attempted to create the impression that it distinguished between fighters and civilians who must not be hurt; but, in actual fact, the statement diminished the definition of "civilian" when it explained who was included in this term: "women, children, and the elderly". This definition omits men, but from the declaration it is clear that only "those who do not take part in hostilities, especially men who deal in humanitarian or communications activity" are protected. Anyone who does not meet this category is to be considered an enemy, and therefore harming him is permissible. On 19 November 2004, a day after the publication of the declaration, al Qaradawi honed the differentiation between fighters and civilians, stating that foreign engineers, laborers, and technicians working in Iraq were not considered protected civilians and were therefore fair prey. In an interview with al Jazeera, al Qaradawi stated: "I have banned killing Americans. When asked a question in this matter, I said that it is forbidden to kill civilians. I explained that it is permissible to kill only those involved in the fighting. Islam forbids the killing of women and children, etc. I have stated this openly, but at the same time I posed the question: 'who is a civilian?' Are engineers, laborers, and technicians coming into Iraq with the American army considered civilians? Is a fighter only someone in a tank, or is it also someone who provides services to the army? I refer to the interpretation of the word 'civilian'. If it is clear that someone is a civilian, then it is forbidden to kill him. We, at the federation of the Muslim *ulema*, published a manifest yesterday stating that the resistance in Iraq must adhere to the laws of the Sharia: it is forbidden to kill a civilian, only a fighter."

The text of the manifest follows:

"The International Federation of the Muslim *ulema* cannot stand by and watch the oppression and aggression against the weak taking place all over the world, as well as the massacres that occur time and again, particularly in Muslim countries. [These things happen] in order to ignite the fire of the destructive wars for no reason other than to sate the avaricious appetite of the minority that profits from these wars, lethal arm dealers, and others whose interests link them to war and agitation. Thus, the International Federation of the *ulema* wishes to clarify the following:

- The resistance of the Iraqi people fighting a jihad against the foreign occupation, which is aimed at liberating Iraqi land and reinstating its national sovereignty, is a Sharia obligation which falls on anyone who belongs to the Muslim nation inside or outside of Iraq, and who has the ability to achieve this.
- Allah permitted this when He said: 'We will give them permission to fight because they were oppressed' [Koran 22:39], and so he said to the Muslims: 'Fight on behalf of Allah against those who fight you' [Koran 190:2]. This fighting is a jihad for the purpose of defense, which does not necessitate the instruction of general leadership [that would declare a jihad], but rather it is implemented according to the personal capability [of each Muslim individual]. In addition, it is recognized that the resistance to occupation is a legitimate right ratified by international conventions and the UN pact.
- The acts perpetrated by the foreign armies invading Iraq are unprecedented atrocities. The US's justification for the invasion of Iraq was

the claim that the latter was concealing non-conventional weapons and aiding terrorism. In actual fact, non-conventional weapons were not found in Iraq; this is a gross violation of the Geneva Convention and other pacts addressing the [handling of] civilians during wartime and [the handling of] the providers of medical treatment and POWs. The use of internationally-banned weapons; the destruction of homes, buildings, mosques, churches, other houses of worship, and [the destruction of] infrastructures; the death of the wounded in mosques and the prevention [of the delivery of] emergency aid and rescue from those hit by disaster; the bombardment of hospitals and preventing medical teams from carrying out their humanitarian duty towards the injured – all this is a mark of disgrace on the foreheads of the states that perpetrate [these deeds].

- The International Federation of the Muslim *ulema* calls on the governments of each and every one of these countries to change their ways, resume humanitarian behavior, and withdraw from Iraq immediately, after temporarily handing over control to a recognized international entity that will supervise free and untainted elections, which will enable the Iraqi people to run their country independently.
- No Muslim is allowed to support [the deeds of] the invaders against the Iraqi people and its noble resistance. This is because this type of support is a way of abetting [the invaders] in their crime and aggression against the oppressed Islamic people. If the situation and conditions necessitate some Iraqis to work in the army or the police, they must try to avoid causing damage to their civilians [the Iraqis]. The resistance will not inflict any harm on them as long as they do not [actively] fight their people and do not form an alliance with the enemy.
- The distinguished resistance fighters must adhere to the commandments of the Sharia during their jihad against the occupiers and refrain from injuring civilians who are not involved in the fighting: women, children, and the elderly, even if they are nationals of the invading forces, if they do not perpetrate hostile acts, especially if they are involved in humanitarian or communications activity, because Allah directed us to fight those who would fight us and forbade acting aggressively. If some of the enemy forces are taken captive, they must be treated kindly during their captivity and be brought to fair trial in order to release the innocent among them.
- It is forbidden to hold hostages and threaten to kill them in order to apply pressure during an interrogation for a certain purpose because, as it says in the Koran [6:164]: 'A soul shall not carry the burden of another soul,' and Muhammad said: 'A violator will be punished for

his deeds alone.' If a person is held in this way, then he is a prisoner of war and it is forbidden to kill him or harm him. Moreover, he will certainly be released, as Allah said: 'Whether to mercy and whether to ransom' [Koran 47:7].

- The distinguished resistance fighters must take note of the existence of many [groups of] fifth-columns interested in inflicting damage upon Islam, and Muslims that carry out acts that would appear to be resistance. However, these [acts] are actually a continuation of the aggression and a distortion of the noble resistance. It is possible that these fifth-column [groups] are connected to the Zionist and world intelligence agencies. The noble resistance must condemn the acts [of these groups] and expose their collaboration [with foreign intelligence entities] and their infiltration [to Iraq], particularly because many of the crimes [that these groups] perpetrate become apparent due to the exposure of the invaders' barbaric behavior. Thus, they perpetrate even more barbaric acts in order to cover up the occupiers' behavior and make the world forget their atrocities.

- Today there is a dangerous plot against Iraq whose aim is to rip its social texture . . . by encouraging hostility on a religious or national basis as well as emphasizing controversial issues. All Iraqis must feel that they are one people united by Islam as a religion and by 'Arabism' as a language and culture. [They must understand] that their religious and national obligation is to cease all controversy and stand together in order to banish the conquest and build a united Iraq for all its residents . . . ."

In contrast to the relatively moderate approach adopted by the International Federation of the Muslim *ulema*, and by al Qaradawi himself in this forum, on other opportunities he took a far more radical stand. Several examples are detailed below:

- At a conference addressing "pluralism in Islam" that took place in August 2004 at the Egyptian Journalists' Association in Cairo, he stated: "All Americans in Iraq are fighters, there is no difference between a civilian and a soldier, and they must be fought because American citizens come to Iraq in order to serve the invasion. The abduction and execution of Americans in Iraq is a [religious] obligation so that they will be forced to leave Iraq immediately. But [in contrast] the mutilation of the dead bodies is forbidden in Islam."
- In September 2004, al Qaradawi published a religious precept permitting the abduction and murder of American citizens in Iraq in order to pressure the American army to withdraw its forces.
- Additionally, the manager of al Qaradawi's office, Atsam Halima,

confirmed that the sheikh had published a religious declaration according to which it is obligatory to fight American citizens in Iraq because they are invaders.

Notes

1. According to *Brookings Iraq Index* (30 November 2010), 312 foreign citizens were kidnapped in Iraq in the years 2003–4. Other sources report higher figures of about 400 hostages.
2. *Gulf Research Center* (GRC), now based in Jeddah, Saudi Arabia.
3. *Brookings Iraq Index*, 30 November 2010.
4. *Ha'aretz*, 10 March 2005.
5. Robert Worth, *The New York Times*, 23 November 2004 (quoted in *Ha'aretz*).
6. *Ha'aretz*, 4 July 2005.
7. *Ha'aretz*, 19 March 2005.
8. "Missing Ohio Soldier's Remains Found in Iraq After 4 Years", *AP*, 31 March 2008.
9. Michael R. Gordon and Andrew W. Lehren, "Leaked Reports Detail Iran's Aid for Iraqi Militias", *The New York Times*, 22 October 2010.
10. "Al Qaeda Attack on Baghdad Church Ends in Massacre", *Asian News*, 1 November 2010.
11. "Al Qaeda Claims Iraq Church Attack", *al Jazeera*, 2 November 2010.
12. "Three Priests Killed in Attack on Baghdad Church", *ACN News*, 2 November 2010.
13. "Al Qaeda Claims Attack", *al Jazeera*, 2 November 2010.
14. *Ibid*.
15. "Al Qaeda Attack Ends in Massacre", *Asian News*, 1 November 2010.
16. "Three Priests Killed", *ACN News*, 2 November 2010.
17. "Al Qaeda Claims Attack", *al Jazeera*, 2 November 2010.
18. *Ibid*.
19. "Al Qaeda Attack Ends in Massacre", *Asian News*, 1 November 2010.
20. *Ibid*.
21. Greg Burke, "Al Qaeda Threat to Christians Serious?", *Fox News*, 3 November 2010.
22. "Al Qaeda Threat: Christians are Legitimate Targets", *Asian News*, 3 November 2010.
23. "Twelve Arrested over Deadly Baghdad Church Siege", *BBC News*, 7 November 2010.
24. "Fear of Jihad Driving Christians from Iraq", *USA Today*, 12 November 2010.
25. Jonathan Adams, "Deadly Baghdad Church Siege Highlights Threat to Iraqi Christians", *The Christian Science Monitor*, 1 November 2010.
26. *Ibid*.
27. *Ibid*.

28 *Asharq al Awsat*, 19 July 2005.
29 Shahar Samuha, "Death News", *Ha'aretz*, 29 June 2004.
30 Amit Cohen, *Ma'ariv*, 2 July 2004.
31 "Islamic Fundamentalists' Global Network Modus Operandi", *Bosnia Documentation Center of the Republic of SRPSKA*, Banja Luka, September 2002, pp. 59–60.
32 Timothy R. Furnish, "Beheading in the Name of Islam", *Middle East Quarterly*, Spring 2005, pp 51–57.
33 "US Hostage's Head Found in Freezer", *CNN*, 21 July 2004, http://edition.cnn.com/2004/WORLD/meast/07/21/saudi.johnson/index.html.
34 Furnish, "Beheading in the Name of Islam", *Middle East Quarterly*, 2005.
35 Based on an article in MEMRI, "The International Federation of the Muslim Alma led by Sheikh al Karochi: The Resistance in Iraq is an Obligation that Applies to Every Muslim", *al Quds al Arabi*, London, 23 August 2004.

7

Terror Abductions in Saudi Arabia

During the last three decades, there have been several terrorist attacks within the Kingdom of Saudi Arabia, the most serious being the siege of the Grand Mosque of Mecca in 1979. In 2003–6, Saudi Arabia suffered a wave of terror attacks in the form of kidnappings, bombings of residential compounds and government offices, and an attack on the US consulate in Jeddah. Suicide bombers killed thirty-five people at a housing compound for westerners in Riyadh in May 2003. The last attack directed at foreign nationals in the kingdom was in 2007.[1]

The Saudi government takes the threat of terrorism seriously and has carried out a number of arrests of suspected Islamist militants in recent years. There are ongoing concerns regarding terrorism in the Saudi peninsula, particularly against western targets and the local oil infrastructure. The most credible terrorist threats in Saudi Arabia stem from al Qaeda in the Arabian Peninsula (AQAP) and Saudi jihadists returning from Iraq.

Western intelligence estimates that there are several hundred Saudi nationals amongst the insurgents in Iraq – other estimates claim there are thousands. According to one analysis, Saudi citizens represented 61 percent of the 154 foreign Arabs killed in Iraq. "They are coming back with security experience, ranging from skills in how to lose people who are trailing them, as well as having the qualities of guerilla fighters. They also know how to do surveillance," said one official.[2]

The Siege of the Grand Mosque in Mecca (1979)
Juhayman ibn Muhammad ibn Sayf al Otaibi

Juhayman was born in 1936 in a small Bedouin village called al Sajr, in the Najd region of the al Qassim province. At the age of nineteen, he joined the Saudi Arabian National Guard and attended talks given by Wahhabi clerics, most notably Sheikh Abdel Aziz ibn Baaz. He stayed with the National Guard until 1955, and then left to study at the University of Medina.

In the 1950s, the Muslim Brotherhood (MB) was outlawed by President Gamal Abdel Nasser in Egypt after a failed assassination attempt on his life. Many members of the MB were persecuted and imprisoned, while others fled to Saudi Arabia, where King Faisal was happy to accept opponents of Nasser's regime. One of the most notable Egyptians to move to Saudi Arabia was Muhammad Qutb, brother of Sayyid Qutb who was employed as a lecturer at Jeddah University. Juhayman met him and other members of the MB during his studies at Medina.

In 1974, Juhayman left the university along with a number of his followers and returned to his hometown of Najd, where he organized a group that he called the *ikhwan* (brotherhood), started preaching his take on Salafist doctrines, and distributed pamphlets denouncing the Saudi regime.[3] Many of his followers were Bedouin who had moved to the big cities from their villages, but eventually returned after becoming upset with the pace of modernization that was taking place on the back of the oil boom. Juhayman preached of his desire to do away with the Saudi regime and to establish a real Islamic state.[4] He believed that the Saudis were violating the Islamic holy places of Mecca and Medina merely by having control of them.[5]

In the late 1970s, Juhayman moved to Riyadh where he organized demonstrations against the monarchy in 1978. This drew the attention of the security services, who arrested him and one hundred of his followers. He was later released after ibn Baaz told the authorities that he was an angry young man, but harmless. After Juhayman's release from prison, he started planning his assault on the Grand Mosque in Mecca.

Juhayman and the Mahdi

The year 1980 (or 1400, according to the Islamic calendar) was seen by Juhayman as having a supernatural significance. Juhayman and his friends saw a number of divine signs and believed that the new century would deliver the prophesied redeemer of Islam: the Mahdi.[6] Juhayman found recruits among those younger than he, including his brother-in-law, Muhammad bin Abdallah al Qahtani. Juhayman, and perhaps a few others, tried to convince al Qahtani that he was the Mahdi. Abdallah was skeptical for a while but, with an adequate application of religiosity, he was eventually won over.[7]

The takeover of the Grand Mosque (November 1979)

Juhayman had co-conspirators who had studied at the Grand Mosque academy and "knew every nook and cranny of the compound".[8] On the eve of the new century, the conspirators parked three pickup trucks in the compound's basement – filled with an abundance of weapons, ammunition, and food – and early on the new century's first day (20 November 1979), the conspirators, "hundreds" in number, were at the Grand Mosque among the more than 100,000 pilgrims from around the world.[9] Juhayman's men closed the gates to the mosque, fired their weapons into the air, and announced their takeover. The pilgrims were now prisoners. One by one, with weapons in hand, the conspirators knelt down, kissed the supposed Mahdi's hand, and offered an oath. Some pilgrims also joined in.

The siege

Before the day was over, Saudi police officers arrived and were shot and killed. The conspirators restricted themselves to shooting at uniformed agents of the government. They were skilled marksmen, with weapons that had good range, and they occupied the top levels of the mosque's minarets.[10] The Saudi government was stunned, slow to understand what was happening, and tried to seal off news of the event to the outside world. Learning later that news of the Grand Mosque takeover had been leaked, the Saudis were outraged.[11]

At the Grand Mosque, Saudi troops attacked with armored personnel carriers (APCs), ·50-caliber machine guns, and heavy weaponry. Snipers were blasted out of their nests high in the minarets. Once the firing began, groups of commandos stormed the Peace Gate, only to be mowed down by rebel fire.[12] Following this major defeat, the Saudi monarchy was determined to continue these small-scale counterattacks. On the next morning, Sixth Battalion rangers managed to inconspicuously approach the Marwa Gate and affix explosives to the perimeter, blowing the gate off its hinges and allowing access to the Marwa-Safa gallery. There, however, they were brutally ambushed.[13]

On Friday 23 November, a *fatwa* issued to permit attacks on the rebels in the mosque stated: "The *ulema* unanimously agreed that fighting inside the mosque had become permissible . . . If they fight you, then you must kill them, because this is the punishment of nonbelievers."[14] Even after receiving the approval of the clerical establishment, the Saudis had much more severe fighting ahead of them before they could rest at ease, despite several of their own public statements. However, the proclamation significantly eased the difficulty of their task as it allowed them the freedom to retake the mosque in whichever way they could. By the time the Saudis were able to begin their full offensive, the rebels had strategically established themselves throughout the mosque, especially along the perimeters, in order to withstand any ensuing government retaliation. Furthermore, snipers atop the minarets could warn their compatriots of upcoming attacks as well as provide protective fire.

The Saudi military was well-equipped with American and European military technology. On November 23rd, the Saudi military brought in a fleet of APCs and artillery support. Their primary goal was to eliminate the snipers using TOW antitank missiles, allowing the Saudis to begin their ground offensive using the APCs to shield them from fire (although this tactic was not totally successful as some rebels managed to toss Molotov cocktails into the cockpits of the vehicles). By mid-Saturday, the armored offensive finally cleared out the Marwa-Safa gallery, opening the path to the main courtyard. The APCs drove into the main courtyard and quickly fired into the surrounding ramparts. The mosque's ground level was cleared of rebels.

The fighting continued in the vast basement area, which Saudi troops again penetrated with armored vehicles. The floor was slippery with blood and human entrails. Pilgrims remained trapped inside, with Saudi troops firing at anything that moved. Mohammed al Qahtani, the supposed Mahdi, was at the forefront of the fighting, apparently believing that he was immortal and impervious to bullets. He picked up concussion grenades tossed his way and threw them back. All that the person throwing the grenades had to do was to count off a couple of seconds after pulling the grenade pin, and then throw the grenade – the grenade would go off before al Qahtani could throw it back. This is indeed what happened, leaving al Qahtani bleeding and out of action on the floor. Under barrages of fire, Juhayman's men were unable to rescue their Mahdi, who writhed in agony amid the toxic haze. Juhayman was asked by his men whether the Mahdi's death meant that their venture was a mistake. In response, Juhayman asked how anyone could question God's command, and what proof did anyone have that the Mahdi was dead? The battle for justice on Earth, he shouted, must go on, and said that he would stay and fight, even if he were the only one who remained. Swayed by his ardor, his men remained.

The Saudi authorities decided that their troops were too slow in defeating the rebels and that the rule of the Saud family was indeed threatened. Reluctant to seek help from the US, Saudi Minister of Defense Prince Sultan finally called on the Pakistani army to handle the situation. Pakistan's President General Zia-ul-Haq, who had become unpopular in Pakistan for having Zulfikar Ali Bhutto (the former president) executed, jumped at the chance, hoping that helping the Saudis would improve his credentials amongst the masses in Pakistan. General Zia directed the Pakistan army to recapture the mosque, which they achieved with the help of three members of the French special forces *Groupe d'Intervention de la Gendarmerie Nationale*.

The fighting in the basement of the Grand Mosque lasted until 4 December. The rebels tried to escape through tunnels around the mosque, but these were filled with water to flush the rebels out. The last of the rebels, including Juhayman, were taken prisoner on 5 December 1979.

For years, Saudi Arabia had been speaking of the threat to it posed by Communism – in addition to the republicanism that had been espoused by Egypt's President Nasser. Now, after assessing the threat to Saudi Arabia from the extremists who had attacked the Grand Mosque, it was recognized that, had Juhayman and his group attacked a vital target rather than a religious symbol, they might have succeeded in their goal of overthrowing the monarchy. Weeks after the battle, Saudi King Khalid is reported to have told foreign visitors that "had Juhayman attacked my palace, he might have met with more success". This was before the age of internet and live satellite news that may have attracted more radical support for Juhayman's uprising.

On 9 January 1980, Juhayman and sixty-three of his followers were beheaded. Among the condemned, forty-one were Saudi Arabia, ten from Egypt, seven from Yemen (six from what was then South Yemen), three from Kuwait, one from Iraq, and one from the Sudan. Saudi authorities reported that 117 militants died as a result of the siege – eighty-seven during the fighting and twenty-seven later from their injuries in hospitals. Saudi security forces suffered 127 deaths and 451 wounded.[15]

The cleric ibn Baaz and other radical clergy, described by some as Wahhabi, had switched sides and now favored Saudi authority. In 1992, ibn Baaz would be appointed Grand Mufti of Saudi Arabia, head of the Council of Senior Scholars, and president of the Administration for Scientific Research and Legal Rulings.

The Shiite rebellion in east Saudi Arabia

A threat to the Saudi government also occurred in an uprising from 25 to 30 November 1980, in Saudi Arabia's eastern oil-producing region along the Persian Gulf. The rebels were youths belonging to the country's Shiite minority, moved by rumors about the events in Mecca. The Saudi government had censored all news of the uprising, but there were many casualties inflicted by the Saudi National Guard using APCs, machine guns, helicopter gunships, and artillery. The uprising ended with the dispersal of the rioting youths, while an older generation of Shiite leaders successfully sued for peace.

The American response

The Carter administration in Washington was affected by fears of its enemy, Iran, which at that time was holding hostages at the US embassy in Tehran under the control of Ayatollah Khomeini, and an assumption was made that the rebels at the Grand Mosque were Shia supporters spreading Khomeini's revolution. This assumption was passed on to the media as fact, with an article in *The New York Times* quoting an American official who described the militants in Mecca as "likely to be responding to Khomeini's call for an uprising by fundamentalist Muslims". President Carter decided that he had to act and ordered a battle group from Subic Bay in the Philippines, including the carrier *Kitty Hawk*, to the Persian Gulf to enhance Saudi Arabia's sense of security.

On 4 December 1979, at a National Security Council (NSC) meeting, Carter accepted the idea, put forward by National Security advisor Zbigniew Brzezinski, that demonstrating weakness could be disastrous and that it was necessary to demonstrate strength. This was the beginning of what would later be called the "Carter Doctrine", intended to demonstrate US strength and commitment to the defense of countries in the Persian Gulf region that were of "vital interest" to the United States. A few days later, US negotiators flew to Oman to discuss the establishment of a new military base.

The American embassy crisis in Pakistan (November 1979)

On 21 November 1979, a crowd chanting "death to American dogs" broke into the secure compound of the US embassy in Islamabad. The marine guards were not allowed to fire their weapons, while demonstrators firing weapons killed one marine and a US-Army warrant officer. A total of 137 embassy personnel huddled inside the embassy vault, nearly overcome by heat and suffocation as the embassy burned around them, while they waited for help from the Pakistani police – which did not arrive. The Carter administration had been misinformed that Pakistan's dictator General Zia had immediately dispatched troops to the embassy. Zia played to the crowd, reluctant to alienate his fellow Muslims. While the lives of the embassy personnel hung in the balance, he promised to make Pakistan "an impregnable fortress of Islam", proclaiming the situation at the Grand Mosque "extremely sad" and stating that "Muslims must pray to God Almighty to bestow His blessing and mercy on the Muslim world." No help to the besieged embassy personnel was forthcoming from the Pakistani authorities. Having since been authorized to defend themselves with firearms, those huddled inside the embassy vault fired back against those assaulting the vault hatch on the embassy's roof. When night fell, the attackers departed.

President Carter and Secretary of State Cyrus Vance praised Zia and his troops for their stellar behavior, leaving those who had suffered through the attack on the embassy livid with anger against the American president. Secretary Vance soon moved to evacuate his diplomatic corps from the Muslim world – except from Saudi Arabia – to forestall similar situations from developing. US embassies in the region became empty shells.

The Iranian response

Iran's foreign ministry was outraged at what it saw as an accusation from Washington. A message from Ayatollah Khomeini was broadcast on Iranian radio, accusing the US and Israel of being responsible for orchestrating the horrors in Mecca. In the days that followed, the Muslim world adopted Khomeini's description of the events at Mecca, without a clear and adamant denial from Saudi Arabia.

The response from the Muslim world

In Pakistan, Bangladesh, Turkey, Libya, Kuwait, and among Muslims in India, places identified as American were targeted – embassies, consulates, US information and culture centers, a Bank of America branch, an American Express office, and Pan Am airline offices. In Hyderabad, India, where there were no obvious American targets, violence was directed against Hindu merchants, who had not shuttered their stores as had the Muslim shop owners. The violence continued for days until security forces overwhelmed the rioters and made more than one thousand arrests.

The Soviet invasion of Afghanistan (December 1979)

Meanwhile, the Soviet Union's military, led by Defense Minister Dmitriy Ustinov, decided that if President Carter could deploy a task force to the Gulf area, tens of thousands of kilometers from US territory, the Soviet Union should also be free to defend its interests in neighboring Afghanistan. On 10 December 1979, the Soviet military began to assemble a force of some 75,000 to 80,000 troops along the Afghan–Soviet border. On December 24th, Soviet troops invaded Afghanistan. The "Carter Doctrine" would now be transformed into an American defense of the Persian Gulf area from Soviet domination.

President Carter responded in a speech, delivered in January 1980: "Let our position be absolutely clear – an attempt by any outside force to gain control of the Persian Gulf region will be regarded as an assault on the vital interests of the United States of America, and such an assault will be repelled by any means necessary, including military force."

The assassination of Anwar Sadat (October 1981)

Juhayman's influence remained. One of the pilgrims who had watched the takeover in Mecca had taken a leaflet explaining Juhayman's religious and political beliefs home with him to Egypt. Yaroslav Trofimov describes this pilgrim as sharing its contents and exciting tales of the events in Mecca with his brother Khalid Islambouli, a first-lieutenant in the Egyptian army, who then began an eighteen-month "path to martyrdom".[16] It was this brother who, on 6 October 1981, would fire several bullets into the "pharaoh" Anwar Sadat, Egypt's president, for the crimes of "betraying Islam and making peace with the Jews".

The assassination attempt on Pope John Paul II (May 1981)

Meanwhile, when the crisis at Mecca broke out, Pope John Paul II was visiting Turkey. A young Muslim radical, Mehmet Ali Ağca, managed to escape from a Turkish prison, later claiming that his reason for doing so was the siege at Mecca. Ağca described the pope's visit as part of an infidel plot, and the pope as masquerading as a man of faith. He warned that "the crusaders" would pay for their misdeeds – it was Ağca who would later shoot and wound the pope in Saint Peter's Square on 13 May 1981.

Juhayman's movement and al Qaeda in Iraq and Jordan

One of those who had a "personal bond" with Juhayman's movement was a Palestinian preacher, Isam Mohammad Tahir al Barqawi, alias Abu Mohammed al Maqdisi. He wrote that Juhayman had been wrong about the Mahdi, but that this was "nothing compared to the enormous crimes of the Saudi government" and argued that by sending soldiers against Juhayman, the Saudi state was the first to violate Koranic prohibitions against waging warfare in "the holy precinct".

One of those influenced by al Barqawi was the person who planted the bomb that destroyed the Saudi National Guard headquarters in Riyadh in November 1995, killing seven people, including five Americans. At the time, al Barqawi was behind bars in Jordan. His cellmate, "a co-conspirator and favored pupil", was Abu Musab al Zarqawi, the future leader of al Qaeda in Iraq.

The Abduction and Murder of Paul Marshall Johnson (June 2004)

Paul Marshall Johnson, Jr. was an American helicopter engineer who lived in Saudi Arabia and worked for Lockheed Martin upgrading Saudi AH-64A "Apache" attack helicopters.[17] In June 2004, he was taken hostage by terrorists, and his subsequent murder was recorded on video.

Johnson was stopped at a fake police checkpoint near Riyadh on 12 June 2004, and then abducted.[18] Al Qaeda in the Arabian Peninsula (AQAP), headed by Abdul Aziz al Muqrin, posted a video of a blindfolded Johnson on an Islamist website on 15 June 2004, and threatened to kill him unless all al Qaeda prisoners were released from Saudi jails within seventy-two hours.[19] The video was released on the same day that Saudi Crown Prince Abdullah promised to increase security and begin investigations against militant Islamic groups in Saudi Arabia.

Immediately after the video was released, American and Saudi Arabian authorities began to deal with the hostage situation. Both asserted that they would not comply with the kidnappers' demands. Those demands included, but were not limited to, releasing all terrorists being held in Saudi custody. Johnson's abduction came during increased violence against foreigners in Saudi Arabia – the previous week, BBC journalists Frank Gardner and Simon Cumbers had been shot and two other Americans had been attacked in Riyadh.

On 18 June 2005, *al Arabiya* and CNN reported that Johnson had been beheaded. The reports were based on three photographs of the murder posted on the internet – one picture showed a severed head sitting on the back of a headless body.[20] The same day, al Muqrin claimed responsibility for Johnson's murder. "As we promised, we, the mujahideen from the Fallujah Squadron, slaughtered the American hostage Paul Johnson after the deadline we gave to the Saudi tyrants," said a statement on a website that was translated from the Arabic. "So he got his fair share from this life and for him to taste a bit of what the Muslims have been suffering from Apache helicopter attacks. They were tortured by its missiles," the statement claimed, adding that the killing was "a lesson for them to learn for whoever comes to our country, this will be their punishment". Muslim friends of Johnson – including some clerics – had pleaded for his release, but the militants were not swayed. The statement addressed those pleas: "A lot of voices were very loud, expressing their anger for taking a Christian military person as a hostage and killing him, while they kept their mouth shut from saying anything supporting those poor Muslims who are in prisons and being tortured by the hands of the cross-believers," in an apparent reference to the abuse of Iraqis held at Abu Ghraib prison.[21]

The response of Saudi Arabia

The Saudi government withheld official proclamation of Johnson's death until the body was found.[22] Al Muqrin was later killed in a firefight with Saudi government forces, finally closing the chapter of Paul Johnson.[23] Shortly before the news broke, Adel al Jubeir, the foreign affairs advisor to Saudi Crown Prince Abdullah, told reporters in Washington that Saudi security forces discovered terrorist suspects fleeing in cars, gave chase, and then battled them in central Riyadh. "A number of terrorists have been killed," he said. "We believe they are part of the al Qaeda network in the kingdom."

Al Arabiya first reported al Muqrin's death. Video from the scene showed police moving people away from a crowded residential area of the capital. Al Muqrin and three other terrorists were killed while disposing of Johnson's body. The three other terrorists turned out to include the second most-wanted man in Saudi Arabia, Rakan Alsaykhan, who had close ties with the al Qaeda mastermind of the October 2000 bombing of the USS *Cole*, and brothers Bandar and Faisal Aldakheel, who were also on the Saudi most-wanted list. Five Saudi security personnel were killed in the shootout.[24]

The al Khobar Massacre (May 2004)

On 29 May 2004, seventeen al Qaeda militants, reportedly dressed in military-style uniforms, attacked two oil industry installations in Saudi Arabia: the Arab Petroleum Investments Corporation (APICorp) building and the Petroleum Center, both in the city of Khobar, four hundred kilometers northeast of Riyadh. Khobar was one of the main centers of the Saudi oil industry, in which foreign workers played a key role, and the incident was part of a series of attacks on the kingdom's oil industry. The gunmen fled into the luxury six-storey Oasis housing compound and took hostages. After a twenty-five-hour siege, forty-one hostages were freed, twenty-five had been injured, and twenty-two killed, among them nineteen foreigners from nine countries. Fourteen attackers were captured or killed, and three escaped.

A group calling itself the "al Quds Brigade" – a local Saudi Arabia-based faction of al Qaeda – claimed responsibility and said it was attacking "Zionists and Crusaders who are in Saudi Arabia to steal our oil and resources".[25]

The al Khobar petroleum center

At 6:45 a.m., a group of four terrorists, separate from the group that attacked the Oasis compound, arrived in a vehicle and shot at guards and employees around the front gate of the al Khobar Petroleum Center. Police arrived and killed the two gunmen, while a third was killed running from the building. The fourth escaped over a wall into the al Hada compound, made his way to the Holiday Inn hotel, and fired at it, causing no casualties, before hijacking a car and escaping.

The Arab Petroleum Investments Corporation building

At 7:15 a.m., terrorists in a vehicle attacked the APICorp compound, using a rocket-propelled grenade (RPG) on the gatehouse, which killed two security guards. A school bus that was exiting at the time was shot at, killing a ten-year-old Egyptian boy, the son of an APICorp employee. The terrorists then tried to escape in their vehicle, but a Saudi civilian rammed their car off the road. The terrorists shot the Saudi man dead before he could get out of his car, but police arrived and killed the terrorists before they could make their escape.

The Oasis-3 compound

At 7:30 a.m., six terrorists scaled the wall of the Oasis-3 residential compound, while another five drove up to the main vehicle checkpoint. A civilian car was in the queue in front of the attackers and a school bus was behind. The checkpoint had two gates: a vehicle drove through one gate, was inspected after the first gate had closed, and then the second gate was opened to let the vehicle through. On the morning of the attack, the second gate was left continuously open, so that when the first gate opened, the terrorists drove straight through, while a terrorist opened the sunroof of their vehicle and killed the two armed guards with a machine gun. Turning back, he fired on the school bus, killing two children and wounding four. A five-year-old and a seven-year-old child were critically wounded.

The terrorists then drove into the main compound area, while a security guard took the surviving children from the school bus and conducted them to a safe area of the compound. The terrorists exited their vehicle and moved on foot into the residential complex, kicking in doors and slitting the throats of any non-Muslims they could find. Most of the killings took place inside the compound's Italian restaurant, Casa Mia, where afterwards the terrorists sat and ate breakfast. They then returned to the first floor with the intention of killing Hindus: eight Indians were killed before fifty-four people were taken hostage on the sixth floor of the Soha Towers hotel in the far east of the compound.[26] Booby traps were placed at the exits.

The rescue operation

By 9:30 p.m., Saudi emergency forces had surrounded the complex and extracted the children from the school bus, who were hiding in an underground parking garage, along with a few British nursery workers who were rescued from the Oasis compound and returned to the Las Dunas compound, where their families and friends were waiting. At 2:00 a.m. the next morning, Saudi forces attempted to enter the booby-trapped hotel. Several commandos were injured in two explosions before the group was forced to pull back after threats by the remaining terrorists to kill the hostages. At 2:30 a.m., two American military officers were injured and subsequently admitted to hospital.

Saudi military forces, in four National Guard KC-113 helicopters, arrived at 6:30 a.m., and were lowered onto the roof of the Soha Hotel to storm the building, while forces on the ground fired into the building as a diversion. Following the operation, Saudi authorities announced that all the hostages had been freed, and that two terrorists had been killed and another captured. Apparently, most of the attackers had fled before the Saudi raid.

Saudi Arabian Security Forces Free Two German Girls Kidnapped in Yemen (May 2010)

Saudi Arabia's security forces freed two German Christian girls kidnapped in June 2009 in neighboring Yemen, but the fate of their abducted parents, their infant brother, and a British engineer remains unknown.[27]

Anna Hentschel, aged three, and her sister, Lydia, aged five, were rescued in an operation on 17 May 2010 that targeted the hideout of their abductors in Yemen. The raid, in which Saudi military helicopters took part, happened in the Shadaa district of the northwestern province of Saada. Saudi officials said the search would continue for the other hostages. The girls were transferred to the care of Saudi authorities before returning to Germany on 19 May 2010.

The girls were part of a group of nine Christians working at the Protestant-run al Jumhuri hospital near Sana'a, who were kidnapped in Saada province in mid-June 2009. Several other members of the kidnapped group had already died: on 12 June 2009, the bodies of three of those abducted – German bible students Rita Stumpp, aged twenty-six, Anita Gruenwald, aged twenty-four, and South Korean teacher Eom Young-sun, aged thirty-three – were found murdered. Some Yemeni officials attributed the kidnapping and murders to forces linked to al Qaeda, assisted by Shiite rebels.

Al Qaeda in Yemen Urge Kidnappings of Saudi Royals and Christians (June 2010)

In June 2010, senior al Qaeda in Yemen commander Saeed al Shehri released an audio message urging his followers in Saudi Arabia to kidnap Christians and members of the Saudi royal family. In the message, distributed by Dubai news channel *al Arabiya*, al Shehri urged "major operations" against the Saudi kingdom after the arrest of female al Qaeda operative Hayla al Qassir.[28] "Form cells to kidnap Christians and princes from the Saud family and their top officials of ministers and officers. We tell our soldiers: 'You have to kidnap in order to release the prisoners,'" he said. "Stop knocking at the doors of the tyrants and their deviant *ulemas*. If you want your relatives to be released from prison, they will only be out by the same way they were taken in." Al Qassir had been accused of recruiting women for the militant group and being responsible for the group's finances. She was also the widow of an al Qaeda operative who was killed six years previously.

The US embassy in Saudi Arabia issues a kidnapping warning to its citizens

In September 2011, the US embassy in Riyadh issued a warning to its citizens in the kingdom that an unidentified terrorist group may be planning to kidnap western nationals in the capital city. American citizens "should exercise prudence and enhanced security awareness at all times", the embassy said. "The US embassy in Riyadh advises US citizens in the kingdom of Saudi Arabia that we have received information that a terrorist group in Saudi Arabia may be planning to abduct westerners in Riyadh," the embassy stated in a message posted on its website.

The former leader of Saudi Arabia's intelligence agency, Prince Turki al Faisal, said the political turmoil across the Middle East had created a fertile ground for terrorist groups in the region, but said the kingdom remained "stable and secure".[29]

A Saudi Diplomat Kidnapped in Yemen (March 2012)

AQAP militants seized Abdullah al Khalidi, Saudi Arabia's deputy consul in the southern port of Aden, on 28 March 2012. In April 2012, a militant who claimed responsibility for al Khalidi's kidnapping threatened to kill him unless a ransom was paid and al Qaeda prisoners were freed from Saudi jails.

Al Khalidi subsequently appeared in two videos posted on the internet, on 25 May 2012, and again on 1 July 2012, begging King Abdullah to meet his captors' demand for the release of five women detainees. "Release those women, they release me the next day," he said in the second video. The women, who were held by Saudi security services, were relatives of al Qaeda fighters.[30]

In a new video, distributed in April 2013 by al Malahem, the extremist group's media arm, al Khalidi appealed to Saudi Arabia's King Abdullah to secure his release by meeting his kidnappers' demands, asking: "Will he release me and return me back to my family and children?"[31] "They are demanding the release of a few women and some clerics" detained by Saudi authorities over their links to al Qaeda, he said. In parts of the video, AQAP included what it said were satellite pictures of a US airbase in Saudi Arabia from which drones targeted al Qaeda militants in Yemen as well as pictures of the destruction caused by those raids. This was al Khalidi's fourth appeal.

On 11 August 2012, five al Qaeda-linked women detainees were freed by Saudi authorities. Asked if they were released to meet the demands of Khalidi's captors, interior ministry spokesman Mansour al Turki said: "The investigation bureau and public prosecution office decided to release two of the women detainees by court order as they were [pregnant] and close to their due dates." The other three were released on bail pending trial, he said. One more woman detainee was serving a jail sentence.[32] "We can not consider this release as heeding to demands of the captors because, on principle, states do not accept to be subject to blackmail," said a Saudi official who declined to be named. "There was a coincidence between the release of the women detainees on humanitarian grounds and the demands of the captors."

The government hoped the move will prompt Khalidi's captors to release him on humanitarian grounds, the official said.[33]

On 12 August 2012, al Qaeda-linked militants released the Saudi Arabian diplomat. A tribal source told news agencies that his release was secured after tribal mediation efforts.[34]

NOTES

1 Claire Ferris-Lay, "US Warns Expats of Kidnap Threat in Saudi", *Business Magazine*, 29 September 2011.
2 Joshua Teitelbaum, "Terrorist Challenges to Saudi Arabian Internal Security", *Middle East Review of International Affairs*, Volume 9, No. 3, September 2005.
3 "Juhayman's Letters", US Embassy Kuwait Cable 5422, *US Department of State*, 29 November 1979.
4 Abu Dharr, "*Thawra fi rihab Makka*" ("Revolution in the Mecca Precinct"), *Sawt al Talia*, 1980. Received from Thomas Hegghammer.
5 Ahmad Rifat Sayyid, "*Rasa'il Juhayman al 'utaybi, qa'id al muqtahimin li-l masjid al haram bi-l Makka*" ("Letters of Juhayman al Utaybi, Leader of the Invaders of the Holy Mosque in Mecca"), *Madbuli*, Cairo, 2004.
6 Yaroslav Trofimov, *The Siege of Mecca: The Uprising at Islam's Holiest Shrine* (New York: Anchor Books, 2007).
7 Muhammad Diab, "Juhayman Three Decades Later", *Asharq al Awsat*, 30 November 2009.
8 Trofimov, *The Siege of Mecca*, 2007.
9 Trofimov and several other scholars, such as Robert Lacey in *The Kingdom: Arabia and the House of Sa'ud* (New York: Avon Books, 1981) list the number to be five hundred, but in American embassy cables the number is listed as being three hundred. See "Conflicting Reports by American Pilots in Mecca and the Military Liaison in Jidda Office in Riyadh's Report on the Uprising", US Embassy Jeddah Cable 7993, *US Department of State*, 21 November 1979, http://www.randomhouse.com/doubleday/siegeofmecca/pdf/7993_21Nov1979.pdf.
10 Angus Deming, Ron Moreau, Nabile Megalli, and David Martin, "Mecca and the Gulf", *Newsweek*, 3 December 1979, quoting Egyptian pilgrims that were at the mosque; "Saudis Promise Harsh Treatment for Mosque Assailants", *AP*, 23 November 1979; "Conflicting Reports by American Pilots in Mecca", US Embassy Jeddah Cable 7993, *US Department of State*, 21 November 1979.
11 Edward Cody, "Saudis Raid Mosque to End Siege", *The Washington Post*, 25 November 1979, quoting an interview on Saudi television.
12 Accounts of the casualties themselves are taken from Trofimov, *op. cit.*, p. 129, and accounts of the attack on the Mecca are combined from a series of American embassy cables discussing the attacks late on Wednesday night. Specifically, the reconnaissance pilots again flew over the mosque

and noticed that, despite the noise, there was no damage to the mosque or much activity on the ground, showing that the attack had not been as successful or as large as the Saudis had proclaimed it to be.
13 This account is taken from Trofimov, *op. cit.*, p. 133, and is based on his interviews with surviving Saudi military personnel that were involved in the attack.
14 "*Fatwa hayi'at kibar al 'ulama fi ahdath al haram*" ("Opinions of the Committee of Senior *ulema* on the Events in the Haram"), via Thomas Hegghammer (n.d.).
15 Pierre Trisan, "Seizure of the Grand Mosque in Mecca", *About*, 1979.
16 Trofimov, *The Siege of Mecca*, 2007.
17 Neil MacFarquhar, "The Reach of War: Saudi Hostage; Kidnappers of American Threaten to Kill Him in 3 Days", *The New York Times*, 16 June 2004, http://www.nytimes.com/2004/06/16/world/reach-war-saudi-hostage-kidnappers-american-threaten-kill-him-3-days.html?partner=rssnyt&emc=rss.
18 "Al Qaeda Site: Police Helped in Johnson Abduction," *USA Today*, 21 June 2004, http://www.usatoday.com/news/world/2004-06-20-saudi-message_x.htm.
19 Jasper Mortimer, "Al Qa'ida Threatens to Kill US Hostage in Saudi", *The Independent*, 16 June 2004, http://www.independent.co.uk/news/world/middle-east/alqaida-threatens-to-kill-us-hostage-in-saudi-732410.html.
20 "Al Qaeda Militants Kill American Hostage", *CNN*, 19 June 2004.
21 *Ibid*.
22 "US Hostage's Head Found in Freezer", *CNN*, 21 July 2004, http://edition.cnn.com/2004/WORLD/meast/07/21/saudi.johnson/index.html.
23 Mahjahieen Agha, "Who Killed Paul Johnson?", *World Media Monitors*, 22 June 2004, http://world.mediamonitors.net/content/view/full/7632/.
24 "Al Qaeda Militants Kill American Hostage", *CNN*, 19 June 2004.
25 "Saudi Troops Raid Hostage Compound", *BBC News*, 30 May 2004.
26 Tim Blair, "Khobar: An Insider's Story", *Wikipedia*, 8 June 2004, http://en.wikipedia.org/wiki/2004_Khobar_massacre#cite_note-Blair-5#cite_note-Blair-5.
27 "Saudi Arabia Security Forces Free 2 German Girls Kidnapped in Yemen", *Voice of America*, 18 May 2010.
28 "Al Qaeda in Yemen Urge Kidnappings of Saudi Royals, Christians", *Digital Journal*, 3 June 2010.
29 Ferris-Lay, "US Warns Expats of Kidnap Threat", *Business*, 29 September 2011.
30 "Saudi Arabia Releases Five al Qaeda-linked Women Detainees", *al Arabiya*, 23 July 2012.
31 "Saudi Diplomat Kidnapped in Yemen in New Video Plea", *Lebanon Daily*

Star, 17 April 2013, http://www.dailystar.com.lb/News/Middle-East/2013/Apr-17/213975-saudi-diplomat-kidnapped-in-yemen-in-new-video-plea.ashx#ixzz2Qkbh7aj8.
32 "Al Qaeda Linked Female Detainees", *Reuters*, 23 July 2012.
33 *Ibid*.
34 "Kidnapped Saudi Diplomat Released in Yemen – Tribal Chief", *Reuters*, 12 August 2012.

8

Terror Abductions in Yemen

Yemen and Islamic Terror

The Republic of Yemen's demographic and social structure, its tribal divisions, perpetual civil wars, and the lack of effective central government control have turned the country into a convenient arena for the development of radical Islam.[1] The British colonial rule in South Yemen also left its mark *vis-à-vis* the population's approach to the west, which still constitutes a source of hostility and hatred today. Until South Yemen's union with North Yemen in May 1990, the Marxist South Yemen Republic served as a haven for a wide range of Palestinian and other terrorist organizations and allowed those groups to establish a terror infrastructure that enjoyed government sponsorship. This tradition of supporting subversive organizations continued after the confederation of Yemen's north and south, but Islamic-oriented organizations subsequently came to replace the Palestinian and radical left-wing movements in the country.

Yemen, which exists in the shadow of affluent and western-oriented Saudi Arabia, traditionally served as a refuge for entities opposing the Saudi Arabian monarchy and sought regional allies to balance the asymmetry between its own status and that of its rich and larger neighbor. Thus Yemen has always been a potential ally for Saudi Arabia's adversaries such as Iran, Iraq, and Egypt. Since the early 1990s, Yemen gradually became both a refuge and a transit area for radical Islamic entities due to the tolerant – indeed enthusiastic – support of the Yemenite authorities; Osama bin Laden (whose father came to Saudi Arabia from the Yemeni town of Hadramawt) was perhaps the most infamous example. In addition, one of bin Laden's wives was of Yemenite descent. Jane's Intelligence Review estimates that, during the years of the jihad against the Soviets in Afghanistan, about three thousand volunteers from Yemen participated in the conflict. The majority of these militants returned to Yemen at the end of the jihad and became the spearhead of radical Islam. Osama bin Laden opened accounts at Yemen's central bank and at one point he had deposited around US$200 million. Some of these funds were held in the account of Sheikh Abdul Majid al Zindani, a prominent Islamic leader in Yemen,[2] who assisted bin Laden to develop a widespread, clandestine financial infrastructure in Yemen, while bin Laden simultaneously developed strong links with radical Islamic leaders, some of whom were familiar to him from the jihad in Afghanistan. The first terror attack initiated in Yemen by bin Laden took place in 1992,[3] enabled by al Qaeda's newly-established local infrastructure under the sponsorship of al Zindani.[4]

In early 1988, during al Qaeda's preparations for the attacks against the American embassies in eastern Africa and as part of the global jihad that bin Laden had declared against the United States, the group established its operational headquarters in Sana'a, the capital city of Yemen, and bin Laden himself was seen in Yemen at that time. During 1998–99, Yemen again served as a base for the activities of al Qaeda and other terror organizations, including the Aden-Abyan Islamic Army that was established in that period. Subsequently, Yemen itself became an arena for terrorist attacks, some of which were thwarted, while others "succeeded", such as the abduction of western hostages and the attack against the USS *Cole*. In the past, and even today, Yemenite citizens have been active partners in bin Laden's terror network: at least seventeen of the al Qaeda prisoners transferred to Guantanamo Bay in Cuba were Yemenite citizens, several Yemenite nationals were involved in the attacks against the American embassies in Kenya and Tanzania, one of the hijackers in the 9/11 attacks was a Yemenite named Khalid al Mihdhar, and Yemenite al Qaeda members were involved in the attack on the USS *Cole*.[5]

During the past decade, the US administration, Britain, and Saudi Arabia have acted to convince the authorities in Sana'a to refrain from offering support to terror organizations and to cooperate with them in the struggle against al Qaeda. A real turning point in Yemen's approach to terror came in the aftermath of the 9/11 attacks and America's declaration of a global "war on terror". Due to Yemen's fear that it would become a target of the US and suffer a fate similar to that of the Taliban regime in Afghanistan, it decided to (at least formally) side with the coalition in fighting global terror.[6] In the framework of these steps, Yemen established a special counter-terror unit within its interior ministry and started to cooperate with international entities in the "war against terror". However, the Yemenite government's steps have been only marginally successful.

The Abduction of Foreign Residents in Yemen

One of the most prominent examples of the ongoing ineffectiveness of Yemen's central government is the phenomenon of the kidnapping of foreign residents by tribal entities, usually with the aim of furthering their interests in the struggle against the Sana'a authorities. Since 1991, there have been over one hundred incidents of the kidnapping of foreign citizens, generally with demands for ransom money to obtain their release. When the ransom is paid, the hostages are usually released unharmed. During the years 1996–2000, Yemenite kidnappers held 150 hostages, including 122 foreign residents.[7]

Examples of kidnappings of foreign residents in Yemen include:[8]

- *26 January 1996*: Seventeen elderly French tourists were kidnapped by tribal members in the Maareb province. The kidnappers demanded the release of one of their tribal members who had been arrested. The hostages were released on 29 January 1996.
- *20 October 1996*: A French diplomat was kidnapped in Sana'a and was released on 1 November 1996, after the Yemenite authorities capitulated to the kidnappers' demands.
- *4 March 1997*: Seven German tourists were kidnapped and the kidnappers demanded US$12 million for their release. The hostages were released on 12 March 1997.
- *27 March 1997*: Four German tourists were kidnapped and the kidnappers demanded US$3 million for their release. They were freed on 6 April 1997.
- *29 November 2001*: Just before Yemen's President Ali Abdullah Saleh arrived on a state visit to Germany, a German citizen named Carl Lehrner, who was employed at the Mercedes dealership in Sana'a, was kidnapped by armed men. The kidnappers transferred the victim to a hiding place in a mountainous area some 170 kilometers east of the capital, pursued by Yemenite security forces who conducted a manhunt.[9] On December 8th, the security forces surrounded the remote village and engaged in a gun battle with the villagers, who were believed to have been involved in the kidnapping. In the exchange of fire, three villagers were killed along with two policemen; many more were injured.[10]

The Arrest of the "British" Terror Network in Yemen (December 1998)

On 23 December 1998, three terrorists were arrested in a car loaded with explosives on their way to perpetrate a terror attack against the British consulate in Aden. As the result of their interrogation, another three terror-cell members were arrested and a safe house was located that contained mines, rocket launchers, computers, encrypted communication devices, and many cassettes belonging to the al Qaeda-affiliated Ansar al Sharia ("Supporters of Sharia Law") group. The members of this organization, which had been planning a series of attacks against British and American targets,[11] were subsequently apprehended in Yemen.

Five of those arrested were carrying (authentic) British passports, and the sixth was carrying original French documentation. Their questioning revealed that they were members of Ansar al Sharia, based in London and headed by Abu Hamza al Masri, a radical Islamic leader associated with bin Laden.[12] Among the cell's members were two relatives of al Masri: his stepson Mohssin Ghailam, who was arrested in Yemen, and his son Muhammad Mustafa Kamel, who succeeded in evading capture.

The network's members arrived in Yemen in mid-December and, according to the testimony of at least one of the arrested suspects, they met with Abu al Hassan (one of the leaders of the Aden-Abyan Islamic Army), who provided them with weaponry and instructions for perpetrating the attacks.[13] Their intention was to carry out a series of attacks on Christmas Eve against western targets in Aden, including the British consulate in Aden, an Anglican church, and a group of Americans dealing in the removal of mines from Yemen, who resided at the Movenpick hotel in Aden.

Al Masri denied any connection with terror activity in Yemen and denied that the detained suspects were members of his "Supporters of Sharia Law" organization, which he claimed dealt solely with religious studies and adhered to the laws of Britain.[14]

The Abduction of Foreign Tourists (December 1998)

On 28 December 1998, sixteen tourists from various countries were kidnapped (twelve British, two American, and two Australian citizens) while they were touring the Abyan region of Yemen in a convoy of five vehicles.[15] The convoy was attacked about sixty kilometers northeast of Aden by a group of armed men who kidnapped the tourists and held them hostage for a time before transferring them to the organization's base camp in a remote mountainous area. On the night of 29 December 1998, a spokesman for the Aden-Abyan Islamic Army stated that members of his organization had kidnapped the tourists and made several stipulations for their release:

- The release of the "British" network's members (sent by al Masri) and members of the Aden-Abyan Islamic Army.
- Cessation of US and British aggression against Iraq.
- Banishment of the British and US presence in the Arabian Peninsula.

The Yemeni authorities refused to accept the kidnappers' demands. Yemeni security forces tracked the abductors to their hiding place and surrounded the kidnappers and their hostages. In the course of the rescue attempt, several hostages were killed and others were wounded. At least three of the kidnappers were killed in the assault and three others were captured, including Abu al Hassan.

During his interrogation, al Hassan confessed that the kidnapping was to have brought about the release of both the organization's members and those of the "British" terror network members incarcerated in Yemeni jails. According to the testimony of one of the kidnapped victims, al Hassan held a telephone conversation during the kidnapping with General Ali Mohsen al Ahmar, a relative of Yemen's President Saleh, in an attempt to get the latter to agree to the abductors' demands, but the Yemeni authorities had already decided to take action to release the hostages. During the 1990s, there were over one hundred incidents of the abduction of foreign residents in Yemen, but this particular incident was the broadest in scale, and one of the few that ended in the deaths of hostages.

The abduction of foreigners did not cease even after the Yemenite government joined the coalition in the "war against terror" in the aftermath of the 9/11 attacks. Abductions continued in Yemen, including:

- *In 2004*, an Australian oil engineer was abducted from Oman together with his two escorts. The three were subsequently freed by their abductors. It is unknown whether a ransom was paid for their release.
- *In November 2005*, two Austrian tourists were abducted. The two were subsequently released. It is unknown whether a ransom was paid for their release.
- *In December 2005*, a senior German diplomat was abducted together with his family. The abductors demanded that the

Yemeni government release prisoners from a certain tribe in exchange for the captives' release. The German hostages were released following negotiations. It is unclear whether the Yemeni government kept its promise to release prisoners.
- *At the beginning of 2006*, five Italian tourists were abducted and were subsequently released. Two of the abductors were later arrested by the Yemeni authorities.
- *On 31 August 2007*, a Canadian of Indian origin, a Syrian, and their Yemeni driver were abducted in the province of Shabwah, where they worked on a contract for a gas firm. They were freed a day later, after the Yemeni military threatened to storm the area to secure their release.
- *On 8 May 2008*, a group of armed tribesmen abducted two female Japanese tourists and held them for several hours in the north-central city of Marib. The tribesmen kidnapped the women to press the Yemeni government to free a jailed relative.
- *On 12 August 2008*, tribesmen, pressing for the release of jailed relatives, abducted a French-Algerian engineer and his two Yemeni drivers in the Habban district, forty kilometers from Ataq, the provincial capital of Shabwah. They were freed hours later.
- *On 14 December 2008*, three Germans (a woman who officials said worked for the United Nations, and her elderly parents) were kidnapped on the outskirts of Sana'a. The kidnappers were tribesmen pressing for an end to a land dispute with another tribe and for the release of jailed fellow tribesmen. The hostages were released on December 19th.
- *On 17 January 2009*, a German engineer and two Yemenis were seized in the Shabwah region in the south of the Arabian Peninsula. The three men, who worked for Yemen LNG Ltd., were freed on January 20th.
- *On 31 March 2009*, a Dutch couple, Jan Hoogendoorn and Heleen Janszen, were seized in the southern city of Taiz. They were released on April 13th.
- *On 11 June 2009*, tribesmen in Saada province kidnapped twenty-four doctors and nurses and demanded that the authorities should free two prisoners. All twenty-four, most of whom were Yemenis, but also included Egyptians, Indians, and Filipinos, were released the next day.
- *On 14 June 2009*, seven Germans, a Briton, and a South Korean were kidnapped from the Saada area of north Yemen. The Briton was an engineer and the South Korean was a female school teacher working with an aid agency. One German was a doctor

at a hospital. The group, which included the doctor's three children, was seized while picnicking. A few days later, the bodies of three women hostages were found. In May 2010, two more hostages were released. No one took responsibility for the abduction and murder, but the Yemeni government claimed that Houthi militants were responsible for the crimes, while the Houthi denied any connection to the crimes.[16]

On 11 January 2010, German Foreign Minister Guido Westerwelle made a surprise visit to Yemen to hold talks with President Saleh and other top officials. Westerwelle discussed the fate of the five Germans, including three children, and the British national. In January, before the visit, a senior Yemeni official had said the six hostages were still alive.[17]

There has been no news of the remaining four hostages.

Three French Aid Workers Abducted in Yemen (July 2011)

Three French aid workers – two women and a man – were kidnapped in Yemen on 28 May 2011. They were part of the French non-governmental organization Triangle Génération Humanitaire, based in Lyon, and were working with a group of seventeen Yemenis in the town of Sayun, six hundred kilometers east of Sana'a. They were seized in Yemen's eastern Hadramawt province, which is home to al Qaeda in the Arabian Peninsula (AQAP) and other radical Islamic groups. An official said that the French aid workers had refused protection from Yemeni authorities, saying they did not need it. "They were kidnapped because they had written a letter to Yemeni security services asking not to be accompanied by anyone for protection," he claimed.

The security services in the province of Hadramawt were mobilized and searched the region for the missing aid workers, but failed to find them. A Yemeni security official said their car (a Hilux pickup) was found on the road some twenty kilometers from Shebam, a city known as the "Manhattan of the Desert" because of its spectacular high-rise mud-brick buildings. After the aid workers' disappearance, Yemeni officials initially feared the group had been taken hostage by tribesmen, who frequently used abductions – of locals and foreigners – to press the government for concessions such as the release of fellow tribesmen in prison.[18]

On 28 June 2011, local security officials said that they had succeeded in identifying the kidnappers, who belonged to "an Islamist extremist group", without naming the particular organization. Yemeni tribal sources said that the three French aid workers were held by al Qaeda members who were seeking a US$12 million ransom for their release. However, al Qaeda did not claim responsibility for the kidnappings. The chief of the Yemeni intelligence department and other senior government officials asked prominent figures in the town of Sayun to try to mediate their release.[19]

The French response

A French foreign ministry spokesman said that the ministry had not heard whether the group was being held by al Qaeda or if they were demanding a ransom. The director of the French aid group, Patrick Verbruggen, also claimed it had had no contact with the kidnappers since the abduction in May, and said he also had no information on whether the aid workers were being held by al Qaeda or if a ransom had been demanded.[20]

The release

In November 2011, after almost six months in captivity, al Qaeda released the three aid workers following mediation by Sultan of Oman Qaboos bin Said and the payment of a ransom. The abductors had demanded US$12 million for their release, but the total ransom paid remained undisclosed. The freed hostages were flown to Oman before returning to France.[21]

Summary

In the past, tribesmen often kidnapped foreigners to wrest concessions on local issues from the government – including ransoms, the release of jailed relatives, or even promises to build local infrastructure – but they usually treated hostages well and released them unharmed. Past abductions by al Qaeda and other jihadi organizations, however, have ended with the deaths of hostages. Al Qaeda's presence in Yemen has strengthened over the past years; al Qaeda militants, including fighters returned from Afghanistan and Iraq, have established sanctuaries among a number of Yemeni tribes, particularly in the three provinces bordering Saudi Arabia. In January 2009, al Qaeda groups in Yemen and Saudi Arabia announced they were merging their operations and said that their joint forces would carry out operations across the Arabian Peninsula, and beyond.

In July 2009, AQAP called for the kidnapping of tourists in Yemen to press for the release of jailed fighters. "It is a duty that detainees be freed through any rough way, such as kidnapping tourists, who are numerous, or through various other ways," read an article in AQAP's e-magazine.[22]

In the same month, Yemen's deputy minister of tourism estimated the cost of the damage to the economy of Yemen at around US$200 million. He said that about two million Yemeni citizens working in the tourism sector, including hotels and travel agencies, had been affected by the kidnappings.[23] In 2009, as a result of the increased number of kidnapping incidents, the interior and tourism ministries provided security escorts and GPS tracking devices to the vehicles of tourist groups and formed an operation center devoted to communication with the vehicles' drivers, while Yemen's government urged parliament to pass tougher security and gun-control laws, saying unrest and kidnappings of westerners were straining the economy.[24]

As mentioned before, the Yemeni government's steps were only marginally successful:

- The government's control in areas remote from the capital is limited and the tribal structure of Yemenite society precludes the existence of an effective central government.
- Strong tribal leaders operate their own policies and support radical Islamic entities for financial and ideological reasons.
- There are strong radical Islamic circles that enjoy widespread popularity in the region.
- Corrupt and ineffective administration and control systems impair the government's control of what takes place in the country.

Yemen's President Saleh vowed to crack down on abductions of foreigners that, along with attacks by al Qaeda, have hindered the state's efforts to boost tourism and the local economy, but this policy has so far met with limited success.

Yemen and the "Arab Spring"

The "Arab Spring" protests started in Yemen in mid-January 2011. Demonstrators initially protested against governmental proposals to modify Yemen's constitution, unemployment and economic conditions, and corruption, but their demands soon included a call for the resignation of President Saleh, who vowed to remain in office, and the unrest and violent government response continued.

In June 2011, President Saleh was injured in a rocket attack and was evacuated to Saudi Arabia. While in Saudi Arabia, Saleh kept hinting that he could return at any time and continued to be present in the political sphere through television appearances from Riyadh. On 23 September 2011, three months since the assassination attempt, Saleh returned to Yemen, but internal and external pressures forced him to resign. On 23 November 2011, Saleh agreed to step down and set the stage for the transfer of power to his vice-president, Abdrabuh Mansur Hadi. A presidential election was then held on 21 February 2012, in which Hadi (the only candidate) won 99.8 percent of the vote. Hadi then took the oath of office in Yemen's parliament on 25 February 2013. President Hadi has largely continued Saleh's policies – the country remains unstable and security conditions have deteriorated; terror attacks and kidnapping of local people and westerners in Yemen continue to be carried out by al Qaeda militants and tribesmen, and the president warned that the al Qaeda branch in the country was expanding and using assassinations and abductions of foreigners as a way to challenge central governmental authority.[25]

Examples of abductions and the responses of various countries are detailed below:

- In March 2012, armed tribesmen kidnapped a Swiss teacher in the western Yemeni port city of al Hudaydah in order to press the Yemen government to free jailed relatives. The Swiss woman was freed by her kidnappers in February 2013, and flown to Doha following mediation by Qatar.
- Three Europeans, a Finnish couple, and an Austrian were kidnapped by tribesmen in the center of Sana'a on 21 December 2012, and moved to different locations around Yemen. In early January 2013, Yemeni security officials said the Europeans were held by al Qaeda-linked tribesmen in the Marib province of eastern Yemen, and were later "sold" to members of al Qaeda and transferred to the small town of Manasseh south of the capital. In February 2013, the Austrian student appeared in a YouTube clip with a gun to his head, saying his captors would kill him unless Austria, Yemen, and the European Union met their ransom demands. At the end of March 2013, the foreign minister of Finland held talks in Sana'a with President Hadi about the fate of the hostages. In May 2013, the kidnappers released the Finnish couple and the Austrian man more than four months after they were seized in the capital. The trio were freed after mediation by authorities in neighboring Oman, who paid a sum of money for their release.[26] Austria's foreign ministry said the three had been flown to Austria and were receiving medical

and psychological treatment. Austrian Vice-Chancellor Michael Spindelegger thanked Oman's Sultan Qaboos for his "personal support". Finland's Foreign Minister Erkki Tuomioja said his country did not pay ransoms, but had no information about whether Oman had done so, adding that freed hostage Atte Kaleva worked for Finland's army, without going into further details, but had visited Yemen while on leave to study Arabic. Finnish media said Kaleva's wife Leila was visiting him when they were kidnapped.[27]

- On 13 May 2013, three staff members from the International Committee of the Red Cross (ICRC) were kidnapped in Yemen's southern province of Abyan, near Jaar.[28] The two international staff from Kenya and Switzerland, and a locally hired employee, were returning from a field trip. The kidnapped workers were safely released on 16 May 2013.[29]

NOTES

1 This section is based on Shaul Shay, *The Red Sea Terror Triangle: Sudan, Somalia, Yemen, and Islamic Terror* (New Brunswick: Transaction Publishers, 2011).
2 Yossef Bodansky, *Bin Laden: The Man Who Declared War on America* (New York: Forum, 1999), p. 314.
3 "International Terror Attacks", *International Institute for Counter-Terror Policy* (ICT), http://www.ict.org.il (n.d.).
4 Bodansky, *Bin Laden*, p. 246.
5 "Yemen Fights Own Terror War", *Christian Science Monitor*, 5 February 2002.
6 "Yemen Quakes in Cole's Shadow", *Christian Science Monitor*, 5 September 2002.
7 *Yemen Times*, Issue 7, 17 February 2002.
8 "Yemen Fights Own Terror War", *Christian Science Monitor*, 5 February 2002.
9 "Yemen New Terrorist Capital", *ABC News*, 8 October 2001.
10 Peter L. Bergen, *Holy War Inc.: Inside the Secret World of Osama Bin Laden* (London: Weidenfield and Nicolson, 2001), p. 193.
11 "International Terror Attacks", *ICT*, (n.d.).
12 *Arabic News*, 6 December 2001.
13 *Ibid*.
14 Bergen, *Holy War Inc.*, pp. 190–191, 193.
15 *Ibid.*, pp. 190–191.
16 "Nine Foreign Hostages Found Dead in Yemen", *CBC News*, 15 June 2009.
17 "Yemen: German Minister Makes Surprise Visit", *Adnkronos International*, 11 January 2010.

18 "Yemen Troops Search for Missing French Aid Workers", *Khaleej Times*, 30 May 2011.
19 "Abducted French Workers in al Qaeda Hands", *France 24*, 27 July 2011.
20 *Ibid*.
21 "Al Qaeda Militants Release Three French Aid Workers Held Hostage in Yemen", *AP*, 14 November 2011, http://www.foxnews.com/world/2011/11/14/al-qaeda-militants-release-three-french-aid-workers-held-hostage-in-yemen/#ixzz2XOv5MAHr.
22 Nasser Arrabyee, "Al Qaeda Calls for Tourist Kidnappings in Yemen", *Gulf News*, 10 July 2009.
23 Khaled al Hilaly, "Kidnappings Cause Decline in International Tourism to Yemen", *Yemen Times*, 1 July 2009.
24 "Yemen Government Wants Tougher Laws to Curb Kidnaps, Unrest", *Reuters*, 14 July 2009.
25 "Kidnapped Red Cross Workers Released in Yemen", *al Jazeera*, 16 May 2013.
26 "Yemen Kidnappers Free Finnish Couple, Austrian", *Reuters*, 9 May 2013.
27 *Ibid*.
28 Cheryl K. Chumley, "Three Red Cross Workers Kidnapped in Yemen", *The Washington Post*, 13 May 2013.
29 "Kidnapped Red Cross Workers Released in Yemen", *al Jazeera*, 16 May 2013.

9

The "Arab Spring" and Terror Abductions in Syria and Lebanon

As a part of the "Arab Spring" revolution in the Syrian Arab Republic, abductions were used by the al Assad regime, the galaxy of Syrian opposition groups, and criminal gangs in order to obtain ransom, revenge, or the exchange of prisoners. The scourge of kidnapping in the Syrian conflict has currently caused at least 1,753 victims, nearly all civilians.[1]

Civilians are exploited by armed or jihadist groups. The fragmentation of these gangs, their heterogeneous origins and identities, their full autonomy in matters of unrest and banditry, and their attempts to pollute the Syrian population all contribute to sectarianism – and thus jihadism spreads. Some kidnappings, as in the case of Father Fadi Jamil Haddad, end in a barbaric manner with the torture and beheading of the hostages.

Abductions have become so frequent that rebels from the Free Syrian Army (FSA) have publicized a helpline number, writing it on walls and publishing it in social media. When they receive a call from relatives of the victim, they track down the kidnappers. Then they either issue threats, or go in for the rescue using force. A brigade of the FSA posted an online video claiming that the forty-eight Iranians it kidnapped in August 2012 were members of Iran's elite Revolutionary Guards and warned of further abductions over Tehran's support for the Syrian government.

The Abduction of Foreign Nationals in Syria

Russians are legitimate targets for attacks in Syria, claimed a member of the opposition National Coalition for Syrian Revolutionary and

Opposition Forces. "Russia, like Iran, supports the Assad regime with weapons and ammunition, as well as in the political arena, so the citizens of these countries are legitimate targets for militants in Syria," stated Haitham al Maleh in an interview with Russian television, claiming that the Geneva Convention allowed for attacks on civilians cooperating with enemy armed forces. However, he called on militants not to kidnap citizens of countries that "do not support the Assad regime."[2] Indeed, Iranians, Russians, and citizens of other countries supporting the al Assad regime are high-value, but not the exclusive, targets of various rebel groups.

The abduction and release of Iranian pilgrims (August 2012)

On 4 August 2012, forty-eight Iranian pilgrims were abducted from a bus in the Syrian capital. Hundreds of thousands of Iranians travel each year to Damascus to visit the Shia shrine of Sayyidah Zaynab, the granddaughter of the Prophet Muhammad. The pilgrims were abducted on their way to the airport after visiting the shrine. At first, the kidnappers claimed the pilgrims were members of Hizballah, but then backtracked and claimed to be holding the men until Hizballah's leader Hassan Nasrallah publicly apologized for voicing support for Assad's regime.

In a video released in October 2012, fighters from the al Baraa brigade of the FSA said that they had "captured forty-eight of the *shabiha* (militiamen) of Iran who were on a reconnaissance mission in Damascus". "During the investigation, we found that some of them were officers in the Revolutionary Guards," said a man dressed in an FSA officer's uniform, displaying documents taken from one of the men, who appeared in the background,[3] and threatened to execute the hostages if the al Assad government did not free rebel prisoners and halt the shelling of civilian areas. The FSA had previously taken hostages, but this was the first occasion that they had threatened to execute prisoners if their demands were not met. The Iranian government rejected the allegations, insisting the men had been merely visiting the shrine when they were abducted. However, the State of Qatar successfully urged the rebels not to carry out their threats.[4]

Tehran is the staunchest ally of Syrian President al Assad and several reports have emerged from opposition groups stating that "Iranian Revolutionary Guards were present fighting with the Syrian army". Iran repeatedly denied that it had sent any military units to Syria and asked Turkey and Qatar to help secure the hostages' release. Ahmet Davutoğlu, the Turkish foreign minister, and Sheikh Hamad bin Jassim bin Jabr al Thani, his Qatari counterpart, agreed to seek the pilgrims' release during separate phone conversations with Iranian Foreign Minister Ali Akbar Salehi.[5]

The release of the hostages

The release of the Iranian hostages came on 9 January 2013, after months of diplomatic efforts which reportedly involved Qatar, Turkey, and the Turkish Islamic aid agency Humanitarian Relief Foundation (IHH).[6] The abductees were set free as part of a deal between the Syrian government and the armed militants. Hüseyin Oruç, a board member of IHH, told the media that the Syrian government freed 2,130 prisoners in exchange for the release of the forty-eight Iranians held by Syrian rebels. "Most of the prisoners swapped were Syrians in exchange for Iranians. The released prisoners include seventy-three women, four Turks, and a Palestinian."[7] A member of the IHH's executive board, Osman Atalay, quoted IHH chief Bülent Yildirim, who was in Damascus to help coordinate the deal, as saying that the prisoner swap had already begun.[8]

The abduction of two Russians and an Italian (December 2012)

On 8 December 2012, three people were kidnapped in the coastal city of Latakia: an Italian engineer and two Russian citizens, all employees of the Syrian-owned Hmisho steel plant. Russia's foreign ministry identified the two Russian nationals as V. V. Gorelov and Abdessattar Hassoun – the latter had dual Syrian–Russian citizenship. The abductors demanded a ransom of over US$700,000 for their release, reports claimed, citing the *Kommersant* daily newspaper.[9]

The three workers remain in captivity.

The abduction of a Ukrainian journalist (October 2012)

In October 2012, Anhar Kochneva, an Ukrainian journalist, was abducted by members of the FSA in the city of Homs. Kochneva, known as an expert on Syrian affairs, had been in Syria since the start of the conflict. An outspoken supporter of President Bashar al Assad, she was freelancing for several Russian media outlets, including the NTV, RenTV, and RT channels, and the Utro.Ru internet news portal.[10]

A month after the kidnapping, a video message from Kochneva was posted on the YouTube site, in which she appealed to the embassies of Ukraine and Russia, as well as the Syrian government, to meet the demands of the kidnappers, and also "confessed" to working for Russian intelligence. Her captors claimed that Kochneva was armed and had acted as an interpreter for Russian officers, and said they would target all Russians, Ukrainians, and Iranians in Syrian territory.

On 28 November 2012, in a second video, Kochneva read a text in Arabic admitting to having participated in the fighting and working as a military interpreter for Syrian and Russian officers. The kidnappers threatened to kill Kochneva if a US$50 million ransom was not paid but, by mid-January, had reduced their ransom demand to US$20 million, and it was reportedly later reduced to US$300,000.[11]

The kidnappers repeatedly threatened to kill her if the ransom was not paid. The rebels claimed that they had planned to put Kochneva to death on 16 December 2012, but had decided to "give her a second chance".[12] Several world powers – including Russia, the US, and France – as well as international human rights organizations, urged the Syrian opposition to release the journalist.

On 12 March 2013, Anhar Kochneva escaped from captivity and returned to the Ukraine.

The abduction and release of UN peacekeepers (March 2013)

On 5 March 2013, fighters from the "Martyrs of Yarmouk", a Syrian opposition group, seized twenty-one Filipino UN peacekeepers on the Syrian Golan Heights, part of the United Nations Disengagement Observer Force (UNDOF) that monitors the ceasefire between Syria and Israel. According to the UN, the peacekeepers were on a regular supply mission when they were stopped by armed men near an observation post. The UN Security Council demanded the unconditional release of the observers, who were held in the village of Jamla, about 1.6 kilometers east of the Syrian–Israeli frontier and ten kilometers north of Jordan. The kidnappers demanded the withdrawal of Syrian government forces from Jamla before they would proceed with the release. The FSA – the main rebel fighting force – condemned the seizure of the UN observers.

The release

A UN team had been due to go into Syria to collect the peacekeepers under a truce between the warring sides. However, the relief convoy was stopped several kilometers away because of continued fighting between government and rebel forces. Instead, the rebels took the hostages to the Jordanian border. The peacekeepers were later welcomed in Amman by Jordanian Foreign Minister Nasser Judeh.[13] The incident was a sign that fighting between rebel groups and government troops of President al Assad was spreading, and indicated a lack of central control among the rebel factions.

The abduction and release of US journalists (December 2012)

On 13 December 2012, Richard Engel, chief foreign correspondent for NBC News, and his entire production team were kidnapped when the group of Syrian rebels with whom they were traveling was ambushed by members of a pro-government militia. "They kept us blindfolded, bound," said Engel, aged thirty-nine, who speaks and reads Arabic. "They made us choose which one of us would be shot first, and when we refused, there were mock shootings."[14]

The group was moved from place to place before their captors were stopped at an unexpected rebel checkpoint while traveling to another location in a northern province. A gunfight ensued, and at least two of the kidnappers were killed before Engel and his crew were able to escape; they spent the night with the rebels before entering Turkey.[15] Engel said his captors talked openly of their loyalty to the Syrian regime and said they were trained by the Iranian Revolutionary Guard and allied with Hizballah. He stated that his kidnappers wanted to exchange the journalists for four Iranian and two Lebanese prisoners being held by the rebels. "They captured us in order to carry out this exchange," he said.[16] NBC did not identify the others who were kidnapped along with Engel, but said there was no claim of responsibility, no contact with the captors, and no request for ransom during the time the crew was missing. The network had not publicized the kidnapping before the captives escaped.[17]

Abductions and Beheadings in Syria

The civil war in Syria appeals to young Muslims from many countries, including those in the west, wishing to join the ranks of the "holy war" as part of the rebel forces in Syria, most of which are identified with radical Islamic streams. Syrian rebels have increasingly resorted to torture and summary execution of government soldiers, suspected informants, pro-government militias, and captured or kidnapped civilians.[18]

In two separate reports reviewing the conduct of the rebels and the Syrian government, Amnesty International said that the killing of government soldiers and suspected government supporters was on the rise as rebel forces continue to gain ground. "Rebel fighters are summarily killing people with a chilling sense of impunity, and the death toll continues to rise as more towns and villages come under the control of armed opposition groups," said the statement. "While the vast majority of war crimes and other gross violations continue to be committed by government forces, the research also points to an escalation in abuses by armed opposition groups," said Ann Harrison, deputy director of Amnesty's Middle East and North Africa Program.[19]

Noting the public sympathy the Syrian opposition continues to receive from the west, Amnesty International said rebel fighters must be held accountable for crimes against humanity: "It's time for the armed opposition groups to know that what they are doing is very wrong, and that some of the abuses they committed amount to war crimes."[20] Amnesty also said it investigated one of the most gruesome videos in the conflict, which showed the beheading of two Syrian army officers abducted from the eastern town of Deir ez-Zor in August 2012. Amnesty said that researchers contacted the families of the slain men, Colonel Fuad Abd al Rahman and Colonel Izz al Din Badr, and were told that the kidnappers had identified themselves as members of the opposition group Osoud al Tawhid ("Lions of al Tawhid") when they initially contacted the family to demand a ransom but, after negotiations, the hostage-takers told the family they had killed the two men.[21]

In November 2012, a video surfaced of a machete-wielding boy – apparently between twelve and fourteen years of age – standing over Colonel Badr, who was shown lying prostrate with his hands bound behind his back. A voice off-camera provoked the youth, shouting: "He doesn't have the strength!" The boy brought the machete down on Colonel Badr's neck as rebel fighters cheered him on. At least one gunman then proceeded to fire six shots into Badr's body. The family of Colonel Rahman learned the gruesome nature of his death after his beheading was aired on Damascus-based Sama television. Amnesty said the footage was most likely authentic.[22]

The "Spillover" of Terror Abductions from Syria to Lebanon

The Syrian civil war and the involvement of Hizballah in the fighting alongside the al Assad regime caused a "war of abductions" across the Syrian–Lebanese border. Extended families with differing allegiances straddle both countries, and the use of hostages signaled the rise of abduction as a tactic by the antagonists in the conflict. The Lebanese Republic's divided government, often unwilling to confront private militias, had already been shaken by clashes between supporters and opponents of the Syrian government, especially near the border with Syria.

The opposition Syrian National Council (SNC) accused the Lebanese authorities of failing to act over a wave of kidnappings and arrests of Syrians in Lebanon, and accused some political parties of complicity. "Syrians in Lebanon have been abducted by political parties, and subject to arbitrary arrests by security agents, without the authorities so much as lifting a finger," the SNC said, implicitly blaming the Shiite militant group Hizballah that is closely allied with the Damascus regime. Hizballah denied any connection with the kidnappings, but said that the group cannot control the "reactions" of people to events in Syria.[23] Several analysts said the abductions may just be the beginning. "We could be heading toward chaos and an uncontrollable security situation," said Talal Atrissi, an analyst in Beirut.[24]

The abduction of eleven Lebanese pilgrims (May 2012)

In May 2012, eleven Lebanese Shiites were abducted in the Syrian city of Aleppo while they were returning to Lebanon from a pilgrimage in Iran. The armed gang allegedly hijacked their bus, then kidnapped the men and released the women. Shia Muslims in Lebanon protested against the abduction and gathered in the southern suburbs of Beirut, closing several roads with burning tires and garbage cans. Meanwhile, Hizballah's Secretary-General Hassan Nasrallah condemned the abduction, saying the Lebanese government should be held accountable. The kidnappers put forward a ransom demand, claiming that the hostages were members of Hizballah, while family members of those kidnapped said they were merely pilgrims returning to Beirut from the Iranian city of Mashhad.

Fears of violent responses and revenge abductions increased in August 2012, when Lebanese television reported that shelling and air strikes by the Syrian military in Azaz, thirty kilometers north of Aleppo, had killed some, or all, of the eleven kidnapped Lebanese pilgrims. By 16th August, their fate had become clear: four had been killed, the Syrian rebel commander said in an interview on Lebanese television. The families of the pilgrims, angered by the reports from Azaz, later kidnapped several Syrians.[25]

The abduction of Hassan Salim al Miqdad (August 2012)

Hassan Salim al Miqdad was abducted in Syria in August 2012. Miqdad's captors said in an online video that he was a sniper from Hizballah sent to support loyalists of President al Assad.[26]

Hizballah denied that al Miqdad was a supporter, while his family said he had moved to Damascus to escape personal debts, but had settled the matter and was en route home when he was kidnapped. Hatem al Miqdad, his brother, said he had communicated with the kidnappers and believed his brother was safe.

The abduction of twenty Syrians in Lebanon (August 2012)

In August 2012, more than twenty Syrians inside Lebanese territory were abducted by members of the powerful Lebanese Shiite Miqdad family. In interviews with reporters, relatives of Salim al Miqdad said that they had taken the hostages to avenge his abduction. Anxiety quickly spread through Lebanon and extra security precautions were taken in Beirut. Lebanese officials said additional guards had been assigned to the embassies of Qatar, Saudi Arabia, and Turkey, the main allies of the Syrian insurgency. Neither the police nor the army responded to the abductions, and officials remained silent even as Shiite militias blocked Beirut's airport road.[27]

Some al Miqdad relatives in the Bekaa Valley near the Syrian border – where the captives appeared to have been captured and held – said that they did not intend to spread Syria's war. "We just want to get him released," one relative said in an interview with *al Mayadeen*, the pan-Arab television network based in Beirut, as a dozen camouflage-clad men with automatic weapons surrounded the hostages. The al Miqdad family said that members of the FSA had abducted al Miqdad, but the FSA denied any role in the abduction. The family also said that it had kidnapped a Turkish man and warned that Saudis in Lebanon would also be targeted.[28] In response to the threats, the embassies of Kuwait, Qatar, and Saudi Arabia advised their citizens to leave the country.[29]

A group of Shiites from the Zeeiter tribe told reporters, on 15 August 2012, that they had kidnapped four members of the FSA from hospitals in the Bekaa Valley in eastern Lebanon, which borders Syria. Another tribe in the area, according to local news reports, kidnapped four other rebel fighters just across the border inside Syria.[30]

The fate of the hostages remains unresolved.

Summary

Two years after the Syrians rose in peaceful protest against their government (the "Arab Spring"), the country is still mired in a bloody civil war between the al Assad regime and its allies, Iran and Hizballah, and the diverse opposition, composed of secular and nationalist parties, al Qaeda, and other global jihad groups. The UN estimates that more than 70,000 people have been killed and over two million internally displaced during the two-year uprising against the government of Syrian President Bashar al Assad.

Armed opposition groups (mainly jihadi groups) have increasingly resorted to hostage-taking and the torture and summary killing of soldiers, pro-government militias, and civilians. Foreign citizens, aid workers, and journalists are among the victims of the opposing parties in the conflict. As long as the civil war continues, the number of abductions will increase as a significant tool to influence foreign decision-makers and public opinion in favor of, or against, the interests of the warring parties within the Syrian conflict.

NOTES

1. Ruth Sharlock, "Epidemic of Kidnappings Breaks Out in Syria", *The Telegraph*, 7 September 2012.
2. "Russia for Stopping Kidnapping Foreigners in Syria", *Voice of Russia*, 20 December 2012.
3. "Syrian Rebels Say Hostages Iranian Soldiers", *al Jazeera*, 5 August 2012.
4. "Iranians Held by Syria Rebels Released", *BBC News*, 9 January 2013.
5. *Ibid.*
6. "Kidnapped Iranian Pilgrims Freed in Syria", *FARS*, 9 January 2013.
7. *Ibid.*
8. *Ibid.*
9. "Russians in Syria are Legitimate Targets: Key Opposition Group Member", *RT*, 19 December 2012.
10. "Ukranian Reporter Escapes from Syrian Captivity", *RIA Novosti*, 13 March 2013.
11. "'If You were a Man, We'd Kill You': Captive Journalist Tells RT How She Escaped Syrian Rebels", *RT*, 13 March 2013.
12. *Ibid.*
13. Tara MacIsaac, "21 UN Peacekeepers Kidnapped in Syria", *Epoch Times*, 6 March 2013.
14. "US Journalists Free after Kidnapping in Syria", *Sky News*, 18 December 2012.
15. *Ibid.*
16. *Ibid.*
17. *Ibid.*
18. "Syrian Rebels Ramp Up Extrajudicial Killings and Kidnappings", *Amnesty International*, 14 March 2013.
19. *Ibid.*
20. *Ibid.*
21. *Ibid.*
22. *Ibid.*
23. "Syria Opposition Points Finger at Lebanon over Kidnappings", *al Arabiya*, 21 August 2012.
24. Dalal Mawad and Damien Cave, "Syrian Conflict Crosses Border into Lebanon in Abductions", *The New York Times*, 15 August 2012.
25. Damien Cave, "In Lebanon, Sunnis Threatens Shiites as Kidnapping of Syrians Rise", *The New York Times*, 16 August 2012.

26 Mawad and Cave, "Syrian Conflict Crosses Border", *New York Times*, 15 August 2012.
27 *Ibid.*
28 *Ibid.*
29 Cave, "Sunnis Threatens Shiites", *New York Times*, 16 August 2012.
30 *Ibid.*

10

Terror Abductions in the Philippines

The Republic of the Philippines faces numerous threats from terrorism. Operating within the country are the Abu Sayyaf Group (ASG), the Communist Party of the Philippines/New Peoples Army (CPP/NPA), Jamaah Islamiyah (JI; literally, "Islamic Congregation"), the Rajah Sulaiman Islamic Movement (RSIM), Moro Islamic Liberation Front (MILF), and Moro National Liberation Front (MNLF).

The Abu Sayyaf Terror Organization

The southern part of the Philippines has a long history of resistance dating back to the Spanish conquest and continuing through the US colonial era. The Spanish occupation sparked a series of so-called "Moro wars" that ran from 1718 to 1878. Those conflicts isolated Mindanao from the rest of the Philippines and contributed to the economic stagnation that lingers in the region to the present day.

After the US took over from Spain as colonial ruler in 1898, Muslims from the Sultanate of Sulu continued to rebel against Washington. The Americans concentrated on eliminating resistance in Luzon and Visayas, and at first avoided conflict with the Mindanao Muslims through the autonomy-granting Bates Treaty of 1899, but later abrogated the treaty and moved to enforce certain cultural values and practices that irked Muslim sensitivities. The US was subsequently involved in attacks on local leaders seen as a threat to consolidating US colonial control over the region, and many Muslim and tribal communities fled to the safety of inaccessible sanctuaries – many in the areas where the ASG now operates.

Many Muslims in the region still harbor bitterness about that past experience and associate the current presence of US military instructors based in Mindanao with that same oppressive history. Mainstream Philippine history overlooks the contribution that Filipino Muslims made in the fight to end colonial rule, although studies have been launched in recent years to address those historical oversights in educational textbooks. In the early 1970s, the Moro National Liberation Front (MNLF) was the main Muslim rebel group fighting in Basilan and Mindanao in the southern Philippines, and later evolved into an established political party, the Autonomous Region in Muslim Mindanao (ARMM), which was established in 1989, fully institutionalized by 1996, and eventually became the ruling government in southern Mindanao.

Abdurajik Abubakar Janjalani, a teacher from Basilan who later studied Islamic theology and Arabic in Libya, Syria, and Saudi Arabia during the 1980s, went to Afghanistan to participate in the jihad against the Soviet forces. During that period, he is alleged to have met Osama bin Laden and been given US$6 million to establish a more Islamic group in the southern Philippines, to be made up of members of the MNLF. The new movement was formally established in 1984 as the Moro Islamic Liberation Front (MILF).

When Janjalani returned home to Basilan Island in 1990, he gathered together radical members of the old MNLF who wanted to resume armed struggle for an independent Islamic state and, in 1991, he established the Abu Sayyaf Group ("Bearer of the Sword"), which is opposed to any accommodation with Christians and believes that violent struggle is the only solution.[1] The first attack by the Abu Sayyaf Group (ASG) was the assault on the town of Ipil in Mindanao in April 1995.

By 1995, the ASG was active in large-scale bombings and attacks in the Philippines. Abdurajik Janjalani died in December 1998 in a gun battle with Filipino forces and was replaced by his brother, Khadaffy.[2] The death of Janjalani marked a turning point in ASG operations, shifting its ideological focus more towards general kidnapping, murder, and robbery as the younger brother succeeded Abdurajik.[3] Khadaffy Janjalani was considered to be the leader of the group until his death in a gun battle on 4 September 2006. His death was officially confirmed on 20 January 2007, through DNA analysis.

The areas where the ASG operates suffer from extreme poverty, making them fertile ground for the recruitment of disenfranchised young men. The region's dire economics has also made kidnapping-for-ransom a lucrative proposition; in the past, the group has targeted luxury beach resorts and gained extensive revenue from kidnapping – including a US$25 million ransom payment from Libya in March 2000. The group later expanded its operations to Malaysia, where it abducted foreigners from two different resorts in 2000.[4]

The ASG has a record of killings and kidnappings, and has had links with al Qaeda, JI, MILF, and the MNLF. Since 2003, the ASG has planned and carried out attacks in cooperation with the JI and the MILF, including bombings in Manila. The ASG and JI were reportedly engaged in joint training that emphasized training in explosives and techniques for urban bombing. By 2005, JI personnel had trained about sixty ASG cadres in bomb assembly and detonation.

Most of the ASG's victims have been Filipinos. However, non-Filipinos have also been taken hostage for large ransom payments, while westerners, especially Americans, have been targeted for political reasons. The abductions of foreign nationals in the southern Philippines attract the most attention, but Filipino locals are victimized more often, and many cases are negotiated quietly and not reported to the authorities. Although the ASG is considered to be a terrorist organization by governments around the world, its motives for kidnapping do not appear to be ideological – the group obtains most of its financing through ransom and extortion.[5] One report estimated its revenues from ransom payments, in 2000 alone, as between US$10 million and US$25 million. According to the US State Department, the group may also receive funding from radical Islamic benefactors in the Middle East and south Asia.[6]

US Involvement in Counter-terror Operations in the Philippines

Philippine military and law enforcement agencies conducted intensive civil-military operations to eliminate terrorist safe havens in the Sulu archipelago and central Mindanao. In 2002, the US included the ASG in its list of foreign terrorist organizations, alongside the al Qaeda network and the Indonesian-based JI.[7] Under US-supported Philippine military pressure since 2002, ASG's armed strength has declined from an estimated one thousand to about four hundred.

Under the George W. Bush administration, southeast Asia was often mentioned as the second front in the US's global "war on terror"; a definition that provided funds and training to the Philippine armed forces to combat the ASG's long-running insurrection. There have been reports – denied by Washington – that US troops assisted their Filipino counterparts in certain combat operations against the ASG, including the killing of one of the group's top leaders, Abu Sabaya, on 21 June 2002.[8]

In its final days, the George W. Bush administration attempted to portray US counter-terrorism efforts in Mindanao as a foreign policy success story. That statement is debatable, particularly in light of the ASG's recent actions, and it remains unclear what new policy US President Barack Obama will take towards the ongoing conflict in the southern Philippines.

Philippine President Gloria Macapagal-Arroyo was the first southeast-Asian leader to hold meetings with the new US administration when she met with US Secretary of State Hillary Clinton in Washington before Clinton traveled to northeast and southeast Asia. It is clear to most observers that the geographically-strategic Philippines will play a larger role in the US's regional gambit to counteract China's growing influence in southeast Asia.

In 2012, the Philippines brokered a peace deal with the largest Muslim separatist group in the region, but the ASG was not included in that agreement and the group continues to carry out attacks. Many governments continue to discourage their citizens from visiting the southern Philippines, while Australia uses some of the strongest language in its warnings.

Examples of ASG Abductions

The Sipadan kidnapping (May 2000)

On 3 May 2000, ASG terrorists occupied the Malaysian dive resort island of Sipadan and took twenty-one people hostage, including ten tourists – a total of nineteen non-Filipino nationals. The hostages were taken to an ASG base at Jolo Island in the Sulu archipelago. Located in the waters that separate Malaysia from the Philippines, the Sulu archipelago consists of hundreds of remote islands. While this event represented an international foray by the ASG, Sipidan's proximity to the Sulu islands was the most likely reason it was chosen.

Two Muslim Malaysians were released soon afterwards, but the ASG made various demands, including the release of 1993 World Trade Center bomber Ramzi Yousef and a ransom payment of US$2.4 million. In July 2000, a Filipino television evangelist and twelve of his crew offered their help to mediate for the release of the remaining hostages – the entire production crew, three French crewmembers, and a German journalist were taken hostage while visiting the ASG on Jolo Island. Most of the hostages were eventually released between August and September 2000, partly due to mediation by the Libyan leader, Muammar Gaddafi, and partly due to an offer of US$25 million in "development aid".[9]

The ASG conducted another raid on the island of Pandanan, near

Sipadan, on 10 September 2000, and seized three more Malaysians. The Philippine army launched a major offensive on 16 September 2000, and succeeded in rescuing all the remaining hostages except Filipino dive instructor Roland Ullah, who was eventually freed in 2003.[10]

The abduction and release of American Jeffrey Schilling (August 2000)

Jeffrey Schilling, a Muslim convert and American citizen, was abducted by the rebels after he visited their base on Jolo Island accompanied by his wife, Ivy Osani, on 31 August 2000. Schilling claimed to have been invited through an ASG member who was a relative of his wife, who was freed soon after the rebels seized Schilling. The ASG demanded that the US release Sheikh Omar Abdel Rahman and Ramzi Yousef, jailed for their involvement in the 1993 World Trade Center bombing. "We have been trying hard to get an American because they may think we are afraid of them," a spokesman for the ASG said, claiming: "We want to fight the American people."[11] The group later demanded a US$10 million ransom for Schilling's release.

In February 2001, the guerillas threatened to behead their hostage. The ASG had threatened to kill Schilling several times earlier in his captivity, but this was the most specific threat and prompted Schilling's mother to fly in from Oakland to make a personal plea for his release.[12]

The Philippine military rescued Schilling on 12 April 2001, after ten days of assaults on Jolo Island by Philippine marines.[13] The offensives, which initially found only abandoned hideouts, continued on the jungle-covered island that lay about 580 miles south of Manila. Four rebels were killed in one clash. The military claimed it killed seven ASG guerrillas after President Arroyo had ordered "all-out war" against them. The US embassy welcomed the rescue, praising Arroyo and the Philippine military. "The US government is thrilled with the news of Mr Schilling's safe release," the embassy statement said. "The embassy has been informed that Mr Schilling is in 'pretty good shape' and will be returning to his family in the US shortly."[14]

The Dos Palmas abductions (May 2001)

On 27 May 2001, an ASG raid abducted about twenty people from Dos Palmas, a luxury resort in Honda Bay, to the north of Puerto Princesa on the island of Palawan, which had been considered "completely safe". The most "valuable" of the hostages were three Americans: Martin and Gracia Burnham (a missionary couple) and Guillermo Sobero (a Peruvian-American tourist, who was later beheaded by his captors); the

ASG demanded US$1 million in ransom to ensure their release.[15] The hostages and hostage-takers returned across the Sulu Sea to Abu Sayyaf's bases in Mindanao, after which ASG operatives conducted numerous further raids, including one at a coconut plantation called Golden Harvest where they took about fifteen people captive, and later used bolo knives to hack the heads off two men. The number of hostages held by the group waxed and waned as some were ransomed and released, new ones were taken, and others were killed.

On 7 June 2002, about a year after the Dos Palmas raid, Philippine army troops attempted a rescue operation in which two of the three hostages were killed – Martin Burnham and a Filipino nurse named Ediborah Yap. The remaining hostage, Gracia Burnham, was wounded, while the hostage-takers escaped.[16] The third American, Guillermo Sobero, had been beheaded by militants on Basilan Island on 12 June 2001. In July 2004, Gracia Burnham testified at the trial of eight ASG members and identified six of the suspects as being her erstwhile captors. In February 2010, Philippine troops arrested a suspected Muslim militant, Jumadali Arad, accused of the high-profile kidnappings and killings of dozens of Filipino nationals, at Manila harbor as he was about to board a ship bound for the southern Philippines; he had been in hiding since the 2001 Dos Palmas abductions after allegedly piloting a speedboat loaded with the hostages.[17] Arad was reportedly on a mission to buy ammunition for ASG commander Isnilon Hapilon when he was arrested. Hapilon had been indicted in the US on kidnapping and murder charges, and Washington offered a US$5 million reward for his capture.

The abduction of three aid workers (January 2009)

In January 2009, a group of unidentified armed men seized three aid workers from the International Committee of the Red Cross (ICRC) in Patikul, Sulu province, where they were working on a water and sanitation project for a local prison. As was the case in previous kidnappings in southern Mindanao, the three workers were delivered by their abductors to a group associated with the ASG, whose leader Albader Parad was said to have been involved in the kidnapping. The three – an Italian, a Swiss, and a Filipino – were in a car on their way to the airport when armed men on motorbikes blocked their path and abducted them.

All three workers were eventually released.[18] According to a CNN report, Parad was killed along with five other militants in an assault by Philippine marines in Sulu province on Sunday, 21 February 2010.

The abduction of Australian Warren Richard Rodwell (December 2012)

Warren Rodwell, a former Australian soldier who worked as a teacher and travel writer and had previously worked as a teacher in China, moved to the southern Philippines in 2011 to join his Filipino wife in her native town of Ipil in the restive region of Zamboanga Sibugay. On 5 December 2012, gunmen riding motorcycles burst into his home, abducted him, and took him by speedboat to nearby islands where kidnap-for-ransom gangs operated. The abductors identified themselves as members of the ASG.[19]

In December 2011, Rodwell was featured in several proof-of-life videos released by his abductors, including one in which a US$2 million ransom was demanded. In the video, Rodwell looked pale and haggard as he stammered and read slowly from a script. "To my family, please do whatever to raise the two million US dollars they are asking for my release," he said, appearing at points to choke with emotion. The Australian government had sent officials to the area to assist in the investigation and negotiations were under way with the kidnappers. Major-General Noel Coballes, commander of the First Infantry Division of the Philippine Army, said that the video showed Rodwell with a wound on his hand. "He was hit in the hand because he resisted," said Coballes, noting that Rodwell had formerly served in the Australian military.[20] Warren Rodwell was released in the coastal town of Pagadian on 23 March 2013, and was evacuated by helicopter to a nearby military base.[21]

The Australian response

Australian Foreign Minister Bob Carr told the ABC network that no ransom had been paid by his government, but he declined to say that none had been paid by other parties. "The Australian government never pays ransoms," he said. "To do so would leave Australians exposed in all parts of the world to kidnappers who'd be motivated by a desire to get money, and to get it fast, from the Australian government. But I won't comment on arrangements that may have been made by Mr Rodwell's family and Abu Sayyaf, the kidnappers, made through the Philippines anti-kidnapping unit and their police force," he stated. Australian Prime Minister Julia Gillard thanked the Philippine government during a news conference: "I do want to pay tribute to the government of the Philippines and their agencies and personnel who worked so hard to secure Mr Rodwell's release, including particularly those who combat kidnapping in the Philippines for the Philippines government. They have done some remarkable work," she said.[22]

The Philippine response

A spokesman for President Benigno S. Aquino III said that the Philippine government was working to reunite Rodwell with his family as quickly as possible. "Our primary concern was to ascertain that Mr Rodwell would receive immediate medical attention," said deputy presidential spokeswoman Abigail Valte. "Presently, his medical condition is being assessed and, as soon as the doctors give clearance, we hope that he will be reunited with his family."[23]

There were allegations that a ransom of seven million pesos (US$171,990) was paid for Rodwell's release, while a report, quoting Basilan vice-governor al Rasheed Sakalahul, said the payment was just four million pesos. The Philippine government reiterated it would continue observing its "no ransom policy" in handling abduction and kidnapping cases. Ms Valte shrugged off reports that at least four million pesos (US$98,280) was paid in exchange for the release of Rodwell; in a radio interview she said she had no information if there was an exchange of ransom that led to the release of the hostage. "It is up to the security and investigating officials to look into the reported ransom payment," she stated. "The policy of the government remains that we do not pay ransom. Having said that, we have no information nor confirmation on that alleged ransom that was paid. The policy of the government has not changed," she said.[24]

In a recent report, the regional corporate-risk mitigation firm Pacific Strategies and Assessments, based in Manila, said that the ASG had lost some support from regional and international militant organizations because of its low level of "Islamic awareness". "By most accounts, the ASG has abandoned its Islamist terror credentials and public facade of ideology in favor of its traditional and more lucrative criminal activities, such as kidnapping and extortion," the firm's report stated.

The abduction of Jordanian journalist Baker Atyani (June 2012)

Jordanian-born Baker Atyani was the Philippines correspondent for the *al Arabiya* TV network. He and two Filipino crewmembers were abducted in June 2012, while reporting on the predominantly-Muslim island of Mindanao.

In February 2013, militants released the two Filipino crewmembers, who said they had been separated from Atyani on the fifth day of their captivity. The well-known journalist had been taken to a more secure location deep in the Sulu forest in order to increase the prospects for a large ransom. The failure – or refusal – of the ASG to fulfill their commitment (sworn on the Holy Koran) to release the Jordanian journalist triggered fighting between the MNLF and the kidnappers at Sangay village, Patikul, on 3 February 2013.[25]

The MNLF secretary-general emphasized that kidnapping *per se* was a crime against humanity that everyone must condemn. He likewise said that the MNLF leadership had been emphasizing that force was to be used only as a final recourse and, given the ASG's unstoppable program of criminality, it was about time to use the final recourse: although the MNLF believed that war was "inhuman, barbaric, and catastrophic, they now had to wage an all-out war against the ASG".[26] He further claimed that even the US had classified the ASG as terrorists; so, if only to achieve total peace and security for the rest of the Bangsamoro people, the work of the Abu Sayyaf bandits and kidnappers must be terminated.

Respected Islamic cleric and MNLF central committee secretary General Ustadz Ibrahim Murshi told *The Manila Times* that Hatib Ahajan and a certain Asman of the ASG had sworn on the Holy Koran to Ustadz Habier Malik, chief of the MNLF's Asadullah National Task Force (ANTF) that they would release Atyani. Asadullah (which means "the Lion of God") was the name of the task force involved in the MNLF's "Operation Purging for Peace", composed of Bangsamoro forces under both national and state command headquarters located in Lupah Sug. More than one infantry division was engaged in this operation.[27]

The Grand Imam of al Azhar, Sheikh Ahmed al Tayeb, the top religious authority for Sunni Muslims, called upon the kidnappers in a statement released by his office in Cairo to "revert to right and religious principles . . . which stress that kidnapping and terrorism are prohibited", and urged Islamist militants in the Philippines to free Atyani. In a statement to the media, he said that killing and violence in the name of religion were an insult to Islam. "This shameful act of kidnapping, terrorism, and putting the lives of people at risk for a small sum of money contradicts the principles of Islam. It also violates the freedoms guaranteed in all conventions and international norms," he added, calling on the kidnappers to release the journalist without conditions.[28]

The journalist remains in captivity.

List of ASG Terror Abductions

23 April 2000: ASG gunmen raided the Malaysian diving resort of Sipadan, off Borneo, and fled across the sea border to their Jolo Island stronghold with ten western tourists and eleven resort workers.

27 May 2000: The kidnappers issued political demands, including a separate Muslim state, an inquiry into alleged human rights abuses in Sabah, and the restoration of fishing rights. They later demanded a multimillion-dollar cash ransom.

1 July 2000: Filipino television evangelist Wilde Almeda of the Jesus Miracle Crusade (JMC) and twelve of his followers were seized while visiting the Abu Sayyaf headquarters. A German journalist was seized the following day.

9 July 2000: A three-member French television crew was abducted.

27 August 2000: French, South African, and German hostages were freed.

28 August 2000: US Muslim convert Jeffrey Schilling was abducted.

9 September 2000: Finnish, German, and French hostages were freed.

10 September 2000: The ASG raided Pandanan Island near Sipadan and seized three Malaysians.

16 September 2000: Government troops launched a military assault against the ASG base in Jolo. Two kidnapped French journalists escaped during the fighting.

2 October 2000: JMC evangelist Wilde Almeda and twelve "prayer warriors" were released.

25 October 2000: Troops rescued the three Malaysians seized in Pandanan.

12 April 2001: Jeffrey Schilling was rescued, leaving Filipino scuba diving instructor Roland Ullah in the gunmen's hands.

22 May 2001: Suspected ASG gunmen raided the luxurious Pearl Farm beach resort on Samal Island, southern Philippines, killing two resort workers and wounding three others, but no hostages were taken.

28 May 2001: Suspected ASG gunmen raided the Dos Palmas resort off the western Philippines island of Palawan and seized twenty hostages, including an American couple and former *Manila Times* owner Reghis Romero II. President Arroyo ruled out a ransom payment and ordered the military to go after the kidnappers.

30 May 2001: US spokesman Philip Reeker called for the "swift, safe, and unconditional release of all the hostages". An Olympus camera and an ATM card belonging to one the hostages were found on the island of Cagayan de Tawi-Tawi, and pictures of ASG leaders were released to the media by the Philippine armed forces.

31 May 2001: The Philippine military failed to locate the bandits and the hostages, despite search and rescue operations in Jolo, Basilan, and Cagayan de Tawi-Tawi.

1 June 2001: Military troops engaged ASG bandits in Tuburan town in Basilan. ASG spokesman Abu Sabaya threatened to behead two of the hostages.

2 June 2001: The ASG invaded Lamitan City and seized the José

Maria Torres Memorial Hospital and Saint Peter's church. Soldiers surrounded the bandits and engaged them in a day-long firefight. Several hostages, including businessman Reghis Romero, were able to escape. Witnesses said the bandits escaped from Lamitan at around 5:30 p.m., taking four medical personnel from the hospital with them.

3 June 2001: Soldiers recovered the bodies of hostages Sonny Dacquer and Armando Bayona in Barangay Bulanting. They had been beheaded.

4 June 2001: Military officials asked for a state of emergency in Basilan; President Gloria Arroyo turned the request down.

6 June 2001: ASG leader Abu Sabaya told the Radio Mindanao network that US hostage Martin Burnham sustained a gunshot wound to the back during an exchange of gunfire.

August 2002: Six Filipino Jehovah's Witnesses were kidnapped and two of them were beheaded.

17 January 2008: ASG militants raided a convent in Tawi-Tawi and killed a Catholic missionary during a kidnapping attempt.

8 June 2008: ABS-CBN journalist Ces Oreña-Drilon and her TV crew were kidnapped. Ten days later, they were released after their families paid a portion of the ransom.

15 January 2009: Three Red Cross officials – Swiss Andreas Notter, Filipino Mary Jane Lacaba, and Italian Eugenio Vagni – were kidnapped. Notter and Lacaba were released after four months, and Vagni was released six months later on July 12th.

14 April 2009: The ASG executed one of the two hostages they took during a raid on a Christian community in Lamitan City. The body of Cosme Aballes was recovered by marines who were in pursuit of the bandits. Aballes and Ernan Chavez were taken hostage by at least forty ASG, rogue MILF rebels, and kidnap-for-ransom elements in a raid on Sitio Arco in Lamitan City on Good Friday, meant to disrupt the Christian activities during the Lenten season and to extort money. On their way out, the kidnappers shot dead a resident, Jacinto Clemente. Including Chavez, the ASG held seven hostages on Basilan, including three teachers kidnapped in Zamboanga City in January 2009.

18 May 2009: ASG gunmen in Basilan beheaded a sixty-one-year-old man who was abducted from that city about three weeks before.

12 July 2009: Italian Red Cross hostage Eugenio Vagni was released.

14 October 2009: An Irish priest was kidnapped from outside his home near Pagadian City in Mindanao. He was released on 11 November 2009.

9 November 2009: A schoolteacher in Jolo who was captured on October 19th was beheaded by ASG militants.

10 November 2009: ASG members captured several Chinese and Filipino nationals in Basilan.

March 2012: Randelle Talania, a nine-year-old boy, was abducted in the town of Titay.

July 2012: US citizen Gerfa Yeatts Lunsmann, her fourteen-year-old son, and a Filipino nephew were kidnapped in a coastal area of Zamboanga City. Mrs Lunsmann was released in October 2012, the nephew in November 2012, and her son in December 2012. There were conflicting reports as to whether a ransom was paid or the son escaped.

September 2012: Luisa Morrison, a Philippine citizen married to a British national, was abducted in Ipil.

NOTES

1 Major Michael E. Carter, *Islamic Terrorism in Southeast Asia: An Effects-Based US Regional Strategy against Jemaah Islamiyah and Abu Sayyaf*, School of Advanced Military Studies, AY 04–05, United States Army Command and General Staff College, Fort Leavenworth, Kansas, May 2004 (US: BiblioScholar, 2012).
2 Simon Elegant, "The Return of Abu Sayyaf", *Time Asia Magazine*, 30 August 2004.
3 *Ibid*.
4 Abu Sayyaf Group, *Council of Foreign Relations*, 27 May 2009.
5 Carter, *Islamic Terrorism in Southeast Asia*.
6 Chip Johnson, "What Was Schilling Thinking? Oblivious Oakland Man Sets Himself Up", *San Francisco Chronicle*, 14 April 2001.
7 Abu Sayyaf Group, *Council of Foreign Relations*, 27 May 2009.
8 "Prominent Abu Sayyaf Commander Believed Dead", *Institute for Counter-Terrorism* (ICT), 22 June 2002, http://www.ict.org.il/spotlight/det.cfm?id=796.
9 "Abu Sayyaf Muslim Rebels Raped Sipadan Dive Tourist Hostages", *CDNN*, 10 September 2000.
10 "Abu Sayyaf Kidnappings, Bombings and Other Attacks", *GMA News*, 23 August 2007.
11 Abu Sayyaf Group, *Council of Foreign Relations*, 27 May 2009.
12 Johnson, "What Was Schilling Thinking?", *San Francisco Chronicle*, 14 April 2001.
13 "Muslim Rebels Raped Hostages", *CDNN*, 10 September 2000.
14 "US Hostage Freed in Philippines", *CBS News*, 12 April 2001.
15 *Ibid*.
16 Abu Sayyaf Group, *Council of Foreign Relations*, 27 May 2009.
17 "Suspected Abu Accused of Kidnapping Americans Nabbed", *AP*, 19 February 2010.

18 Julie Alipala, "3 Red Cross Kidnap Victims Alive, Safe", *Philippine Daily Inquirer*, 17 January 2009.
19 Floyd Whaley, "Kidnappings Point to Security Breakdown in Southern Philippines", *The New York Times*, 5 January 2012.
20 *Ibid.*
21 Floyd Whaley, "Kidnapped Australian is Freed in Southern Philippines", *The New York Times*, 23 March 2013.
22 *Ibid.*
23 *Ibid.*
24 "Philippines Gov't Persists in 'No Ransom Policy' on Abduction Cases", *Global Times*, 24 March 2013.
25 "ASG Refusal to Release Jordanian TV Journalist Triggered MNLF Action", *The Manila Times*, 10 February 2013.
26 *Ibid.*
27 *Ibid.*
28 "Al Azhar Grand Mufti Urges Abu Sayyaf Captors to Free Jordanian Reporter", *Inquirer Global Nation*, 28 February 2013, http://globalnation.inquirer.net/65889/al-azhar-grand-imam-urges-abu-sayyaf-captors-to-free-jordanian-reporter#ixzz2PyBAeSVQ.

11

Al Qaeda and Terror Abductions in the Maghreb

The region of northwest Africa known as the Maghreb is dominated by the al Qaeda in the Islamic Maghreb (AQIM) organization,[1] previously known as the Salafist Group for Preaching and Combat (GSPC), an Algeria-based Sunni Muslim jihadist group originally formed in 1998 by Hassan Hattab, a former Armed Islamic Group (GIA) regional commander who broke with the GIA in protest over its slaughter of civilians.[2] In September 2003, it was reported that Hattab had been deposed as emir of the GSPC and replaced by Nabil Sahraoui (Sheikh Mustapha Abu Ibrahim), a thirty-nine-year-old former GIA commander.[3] Following the death of Sahraoui in June 2004, Abdelmalek Droukdal (also known as Abu Musab Abdel Wadoud), a university-educated science student well known for his bomb-making abilities, became the new leader of the GSPC.[4] The GSPC had close to thirty thousand members at its height, but the Algerian government's counter-terrorism efforts have reduced the group's ranks to several thousand.

The GSPC declared its allegiance to al Qaeda as early as 2003, although its merger with al Qaeda was officially sanctioned[5] only in a videotape released on 11 September 2006 by bin Laden's deputy, Ayman al Zawahiri.[6] Since then, the AQIM has claimed responsibility for attacks under its new name. The group's original aims included the overthrow of Algeria's secular military government and the establishment of an Islamic caliphate in that country.

The AQIM has become a regional terrorist organization recruiting and operating throughout the Maghreb and beyond, to Europe itself. AQIM's vocal support of al Qaeda and its declaration of solidarity with Islamic extremists in the Palestinian territories, Iraq, Somalia, and

Chechnya indicate its broader intent.[7] "Our general goals are the same goals of al Qaeda, the mother," stated AQIM's leader, Droukdal.[8]

Jihadist groups in North Africa and the Sahel states are increasingly turning to hostage-taking, both for political gain and to fill their war chests with ransoms. The Saudi daily newspaper *Asharq al Awsat* published a letter from AQIM entitled "Call for Help from the Islamic Maghreb" in which AQIM acknowledged that it was suffering from a lack of operatives and, most importantly, that its elements have "an urgent need of cash".[9]

In economic terms, kidnapping has proved highly profitable for AQIM. In this regard, it should be noted that abductions have long been a favored tactic of AQIM (and GSPC before it); most of its past victims tended to be wealthy Algerians kidnapped for money. AQIM has made no secret that the targeting of foreign nationals has become one of its priorities. In Algeria, AQIM targeted US and Russian contractors and the UN compound in Algiers, while western nations have warned their citizens of the risks associated with remaining in the country. AQIM also nearly succeeded in kidnapping two French executives, after which a number of French nationals (mostly women and children) left Algeria to return to safer ground. The goal behind AQIM's strategy is to destroy the tourism industry and dry out foreign investment in the region.[10]

The abductions since 2008 illustrate the increase in AQIM's antiwestern activity. In particular Algeria, Mali, and Mauritania have experienced a rise in attacks on foreign interests and nationals. The abduction cases in 2009 indicate that this threat also applies to other countries in the region.

GSPC and AQIM Abductions (2000–2008)

AQIM has a tradition of self-financing its operations, mostly through kidnappings, racketeering, and smuggling of all kinds. In February 2003, the Algerian GSPC, under the command of Amari Saifi (also known as Abderrazak al Para), kidnapped thirty-two European tourists (including Austrian, Swiss, and German nationals) in the Algerian Sahara. Seventeen of them were freed thanks to a military operation led by Algerian forces, and the remaining fourteen – one hostage had died – were released six months later, after a large ransom (reportedly US$10 million) was allegedly paid by German authorities; this money was used to buy substantial quantities of sophisticated weapons, including surface-to-air missiles, heavy machine guns, mortars, and satellite-navigation equipment. The Algerian security services seized a part of this arsenal in January 2004 and, in the same year, Saifi was captured in Chad and extradited to Algeria, where an Algerian court sentenced him to death.[11]

In 2007, a group of French picnickers was killed. The gunmen were believed to be linked to AQIM, and the incident prompted the organizers of the famous Dakar Rally to cancel the annual trans-Sahara car race.[12] On 22 February 2008, AQIM kidnapped two Austrian citizens in Tunisia. The hostages were reportedly taken to Mali and held there until released after payment of a ransom. At first, AQIM demanded the release of Abderrazak al Para and other of its members imprisoned in Algeria, but then changed their demands to include two Muslims imprisoned on terrorism charges in Austria. The hostages were finally released in October 2008, in return for a ransom payment of US$4 million, paid by Vienna, and the release of several jihadists held in Mauritania, including a veteran fighter named Oussama al Boumerdassi.[13]

On 14 December 2008, two Canadian diplomats – the UN special envoy to Niger, Robert Fowler, and his aide, Louis Guay – mysteriously disappeared while on a field trip. The fate of the two Canadians long remained shrouded in uncertainty. At first, a Nigerian Tuareg rebel group claimed responsibility for their abduction, but this claim was quickly retracted. AQIM later released an online statement[14] in which it claimed responsibility for the abduction of Fowler and Guay, and other Europeans.[15] On 29 April 2009, Fowler and Guay, along with a Swiss and a German, were released by AQIM in exchange for four mujahideen who had been jailed in Mali since February 2008. One of the released terrorists was Algerian al Qaeda member al Boumerdassi, who had fought with the then US-backed mujahideen resistance to the Soviet presence in Afghanistan, staying on until 1992. Two of the other released terrorists were Mauritanian, while the remaining one was either Jordanian or Syrian.[16]

At the heart of the negotiations seeking the release of the hostages were Saif al Islam Gaddafi, son of the Libyan leader Muammar Gaddafi, and a relative of Burkina Faso President Blaise Compaoré, identified as Mauritanian businessman Abdallah Chaffei. In 2008, Saif Gaddafi, who headed the Gaddafi Foundation charity, also mediated in the case of two Austrians held by AQIM in Mali.[17]

Canadian Prime Minister Stephen Harper specifically thanked both Mali and Burkina Faso during a press conference in which he announced the Canadians' release. AQIM declared in an unofficial manner that "four of its members . . . have been delivered to the north of Mali as a result of a major transaction led by the Malian president".[18]

The abductions of 2009

On 4 January 2009, a local criminal gang tried to kidnap a group of four Saudi tourists hunting birds in the desert region of Tillabéri in western Niger. The attack triggered a gunfight in which one Saudi Arabian was murdered by his captors and two other Saudis were wounded. The *Asharq al Awsat* Arabic-language newspaper reported that the brigands wanted to sell the Saudis to Mokhtar Belmokhtar, an elusive al Qaeda leader who operated in the region and was associated with the Algeria-based AQIM.[19]

On 22 April 2009, four Europeans (two Swiss, one German, and a Briton) were kidnapped as they were returning from the Anderamboukane nomad culture festival in the border area between Mali and Niger. Their three-car convoy was ambushed: the first vehicle got away and alerted the security forces, but the second and third cars that were carrying the tourists were captured by Tuareg rebels, and the occupants were later "sold" to jihadists who demanded the release of Jordanian militant leader Abu Qatada (held in Britain since 2005) and threatened to kill Edwin Dyer, a British hostage, if their demands went unmet. The Algerian media reported that the group also demanded US$14 million and the release of twenty of its members held in Mali.[20]

The Swiss and German women were freed in April 2009, along with the two Canadian diplomats who had been abducted in Niger on 14 December 2008. The Swiss man was later released in July 2009.[21] The Briton Edwin Dyer was murdered by his kidnappers and became the first British hostage executed by al Qaeda outside Iraq. Britain's Prime Minister Gordon Brown condemned the killing as "an appalling and barbaric act of terrorism" and said it reinforced Britain's commitment to confront terrorism. "I want those who would use terror against British citizens to know beyond doubt that we and our allies will pursue them relentlessly, and that they will meet the justice they deserve," he vowed.[21]

On 25 June 2009, AQIM claimed responsibility for the killing of an American aid worker in Mauritania's capital city of Nouakchott.[22] The attack was described as a botched kidnapping attempt.[23] The Arabic television channel *al Jazeera* said it had received an audio statement from AQIM, in which the group said thirty-nine-year-old Christopher Ervin Leggett, an American aid worker, was killed for allegedly trying to convert Muslims to Christianity. "Two knights of the Islamic Maghreb succeeded Tuesday morning at 8:00 a.m. to kill the infidel American Christopher Leggett for his Christianizing activities," the group said. Mauritania's interior ministry said it was investigating the death and security forces were doing "all they can to catch the criminals".[24]

On 25 November 2009, Frenchman Pierre Camatte was snatched from a hotel in Ménaka, in the Sahel region of northern Mali, more than 1,500 kilometers from the capital Bamako. In a message delivered in early January 2010, AQIM threatened to kill the French hostage if France and Mali did not meet the group's demand for the release of four militants imprisoned by Mali's authorities. The message included a call to the French public and the Camatte family to pressure French President Nicolas Sarkozy to accept their demands if they wanted the Frenchman to avoid the fate of English hostage, Edwin Dyer.[25] On 23 February 2010, AQIM released Pierre Camatte following the freeing of the four Islamist prisoners by Mali.

Algeria and Mauritania recalled their ambassadors to protest against the prisoner swap. Algerian media said two of the freed men were Algerian, and the Mauritanian government stated that one was Mauritanian.[26] French President Sarkozy said in a statement that he was delighted that Camatte had been freed, thanked Malian President Amadou Toumani Touré for his handling of the crisis, and pledged future French support for the struggle against terrorism.[27]

On 29 November 2009, three Spanish volunteers – Albert Vilalta, aged thirty-five, Alicia Gamez, thirty-five, and Roque Pascual, fifty – were traveling in Mauritania in a convoy delivering humanitarian aid for the Spanish charity Barcelona Acció Solidària when they were kidnapped. AQIM claimed responsibility for the kidnapping, as well as that of Camatte, in an audiotape released on 16 December 2009 by *al Jazeera* television. In the tape, AQIM spokesman Saleh Abu Mohammad said: "Two units of the valiant mujahideen managed to kidnap four Europeans in two distinct operations: the first in Mali, where Frenchman Pierre Camatte was seized on November 25th, and the second in Mauritania, where three Spaniards were held on November 29th. France and Spain will be informed later of the legitimate demands of the mujahideen."[28]

On 12 March 2010, AQIM said in a statement posted on militant websites that it had released a Spanish woman held captive for one hundred days in Mauritania because she voluntarily converted to Islam. AQIM claimed it also took into account health reasons in choosing to free Alicia Gamez. "The Spanish woman converted to Islam voluntarily after the mujahideen exposed her to Islam and its teachings. She took the name of Aicha," the brief message said. The two male Spanish volunteers were still being held captive by AQIM.[29]

On 18 December 2009, an Italian couple was kidnapped in southeastern Mauritania – sixty-five-year-old Nicola Sergio Cicala and his wife, thirty-nine-year-old Philomen Kabouree (originally from Burkina Faso). They were abducted on the road from Aioun in Mauritania to

Kayes in Mali. AQIM claimed responsibility for this kidnapping in two separate messages. The first message appeared on *al Arabiya* television, where a picture of the couple was shown along with an audio message. The second message was posted on the internet, where it clearly stated that the kidnapping was linked to the role that Italy had played in the wars in Afghanistan and Iraq, and because of Italy's support for the "crusade against Islam".[30] AQIM demanded that Mali's government free imprisoned militants before March 1st in exchange for the couple. Shortly before the deadline expired, in a purported audio message posted on the internet, Cicala urged Italian Prime Minister Silvio Berlusconi to intervene.

In April 2010, AQIM freed the couple. Local officials in Mali said that Cicala and Kabouree were picked up by an army patrol in the eastern Gao region. Italy's foreign minister said they were "in the hands of Malian authorities" and were being taken to a "safe place". In Rome, Italian Foreign Minister Franco Frattini said the Italians' release had been "the fruit of intense diplomatic work that led authorities in Mali to take decisive actions to reach this solution".[31]

The abductions of 2010–11

In April 2010, French engineer Michel Germaneau, aged seventy-eight, was kidnapped as he supervised the construction of a school for an aid organization in the north of Niger. He was killed in July 2010 by AQIM, which said it was taking revenge for the deaths of AQIM fighters three days before in a French-Mauritanian raid in Mali.

On 6 September 2010, gunmen kidnapped five French nationals and two Africans (one from Madagascar and one from Togo) in the town of Arlit in northern Niger. The men, who were snatched from their homes in the remote desert, worked for France's state-owned nuclear giant Areva and a subsidiary of the French construction company Vinci.[32]

The attackers entered the town at around 2:00 a.m., made their way through streets patrolled by 350 soldiers, and passed through a gate into a residential area where the foreign employees of the nuclear company lived. Both the gate and each of the houses where the employees lived was guarded by security personnel.[33] Officials said they believed the kidnappers took the hostages to a mountainous area in neighboring Mali.[34]

On 23 September 2010, AQIM claimed responsibility for the kidnapping when AQIM spokesman Saleh Abu Mohammad warned the French government against any sort of "stupidity". "In announcing our claim for this operation, we inform the French government that the mujahideen will later transmit their legitimate demands," said Mohammad on the audiotape. "Despite the high military preparations in the area and the security belt around it, those lions of Islam were able to break in and kidnap five nuclear experts who work for Areva," the message said. "So we claim our responsibility to this blessed operation and we tell the French government that our fighters will deliver their lawful demands to them." The message noted that the Niger region "is one of the world's most important uranium-producing areas" and claimed that France had "stolen the strategic resource for decades". "We want to remind our Muslim brothers and public opinion that the uranium thieves caused the killing of thousands of poor Muslims in the area and abusing them in those mines and exposing them to dangerous radiation from radon gas while denying them any protection or health care," the message continued. "The crusaders' companies who steal our resources and abuse our sons should know that the fighters' goals are lawful and they must leave." The message was posted on Islamist websites that had carried messages from AQIM in the past. On 1 October 2010, the Qatar-based *al Jazeera* television station aired pictures of the seven French and African hostages sitting on the ground with armed men behind them.

Areva's uranium mining operations in Niger are of crucial importance to the local economy, and to France. About half of France's nuclear energy derives from Niger's huge uranium deposits and the French uranium trade accounts for about 75 percent of revenue in Niger, whose per capita annual income is just US$353.[35]

Areva had had ample warning of an al Qaeda attack – two weeks before the kidnapping, a local police commander in northern Niger had faxed a letter to French companies in the area, warning them that al Qaeda seemed to be planning an assault on foreign workers.

President Sarkozy said that France planned to mobilize all of its state agencies to free the captives and considered this a very serious affair. France sent a military intelligence unit to the region, but said it wanted to open communication with the militants in the hope of freeing the five French nationals and two Africans. A source close to the Niger government said that around one hundred French anti-terrorism specialists had arrived in Niger to help hunt for the hostages.

On 25 February 2011, three of the hostages (from France, Madagascar, and Togo) were released. One of the freed hostages, Frenchwoman Françoise Larribe, suffered from cancer and was undergoing chemotherapy treatment shortly before she was abducted.[36] The details of how they were freed were unclear, but a source said that a ransom had been paid, although declined to disclose the amount.

On 25 April 2011, AQIM released a video showing pictures of the four French nuclear workers (Pierre Legrand, Daniel Larribe, Thierry Dol, and Marc Féret), and urged France to pull its troops out of Afghanistan. Accompanying the photos was an audio track that appeared to be a recording of the men reading a prepared statement: "We urge the president of the French republic, Nicolas Sarkozy, to respond positively to al Qaeda's demand he withdraw French troops from Afghanistan, as the French have really no interest in the war in Afghanistan," they said.[37]

On 16 September 2013, a new video was released that appeared to show the French hostages alive and in good health. One of the hostages, sixty-one-year-old Daniel Larribe, said on the video that his life had been endangered by the French military intervention. "I am in good health but threatened with death," Larribe said, adding that he held French authorities responsible for his fate.[38]

On 6 January 2011, two Frenchmen – Antoine de Leocour, an aid worker in Niger, and his friend Vincent Delory, both aged twenty-five – were kidnapped from a restaurant in the Niger capital, Niamey. They were reportedly abducted at gunpoint by four armed men wearing turbans who tried to take them into Mali. The hostages were pursued by Niger's military, with French military help, and were intercepted at the border with Mali. After a firefight, the hostages were found dead. French Defense Minister Alain Juppé said in a statement: "The terrorists were intercepted at the Mali border and several of them were neutralized. After the fighting, the two hostages were found dead." He said that the operation was "coordinated" by French forces based in the region that participated in the firefight at the border.[39]

French military spokesman Thierry Burkhard said that Niger's National Guard and a French surveillance plane pursued the kidnappers into the desert. Reports suggested that the troops mounted an attack some one hundred kilometers from Niamey that resulted in one Nigerian officer being injured. A second attack followed shortly afterwards when soldiers and French commandos intervened to prevent the kidnappers from crossing the Malian border. Three Nigerian soldiers were killed, two French soldiers were injured, and four militants were killed.[40]

An audio message attributed to AQIM was broadcast on the *al Jazeera* television channel.[41] In the message, an AQIM spokesman said: "A group of mujahideen carried out on Friday 7th January a brave operation in the heart of the Niger capital, Niamey, where they broke into the secured diplomatic neighborhood and succeeded in kidnapping two Frenchmen," he said. "Two battles took place between the mujahideen and French-Nigerian forces, resulting in a major failure in the attempt to rescue the hostages." He claimed that two French soldiers were killed and that twenty-five Nigerian officers were injured.[42] French President Sarkozy said he learned with "profound sadness" of the Frenchmen's deaths, and condemned the kidnapping and deaths of the two hostages as "a barbaric and cowardly act".[43]

The In-Amenas Hostage Crisis in Algeria (January 2013)

The four-day hostage crisis at the In-Amenas gas facility in the Sahara reached a bloody conclusion when the Algerian army carried out a final assault on the gas field taken over by Islamist militants, killing most of the kidnappers and raising the total number of hostages killed to at least thirty-seven.[44] In all, 790 workers were on the site when it was seized, including 134 foreigners from twenty-six nations. Algerian Prime Minister Abdelmalek Sellal detailed the timeline of the sequence of events, breaking it down into three episodes:

First, on 16 January 2013, the militants attacked an armored bus carrying foreign workers to the airport at In-Amenas, and two people aboard were killed. "They wanted to take control of this bus and take the foreign workers directly to northern Mali so they could have hostages to negotiate with foreign countries," he said. "But when they opened fire on the bus, there was a strong response from the gendarmes guarding it." After the terrorists failed to capture the bus, they split into two groups: one tried to seize the complex's living quarters, while the other attempted to capture the gas plant itself, a maze of pipes and machinery. They invaded both sections, taking dozens of hostages and booby-trapping the plant by attaching explosives to machinery. At this point, the facility was surrounded by security forces.

Second, late on the night of Wednesday, January 17th, or early on the morning of Thursday, January 18th, the kidnappers attempted a breakout. "They put explosives on the hostages. They wanted to put the hostages in four-wheel-drive vehicles and take them to Mali. A great number of workers were put in the cars; they wanted to use them as human shields," the prime minister said. Government helicopters immobilized the kidnappers' vehicles. Witnesses described an intense army assault, resulting in the deaths of both militant and hostages. "There was a strong response from the army, and three cars exploded," he said. One contained an Algerian militant, whom the prime minister identified as the leader, Mohamed Lamine Boucheneb.

The final operation happened on Saturday, January 20th, Sellal said, when the eleven remaining kidnappers moved into the gas-producing part of the complex – a hazardous area that they had already tried to ignite. "The aim of the terrorists was to explode the gas compound," he said. In this second assault, he said, there were "a great number of hostages" and the terrorists were ordered to kill them all. It was then that army snipers killed the kidnappers.

The target: In-Amenas gas field

The gas facility, located close to the Libyan border, was operated by jointly by the Algerian state oil company Sonatrach, the British firm BP, and the Norwegian firm Statoil. The plant refined 10 percent of Algeria's natural gas production.[45] Sonatrach said that the attackers had evidently mined the facility with the intention of blowing it up, and that the company was working to ensure the safety of the plant. A government official, meanwhile, said that the militants had set fire to the plant's control tower on the Friday night, and that the fire was later extinguished by soldiers and workers. The militants also tried to blow up a pipeline, he claimed, leading officials to worry about the stocks of gas at the plant. "The authorities were afraid they were going to blow up the reserves," said the official, who believed the militants had planned all along to destroy the complex.

The militants: The "Masked Brigade"

Whatever the goal, the message of the militant takeover of the gas complex, in a country that has perhaps the world's toughest record for dealing with terrorists, seemed clear (at least to Algerian officials): the Islamist mini-state in northern Mali, under assault by French and Malian forces, had given a new boost to transnational terrorism.

Some thirty-two multinational Islamists captured the plant; only three Algerians were members of the al Qaeda-affiliated group al Mulathameen ("Masked Brigade"), established by Mokhtar Belmokhtar after his split with AQIM. The militants who attacked the plant said it was in retaliation for French troops sweeping into Mali to stop an advance of Islamist rebels south toward the capital, although they later said they had been planning an attack in Algeria for some time. The militants demanded an end to French military operations against Islamists in northern Mali in return for the safety of the hostages.[46] Another report mentioned a demand for the release of Aafia Siddiqui and Omar Abdel Rahman, both held in American prisons on terrorism-related convictions.[47] Other reports suggested the hostage-takers demanded the release of about one hundred Islamist prisoners held in Algeria.[48] The group that attacked the plant, thought to be based in Gao, Mali, was previously little known and had split off the previous year from AQIM. Indeed, a spokesman for those militants – in a report on a news site that often carried their statements – said that they planned more attacks in Algeria.

Mokhtar Belmokhtar

AQIM originated from Algerian Islamists who fought against their government during a bloody civil conflict in the 1990s. Over the past decade, AQIM has kidnapped dozens of foreigners, including diplomats, aid workers, field doctors, and tourists.

The driving force behind jihadism in the Sahara region was the competition between two leaders of AQIM: Abdelhamid Abu Zeid and Mokhtar Belmokhtar. Until December 2012, both men were emirs of their own *katiba* (brigade) of the AQIM. Although they were both from southern Algeria, they chose to embed themselves in northern Mali, in the immense, ungoverned desert that ranges from feather-soft dunes to flat, rocky plains. And both made tens of millions of dollars by kidnapping French, Canadian, Spanish, Swiss, German, English, and Italian nationals.

Mokhtar Belmokhtar, the warlord who led the attack on the Algerian gas field, was an Algerian in his forties (known in Pentagon circles as "MBM") who split from AQIM to start his own franchise, the "Masked Brigade".[49] Belmokhtar generated millions of dollars for the al Qaeda group through the kidnapping of westerners and the smuggling of tobacco, which earned him one of his nicknames, "Mr Marlboro". But Belmokhtar bridled under authority and, in 2012, was forced out of the organization by his rival.

Belmokhtar was a contrast to his more ruthless colleague Abu Zeid, who beheaded a British national and executed a seventy-eight-year-old Frenchman in retaliation for an attempted raid to save the hostage in 2010 that killed six militants. Although Belmokhtar's hostages were forced to endure months of privation and to live with the constant threat of execution, he has not yet executed a captive – with the notable exception of the 2011 kidnapping of two French nationals from a bar in the capital of Niger, both of whom were killed when the French military tried to rescue them. It is still unclear if the two died from friendly fire or were executed by their captors. Belmokhtar usually preferred to trade his hostages for money – a strategy which allowed him to build one of al Qaeda's best-financed cells and may also explain how he was able to create the "Masked Brigade" and strike out on his own inside Algeria.

In targeting the Algerian gas facility, Belmokhtar attained the triple achievements of capturing an important symbol of the energy sector that dominates Algeria's economy and political system, defying an Algiers regime infamous for its brutality in dealing with Islamist militants, and claiming scores of foreign lives in defense of the jihad in Mali.[50] Belmokhtar also provoked collateral damage: deadly counterattacks by Algerian forces to end the siege sparked criticism in some foreign capitals suggesting that Algiers made the killing of insurgents a bigger priority than saving hostages' lives.[51] Questions also arose[52] about how a supposedly high-security Algerian installation was so easily overrun by about forty intruders.[53]

The Algerian response

At a news conference in Algiers, Prime Minister Sellal offered an unapologetic defense of the country's tough actions to end the hostage crisis, saying that the militants who had carried out the kidnappings intended to kill all their captives and that, by attacking, the army saved many from death.[54] Sellal portrayed the military's deadly assaults on the Islamist militants who had stormed and occupied an internationally-run gas-producing complex in remote eastern Algeria as a matter of national character and pride. "The whole world has understood that the reaction was courageous," he claimed, calling the abductions an attack "on the stability of Algeria". "Algerians are not people who sell themselves out," he said. "When the security of the country is at stake, there is no possible discussion." This was the Algerian government's first detailed public explanation of its actions during the siege.

Sellal said that the thirty-seven foreign workers killed during the episode came from eight countries, and that five captives remained unaccounted for. It was unclear how many had died at the hands of the kidnappers or the Algerian army. The prime minister also said that twenty-nine kidnappers had been killed, including their leader, and that three had been captured alive. The militants were from Egypt, Mali, Niger, Mauritania, Tunisia, and Canada. Sellal said the group began the plot in Mali and entered Algeria through Libya, close to the site.

The response of the United States

The United States said that three Americans were among the dead and seven had survived. The US did not publicly criticize Algeria, which it regarded as an ally in the fight to contain jihadist groups in Africa, but US law-enforcement and military officials said that they almost certainly would have handled such a crisis differently.

Firstly, the US would have engaged in longer discussions with the captors to identify the leaders and buy time, the officials said. In the meantime, the Pentagon, CIA, and possibly allied security services could have moved surveillance drones, high-altitude reconnaissance aircraft, and electronic eavesdropping equipment into position to help identify the locations of the hostages and the assailants. "It would have been a precision approach, as opposed to a sledgehammer approach," said Lieutenant-General Frank Kearney, a retired deputy commander of the US military's Special Operations Command. American officials said they had offered sophisticated surveillance assistance that could have minimized casualties, both before and during the military operation to retake the seized gas field complex in the Algerian desert. At least some of the assistance was accepted, they said, but there were still questions about whether Algeria had taken all available steps to avert such a bloody outcome. But others declined to second-guess the Algerians, saying events had unfolded so rapidly that the government might have felt it had no choice but to kill the kidnappers, even if hostages died in the process. A senior American official said the Algerians had allowed an unarmed American surveillance drone to fly over the gas field, but it was unclear what role, if any, it had played in the Algerian army's assault that day. US officials said they had not been told of the strike in advance.

France

French officials publicly supported Algeria's actions, in part because France needed to use Algerian airspace for its military intervention in Mali and wanted Algeria to work harder to seal its borders with Mali. "There isn't a military unit that would have done better, given the strategic conditions, the place where this unfolded, the number of assailants, and the number of hostages," said Christian Prouteau, who was chief of security under President François Mitterrand. "I challenge any western country confronting this kind of operation to do better."

United Kingdom

British Defense Minister Philip Hammond called the loss of life "appalling and unacceptable" after reports that up to seven hostages were killed in the final hours of the hostage crisis, and said that the leaders of the attack would be tracked down. Britain's Foreign Secretary William Hague said that five Britons and one British resident had died in the final rescue attempt or were unaccounted for, and stated that police forces were fanning out across Britain, visiting each of the families involved.

The Algerian government was relatively silent after the start of the crisis, releasing few details. It faced withering international criticism for rushing ahead with its first assault on the militants while those governments whose citizens were trapped inside the plant pleaded for more time, fearing that rescue attempts might lead to workers dying. The Algerians responded by saying they had a better understanding of how to handle militants, after fighting Islamist insurgents for years.

Conclusions

Algeria's authoritarian government is seen by France and other western countries as a crucial intermediary in dealing with Islamist militants in northern Africa. In the last decade, the Algerians have made a virtue out of keeping a lid on the Islamic militants, pushing them toward Mali in a strategy of modified containment and ruthlessly stamping them out when they attempt an attack in the Algerian interior. So far, these tactics have worked and Algeria's extensive oil and gas fields, which are essential sources of revenue, have been protected. That relative success has allowed Algeria to take a hands-off approach to the Islamist conquest of northern Mali, even as western governments pleaded with it to become more directly involved in confronting militants who cross the hazy border between the two countries.

The terrorists came with a precise plan: to kidnap foreigners and destroy the gas plant.[55] If the terrorists were shooting hostages, or at least putting explosives around their necks, and their intent was to sabotage the plant, this might have been a suicide mission to blow up the plant, not to negotiate. According to Mansouria Mokhefi,[56] from the start of the siege, the Algerians were bound to respond with force; the question was, how bloody would the outcome be? "Everyone knows the Algerians do not negotiate," she said, and surely the attackers knew this as well. After all, she states, the foundation of the Algerian government is its long-standing defeat of Islamist militancy and its restoration of a "certain peace" to the country after the civil war during the 1990s when tens of thousands died. "The legitimacy of this government in Algeria is its fight against terrorism and the security of the country." Criticizing the Algerians for their harsh tactics, as the British and Japanese have done, simply shows "a deep lack of knowledge about this regime, of its functioning", she claims.

Algeria has shown reluctance to become too involved in a broad military campaign whose success could be very risky for them – international action against the Islamist takeover in northern Mali could push the militants back into southern Algeria, from where they started. That result would undo the years of bloody struggle by Algeria's military forces that have largely succeeded in pushing the jihadists outside their borders. The Algerians also have little patience with what they see as western naïveté about the "Arab Spring". But now Algeria may have to rethink its approach, analysts suggest.

If the eventual outcome the assault on the gas plant represented a relative setback for Algeria, it could also be viewed as a victory for the Islamists who achieved two of their perennial goals: killing large numbers of westerners and disrupting numerous enemy states – a list that includes Algeria.

Criminal and Terrorist Cooperation in Abductions

The weak and ineffective control of the Sahelian states over their territories has played a major role in the development of the current situation. Kidnappings have taken place in Tunisia, Mali, Niger, and Mauritania, usually by local criminal gangs; hostages have then been moved to northern Mali, where a complex political and security situation, pitting local Tuareg tribes against the central government, has allowed various terrorist groups to establish their own bases and training grounds there.

There are loose agreements between AQIM and a multiplicity of groups operating in the Sahel area.[57] The most renowned of these alliances is with the al Mulathameen group, headed by Belmokhtar who had several disagreements with AQIM leader Abdelmalek Droukdal and subsequently acted in a semi-independent fashion.[58] This uneasy collaboration was behind the kidnapping of three Spanish aid workers at the hands of the "Masked Brigade".[59]

The other main group in the area is the Tariq ibn Ziyad Brigade (TIZB), led by Yahia Abu Amar Abid Hammadou (also known as Abdelhamid Abu Zeid) who created the group in AQIM's fifth zone of operations (northeastern Algeria) in 2003, and subsequently moved to the Sahel area. Abu Zeid, who was allegedly responsible for the execution of British hostage Edwin Dyer, is also the leader of the Talaia al Salafiya, Nasr Aflou, and al Muhajiroun groups. The TIZB kidnapped French national Pierre Camatte, in addition to an Italian couple who were held by a TIZB lieutenant, Abu Yahya Amane. Abu Zeid may have tried to exploit these abductions to mark his own territory in the Sahel region and to gain operational independence from the two other groups in the area.

Summary

Statistics kept by regional security services show that 115 people, mostly businessmen, were abducted in the region by Islamist groups in 2007, with billions of dinars paid in ransoms.[60] It seems that AQIM is following the modus operandi of al Qaeda in Iraq: from having imported suicide bombings to Algeria (mostly since the 11 April 2007 attacks), then recruiting teenagers, AQIM is now kidnapping foreign nationals.[61]

AQIM has claimed responsibility for most of the kidnappings across the region in recent years. In most cases, the jihadists make political, as well as financial, demands. The scope of abductions since 2008 illustrates AQIM's extended geographical reach (to Tunisia, Algeria, Mali, and Niger). Whether the AQIM presence is direct or indirect, it continues to pose significant operational implications.

The rate of kidnappings has risen consistently since December 2008, and there are several reasons for this:

- AQIM has intensified its presence in Mauritania, Algeria, Mali, Niger, and the whole Sahel region.
- The security services in Mauritania, Mali, and Niger have neither the equipment nor the ability to effectively fight AQIM and other insurgents, and the liberation of hostages by military means is extremely difficult to achieve.
- Most ransoms are paid, although governments rarely admit this is so.
- The "Arab Spring", the fall of the Gaddafi regime, and the chaotic environment in Libya turned that state into a new safe haven for Islamic terror organizations. The attack against the In-Amenas facility was planned and launched from Libyan territory.

AQIM's growing presence in the Sahel region and the increasing number of abductions of European tourists in Mauritania, Niger, Tunisia, and Mali show that a profitable kidnapping industry has led to an increase in terrorism activity in this region. AQIM's activities were previously based along Algeria's Mediterranean coast, but security crackdowns by the Algerian military forced the group into the largely-ungoverned Sahara desert area of Mali along Algeria's northern border. Owing to the weakness of these states and their ineffective control of the area, AQIM militants are free to move across borders and to establish their bases in the region. This situation enables AQIM to combine its ideological goals with a series of tactical advantages and to rely upon the local communities of the Sahara for sanctuary.

AQIM's flexible structure in the region has led to a win-win situation for the group, where a profitable kidnapping network benefits local criminal groups, local AQIM-affiliated groups, and the AQIM leadership. In this context, local criminals carry out abductions and then sell the hostages to AQIM-affiliated groups for a profit; however, the terrorist groups earn the highest profits, as they bear the highest risk, while the rewards are enormous if they can extort ransom payments from European governments fearful that the failure of negotiations could lead to the death of hostages. This lucrative business also profits local criminal gangs that have become almost natural allies of AQIM in the region.[62]

The US and other western countries have warned that, unless the governments of the region join forces, al Qaeda could turn the Sahara desert into an inter-state safe haven and use it as a base for launching large-scale attacks. Fearing these groups could become too powerful in such vast desert zones where governments hold little sway, western nations, led by France and the US, have stepped up their involvement and improved coordination in the region. US government representatives met French, British, and European Union officials in Paris on 10 September 2010, to review efforts to address the security threat posed by terrorism in Africa's Sahel and Maghreb regions.[63]

In April 2010, four Sahara desert nations (Algeria, Mali, Mauritania, and Niger) opened a new joint military headquarters, based in Tamanrasset in southern Algeria, to coordinate their efforts against AQIM. These countries hope to strengthen their intelligence cooperation and plan to move toward joint military operations against terrorism, kidnapping, and the trafficking of drugs and weapons.

The terrorist threat in the Sahel region has become one of France's biggest foreign policy preoccupations over the past years. President Sarkozy spoke of the country being "at war" in the region and made clear that France's determination to fight terrorism remains intact. In July 2010, France declared war on al Qaeda and matched its fighting words with attacks on AQIM camps in Mali (July 2010) and Niger (January 2011), after the terror network killed a French aid worker it had abducted in April 2010. "We are at war with al Qaeda," Prime Minister François Fillon said a day after President Sarkozy announced the death of seventy-eight-year-old hostage Michel Germaneau.[64] Both the declaration and the attacks marked a shift in strategy for France, usually discrete about its behind-the-scenes battle against terrorism.

The January 2011 AQIM kidnapping represented a significant widening of its area of operation. Previous kidnappings had occurred in Niger's northern desert, hundreds of kilometers from Niamey, and the capital had been considered relatively safe for westerners. The raids in Mali and Niger could be considered as the first steps in a new strategy of direct French involvement in military operations against the AQIM infrastructure in the region, implemented in 2013 in a large-scale military operation in Mali.

The AQIM attack on the In-Amenas gas field was the largest and most sophisticated hostage-taking operation in the region, and could be a source of inspiration for future attacks. AQIM attacks on foreigners can be expected to grow as western companies increase investment in oil and gas exploration in the region. As long as the European states continue paying ransom money, AQIM and its allies in the Sahel region will continue with their campaign of kidnappings. In 2009, Algerian President Abdelaziz Bouteflika pleaded before the United Nations General Assembly for a ban on paying ransoms to kidnappers, which he said had reached "worrying proportions".[65] In 2013, Algeria followed its policy of "no compromise" with terrorists and conducted a rescue operation that inflicted a high death toll upon the hostages.

Recommendations

Only a comprehensive international campaign can lead to the long-term reduction of kidnappings in the Sahel region and the defeat of the AQIM. Such a campaign should include:

- Military operations against the AQIM infrastructure in the region (like the operation in Mali in 2013).
- Economic and military support to the local "weak" states (Mauritania, Niger, and Mali).
- A strategy of "no surrender" to the demands of terrorists.

Notes

1 This article was published first on the Institute for Counter-Terrorism (ICT) website.
2 "Al Qaeda Organization in the Maghreb", *Wikipedia*.
3 "Algerian Group Backs al Qaeda", *BBC News*, 23 October 2003, http://news.bbc.co.uk/2/hi/africa/3207363.stm.
4 "Al Qaeda Organization in the Maghreb", *Wikipedia*.
5 "Merger with Al Qaeda Deepens Threat from Algerian Radicals", *Christian Science Monitor*, 3 October 2006, http://www.csmonitor.com/2006/1003/p05s01-woaf.htm.
6 "Al Qaida Joins Algerians Against France", *AP*, 14 September 2006.
7 "Al Qaeda: The Next Goal Is to Liberate Spain from the Infidels", *Global*

Terror Alert, 11 October 2007, http://www.globalterroralert.com/pdf/0107/gspcwadoud0107.pdf.
8 "Interview with Abu Musab Abdul Wadoud", *The New York Times*, July 2008.
9 "Call For Help From the Islamic Maghreb", *Asharq al Awsat*, March 2008.
10 Olivier Guitta, "AQIM New Kidnappings Strategy", *Middle East Times*, 23 March 2008.
11 "Jihadist Kidnappers Plague North Africa, Algeria", *UPI*, 4 January 2009.
12 *Ibid*.
13 *Ibid*.
14 "AQIM Abduct UN Representatives and European Tourists", *Jihadica*, 18 February 2009, http://www.jihadica.com/wp-content/uploads/2009/02/02-18-09-aqim-abduction-un-representatives-and-european-tourists.pdf.
15 Hana Rogan, "New AQIM Abduction Cases", *Jihadica*, 24 February 2009.
16 "Niger Kidnapping: Mujahedeen Fighters Released in Exchange for Diplomats", *Niger Watch*, 29 April 2009.
17 *Ibid*.
18 *Ibid*.
19 "Jihadist Kidnappers Plague North Africa, Algeria", *UPI*, 4 January 2009.
20 Rogan, "New AQIM Abduction", *Jihadica*, 24 February 2009.
21 "Qaeda Branch Steps Up Raids in North Africa", *The New York Times*, 9 July 2009, http://www.nytimes.com/2009/07/10/world/africa/10terror.html?scp=1&sq=al%20qaeda%20north%20africa&st=cse.
22 "Al Qaeda Claims Slaying of US Aid Worker", *CBS News*, 25 June 2009.
23 "Qaeda Branch Steps Up Raids", *New York Times*, 9 July 2009.
24 "Al Qaeda Claims to have Killed American Aid Worker in Mauritania", *al Jazeera*, 25 June 2009.
25 *Radio France Internationale*, (RFI), 11 January 2010.
26 "Al Qaeda Released Frenchman in Prisoners Swap", *Alert Net*, 23 February 2010.
27 *Ibid*.
28 Mark Tran, "Three Spanish Aid Workers Kidnapped in Mauritania", *The Guardian*, 30 November 2009.
29 "Spanish Hostage Converted to Islam", *AP*, 12 March 2010.
30 Dario Cristiani and Riccardo Fabiani, "AQIM Funds Terrorist Operations with Thriving Sahel-based Kidnapping Industry", *Terrorism Monitor*, Volume 8, Issue 4, 28 January 2009.
31 "Al Qaeda Frees Two Italian Hostages in Mali", *AFP*, 16 April 2010.
32 Vivienne Walt, "Kidnappings Escalate France's Desert War on Al Qaeda", *Time Magazine*, 22 September 2010.
33 Rukmini Callimachi, "Niger Kidnappings Show Al Qaeda Group Getting Bolder", *Christian Science Monitor*, 23 September 2010.

34 *Ibid.*
35 Walt, "Kidnappings Escalate", *Time*, 22 September 2010.
36 "Niger: French, Malagasy, Togolese Hostages Freed", *All Africa*, 25 February 2011.
37 "Al Qaeda Releases Video of French Hostages", *al Jazeera*, 27 April 2011.
38 Robbie Corey-Boulet, "Website Says Video Shows 7 Hostages are Alive", *AP*, 16 September 2013, http://abcnews.go.com/International/wireStory/website-video-shows-hostages-alive-20272430.
39 "Two French Hostages in Niger Killed in Rescue", *BBC News*, 8 January 2011.
40 Ruadhan MacCormaic, "French Hostages Killed in Niger After Abduction", *The Irish Times*, 10 January 2011.
41 "Al Qaeda Claims Responsibility for Niger Kidnappings", *BBC News*, 13 January 2011.
42 Angela Donald, "TV Report: Al Qaeda Arm Claims Responsibility for Taking 2 Frenchmen Hostages in Niger", *Los Angeles Times*, 13 January 2011.
43 "Two French Hostages in Niger Killed in Rescue", *BBC News*, 8 January 2011.
44 Adam Nossiter, "Hostages Dead in Bloody Climax to Siege in Algeria", *The New York Times*, 19 January 2013.
45 "In-Amenas: Timeline of Four-day Siege in Algeria", *The Guardian*, 25 January 2013, http://www.guardian.co.uk/world/2013/jan/25/in-amenas-timeline-siege-algeria.
46 "Foreigners Seized After Deadly Algeria Attack", *al Jazeera*, 16 January 2013, http://www.aljazeera.com/news/africa/2013/01/2013116154848726750.html.
47 "Algeria Hostage Deal: Kidnappers Offer to Swap US Hostages for Jailed Militants", *ANI*, reported by *Reuters* (via *The Huffington Post*), 18 January 2013.
48 "Foreigners Held Hostage by Terrorists in Algeria", *BBC News*, 16 January 2013, http://www.bbc.co.uk/news/world-africa-21042659.
49 Rukmini Callimachi, "Algeria Terror Leader Preferred Money to Death", *AP*, 20 January 2013.
50 Bruce Crumley, "Algeria's Hostage Crises: Did the Jihadists have Inside Help?", *Time Magazine*, 21 January 2013.
51 "US, UK Defense Chiefs Bemoan Hostage Deaths in Algeria", *ABC News*, 19 January 2013, http://abcnews.go.com/International/wireStory/defense-chiefs-bemoan-hostage-deaths-algeria-18257710.
52 "Algeria Hostage Crisis", *CNN*, 21 January 2013, http://edition.cnn.com/2013/01/21/world/africa/algeria-hostage-crisis/index.html.
53 Crumley, "Algeria's Hostage Crises", *Time*, 21 January 2013.
54 Adam Nossiter and Eric Schmitt, "Algeria Defends Tough Response to Hostage Crises as Toll Rises", *The New York Times*, 21 January 2013.

55 According to Hamid Guemache, a journalist at the online news site *TSA-Tout sur l'Algérie*.
56 Mansouria Mokhefi, a professor who heads the Middle East and Maghreb program at the French Institute for International Relations in Paris.
57 Cristiani and Fabiani, "AQIM Funds Terrorist Operations", *Terrorism Monitor*, 28 January 2009.
58 *al Watan*, 1 August 2007.
59 *AFP*, 11 January 2010.
60 "Jihadist Kidnappers Plague North Africa", *UPI*, 4 January 2009.
61 Olivier Guitta, "AQIM New Kidnappings Strategy", *Middle East Times*, 23 March 2008.
62 Cristiani and Fabiani, "AQIM Funds Terrorist Operations", *Terrorism Monitor*, 28 January 2009.
63 "US Franco-EU Discuss Sahel Security Issues", *US Embassy London*, 30 September 2009 (via Wikileaks).
64 "France Declares War Against Al Qaeda", *CBS News*, 27 July 2010.
65 "Kidnapping is Lucrative for Al Qaeda in North Africa", *AFP*, Dakar, 1 December 2009.

12

Terror Abductions in the Horn of Africa

Terror Abductions in Somalia

The Federal Republic of Somalia has been in a state of lawlessness for the past two decades after plunging into a bloody civil war with the 1991 ouster of President Mohammed Siad Barre. Abductions in Somalia are fairly common – usually of Somalis, sometimes of foreigners, and, increasingly, the kidnap-for-ransom of the crews of coastal vessels, carried out mainly by Somali pirates in the Gulf of Aden and Indian Ocean. Islamic terror organizations are also involved, directly and indirectly, in the abduction of foreign citizens from Somalia and across its borders.

Somali gunmen have attacked westerners just across the border with Kenya on several occasions since 2008:

- Two Western nuns were kidnapped in November 2008.
- Three aid workers were kidnapped by armed Somali men in a raid on the Kenyan border town of Mandera in July 2009.
- Three cases of the abduction of foreigners from Kenya occurred in 2011.

Most foreigners kidnapped in Somalia in the past have been released unharmed after ransom payments were made. One government minister and a number of senior officials have been killed since Islamist extremists launched an assault on the western-backed government in May 2009.

French security advisors abducted in Somalia (July 2009)
On 14 July 2009, two French security advisors were kidnapped in

Mogadishu, Somalia's capital. The French foreign ministry said that the two advisors were in Mogadishu on an official mission – they had been invited to train Somali President Sharif Sheikh Ahmed's bodyguards.

The abduction took place in a government-held area of Mogadishu. Gunmen wearing police uniforms entered the Sahafi Hotel where the two were staying, which often accommodated foreign journalists and Somali government ministers, and took them away. The hostages were delivered to two separate hard-line militant groups in order to resolve a dispute between the Islamist factions over who would hold them.[1] Abdiqadir Odweyne, a police officer in Mogadishu, said: "The higher-ranking French official was taken by al Shabaab, and the second hostage was held by the Hizb al Islam group, which is led by Sheikh Hassan Dahir Aweys, a Somali warlord who is wanted as a terrorist by the United States." Al Shabaab and its allies had been trying to topple the fragile interim government, led by moderate Islamist President Ahmed, and the kidnappings came two days after Somali government troops and African Union peacekeepers forced Islamist militants from positions around the presidential palace.

On 9 September 2009, the al Shabaab rebels issued a set of demands to the French government asking for an immediate end to all political and military support for the "apostate government of Somalia" and the withdrawal of French personnel and advisors from the country. Bernard Kouchner, France's foreign minister at the time, rejected the demands and pledged support for the troubled government in Mogadishu.[2]

One of the French hostages, Marc Aubriere, was held by the Hizb al Islam group, but escaped on 26 August 2010 and returned to France. He had walked for five hours until he reached the presidential palace in Mogadishu, and denied rumors that he had killed three militants while fleeing. France said that no money was paid for his release. French government spokesman Eric Chevalier said: "France did not pay a ransom. This is very clear. He succeeded in escaping his kidnappers, and then getting to safety."[3] The second hostage, Denis Allex, remained in captivity.

On 6 June 2010, al Shabaab released a video message from Allex, showing him clothed in an orange outfit and surrounded by armed men as he read a statement in French in which he repeated the group's demands and stated that the group would issue a list of names of prisoners it wanted released. The statement claimed the defeat of President Nicolas Sarkozy's party in French regional elections showed that France opposed his policies. "We ask the French people to do everything for my liberation . . . you can imagine my state of mind . . . I miss my family a lot and hope to see them as soon as possible," Allex said, adding that he had not been mistreated. "Even though they have not and they are not physically abusing me, it is severely affecting my mental and psychological health. The Shabaab movement made its demands to the government without any response, and it is me who is paying the price by remaining in their hands as a hostage for a long time," he concluded.[4] The militant group accused Allex of gathering intelligence for the French government, which it alleged was working in support of foreign "forces of the crusade" – an apparent reference to the presence in Somalia of African Union peacekeeping forces, comprising some five thousand troops from Uganda and Burundi.

In December 2010, French authorities received new evidence that Allex was still alive after being held hostage for nearly eighteen months.[5] An unnamed source in France's international intelligence agency, the Direction Générale de la Sécurité Extérieure (DGSE), said the service had received from the kidnappers "a reply to a personal question" to which Allex was able to respond, proving he was still alive. "No detail was given by his captors on the state of his health, nor on his location or the conditions in which he is being held," the source added. A spokesman for the DGSE said it was in negotiations with the hostage-takers that were "rather hard".[6]

In January 2011, in an audiotape aired by the *al Jazeera* television channel, Osama bin Laden warned French President Sarkozy that if France did not comply with al Qaeda's demands and withdraw its troops from Afghanistan, French hostages held by al Qaeda would be killed – specifically mentioning a certain French hostage held in Somalia.[7] According to the French media, President Sarkozy made it clear that he would not agree to the demands of al Qaeda.

In June 2010, France's Foreign Minister Bernard Kouchner said that Allex may have been held in the autonomous Puntland region of northern Somalia.[8] In 2011, a local source said that the French hostage was being held in Kismayo, the third largest city in Somalia, which was under the firm control of al Shabaab and Islamist fighters. Allex appeared in a final video in October 2012, looking gaunt and calling on the French president to work for his release.

The French rescue operation (January 2013)

On 13 January 2013, a French commando unit tried to rescue Denis Allex from captivity. One French soldier was killed during the failed bid to free the French hostage. The French defense minister said the raid in Bulo Marer, about 110 kilometers south of the Somali capital, Mogadishu, was sparked by the "intransigence of the terrorists who have refused to negotiate for three-and-a-half years and were holding Denis Allex in inhuman conditions". A Somali government official in Bulo Marer also confirmed the raid in which about seventeen militants were reportedly killed. The subsequent al Shabaab statement said "the helicopters attacked a house . . . upon the assumption that Denis Allex was being held at that location, but, owing to a fatal intelligence blunder, the rescue mission turned disastrously wrong. Several French soldiers were killed in the battle and many more were injured before they fled from the scene of battle, leaving behind some military paraphernalia and even one of their comrades on the ground." A spokesman for al Shabaab told *al Jazeera* in an exclusive interview that French troops attacked a house in Bulo Marer, but it was al Shabaab fighters who pushed them back. "When the [French] soldiers could not get anywhere, they used helicopters to bomb indiscriminately," said Ali Mahmoud Rage, who added that the French were unable to successfully achieve their mission. "[The French] also killed more than ten civilians, including women, men, and the elderly," he said. "They also failed to capture the French soldier, and he is still in our custody."

A few days later, al Shabaab announced that Allex was to be killed after the group had "reached a unanimous decision". On Thursday, 17 January 2013, al Shabaab announced that Allex had indeed been executed. "16:30 GMT, Wednesday, 16 January, 2013. Dennis Allex is executed," al Shabaab said on its official Twitter account.[9] François Hollande, the French president, expressed his condolences to the dead soldier's family. "This operation confirms France's determination not to give in to the blackmail of terrorists," he said.

Summary

France is at the forefront of the fight against terrorism in the Horn of Africa. It has had a long history of struggle with various forms of terrorism, and over the past decade has achieved particular success against those Algerian Islamic terrorist groups with close links to al Qaeda – the al Jamaah al Islamiyah al Musallaha ("Armed Islamic Group" [GIA]) and the al Jamaah as Salafiyyah lid Dawah wal-Qital ("Salafist Group for Preaching and Combat" [GSPC]), later known as al Qaeda in the Islamic Maghreb (AQIM).

President Sarkozy preferred a muscular response to terrorism. The French declaration of war against al Qaeda following the AQIM's murder of a French hostage and their raids in Mali (July 2010) and Niger (January 2011) can be considered as the first step in a new strategy that includes a readiness to conduct rescue operations. On the other hand, France maintained the option of indirect negotiations with the terrorists in case there was no military option to release the French hostages. President Hollande later followed the same policy when he approved the rescue operation in Somalia and, at the same time, a large-scale counter-terrorist operation in Mali.

The Abduction of Foreign Nationals from Kenya

The Republic of Kenya has suffered several incidents of the abduction of foreign nationals from its territory, perpetrated mainly by terror organizations based within neighboring states such as Sudan and Somalia; these groups conduct their operations into Kenya from across its borders.

British woman abducted in Kenya (September 2011)

On 10 September 2011, armed men killed a British man, David Tebbutt, and kidnapped his wife Judith from a beach resort in northern Kenya near the border with Somalia.

The kidnapping

A British diplomat in Nairobi said that the attackers broke into the couple's accommodation at the Kiwayu Safari Village resort, consisting of eighteen luxury cottages spread along a private beach, about fifty kilometers north of the island resort of Lamu. The couple was attacked minutes after midnight. Police Commissioner Mathew Iteere said they were the only guests at the resort.[10] The kidnappers murdered the husband, abducted his wife, fifty-six-year-old Judith Tebbutt, from the beachside cottage, and escaped in a speedboat.[11]

Kenyan detectives arrested a hotel worker, Ali Babitu Kololo, who claimed that the gang forced him to lead them to the tourists and held him captive at gunpoint for several hours. Kololo said the kidnappers, believed to be al Shabaab militants from Somalia, let him go when they entered the couple's cottage. A police source said: "They apparently knew he had worked at the hotel, and waited until dark before forcing him to lead them into the grounds."[12] On 15 September 2011, Kenyan police arrested a second man over the kidnapping, suspected of being an associate of the first suspect. Both men were questioned in custody and apparently admitted to helping the raiders under duress after they themselves had been held at gunpoint.[13]

Kenyan Western District Commissioner Stephen Ikua said that a Kenyan national, Famau Kahale, was identified as the leader of the Somali group that abducted the British tourist. "He defected to the other side of Somalia in 2006 and joined the former Somalia Islamic Courts, and later al Shabaab. He is now a ringleader of a small group of pirates," said Ikua, adding that the suspect had been sending threatening messages to government officials. "He has been a fugitive for close to seven years, and has been writing messages and calling to threaten our officers. We have been looking for him. It is just a matter of time before we apprehend him," he said, and claimed the suspect, who lived in the Lamu East constituency, was holed up in southern Somalia's port town of Kismayu: "He was part of pirates who hijacked a fishing vessel and held some Indian sailors hostage last year. We tried to arrest him, but he fled to Somalia and has remained there."[14]

No group claimed responsibility, but the way in which the attack occurred and its proximity to the border with Somalia pointed to the involvement of Somali bandits or Islamist terrorists. A Kenyan police source said that Mrs Tebbutt was probably being held in Somalia: "We suspect they were taken by al Shabaab – that is why the search is concentrated at the Somalia border." The attack may have been timed to mark the tenth anniversary of the 9/11 attacks and a ransom demand was expected to be received from al Shabaab.[15]

The response of al Qaeda-affiliated organizations

Sheikh Abdul Rahman Dehere, one of the leaders of the Somali-based Islamist insurgent group Muaskar Ras Kamboni ("Ras Kamboni Brigade"), claimed that Judith Tebbutt was seized in response to an attack by a US drone on one of its weapons stores at Kismayo, about 520 kilometers southwest of Mogadishu. In a telephone call to a Nairobi-based Somali journalist who had built links with al Shabaab during the previous kidnapping of Britons Paul and Rachel Chandler, he said: "We do not wish to harm her; we would not kill an innocent woman . . . but any further attack of force, we will kill the lady," and added: "The lady is not feeling well. She is not talking. She is finding it hard to speak. Her health is good, but she is traumatized," while threatening to parade the terrified hostage as a trophy at a press conference.[16]

The Ras Kamboni Brigade was the largest and the best-armed of the four Islamist factions that formed the Hizb al Islam ("Islamic Party") coalition in early 2009. Hizb al Islam subsequently forged an alliance with al Qaeda-linked al Shabaab militants to oppose the UN-backed transitional federal government in the region. But the Hizb al Islam/al Shabaab alliance began to unravel in October 2009, after the two groups clashed over control of the southern port of Kismayo when Hizb al Islam forces, led by Ahmed Madobe, were forced to leave the city. Since that time, Madobe's determination to challenge al Shabaab for regional dominance has intensified.[17] After Ras Kamboni's conservative Islamist leader Hassan Turki defected to al Shabaab in February 2010, Madobe replaced him as the leader of the group and declared that the al Shabaab group was Somalia's greatest enemy.

Separately, an al Shabaab radio broadcast on 14 September 2011 claimed that it was holding Mrs Tebbutt and that her husband had been killed because he refused to obey their orders.[18] However, on the following day, al Shabaab claimed it was *not* behind the kidnapping of the British woman, but made no mention of its shadowy faction, Ras Kamboni. "Al Shabaab has not abducted any Briton from Kenya. We believe bandits carried out the attack," stated a senior official of the al Qaeda-linked group by telephone from an undisclosed location. "We shall release a statement later that al Shabaab is not involved," the rebel official concluded.[19]

An al Shabaab recruitment officer in Kismayo, two hundred kilometers north of the Kenyan border, said that Mrs Tebbutt had been brought to the port city, but her whereabouts were unknown. He claimed the attack had been carried out by militia fighters normally sympathetic to al Shabaab, but on this occasion were funded by local financiers. "Private investors provided a boat and weapons for the raid. The pirate gang want now to demand a ransom, but al Shabaab are against the idea," said the rebel recruiter.[20]

According to a Somali daily newspaper, Mrs Tebbutt was taken by her kidnappers to Kismayo by speedboat, later moved to Baidoa in southern Somalia (some 250 kilometers northwest of Mogadishu), and then to Hiin Dawa'o, a town between Hararhdere and the port of Hobyo.[21]

The response of the Kenyan authorities

A Kenyan police spokesman said that Kenyan security services, including crack commando forces similar to Britain's Special Air Service (SAS), had launched a mission to track down and rescue Mrs Tebbutt; helicopter gunships, speedboats, and scores of soldiers and police officers were deployed. Police commander Aggrey Adoli said: "We are using all tactics and resources available. We hope to find her safe." Kenyan and British security forces continued to patrol border areas, both on land and far out at sea. A senior Kenyan military officer said that the marine operation was led by a specialized team from the British Royal Navy.[22]

The Somali response

Mogadishu's ambassador to Kenya, Mohammed Ali Nur, said that Somalia's government forces joined the search for Mrs Tebbutt. "We wish to send our sincere condolences to the British government and the bereaved family. We condemn strongly the killing of David Tebbutt and the abduction of his wife," he said in a phone call, adding that his country's troops were in touch with Kenyan and British detectives who had set up an operational base at Kiunga, on the Kenya–Somalia border. Forces from the African Union Mission in Somalia (AMISOM) were also involved in the operation.[23]

The British response

Britain's foreign office confirmed that two British citizens were attacked near Kenya's border with Somalia, and that one was killed. A team from the British embassy in Nairobi was dispatched to the scene to help secure Mrs Tebbutt's release, while a team of Metropolitan Police officers traveled to Kenya to help local authorities with their investigations.[24]

British Prime Minister David Cameron said he had chaired a crisis meeting on the kidnapping. "We are doing everything we possibly can on this desperately tragic case," he told parliament. "The foreign secretary [William Hague] has met with the family. I think on some of these cases it is not right to air all of these issues in public, but I can reassure . . . the Tebbutt family [that] we will do everything possible to help." A statement posted on the British Foreign Office travel advice website said: "We continue to advise against all but essential travel to within thirty kilometers of Kenya's border with Somalia. There have been previous attacks by Somali militia into Kenya. Three aid workers were kidnapped in July 2009, and two western nuns in November 2008."

The release

Judith Tebbutt was released in March 2012, after her family paid a ransom to her abductors to secure her freedom, and was flown to Nairobi before returning to Britain. The amount of the ransom paid was not disclosed, but was rumored to have been around US$1 million.[25]

The abduction of a British couple from their yacht (October 2009)

A British couple, Paul and Rachel Chandler, had been sailing on their yacht when they were kidnapped by pirates near Somali waters on 23 October 2009. In January 2010, a British Special Boat Service (SBS) mission to rescue the couple was aborted after technical problems and delays. Kenyan police said they believed the gang were acting on the orders of a larger militia group, and probably fled to Somalia. However, al Shabaab denied having anything to do with the kidnapping, although in practice no pirate could operate in southern Somalian waters without al Shabaab's authority.

The couple was eventually released in November 2010, after 388 days in captivity.[26] Reports suggested that a ransom of up to US$1 million was paid to secure the couple's release; due to the British government's policy of not paying ransom demands, the money is said to have come from a mixture of private investors and the Somali government. A British foreign office spokesman said: "Although there is no

UK law against third parties paying ransoms, we counsel against them doing so because we believe that making concessions only encourages future kidnaps. This is why the Government does not make or facilitate substantive concessions to hostage takers."[27]

Disabled French woman abducted in Kenya (October 2011)

A disabled French woman, Marie Dedieu, aged sixty-six, was kidnapped by an armed gang from her bungalow at Ras Kitau on a northern Kenyan resort island and taken to Somalia. Kenya's government said it believed the abductors were al Shabaab militants.[28] Ms Dedieu, who used a wheelchair, was a retired French journalist who spent more than half of each year at a house she had bought on Manda Island.[29]

The abduction

At 3:00 a.m. on 1 October 2011, at least ten armed gunmen landed on Manda's main beach from two small speedboats. Six of the men stormed into the residential area, shooting at guards and shepherding staff into a separate room, while four others remained with the boats that had docked on the beach in front of Ms Dedieu's house. The French woman was dragged down to the beach, thrown over the shoulders of one of the kidnappers, and put into one of the speedboats. Her abductors did not bring her wheelchair with them, and no ransom demand was publicly made.

The Kenyan response

By mid-afternoon, Kenyan forces had spotted the boat with the gang and the Frenchwoman still on board, claimed Kenya's Tourism Minister Najib Balala. Kenyan coast guard and navy speedboats gave chase, assisted from the air at first light by an army helicopter that spotted the kidnappers more than halfway to the Somali border. The rescuers fired warning shots to halt the kidnappers, but the gang fired back, targeting the helicopter as it hovered above the boat on the open seas.[30] Despite repeated attempts to force the vessel to stop and sustained gunfire which injured several of the gang, Kenya's government admitted that it had been unable to rescue the woman before her kidnappers crossed into Somalian waters: "In the ensuing shoot-out between the abductors and the Kenyan navy, several of the abductors were injured." Despite this, they "managed to enter" Ras Kamboni, a town just over the border in Somalia. Two Kenyan naval troops were missing after their boat capsized as they were chasing the kidnappers, while six others on board were rescued.[31]

On 2 October 2011, Kenyan Foreign Affairs Minister Moses

Wetangula said his government would not sit and watch as al Shabaab continued to launch attacks on its citizens and foreign tourists, and declared that Kenyan forces had the ability and the resources to wipe out the militias.[32] A security official, speaking on condition of anonymity, said Kenya had "already sent envoys to Somalia to establish contact with the abductors", and that negotiations were ongoing. "With negotiations such as this, and considering there is no government on the other side, it may take quite some time, and patience is required. We are just pleading with them not to harm the woman," the official said.[33]

The French response

A source at France's defense ministry said that its forces based at Djibouti and its troops with the international anti-piracy force were "involved" in the search for Ms Dedieu. The French government revised its travel advice for Kenya, warning its citizens against visiting Lamu. "It is advised against staying on the Lamu archipelago and its region near the Somali border," the French foreign ministry said on its website.[34] In the past, France had mounted special operations to free its nationals taken hostage by Somali pirates. At least one hostage died during the previous such mission in 2009.

The death of the hostage

Ms Dedieu died in captivity within a month of her abduction, probably due to her illness, although there were reports that her abductors had refused to allow her to receive the necessary medication.[35]

French Prime Minister François Fillon spoke of the "indignation that is ours in the face of this act of cruelty, this act of barbarity", noting that Ms Dedieu was aged, disabled, and sickly. "This speaks to the humanity of those who kidnapped her," Fillon said, claiming the government had tried to send medication to Ms Dedieu, but it was believed that her captors had refused to give it to her. In a statement announcing Ms Dedieu's death, a spokesman for the French foreign ministry called for her body to be returned to French authorities "without delay and without conditions". The date and exact circumstances of Ms Dedieu's death could not be confirmed, he said.[36]

Summary

The kidnapping of Marie Dedieu was the second attack in Kenya in less than a month that targeted foreigners staying on the string of islands that make up the Lamu archipelago, lying one hundred kilometers south of the border with Somalia. If the al Shabaab Islamic terror organization was behind the attacks, these assaults showed that the organization had changed tactics and now appeared keen to add economic sabotage against Kenya to their arsenal of threats. By targeting isolated resorts in areas like Manda Island where the presence of security forces was minimal, the terrorists sent a chilling message that they could undermine that country's tourism. Both kidnapped women hailed from the key Kenyan tourist markets, Britain and France.[37] The two kidnappings severely damaged Kenya's coastal tourism after it had rebounded following two months of violence after the 2007 presidential elections that left 1,100 people dead.

The abduction of two Spanish aid workers (October 2011)

On 13 October 2011, two Spanish women – Blanca Thiebaut, aged thirty, and Montserrat Serra, aged forty – both working for Médecins Sans Frontières (MSF) in the Dadaab refugee camps near the border with Somalia, were kidnapped by gunmen. This kidnapping was the third attack in Kenya within six weeks that had targeted foreigners staying close to the border with Somalia.

The abduction

The attackers, armed with AK-47 assault rifles, waited for the victims outside the refugee camp. As soon as the vehicle carrying them exited the compound, they blocked the gate, shot the driver, and abducted the two foreigners to an unknown destination.[38]

Kenyan Regional Police Chief Leo Nyongesa said: "Two aid workers of Spanish nationality have been kidnapped by the Shabaab, they are working for MSF." A police spokesman added that the women's Kenyan driver was wounded: "A driver who was taking them around was shot and seriously wounded before he was thrown out."[39] Al Shabaab denied that it was responsible for the kidnappings.[40]

Dadaab, the world's largest refugee complex, was home to some 450,000 refugees, most of whom came from Somalia fleeing either drought, war, or a combination of the two. Security had long been a concern at the camp where representatives from various Somali factions sought to recruit disaffected young male refugees as fighters. On several occasions, the Kenyan authorities had expressed fears that Islamist extremists would infiltrate the Dadaab camps from Somalia as the border lay barely one hundred kilometers away. Foreign aid workers lived in guarded compounds surrounded by high barbed-wire fences and the UN required its staff to travel in the camps with armed escorts.[41]

Following the kidnapping, the UN temporarily suspended all non-essential aid operations in the Dadaab camps, which potentially could have severely affected much-needed services in the camps for a long time afterwards.[42] In an earlier abduction, a Kenyan driver working for international aid organization Care International was abducted in September 2011 from the Dadaab Hagadera camp. More than one year later, the three were still missing.[43]

The Kenyan armed forces offensive into Somalia (October 2011)

On 16 October 2011, Kenya's government ordered the Kenya Defense Forces (KDF) to launch a military operation against al Shabaab in the southern part of Somalia, accusing the group of being behind several kidnappings of foreigners. Joshua Orwa Ojode, assistant minister for provincial administration and internal security, said: "al Shabaab is like a snake whose tail is in Somalia, but the head is here in Nairobi."[44]

The Kenyans sensed an opportunity to deliver a knockout blow against al Shabaab, which had already been driven from most of the Somali capital.[45] The military operation started a day after two security ministers, Internal Security Minister Professor George Saitoti and his defense counterpart, Mohamed Yusuf Haji, announced that the government would no longer tolerate actions by the al Shabaab Somali militant group, claiming that the group intended "to undermine Kenya's territorial integrity and national economy". "In light of this, the Kenyan government has decided to take robust measures to protect and preserve the integrity of the country and national economy and security. These measures will involve invoking Article 51 of the UN Charter that pronounces self-defense as an inherent right and which is also in keeping with the Kenyan Constitution," their joint statement said. "If you are attacked by an enemy, you are allowed to pursue that enemy until where you get him. We will force them far away from our border," Haji said.[46] Professor Saitoti branded al Shabaab "the enemy" and vowed to attack them "wherever they will be", stating that the scheduled offensive into Somalia hoped to rescue the Spaniards and two other women – French and British – who had been seized from Lamu three weeks previously.[47]

Summary

Attacks on tourists are unusual in Kenya, which is popular for its safari vacations and pristine beaches. The southern area of Somalia bordering Kenya is controlled by al Qaeda-linked al Shabaab insurgents who have been fighting the western-backed government in the capital Mogadishu for many years.[48]

Piracy and Terror in the Gulf of Aden

Three-quarters of the world's surface is covered by water, and about 80 percent of global trade is shipped by sea, laden on over fifty thousand large vessels and many more smaller ships, while around 60 percent of the world's oil is transported by approximately four thousand oil tankers.

The Gulf of Aden is situated at the southern end of the Arabian Peninsula between Somalia and Yemen. The 4,000-kilometer waterway is one of the most important trade routes in the world, being the southern gateway to the Suez Canal that connects Europe and North America with Asia and East Africa. About 1,500 ships – 10 percent of global shipping traffic – pass through it every month, including 4 percent of the world's daily supply of crude oil. The only alternative route, around South Africa's Cape of Good Hope, is thousands of kilometers longer, and much more expensive. The global economy depends on the free and undisturbed flow of goods and energy resources, and the main threats to the regional maritime trade are terror attacks and piracy.[49]

Piracy in the Gulf of Aden

In 2010, Somali pirates kidnapped a record number of seafarers and left eight sailors dead. Pirates in the region hijacked fifty-three ships and captured 1,181 seafarers that same year, according to a report by the ICC International Maritime Bureau (IMB): "More people were taken hostage at sea in 2010 than in any year on record." The number of pirate attacks against ships had risen every year over the previous four years, the report claimed. There were 445 attacks reported in 2010, up 10 percent from 2009; some 188 crew members were taken hostage in 2006, 1,050 in 2009, and 1,181 in 2010. Hijackings off the coast of Somalia accounted for 92 percent of all ship seizures in the year 2010, with forty-nine vessels captured and 1,016 crew members taken hostage. Somali pirates were still holding twenty-eight vessels and 638 hostages for ransom as of December 2010, the report concluded.[50]

Somali pirates have extended their reach, threatening not only the Gulf of Aden and the east coast of Somalia, but also the southern region of the Red Sea, the Bab al Mandab straits, and the east coast of Oman. This area now ranks as the number one piracy hotspot. The IMB estimated that about one thousand pirates, organized in about twenty-five groups, were active in the Gulf of Aden, counting those who help the pirates on land.[51]

One sailor, a prisoner of the pirates for 174 days, said his captors were well-organized in groups of fifteen to twenty. Armed with Kalashnikov assault rifles, rocket-propelled grenades, and scaling ladders, they operated hundreds of miles offshore from two or three larger "mother" ships, from which they launched their attacks in speedboats against unsuspecting victims. On the seas off Somalia, heavily-armed pirates overpowered ocean-going fishing or merchant vessels to use as bases for further attacks, capturing the crews and forcing them to sail to within attacking distance of other unsuspecting vessels.[52]

Security experts fear the ransom payments received by the pirates allowed them to buy better equipment and weapons for larger operations. Another concern focuses on the threat to the world's energy supply.[53] The threat that piracy around the Horn of Africa poses to international trade and to freedom of movement is substantial. The region's pirates stood to gain an estimated US$50 million in ransom money in 2009, but this sum does not include losses incurred by shipping companies for their ships' inactivity after capture. Increased insurance rates, and thousands of dollars in extra fuel consumption costs from ships traversing the gulf at increased speeds to avoid pirates, are additional financial burdens facing owners.[54]

Al Qaeda and the maritime jihad

Maritime attacks in the years 2000–9 offered a stark picture of al Qaeda's growing interest in maritime targets.[55]

Abu Musab al Suri, a senior al Qaeda ideologist, wrote:

> "Most of the world's commercial and oil economy passes through these marine passages. Furthermore, fleets of ships, aircraft carriers, and missiles of death pass through them, destined for our wives and children. These passages must be closed down, so that these invasive voyages will disappear. This will be done by attacking American ships and those of its allies, by planting mines and sinking the ships, or through threats to perpetrate suicide attacks and acts of piracy against them, and by the use of weapons whenever possible."[56]

Captured al Qaeda commanders, like Abdel Rahim al Nashiri, the mastermind of the attack on the USS *Cole*, and Omar al Farouq, who was captured in Indonesia on 5 June 2002, confessed that al Qaeda planned future attacks against maritime targets. In the area of the Arabian Peninsula and the Horn of Africa, al Qaeda's goal is the removal of western influence and military presence, and the organization is intensively collecting intelligence about potential targets such as ships and port facilities. Al Qaeda and other global jihad terror organizations are improving their operational capabilities, including scuba diving skills, hijacking ships, and even turning vessels into "Trojan Horses" loaded with conventional explosives or "dirty bombs". In 2009, al Qaeda's central leadership published a message entitled "Maritime Terrorism – A Strategic Need" in which the organization claimed that establishing naval terror cells and controlling the seas around Yemen was a "vital step" in achieving a global caliphate. Both the Bab al Mandab waterway and the Gulf of Aden were termed "of supreme strategic importance" in al Qaeda's long-term plan.[57]

In April 2009, the deputy leader of al Qaeda in the Arabian Peninsula (AQAP), Said Ali Jabir al Khathim al Shihri (also known as Abu Sufyan al Azdi), released a message calling on Somali jihadists to step up their attacks on "crusader" forces at sea in the Gulf of Aden and on land in neighboring Djibouti, which hosted France's largest military base in Africa: "To our steadfast brethren in Somalia, take caution and prepare yourselves, and increase your strikes against the crusaders at sea and in Djibouti." Al Shihri opened his message by addressing the jihadi leaders – Taliban supreme leader Mullah Omar, Osama bin Laden, and his deputy Ayman al Zawahiri. He assured them that their warriors (*mujahideen*) in the Arabian Peninsula were not letting them down and pledged to open a new front in the region: "We say to you, we are not just sitting there watching you as the crusader countries prepare themselves to eradicate you and wipe out your group. By Allah, we shall open against them a major front in the Arabian Peninsula which would, Allah willing, be the key to victory that would purge the crusader campaign and put an end to the ambitions of the crusaders and the Jews in the region." Al Shihri warned Somali militants against a conspiracy led by "the crusaders, the Jews, and traitor Arab rulers" to put an end to the Muslim extremists' progress in Somalia: "The crusaders, the Jews, and the traitorous rulers did not come to the Arabian Sea and the Gulf of Aden except to wage war against you in Somalia and abolish your newly established emirate, and by Allah, they shall be defeated. They shall bring a curse upon their people . . . We shall not leave them this time until we get to their own countries with the help of Allah."[58]

In a another message, al Qaeda claimed responsibility for the 2009 surge in pirate attacks and called its maritime campaign "a new strategy which permits the mujahideen to hijack shipping" since "fighters who aspire to establish the caliphate must control the seas and the waterways".[59]

The goals of the pirates in the Gulf of Aden were almost always ransom payments or loot – they were not motivated by Islamic fundamentalism. When dealing with Muslim Somalis, it proved easy to recruit them to contribute to the jihad in order to receive legitimacy and freedom of operation in return. One of these groups was the al Qaeda-affiliated Somali "al Shabaab al Mujahideen" group, which controlled a significant area of Somalia and received ransom money from the pirates. According to Jane's Intelligence Review, "the al Shabaab allow the pirates to operate undisturbed and receive a variety of services in return – the smuggling of guns and foreign fighters via the sea, training of Islamic marine forces, and mostly a nice piece of the profits".[60]

Since the 1990s, al Qaeda has had links to Islamic extremist groups operating in Somalia such as AIAI (al Itihaad al Islamiyah, "The Islamic Union"), the Islamic Courts, and al Shabaab but, thus far, piracy and al Qaeda's brand of terrorism have remained largely separate. In 2009, for the first time, western intelligence sources found that the number of interactions between pirate groups and Somalia's al Qaeda-linked groups continued to rise.[61]

Counter-piracy and counter-terrorism

On 2 June 2008, the United Nations Security Council passed Resolution 1816 that gave foreign warships the right to enter Somali waters for the purposes of repressing, by all means necessary, acts of piracy and armed robbery at sea. France, Russia, India, and many other countries sent warships and commando units to rescue their crews and protect their ships from Somali pirates.[62]

The US played a key role in combating terror and piracy in the region; the US-led coalition formed the Combined Task Force 150 (CTF-150), under the command of the US Fifth Fleet, to patrol the Gulf of Aden, Gulf of Oman, Arabian Sea, and the Indian Ocean. The primary task of the CTF-150 is to assist in the "war against terror", so piracy is lower on its list of priorities. In August 2008, as an anti-piracy measure, the US established a protected shipping corridor in the Gulf of Aden protected by the CTF-150. But although the CTF-150 has since thwarted twelve pirate hijackings, ships are still being attacked, even in the protected zone, indicating the extent and strength of the piracy problem. Captains are even being advised to traverse the gulf in convoy.

Conclusions

Growing cooperation between Somali pirates backed by al Qaeda and other jihadi organizations poses a significant threat to international trade, the world's energy supply, and to freedom of movement on the high seas. Piracy is an extremely profitable business, and al Qaeda and other Islamic terror organizations see it as a lucrative source of finance for their activities.

The disruption of international trade would serve one of al Qaeda's goals: the organization has long targeted the financial systems of western economies ("The Economic Jihad"). Al Qaeda also wants to draw the US and its allies into a new theater of war in order to drain their resources.

Terror organizations allied with pirates pose a threat of further, even more serious, terror attacks of the following types:

- Missile attacks against ships.
- Suicide attacks against ships, like the attacks against the USS *Cole* and the *Limburg* oil tanker.

The growing threat of piracy and terror demands a comprehensive response of the international community in two spheres:

- Stabilizing the political and security situation in Somalia and Yemen.
- Combating the piracy and terror networks in the region.

Only a decisive, well-coordinated, and comprehensive international campaign can reduce the threat to the freedom of shipping and the global economy.

Notes

1. Tristan McConnell, "French Hostages in Somalia are Split Up Between Two Islamist Groups", *The Times*, 19 July 2009.
2. "Al Shabab to Release Video with French Hostage", *Global Jihad*, 6 August 2010, http://www.globaljihad.net/view_news.asp?id=1497.
3. "French 'James Bond' Escapes Captors", *Euro News*, 27 August 2009.
4. "Somali Group Issues Video of French Hostage", *Reuters*, 9 June 2009.
5. "French Spy Hostage Still Alive in Somalia", *AFP*, 28 December 2010.
6. "France Hostage is a Life [*sic*] in Somalia", *Diirad Media*, 29 December 2010.
7. Hassan Ali Gesey, "Osama Bin Laden Threatens to Kill French Hostage in Somalia", *News Blaze*, 23 January 2011.
8. "French Spy Hostage Still Alive", *AFP*, 28 December 2010.
9. Bill Roggio, "Shabaab Executes French Hostage Denis Allex", *The Long War Journal*, 16 January 2013, http://www.longwarjournal.org/archives/2013/01/shabaab_executes_fre.php#ixzz2XJLNp3tM.

10 Galgalo Bocha, "Somalia Joins Search for Seized Briton", *Daily Nation*, 14 September 2011.
11 Katharine Hourled, "Kenya Diplomat: Briton Killed, Wife Kidnapped", *Security Network*, 11 September 2011.
12 "Somali Kidnappers Tipped Off About Tourists", *9 News*, 15 September 2011.
13 Sam Greenhill, "British Woman Kidnapped in Kenya Will be Used as Human Shield by Al Qaeda", *The Mail*, 14 September 2011.
14 "Kenya: Local Linked to Lamu Kidnap Terrorist Group", *Daily Nation*, 22 September 2011.
15 Hourled, "Briton Killed", *Security Network*, 11 September 2011.
16 Greenhill, "British Woman Kidnapped", *Mail*, 14 September 2011.
17 "Somalia's Powerful Hizbul Islam Insurgent Group Splits", *Ethiopian Journal*, 14 May 2010.
18 Greenhill, "British Woman Kidnapped", *Mail*, 14 September 2011.
19 Feisal Omar, "Somalia's al Shabab Say it Didn't Kidnap Briton", *Reuters*, 15 September 2011.
20 *Ibid.*
21 Mohamed Odowa, "Al Shabaab/Al Qaeda Terror Plan Uncovered", *Somalia Report*, 18 September 2011.
22 Bocha, "Somalia Joins Search", *Daily Nation*, 14 September 2011.
23 *Ibid.*
24 "Pirates Kidnap British Wife: Husband Shot Dead in Raid on Luxury Kenyan Holiday Resort", *Daily Mail*, 13 September 2011.
25 "British Hostage Judith Tebbut's Family 'Paid Somali Pirates £600,000 Ransom' to End Her Six-Month Ordeal", *Daily Mail*, 22 March 2012.
26 "British Yacht Couple Kidnapped by Somali Pirates are Finally Released after 388 Days of Captivity", *Daily Mail*, 14 November 2010, http://www.dailymail.co.uk/news/article-1329577/Paul-Rachel-Chandler-kidnapped-Somali-pirates-released-388-days.html#ixzz1ZcSdIu3j.
27 David Williams and Vanessa Allen, "So Happy to be Alive, So Happy to be Free", *The Mail*, 15 November 2010.
28 "French Woman Kidnapped in Kenya Resort", *BBC News*, 1 October 2011.
29 "Disabled French Woman Kidnapped in Kenya", *The Telegraph*, 2 October 2011.
30 *Ibid.*
31 "Kenya Tries to Contact French Woman's Abductors in Somalia", *France 24*, 2 October 2011.
32 Philip Mwakio, "Search for Missing Tourist Intensifies", *The Standard*, 2 October 2011.
33 "Kenya Holds Kidnapped Frenchwoman's Employee", *France 24*, 3 October 2011.
34 "French Woman Kidnapped", *BBC News*, 1 October 2011.

35 Scott Sayare, "Frenchwoman Abducted in Kenya Dies", *The New York Times*, 19 October 2011.
36 *Ibid.*
37 "Kidnappings Signal Change of Tack by Militia", *The Standard*, 3 October 2011.
38 "Al Shabaab Kidnap Aid Workers at Kenyan Camp", *Sunday Nation*, 16 October 2011.
39 "Two Spanish Aid Workers Kidnapped in Kenya", *France 24*, 13 October 2011.
40 Katerina Nikolas, "Al Shabaab Deny Responsibility for Kidnap of Aid Workers in Kenya", *Digital Journal*, 19 October 2011.
41 "Abductions Halt Aid to Kenyan Refugee Camp", *al Jazeera*, 14 October 2011.
42 *Ibid.*
43 "Two Spanish Aid Workers", *France 24*, 13 October 2011.
44 "Horn of Africa RW Updates", *UN Office for the Coordination of Humanitarian Affairs* (UNOCHA), http://www.unocha.org/aggregator/sources/87?page=4 (n.d.).
45 Paul Cruickshank and Zain Verjee, "Kenya's High Stakes Shabaab Offensive", *CNN*, 24 October 2011.
46 Bernard Nomanyi, "Kenya Readies Anti Al Shabaab Offensive Inside Somalia", *CapitalFM News*, 16 October 2011.
47 "Two Spanish Aid Workers", *France 24*, 13 October 2011.
48 "Pirates Kidnap British Wife", *Daily Mail*, 13 September 2011.
49 Stephen Brown, "Jihad on the High Seas", *Frontpage Magazine*, 30 September 2009.
50 "Piracy and Armed Robbery Against Ships", *ICC International Maritime Bureau*, 2010 Report, 28 January 2011, http://www.icc-deutschland.de/fileadmin/icc/Meldungen/2010_Annual_IMB_Piracy_Report.pdf.
51 *Ibid.*
52 *Ibid.*
53 *Ibid.*
54 Brown, "Jihad on the High Seas", *Frontpage*, 30 September 2009.
55 "Maritime Terrorism in the Eyes of Al Qaeda", *Jihadi Websites Monitoring Group Insights* (JWMG), ICT, November 2009.
56 *Ibid.*
57 "Marine Terrorism: A Strategic Need", *Jihad Press*, May 2009.
58 Khaled Waseef, "Al Qaeda Urges Somalis to Attack Ships", *CBS News*, 16 April 2009.
59 Brown, "Jihad on the High Seas", *Frontpage*, 30 September 2009.
60 "Maritime Terrorism", *JWMG*, November 2009.
61 Waseef, "Al Qaeda Urges Somalis", *CBS News*, 16 April 2009.
62 Brown, "Jihad on the High Seas", *Frontpage*, 30 September 2009.

13

Islamic Terror Abductions in the Russia–Chechnya Conflict

Background

The Chechen Republic is a primarily-Muslim region of the Russian Federation, located in the southernmost part of eastern Europe in the area of the Caucasus Mountains. It is bordered by another republic, Ingushetia, to the west, Georgia to the south, and Dagestan to the north. Its capital is Grozny.

Between 1824 and 1859, Russians and Chechen Muslims fought a protracted war that ultimately resulted in a Russian victory. Following the Bolshevik Revolution of 1917, Joseph Stalin's policies provoked a new Chechen uprising in the 1930s that was put down with characteristic Russian firmness, with thousands of Chechens executed or imprisoned. During World War II, the Chechens once again saw an opportunity to throw off the yoke of Russian domination, and sided with the Germans. In 1944, Stalin's forces, emulating the Nazi policy of ethnic cleansing, rounded up virtually the entire Chechen population and shipped them by train to Siberia. In 1957, during Russian Premier Nikita Khrushchev's de-Stalinization program, those Chechens that had survived their harsh thirteen-year exile were permitted to return to their homeland, imbued with a renewed hatred of their Russian oppressors who once again dominated the republic of Chechnya.

After the breakup of the Union of Soviet Socialist Republics (USSR) in the late 1980s, the Chechen Assembly adopted a resolution of sovereignty and, in October 1991, elected Dzhokhar Dudayev as president – Dudayev declared Chechnya's independence, in November 1991, as the Chechen Republic of Ichkeria. In response, Russia imposed an economic blockade and threatened further action. As Dudayev consolidated his position, criminal elements surfaced and local clans fought for power while Russia attempted to destabilize the Dudayev regime by supporting armed rebels. Chechnya languished in discord and dissention until 1994, when Russia proposed autonomy agreements with the breakaway republics of Chechnya and Tatarstan. The latter agreed, but Dudayev maintained his claim of independence and, in December 1994, Russian Premier Boris Yeltsin ordered Russian troops to invade Chechnya, provoking the first Chechen war. As Russian casualties mounted, public opinion turned against the war and, in 1995, Russia agreed to a ceasefire – but, without a settlement of the political issues, the violence soon resumed. Dudayev was killed by Russian missiles on 21 April 1996, and a new ceasefire agreement was agreed to calling for the withdrawal of Russian forces and a political resolution by 2001.

With Russian military forces out of the country, the Chechens elected their own president in January 1997 – Aslan Maskhadov, a former Soviet artillery officer who had been the main rebel military commander during the first Chechen war. Russia recognized his government, although, in accordance with the peace deal negotiated with Moscow, a decision on Chechnya's final political status was delayed for five years. However, in this time of peace, President Maskhadov was unable to control his more radical field commanders such as Shamil Basayev who turned against him and took control of large portions of the country. Chechen guerrillas began incursions into neighboring Dagestan seeking to unify Dagestan and Chechnya as an Islamic state, which provoked intervention by Russian troops. The breakaway Chechen Republic descended into anarchy – in the process becoming one of the hostage-taking capitals of the world.[1]

Victims included British aid workers Jon James and Camilla Carr, who were freed in September 1998 after a year in captivity, and four engineers who were kidnapped and later found beheaded. Herbert Gregg, an American missionary held hostage for seven months and released in July 1999, said much of his treatment was good – despite the fact that the rebels videoed themselves cutting off one of his fingers. In 1998, security firm Kroll Associates UK Ltd. said that there were about one hundred expatriates being held hostage in Chechnya.[2]

Russia escalated its response following a wave of bombings of residential apartment buildings in Moscow and other Russian cities that were widely blamed on Chechen rebels. On 1 October 1999, Russian Prime Minister (later President) Vladimir Putin sent troops once again to invade Chechnya and launched massive, indiscriminate air strikes at Chechen cities, forcing as many as 400,000 civilians to flee. President Maskhadov fled Grozny in 1999 and, after a prolonged and bitter resistance, the Russians finally recaptured the Chechen capital in early 2000.

In June 2001, President Putin installed a new Chechen administration that answered to Moscow, led by a Muslim cleric, Akhmed Kadyrov. The brutality of the Russian tactics had drawn widespread condemnation, but the Kremlin responded to these criticisms by saying that such tactics were justified in order to combat Chechen terrorism. Subsequently, after the 9/11 attacks in the US, President Putin eagerly jumped on the bandwagon of President Bush's "war on terror", characterizing the Chechen separatists as Islamist terrorists and vowing to track them down.

In spite of the Russian victory, the Chechen insurgency and terror campaign in Chechnya continued, and even escalated, during the following years:

- In March 2001, three people were killed when Saudi Arabian security forces stormed a plane that was diverted to Medina after it had been hijacked by Chechen rebels on a flight from Istanbul to Moscow.
- A week later, several pro-Chechen gunmen seized about 120 tourists at a luxury Istanbul hotel in protest against the war.
- In July 2001, up to thirty people were held in searing heat on a bus in southern Russia by a Chechen man demanding the release of five Chechens who had been captured in a previous hijacking.[3]
- In May 2002, a lone gunman held about ten people hostage – again at an Istanbul hotel. They were all released unharmed.[4]

However, the Chechen terrorist campaign again reappeared on Moscow's doorstep: in October 2002, Chechen terrorists seized a Moscow theater, taking over eight hundred hostages. Russian commandos stormed the theater, killing all forty-one terrorists (along with 129 hostages) in the rescue attempt.

One of the key figures in the Chechen insurgency was Shamil Basayev, whose reputation as a terrorist began in 1991 when, during the first Chechen war, he hijacked a Russian plane to Ankara to hold a press conference to publicize the Chechen cause. Basayev became head of the Chechen rebels during the 1994 war, and later served as prime minister of Chechnya before returning to guerrilla fighting in neighboring Dagestan. His attacks during this period included:

- In August 2004, two female suicide bombers destroyed two Russian airliners leaving Moscow, causing the deaths of eighty-nine people.

- In the same month, a suicide bomber killed ten people outside a Moscow metro station.
- In October 2005, Chechen terrorists carried out a raid on the city of Nalchik, the capital of the republic of Kabardino-Balkaria, in which more than one hundred people died.

However, Basayev's most notorious attack was the raid on a school in Beslan that left 331 dead, of whom more than half were children. Basayev was killed in July 2006, in an accidental explosion while inspecting a delivery of weapons.

Beginning in July 2006, both Russia and Ramzan Kadyrov (the Russian-allied president of Chechnya and a former rebel) promoted an amnesty program and invited militants to avoid prosecution by turning themselves in before the end of January 2007. At the end of the program, about five hundred militants were reported to have applied for amnesty. However, the remaining rebels claimed that most were not reformed separatists at all, but rather "prisoners and kidnapped relatives of militants who had been forced into role-playing by Ramzan A. Kadyrov, the pro-Kremlin Chechen premier". Russia and Kadyrov claimed the program was a success.

By the beginning of 2008, Russia could claim to have been stabilized and, although separatist militants continued to operate, their attacks were small and intermittent. However, according to human rights observers, stability came at a high price – Chechnya had been at war for most of the previous twenty years, low-level violence continued, and the republic remained the main source of instability in the volatile Caucasus region.

The Budyonnovsk Hospital Hostage Crisis (June 1995)

Until 6 March 1995, as a part of the first Russian–Chechen war, Russian forces occupied most the territories of Chechnya, including the capital Grozny. As the conflict continued, the Chechen separatists resorted to mass hostage-takings in an attempt to influence both the Russian public and Russian leadership.

The Budyonnovsk Hospital hostage crisis took place from 14–19 June 1995, when a group of eighty to 150 Chechen separatists, led by Basayev, attacked the southern Russian city of Budyonnovsk, over one hundred kilometers north of the border with the Russian republic of Chechnya. The separatists crossed into neighboring Stavropol Krai concealed in military trucks supposedly transporting coffins from the war zone in Chechnya, while others had earlier infiltrated the city in small groups. At about noon on June 14th, they stormed the police station, city hall, and government offices – at least twenty policemen and soldiers were killed, and twenty-one others wounded. After several hours, in the face of Russian reinforcements, the separatists retreated to the residential district and seized a hospital, taking between 1,500 and 1,800 people hostage, most of them civilians.[5]

The hostage crisis

The hostage-takers issued an ultimatum threatening to kill the hostages unless their demands, including an end to the war and direct negotiations with Chechen regime, were met. Russian President Boris Yeltsin immediately vowed to do everything possible to free the hostages.

On June 15th, Basayev demanded that journalists be let into the hospital building to conduct a press conference but, when he decided the Russian authorities were too slow in granting this demand, he ordered five or six hostages killed. After several days of siege, Russian Ministry of Internal Affairs (MVD) and Federal Security Service (FSB) forces tried to storm the hospital compound at dawn on the fourth day, but were met with fierce resistance. After many hours of fighting, wherein more than thirty hostages were killed, a ceasefire was agreed upon and 227 hostages were released. A second Russian attempt to take control of the hospital few hours later also failed, as did a further operation that resulted in more casualties. The Russian authorities accused the Chechens of using the hostages as human shields.

Resolution of the crisis

On June 18th, negotiations between Russian Prime Minister Viktor Chernomyrdin and separatist leader Shamil Basayev led to a compromise: in exchange for the release of the hostages, Chernomyrdin agreed to declare a ceasefire in Chechnya, resume peace talks, and give the terrorists safe passage to Chechnya.[6] On June 19th, most of the hostages were released and Basayev's group, under cover of 120 volunteer hostages (including sixteen journalists and nine State Duma deputies), departed for the Chechen village of Zandak near Chechnya's border with Dagestan. After the village was reached without event, the remaining hostages were released. Basayev, accompanied by some of the journalists, moved to the village of Dargo, where he was welcomed as a hero.

The raid was widely considered to be the turning point in the first

Russian–Chechen war. It boosted morale among the Chechens, shocked the Russian public, and discredited the Russian government.

Casualties

According to official figures, 129 civilians were killed or died of their wounds and 415 were wounded in the incident. However, according to an independent estimate, 166 hostages were killed in the storming of the hospital. At least eleven Russian policemen and at least fourteen soldiers were killed and nineteen wounded, not including the military casualties. Basayev's group suffered eleven militants killed. About 160 buildings in the town were destroyed or damaged, including fifty-four municipal buildings and 110 private houses.[7]

Aftermath

The Kremlin had endured a firestorm of criticism over President Boris Yeltsin's decision to attend the G-7 meeting rather than to stay and deal with the crisis. The just-released hostages and families of the victims were especially angered by Yeltsin's order to use force against the terrorists in the hospital. Reacting to the perceived inept handling of the hostage situation, the State Duma voted 241 to 72 in favor of a motion of "no confidence" in the government led by Viktor Chernomyrdin; the vote, however, was widely seen as purely symbolic and the government did not step down. Still, the debacle cost both Security Minister Sergei Stepashin and Interior Minister Viktor Yerin their jobs. They resigned on 30 June 1995.

In the years following the hostage-taking, more than thirty of the surviving attackers were killed, including Aslambek Abdulkhadzhiev (in 2002) and Shamil Basayev (in 2006), and more than twenty were sentenced to various terms of imprisonment by the Stavropol territorial court.

The Kizlyar–Pervomayskoye Hostage Crisis (January 1996)

The Kizlyar–Pervomayskoye hostage crisis of January 1996 started as a guerrilla raid conducted by Chechen separatists during the first Russian–Chechen war, and turned into a massive hostage situation involving thousands of civilians. More than one hundred people died during the crisis, including at least forty-one civilians.

The Kizlyar airbase raid

On 9 January 1996, a group of around two hundred Chechen separatists, led by Salman Raduyev (allegedly acting on Dzhokhar Dudayev's orders), launched a raid against a Russian military helicopter airfield, and later a civilian hospital, in the city of Kizlyar, located in the republic of Dagestan. Only two or three helicopters were destroyed at the airbase, but at least thirty-three people were killed in the assault and scores were injured. The Chechen fighters then entered the town itself, where they took over two thousand hostages and held them at a local hospital.[8]

After fierce fighting, the Chechen fighters and the Russian authorities started negotiations to solve the crisis. The authorities demanded that the Chechens first release the hostages, and in return they would be granted safe passage back to Chechnya. The next day, most of the hostages were released, but about 160, some of them reportedly volunteers, accompanied the Chechen terrorists to act as human shields in order to deter a Russian ambush along the route to Chechnya.[9]

The terrorists headed in the direction of Chechnya in a column of buses and trucks, but were stopped by a Russian helicopter gunship that suddenly opened fire on their convoy as it approached the border between Dagestan and Chechnya.[10] A group of Russian policemen escorting the convoy were caught in the crossfire and surrendered to the Chechens, who rushed for shelter in the nearby village of Pervomayskoye where they held the hostages in the school and the mosque, and forced the captured policemen to build trenches. The terrorists seized an additional one hundred hostages from among the population of the village and forced some of the civilians to help with constructing defenses.

Russian forces surrounded the village and prepared for a military operation. Before launching their assault, Russian officials falsely stated that the terrorists had "hanged six Russian soldiers". For the next three days, Russian commandos tried to break into the village, supported by helicopters and artillery. On 12 January 1996, the terrorists released the women and children and said they would release the rest of the hostages if four high-ranking Russian officials would take their place.[11]

After the assault attempts had failed, Interior Minister Anatoly Kulikov and FSB Director General Mikhail Barsukov falsely declared that Raduyev's men had "executed all of the hostages". The Russian commanders then ordered their forces to open fire on the village with tanks and rockets.[12] Prime Minister Viktor Chernomyrdin stated that no live hostages remained in the village – in fact, many were still alive and appealed desperately to the Russian security forces to cease firing on the village. The Russian shelling reportedly killed sixteen hostages.[13]

The Chechen terrorists' breakout

On 18 January 1996, Raduyev and his men managed to break out of the encirclement and escape, taking with them about twenty Russian police and a number of civilians as hostages. About twenty seriously-injured Chechen fighters could not be transported and were left behind. During the escape, the Chechen terrorists suffered heavy losses from Russian forces and several hostages were killed. The breakout column eventually crossed a freezing border river by using a gas pipeline and escaped into Chechnya.

At the same time, in order to support the breakthrough, Dudayev sent another unit of almost three hundred Chechen guerrillas to cross the border into Dagestan and attack the Russian lines from behind. This Chechen unit briefly took over a schoolhouse in the neighboring village of Sovetskoye, just a few kilometers outside Pervomayskoye, until Raduyev's column had entered Chechnya – at which point they also withdrew.[14]

The hijack of a Turkish ferry

On 16 January 1996, the situation was further complicated when pro-Chechen gunmen hijacked a Panamanian-registered ferry, the *Avrazya*. The terrorist group included nine Turkish citizens of Caucasian origin who were sympathetic to the rebels besieged at Pervomayskoye. The gunmen threatened to blow up the ship – and the 255 hostages on it – if the Russians did not halt their offensive against the Kizlyar hostage-takers.

However, the Turkish authorities coped effectively with the hijackers. In constant communication and negotiation with the captors – and while ignoring Russian demands for tough action – the Turks secured the safe release of the captives (177 mostly-Russian passengers and a Turkish crew of fifty-five) unharmed and the surrender of the gunmen without bloodshed.[15]

Casualties

When the fighting was over, President Yeltsin stated that eighty-two of the 120 hostages had been found alive, while 153 of the three hundred Chechen separatists had been killed and thirty captured. The rest of the rebels were unaccounted for and may have escaped back into Chechnya.

According to Maskhadov, the Chechen-separatist chief of staff, ninety Chechen fighters died during the attack. The full extent of the civilian and Russian military casualties remains unknown, but it is certain that more than one hundred people lost their lives in the crisis.

The Moscow Theater Hostage Crisis (October 2002)

On 23 October 2002, a highly-organized detachment of about forty male and female Chechen terrorists seized the Palace of Culture (also known as the Dubrovka Theater) on Melnikova Street in southeast Moscow, where the popular patriotic musical "Nord-Ost" was being staged.

The attackers, wearing balaclavas and armed with grenades, bombs, explosive belts, and other weapons, fired shots in the air and ordered everyone to be seated. The terrorists took approximately 850–900 people hostage, including both members of the audience and performers.[16] They later released children, pregnant women, and Muslims, while some performers who had been resting backstage escaped through an open window and called police. The terrorists booby-trapped the building and threatened to detonate their explosives, killing themselves and the hostages, if Russian forces attempted to penetrate the theater.

A Chechen rebel-sponsored website claimed responsibility for the raid and said it was under the command of Movsar Barayev, a Chechen warlord whose uncle, Arbi Barayev, was killed fighting Russian troops in 2001.

The terrorists demanded that Russian forces be immediately and unconditionally withdrawn from Chechnya, and set a deadline of one week, after which they would start killing the hostages.[17]

The Russian authorities opened negotiations with the terrorists in order to find a non-violent solution to the crisis and offered the terrorists the opportunity to leave for any third country, but the latter refused and called on President Putin to halt hostilities in Chechnya, asking him to refrain from assaulting the building, and again threatened to start shooting the hostages if Russia failed to take their demands seriously.[18]

The rescue operation

On 26 October 2002, after fifty-eight hours of siege and negotiations, and shortly before the expiration of the terrorists' deadline, Russian commandos stormed the theater. They pumped fentanyl gas into the building to neutralize the terrorists and prevent them from detonating their explosives and killing all of the hostages inside. Scores of terrorists, some of them women wearing explosive belts, were unable to press the electric detonators that they held in their hands.[19] The Russian commandos poured into the hall from the basement while a diversionary force attacked the main entrance. In a fierce firefight, the commandos gunned down those terrorists who were still conscious and systematically shot those who had succumbed to the gas.

The decision to use gas came from fear that the vast amount of explosives planted at sensitive points around the hall would cause the structure to collapse upon the heads of hundreds of hostages – and in this regard the plan succeeded. At least thirty-three terrorists and 129 hostages died as a consequence of the raid, while the majority of the surviving hostages recovered from the effects of the gas. The Russian authorities initially claimed that none of the deaths among the hostages had occurred due to gas poisoning. President Putin defended the operation, claiming that the Russian government had achieved the almost impossible, saved hundreds of lives, and that the operation proved it was impossible to bring Russia to its knees.

Summary

The Moscow theater incident was an example of the mega-terror tactic propounded by the "Afghan alumni" after the events of 9/11, and was unique in the large number of terrorists taking part who signaled their willingness to die in a massive suicide attack, including many women. However, the presence of both male and female suicide bombers was nothing new for the Chechen rebels – they had often utilized women operatives in their previous actions – but the use of so many was an innovation that indicated the emergence of new groups of suicidal radicals from within Islamic terror organizations. The Chechen terrorists had previous experience in large-scale hostage-taking, but this was the first time that an operation had combined both abduction and suicide attack.

The use of gas by the Russian forces was widely condemned by states worldwide due to the high number of hostages that died during and after the rescue operation, and remains controversial. It was reported that efforts to treat victims were complicated because the Russian government refused to inform doctors of what type of gas had been used.

The Beslan School Hostage Crisis (September 2004)

The Beslan school hostage crisis began on 1 September 2004, when a group of armed terrorists demanding an end to the Chechen war took more than 1,100 people (including 777 children) hostage at School Number One in the town of Beslan, located in the republic of North Ossetia-Alania.[20] The attack was carried out by the Riyadus-Salikhin Reconnaissance and Sabotage Battalion of Chechen Martyrs group, led by Basayev who was an independent warlord at that time.

On the third day of the standoff, Russian security forces stormed the building using tanks, thermobaric rockets, and other heavy weapons. A series of explosions shook the school, followed by a fire which engulfed the building and a chaotic gun battle between the hostage-takers and Russian security forces. Ultimately, at least 334 hostages were killed, including 186 children, and hundreds more were wounded or reported missing.

The tragedy led to security and political repercussions in Russia, most notably a series of government reforms consolidating power in the Kremlin and strengthening of the powers of the Russian president.

As of 2011, there were many aspects of the crisis still in dispute, including how many militants were involved, their preparations, and whether some of them had escaped. Concerns about the government's management of the crisis also persisted.

Day one

The initial attack took place on September 1st, the traditional start of the Russian school year (referred to as "First September" or "Day of Knowledge").[21] On this day, schoolchildren, accompanied by their parents and relatives, attend ceremonies hosted by their schools. Due to the family members attending the "Day of Knowledge" festivities, the number of people present was considerably higher than usual for a normal school day.

Early in the morning, a group of several dozen heavily-armed rebel guerrillas left a forest encampment in the vicinity of the village of Psedakh in the nearby Russian republic of Ingushetia. On their way to Beslan, they captured an Ingush police officer, Major Sultan Gurazhev, on a country road near the North Ossetian village of Khurikau. Gurazhev escaped after reaching the town and went to the district police department to let them know that his pistol and badge had been taken away.

At 9:10 a.m. local time, attackers wearing military camouflage and black balaclava masks, and in some cases also wearing explosive belts, arrived in a stolen police van and a GAZ-66 military truck at School Number One on Comintern Street, located next to the district police station. Many witnesses and independent experts claimed that there were, in fact, two groups of attackers, and that the first group was already at the school when the second group arrived.[22]

At first, those at the school mistook the terrorists for Russian forces practicing a security drill. However, the attackers resolved this misconception by shooting into the air and forcing everybody from the school grounds into the building. During this initial chaos, up to fifty people managed to flee and alert authorities to the situation, and a number also managed to hide in the boiler room. After an exchange of gunfire with local police and an armed civilian, in which it was reported that one attacker was shot dead and two were wounded, the school buildings were seized by the terrorists. Reports of the death toll from the shootout ranged from two to eight people, with more than a dozen wounded.

The attackers took approximately 1,200 hostages (the number was initially downplayed by the government to merely 200–400 and then, for an unknown reason, announced to be exactly 354 – in 2005, the number was set at 1,128). The militants herded their captives into the school's gym, confiscated all mobile phones, and ordered everyone to speak in Russian and to speak only when spoken to, on pain of death.

After gathering the hostages in the gym, the attackers singled out the fifteen or twenty strongest adults from among the male teachers, school employees, and fathers, apparently thinking they represented a possible threat, and took them into a corridor next to the cafeteria on the second floor. There, a deadly blast took place – an explosive belt worn by one of the women bombers had detonated, killing several of the selected hostages and another female terrorist (it was also claimed later that the second woman died from a bullet wound) as well as mortally wounding a male terrorist. According to the version presented by the single surviving hostage-taker, the blast was actually triggered by remote control by the group leader – known as *Polkovnik* ("Colonel") – in order to kill those who openly disagreed with him about taking children hostage and to intimidate other possible dissenters. Those still alive in the corridor were ordered to lie down and then shot with an automatic rifle by another gunman – all but one were killed.[23] The militants then forced the other hostages to throw the bodies out of the building and to wash the blood off the floor.

The beginning of the siege

A security cordon was soon established around the school by *militsiya* (police) and Russian army forces, which included the elite Alfa and Vympel units of the FSB and OMON (*Otryad Mobilniy Osobogo Naznacheniya*, "Special Purpose Mobile Unit") units from the MVD. A line of three apartment buildings facing the school gym was evacuated and taken over by the security forces, and a perimeter was set up within 230 meters of the school – inside the range of the terrorists' grenade launchers. The chaos was worsened by the presence of *opolchentsy* (Ossetian militiamen) and armed civilians among the crowd of up to five thousand relatives who had gathered at the scene.

The attackers mined the gym and the rest of the building with improvised explosive devices, and surrounded it with tripwires. In a further bid to deter rescue attempts, they threatened to kill fifty hostages for every one of their own members killed by the police and to kill twenty hostages for every gunman injured. They also threatened to blow up the entire school if government forces attacked. To avoid being overwhelmed by gas like their comrades in the 2002 Moscow theater siege, the rebels quickly smashed the school's windows. The captors prevented the hostages from eating and drinking (calling it a "hunger strike" that they claimed they joined too) until the arrival of North Ossetia's President Aleksander Dzasokhov to negotiate with them. However, the FSB had set up their own crisis headquarters from which Dzasokhov was excluded, and threatened to arrest him if he tried to go to the school.[24]

The Russian government announced that it would not use force to rescue the hostages, and negotiations towards a peaceful resolution took place on the first and second days. At Russia's request, a special meeting of the United Nations Security Council was convened on the evening of September 1st, at which council members demanded "the immediate and unconditional release of all hostages of the terrorist attack". US President George W. Bush made a statement offering "support in any form" to Russia. That night, the hostage-takers began exploring the area surrounding the school in preparation for an exit strategy once their demands had been met.

Day two

On 2 September 2004, negotiations with the hostage-takers proved unsuccessful. The attackers refused to allow food, water, or medicines to be taken in for the hostages, or for the bodies of the dead to be removed from the front of the school.[25] The immediate response to the crisis from President Putin and the rest of Russia's political leadership was near-total silence. Only on the second day did Putin make his first public comment on the siege, during a meeting in Moscow with King

Abdullah II of Jordan: "Our main task, of course, is to save the lives and health of those who became hostages. All actions by our forces involved in rescuing the hostages will be dedicated exclusively to this task." This was the only public statement made by Putin about the crisis until one day after its bloody end.

On the afternoon of the second day, the terrorists allowed the former president of Ingushetia, retired Soviet Army general Ruslan Aushev, to enter the school building and released twenty-six hostages (eleven nursing women and fifteen children) personally to his care. The rebels also gave Aushev a videotape made in the school and a note containing the demands from their leader Basayev, who was not himself present at the scene. In the note, Basayev demanded recognition of a "formal independence for Chechnya" in the framework of the Commonwealth of Independent States (CIS). He also said that, although the Chechen separatists "had played no part" in the bombings of Russian apartment buildings, they would now publicly take responsibility for them if needed.

The lack of food and water took its toll on the young children, many of whom were forced to stand for long periods in the hot, tightly-packed gym. Many children fainted and their parents feared they would die. At around 3:30 p.m., two grenades were fired by the hostage-takers, approximately ten minutes apart, at security forces outside the school, setting a police car ablaze and injuring one officer. However, the Russian forces did not return fire. As the evening and night wore on, the combination of stress and sleep deprivation – and possibly drug withdrawal – made the hostage-takers increasingly hysterical and unpredictable. The crying of the children irritated them, and on several occasions children and their mothers were threatened with being shot if they would not stop. Overnight, a police officer was wounded by shots fired from the school. Talks were broken off, and resumed again the next day.

Day three

Early on the morning of the third day, 3 September 2004, contact was made with Maskhadov, the separatist president of the Chechen Republic of Ichkeria. Maskhadov's sole demand was his unhindered passage to the school; however, the assault on the school began one hour after an agreement was made regarding his arrival.

Around 1:00 p.m., it was agreed to allow four Ministry of Emergency Situations medical workers in two ambulances to remove twenty bodies from the school grounds, However, at 1:03 p.m., when the paramedics approached the school, an explosion was heard from the gymnasium. The hostage-takers then opened fire, killing two paramedics, while the other two took cover behind their vehicle.[26]

A second, "strange-sounding" explosion was heard twenty-two seconds later. At 1:05 pm., a fire started on the roof of the sports hall, and soon burning rafters and lagging fell onto the hostages below, many of them wounded, but still alive. Eventually, the entire roof collapsed. The flames reportedly killed some 160 people – more than half of the total hostage fatalities.

The assault by Russian forces

Part of the wall of the sports hall had been demolished by the explosions, allowing some fourteen hostages to escape. Local militias fired shots, causing the militants to return fire, and a number of people were killed in the crossfire. Russian officials said that, when militants shot hostages as they ran, the military fired back, and asserted that, once the shooting had started, troops had no choice but to storm the building.

A chaotic battle broke out as the commandos fought to enter the school. The assault forces were supported by a number of tanks from Russia's Fifty-Eighth army, BTR-80 armored personnel carriers, and armed helicopters, including at least one Mi-24 attack-helicopter. Many local civilians also joined in the chaotic battle, having brought along their own weapons (at least one of the armed volunteers is known to have been killed).

By 3:00 p.m., two hours after the assault began, Russian troops had reclaimed control of most of the school. However, as evening fell, fighting still continued on the school grounds and included a group of militants holding out in the basement. During the battle, a group of thirteen hostage-takers broke through the military cordon and took refuge nearby. Several others were believed to have entered a nearby two-storey building, which was destroyed by tanks and flamethrowers at around 9:00 p.m., according to the findings of the Ossetian investigative committee, later published as the Kesayev Report. Another group of militants appeared to head back over the railway and were chased by helicopters into the town.

Sporadic gunfire and explosions continued that night until some twelve hours after the first explosions, despite reports from the Russian authorities that all resistance by militants had been suppressed. Early the next day, President Putin ordered the borders of North Ossetia to be closed, apparently because some hostage-takers were still being pursued by Russian forces.

Aftermath

At least 396 people, mostly hostages, were killed during the crisis. By 7 September 2004, Russian officials revised the death toll down to 334, including 156 children, while almost two hundred people remained missing or unidentified.[27] After the bloody conclusion of the crisis, many of the injured died in the only hospital in Beslan, which was highly unprepared to cope with the casualties, before the patients were finally sent to better-equipped facilities in Vladikavkaz. The day after the storming, bulldozers razed the buildings and removed the debris, including the body parts of the victims, to a garbage dump. The first of the funerals was conducted on September 4th, the day after the final assault. Many more followed soon after, including one mass burial of 120 victims.

President Putin reappeared in public during a hurried trip to the Beslan hospital in the early hours of September 4th to see several of the wounded victims – his only visit to Beslan. After returning to Moscow, he ordered a two-day period of national mourning on 6 –7 September 2004. In his televised speech, Putin paraphrased Joseph Stalin, saying: "We showed ourselves to be weak, and the weak get beaten."[28] On the second day of mourning, an estimated 135,000 people joined a government-organized rally against terrorism in Moscow's Red Square, while an estimated 40,000 people gathered in Saint Petersburg's Palace Square.

The identity of the hostage-takers, motives, and responsibility

On 17 September 2004, Basayev issued a statement claiming responsibility for the Beslan school siege, saying his Riyadus-Salikhin "martyr battalion" had carried out the attack and also claiming responsibility for a series of terrorist bombings in Russia in the weeks before the events in Beslan. Basayev said that he had underestimated the Kremlin's determination to end the Beslan crisis by all means possible, and stated that he had originally planned to seize at least one school in either Moscow or Saint Petersburg, but lack of funds forced him to pick North Ossetia, "the Russian garrison in the North Caucasus". Basayev blamed the Russian authorities for "a terrible tragedy" in Beslan, saying he was "cruelly mistaken" and that he "was not delighted by what happened there", but also added: "We are planning more Beslan-type operations in the future because we are forced to do so."[29]

However, this was the last major act of terrorism in Russia, as Basayev was soon persuaded to give up indiscriminate attacks by the new rebel leader, Abdul Halim Sadulayev, who made Basayev his second-in-command, but banned hostage-taking, kidnapping, and operations targeting civilians. Chechen separatist leader Maskhadov immediately denied that his forces were involved in the siege, calling it "a blasphemy" for which "there is no justification" and describing the perpetrators of the Beslan massacre as "madmen" driven out of their senses by Russian acts of brutality. He condemned the action and all attacks against civilians via a statement issued in London by his envoy, Akhmed Zakayev, blaming the attack on what he called "a radical local group" and agreeing to a North Ossetian proposition to act as a negotiator.[30] Later, Zakayev also called on western governments to initiate peace talks between Russia and Chechnya, and added his wish to "categorically refute all accusations by the Russian government that President Maskhadov had any involvement in the Beslan event".[31] In response, Putin vowed not to negotiate with "child-killers", comparing calls for negotiations with those for the appeasement of Hitler and putting a US$10 million bounty on Maskhadov's head (the same bounty that he offered for Basayev).[32] Maskhadov was killed by Russian commandos in Chechnya in March 2005, and was buried in a secret location.[33]

Shortly after the crisis, official Russian sources stated that the attackers were part of an international group led by Basayev that included a number of Arabs with connections to al Qaeda, and said they had intercepted phone calls in Arabic from the Beslan school to Saudi Arabia and another undisclosed Middle Eastern country. Two English-Algerians were among the identified rebels who actively participated in the attack: Osman Larussi and Yacine Benalia. Another UK citizen – Kamel Rabat Bouralha, arrested while trying to leave Russia immediately following the attack – was suspected to be a key organizer. All three were linked to the Finsbury Park Mosque in London.

The hostage-takers in Beslan were reported to have made the following demands:[34]

- The withdrawal of Russian troops from Chechnya, and independence for Chechnya.
- The presence of the following people in the school:
    - Aleksander Dzasokhov, president of North Ossetia.
    - Murat Zyazikov, president of Ingushetia.
    - Ruslan Aushev, former president of Ingushetia.
    - Leonid Roshal, a pediatrician.

It was also claimed that the terrorists demanded the release of some twenty-eight or thirty mostly-Ingush insurgents jailed after the June 2004 raids in Ingushetia.

The hostage-takers

According to the official version of events, of the terrorists that participated directly in the attack, one was taken alive while the rest were killed. The number and identity of attackers remains a controversial topic, fueled by often-contradictory statements and official documents. The government statements of September 3–4th said that a total of twenty-six or twenty-seven militants were killed during the siege while at least four militants, including two women, had died prior to the storming of the school.

According to Basayev: "Thirty-three mujahideen took part in Nord-West. Two of them were women. We prepared four [women], but I sent two of them to Moscow on August 24th. They then boarded the two airplanes that blew up. In the group there were twelve Chechen men, two Chechen women, nine Ingush, three Russians, two Arabs, two Ossetians, one Tartar, one Kabardinian, and one Guran."

On 6 September 2004, the names and identities of seven of the assailants became known after interviews with surviving hostages and the captured assailant. Forensic tests also established that twenty-one of the hostage-takers had taken heroin and morphine in a normally-fatal amount – the investigation cited this drug use as a reason for the militants' ability to continue fighting despite being badly wounded and presumably in great pain. In November 2004, Russian officials announced that twenty-seven of the thirty-two attackers had been identified. However, in September 2005, the lead prosecutor in the case against Nur-Pashi Kulayev, the surviving attacker, stated that only twenty-two of the thirty-two bodies had been identified, leading to further confusion over which identities had been confirmed.

The commander of the hostage-takers was tentatively identified by the Russian government as an ethnic Ingush and native of Galashki, Ruslan Tagirovich Khuchbarov, aged thirty-two, who was nicknamed *Polkovnik* ("Colonel"). Basayev identified him as "Colonel Orstkhoyev". Reportedly also referred to by the hostage-takers as "Ali", he had led the negotiations on behalf of the hostage-takers. However, his identification was disputed and it is possible that he escaped and remains at large.

The captured terrorist's interrogation and trial

The captured terrorist, twenty-four-year-old Nur-Pashi Kulayev, born in Chechnya, was identified by former hostages. The state-controlled Channel One showed fragments of his interrogation in which Kulayev said the group was led by a Chechnya-born terrorist nicknamed

Polkovnik and by a North Ossetian native, Vladimir Khodov.[35]

On 17 May 2005, Kulayev was tried in a court in the republic of North Ossetia charged with murder, terrorism, kidnapping, and other crimes, and pleaded guilty to seven of the counts. On 26 May 2006, Nur-Pashi Kulayev was sentenced to life in prison.[36]

Soviet Union and Russian Counter-abduction Doctrine

Over the past two centuries, Russia developed some very successful techniques for dealing with terror: when confronted with attacks like these, the Russians played by the terrorist's rules – they terrorized the terrorists.

Back in the 1980s, for example, Islamic terrorists in Lebanon kidnapped a Russian diplomat. The Russians (then the Soviets, a distinction that made little difference in these matters) quickly found out which faction held their man, abducted a relative of one of the kidnappers, and delivered a body part to the terror group. The message was: release the Russian diplomat unharmed or the KGB (Soviet secret police) would keep grabbing the kinfolk of the kidnappers and delivering body parts. The Russian diplomat was released.

Notes

1 "Q&A: The Chechen Conflict", *BBC News*, 10 July 2006.
2 "Chechen Rebels' Hostage History", *BBC News*, 1 September 2004.
3 *Ibid.*
4 *Ibid.*
5 "Assault at High Noon", *Time Magazine*, 26 June 1995.
6 "Russia", *Time Magazine*, 23 January 1995, http://www.time.com/magazine/domestic/1995/950123/950123.russia.html.
7 "History of Chechen Rebels' Hostage Taking", *Gazeta RU*, 24 October 2002.
8 "Chechen Rebels Hold at Least 1,000 Hostages in Hospital", *CNN*, 9 January 1996.
9 "Chechens Threaten to Kill Remaining Hostages", *CNN*, 11 January 1996.
10 Robert W. Schaefer, *The Insurgency in Chechnya and the North Caucasus: From Gazavat to Jihad* (Santa Barbara, CA: Preager, 2010), p. 138.
11 "Chechens Offer Trade: Hostages for Politicians", *CNN*, 13 January 1996.
12 Michael Specter, "10 Days That Shook Russia: Siege in the Caucasus", *The New York Times*, 22 January 1996.
13 "Scores Dead at End of Hostage Siege", *CNN*, 18 January 1996.

14 "Chechen Rebels Counterattack", *CNN*, 18 January 1996.
15 "Pro-Chechen Ferry Hijackers Surrender to Turks", *The New York Times*, 20 January 1996.
16 "Chechen Gunmen Seize Moscow Theatre", *CNN*, 24 October 2002.
17 "Hostage-Takers 'Ready to Die'", *BBC News*, 25 October 2002.
18 Johanna McGeary and Paul Quinn, "Theatre of War", *Time Magazine*, 4 November 2002.
19 Yevgenia Borisova, "The Gas Saved Them, The Gas Killed Them", *The Moscow Times*, 28 October 2002.
20 "When Hell Came Calling at Beslan's School No 1", *The Guardian*, 5 September 2004.
21 John Deever, "Mr John and the Day of Knowledge", *Peace Corps*, http://wws.peacecorps.gov/wws/stories/stories.cfm?psid=166. Retrieved 27 March 2007.
22 "Our Native Wiesenthal", *The Moscow Times*, 9 January 2008.
23 "One Little Boy was Shouting: 'Mama!' She Couldn't Hear Him. She was Dead", *The Daily Telegraph*, 5 September 2004.
24 "Critics Detail Missteps in School Crisis", *The New York Times*, 17 September 2004.
25 "Timeline: The Beslan School Siege", *The Guardian*, 6 September 2004.
26 "When Hell Came Calling", *Guardian*, 5 September 2004.
27 "The Beslan School Siege", *Guardian*, 6 September 2004.
28 "Speeches", *The Kremlin*, 4 September 2004, http://www.kremlin.ru/eng/speeches/2004/09/04/1958_type82912_76332.shtml.
29 "Chechen Claims Beslan Attack", *CNN*, 17 September 2004.
30 "President Maskhadov on the Events in Beslan", *Kavkaz Center*, 18 September 2004.
31 "Obituary: Aslan Maskhadov", *BBC News*, 8 March 2005.
32 "Russia: Putin Rejects Open Inquiry Into Beslan Tragedy As Critical Voices Mount", *Radio Free Europe/Radio Liberty*, 7 September 2004.
33 "Chechen Leader Maskhadov Killed", *BBC News*, 8 March 2005.
34 "Beslan Terrorists Confused Roshal with Rushailo", *Russian Information Network*, 7 October 2005. Retrieved 14 February 2007.
35 "Ingush Ex-Cop Reportedly Among Hostage-Takers", *The Jamestown Foundation*, 8 September 2004.
36 "Victims of Beslan Hostage Crisis Demand Death Penalty to the Only Arrested Terrorist", *Pravda*, 18 May 2006.

14

Summary and Conclusions

Points of Emphasis and Lessons to be Drawn

The examination and comparison of the abduction arenas detailed in the previous chapters indicate that Islamic terror organizations adopted terror abductions as a tactic to achieve the following strategic goals:

- Political goals (the withdrawal of military forces from Afghanistan, Iraq, Mali, and Chechnya).
- Release of terrorists from prison (Israel, US, UK, France, and Saudi Arabia).
- Ransom money (Iraq, Afghanistan, Yemen, the Maghreb and Sahel regions, and East Africa).
- A combination of the preceding goals.

There are some unique characteristics involved in Islamic terror abductions:

- The targeting of holy places (the Grand Mosque in Mecca, and Christian churches in Iraq).
- "Mega-terror abductions" involving hundreds or thousands of hostages and dozens of kidnappers (Chechnya, Russia, and Algeria).
- A combination of kidnapping and suicide attacks where terrorists, armed with explosive belts, are ready to die along with their hostages (Chechnya, Algeria, Russia, and India).
- The decapitation of hostages (Iraq, Pakistan, Saudi Arabia, and the Philippines).

In most of these arenas, "waves" of abductions of foreign citizens (many of whom are westerners) are apparent, occurring mainly in regions where there is no effective central government and where the terror organizations enjoy relative freedom. These "waves of abductions" cease when local, regional, or strategic circumstances change.

Abductions are generally regarded as a tactic whose aim is to extract strategic demands from various countries. A state that supports terror, such as Iran, constitutes a central factor in the initiation and encouragement of such "waves of abductions", as is evidenced by an ability to put a stop to such attacks when it so chooses.

Since the late 1990s, the global jihad and al Qaeda have served as a central factor *vis-à-vis* the encouragement and initiation of terror abductions. Those abductions that take place in an arena where intelligence capabilities are absent or restricted, and where the ability of the country whose citizens are being held to launch a military operation is limited, usually culminate in a victory for the abductors.

Most of the hostage rescue operations in the last two decades have ended with the deaths or disappearance of the hostages. In "megaterror abductions", rescue operations caused a high loss of life among the hostages, but most of the hostages were rescued and all of the abductors were killed or captured.

Capitulation to terrorists' demands sometimes discouraged additional future abductions of citizens of that country but, at the same time, encouraged the abduction of citizens of other countries based on the assumption that those countries would also give in to the demands of the abductors. It is impossible to unequivocally determine whether taking a firm, principled stand against terror extortion has brought about a decrease in the number of abductions because sometimes the refusal of those countries to capitulate has triggered repeated attempts to abduct their citizens in order to bring about the desired capitulation. Nevertheless, it is reasonable to assume that a broad and coordinated consensus advocating a uniform policy of refusal to give in to terrorist extortion, shared by as many countries as possible, would diminish the phenomenon.

Kidnapping will remain a tactic, technique, and procedure to intimidate people in order to create anxiety, fear, and mayhem in support of the terrorists' immediate, intermediate, or long-term objectives.

There is no "magic formula" for the resolution of the issue of abductions, but there is no doubt that international action involving the formulation of a treaty defining terror abductions as "crimes against humanity" (which, in fact, they are) and bringing the perpetrators and leaders of the organizations behind these acts to justice, would certainly contribute to the eradication of this phenomenon.

Epilogue

Occurring shortly before publication, the scope and scale of the September 2013 mass hostage-taking attacks in the Philippines and Kenya necessitated their inclusion in a work of this nature.

The Zamboanga Hostage Crises (September 2013)

In August 2013, Moro National Liberation Front (MNLF) founding-chairman Nur Misuari declared the establishment of a "United Federated States of Bangsamoro Republik" to a gathering of his followers in his Sulu stronghold, and named himself president. According to the MNLF website, the new entity envisions a territory consisting of Mindanao, Basilan, Sulu, Tawi-Tawi, Palawan, and Sabah in northern Borneo.

Misuari's declaration came after President Benigno Aquino III's administration announced it was in final stages of negotiations for a peace deal with the Moro Islamic Liberation Front (MILF) that would result in a Bangsamoro political entity replacing the existing Autonomous Region in Muslim Mindanao (ARMM).

Misuari accused the Philippine government of violating the terms of a 1996 treaty by negotiating a separate deal with a rival faction, and repeatedly declared that he considers the terms of that deal to be long dead.

The Philippine government refused to recognize the Bangsamoro Republik. President Aquino stated that there was only one legitimate government in the nation, and charges of sedition charges were readied against Misuari immediately after his unilateral declaration of independence.

On 9 September 2013, several hundred MNLF fighters landed on the coast of Barangay Rio Hondo in Zamboanga City and routed an elite navy special operations group that opposed them, killing one soldier and wounding six others.

Their goal was to march to City Hall, raise their flag, and declare independence from the national government. A group spokesman claimed that the rebels had planned a peaceful march, but were attacked by the military.[2] By dawn, MNLF fighters – joined by around one hundred who had slipped into the city earlier – had occupied six coastal barangays (the smallest administrative division in the Philippines), holding hostage some two hundred civilians in multiple locations as human shields to deter attacks by the Philippine army, and had secured their perimeter with improvised explosive devices and snipers deployed in strategic positions.[3]

The government responded by sending military and police forces to surround the rebels, exchanging mortar fire, firing rockets from helicopters, and battling street-by-street to retake occupied neighborhoods. More than ninety police officers, soldiers, civilians, and rebels were killed during eight days of fighting.[4] According to social welfare and development sources, over 112,000 residents were displaced.[5]

At the time that this epilogue was written – 26 September 2013 – Philippine security forces were still battling MNLF rebels in Zamboanga City.

The Nairobi "Westgate Mall" Hostage Crisis (September 2013)

The siege began when a number of gunmen invaded Nairobi's upmarket Westgate mall firing automatic weapons and throwing grenades at weekend shoppers. At least sixty-one civilians and six security officers were killed. Responsibility for the 21 September 2013 attack was claimed by al Qaeda's Somali-based offshoot, "al Shabaab al Mujahideen".

Four days after the start of the siege, Kenya's President Uhuru Kenyatta announced that his country had "ashamed and defeated" its attackers. Four terrorists were dead and the bodies of at least three more were thought to remain in the rubble of the mall; the final death toll was expected to rise as Kenyan forces sifted through the ruins left after three floors collapsed during the final hours of fighting. President Kenyatta declared three days of national mourning, saying: "Fellow Kenyans, we have been badly hurt and feel great pain and loss – but we have been brave, united, and strong."[6]

The preparations

The plot was hatched weeks or months before, on Somali soil, by al Shabaab's "external operations arm". To enable effective operation in Kenya (where English and Swahili are national languages), English-speakers (some from the US, and possibly from other western countries) were picked to assault the carefully selected target – Nairobi's landmark Westgate consumer mall.[7]

The building's blueprints were studied down to the ventilation ducts, the attack was rehearsed, and the team was dispatched, slipping undetected through Kenya's porous borders. US security experts suspected the group must have had a safe house in Kenya, a place to store weapons and finalize plans for their rampage – suspicions borne out when Kenyan authorities discovered that the assailants had rented a shop in the mall over the preceding three months. A day or two before the attack, powerful belt-fed machine guns were secretly stashed there with the help of a colluding employee.[8]

Witnesses statements claimed several assailants toted Heckler & Koch G3 assault rifles (a bulky weapon used by Kenyan security services), suggesting that militants may have acquired weapons from corrupt army officers known to sell their guns or rent them for a few dollars per hour.[9]

Saturday, September 21

At midday on a busy Saturday, up to a dozen armed militants marched into the four-storey Westgate shopping mall in the Highridge suburb of north Nairobi, popular with wealthy Kenyans and expatriates, and sprayed the packed weekend shoppers with machine-gun fire and hand grenades. Gunmen went from store to store interrogating customers, allowing Muslims to escape from the mall, but shooting or taking hostage those not of that faith.[10] After killing scores of civilians, the militants retreated to a supermarket where they used the smuggled machine guns to hold off Kenyan forces, killing at least six security members.[11] The chaos included an early report on deaths: by the day's end, thirty-nine people had been killed. That figure that would soon grow.

Somalia's Islamist al Qaeda-linked al Shabaab rebels claimed responsibility. Using its official Twitter account, the group justified the attack as retaliation for Kenya's recent military intervention in Somalia and claimed its fighters had killed one hundred people. The international community condemned the terror along with Kenya's president, whose nephew and his fiancée were among those murdered.

Sunday, September 22

Kenyan security forces continued the siege, and confusion prevailed over the number of hostages and fatalities. Sporadic gunshots punctuated the day, between which were moments of silence. Authorities estimated the number of gunmen involved in the attack as between ten and fifteen. Later, unconfirmed reports hinted at who they may be: sources within al Shabaab spoke to CNN about nine names it published on Twitter – purportedly those of the perpetrators, they included up to three from the US, two from Somalia, and one each from Canada, Finland, Kenya, and Britain.[12]

The Kenyan authorities said that an unknown number of hostages were being held "in several locations" at the mall and that no communication had yet been established with the assailants, but claimed that more than a thousand people had been moved to safety since the previous day. Later that evening, the Kenyan army announced it had rescued most of the hostages, secured most of the complex, and was seeking to bring a "speedy conclusion" to the events.

Monday, September 23

The first announcement was made regarding deaths on the other side of the siege: three terrorists had been killed and more than two hundred civilians had been rescued, at a cost of eleven wounded Kenyan soldiers, according to statements by the Kenyan military.[13]

Barrages of heavy gunfire and loud explosions were heard as Kenyan troops continued to battle the militants inside the mall. Ali Mahmoud Rage, al Shabaab's spokesperson, threatened to order the killing of the remaining hostages. Towards the end of the security operation, three floors of the shopping center collapsed.[14]

Kenya's police chief said that some, but not all, of the hostages had been rescued, claiming "we're increasingly gaining advantage of the attackers". The Kenyan army announced that the mall attackers originated from various other countries. That afternoon, Interior Minister Joseph Ole Lenku said that two terrorists had been killed and security forces would soon end the siege: "We are in control of all the floors, the terrorists are running and hiding in some stores . . . There is no room for escape."[15]

Authorities released few details about the death toll. Apparently, most of those slain were Kenyans, but the dead included six British citizens, two French nationals, two Indians, and two Canadians, according to the governments of those countries. The US State Department said that five Americans were among the 175 people wounded.[16]

Tuesday, September 24 – The end of the crisis

Officials said at least 62 people were killed in the attack on the mall, and more than 170 wounded. The dead included six Britons, two French women, two Canadians including a diplomat, a Chinese woman, two Indians, a South Korean, a South African, and a Dutch woman. Also killed was seventy-eight-year-old Ghanaian poet (and formerly UN envoy) Kofi Awoonor, whose son was also injured. Final casualty figures were expected to rise once the siege was concluded and the mall secured.

Western security officials were concerned that several terrorists left the mall during the mayhem, dropping their guns and disguising themselves as civilians – a fear echoed by certain witness accounts.[17]

In a series of "tweets" from an account believed to be genuine, al Shabaab claimed that "having failed to defeat the mujahideen inside the mall, Kenya disseminated chemical gases to end the siege", then, "to cover up their crime, the Kenyan government carried out a demolition of the building, burying evidence and all hostages under the rubble".[18] A government spokesperson immediately denied the claim, insisting that no chemical weapons had been used and saying that part of the mall collapsed after a fire started by the assailants caused structural weakness in a third-level parking lot, which then collapsed down to the ground floor. The official civilian death toll remained at sixty-one.[19]

President Kenyatta finally announced that the siege of Nairobi's Westgate mall had ended, calling for three-days of national mourning for the victims. Sixty-seven people had been killed in the attack, with four terrorists dead and eleven suspects held in custody. In a televised address to the nation, he said: "We have been badly hurt, but we have been brave, united and strong. Kenya has stared down evil and triumphed. We have defeated our enemies and showed the whole world what we can accomplish," and vowed that his government would not be dissuaded by the assault: "I want to be very clear and categorical: We shall not relent on the war on terror. We will continue that fight."

In a speech on 23 September, Somali President Hassan Sheikh Mohamud described al Shabaab as a threat to the world: "They are a threat to the continent of Africa, and the world at large."[20]

The mystery of the women terrorists

Many witnesses claimed they saw at least two female militants, armed to the teeth and dressed in fatigues. Kenyan officials had asserted earlier that there were no women among the shooters, but on Tuesday, 24 September, President Kenyatta seemed to revive the possibility that one of the assailants was a British woman.[21]

Several intelligence analysts speculated that the woman was Samantha Lewthwaite, a Muslim convert who had been married to one of the suicide bombers who struck London in 2005. Kenyan authorities had previously suspected that Lewthwaite (also known as the "white widow") had risen through the ranks of extremist groups and was leading a terrorism cell on the Kenyan coast. They had nearly captured her in a 2011 operation, but she escaped.

Conclusions

Since 2008, al Qaeda and its affiliated terror organizations have adopted a modus operandi that may be defined as *self-sacrifice mega terror abduction*, which was first introduced by Chechen rebels against Russian civilian targets. The Westgate mall attack in Nairobi is itself a variation of previous attacks in Mumbai in 2008 and Algeria in 2013. This new type of terror combines a suicide operation with the taking of hostages to be used primarily as "human shields", not as real bargaining chips in negotiation. The terrorists' goals are to kill as many civilians as possible and to extend the battle against security forces for as long as possible (usually about 3–4 days) in order to gain maximum media coverage.

These latest attacks are to be considered a relatively complex type of terrorism that requires detailed planning and advanced operational skills, and, to a great extent, match the theoretical model that describes terror as a type of theater in which each participant plays a role designated to transmit the terrorists' message.

The main characteristics of these recent terror attacks are:

The perpetrators
- The Mumbai attack (November 2008) was perpetrated by Lashkar-e-Taiba, a Pakistan-based al Qaeda–affiliated terror organization.
- The In-Amenas gas facility in Algeria (January 2013) was assaulted by al Qaeda of the Islamic Maghreb (AQIM).
- The attack on the Westgate mall in Nairobi (September 2013) was carried out by al Shabaab al Mujahideen – al Qaeda's franchise in eastern Africa.

The targets
- The targets chosen were prominent, public places important to the economy and tourism (Mumbai's hotels, Algeria's major gas refinery, Kenya's flagship shopping mall).
- The targets contained foreign victims (tourists and businessmen in the hotels and Israeli Jews in Mumbai's Chabad House, workers at Algeria's In-Amenas gas facility, and expatriates at Nairobi's Westgate shopping center).

Strategic demands
- The withdrawal of French forces from Mali.
- The withdrawal of Kenyan forces from Somalia. The terror organizations knew that such demands would prove unacceptable to the governments concerned.

Neighboring countries
- In all cases, the attackers had a safe haven in a neighboring country (Pakistan for the India attack, Libya in the case of Algeria, and Somalia for the attack in Kenya).

Large groups of terrorists
- Ten terrorists in Mumbai.
- Around 30–40 terrorists in Algeria.
- Up to ten in Kenya.

A large number of hostages
- Hundreds in Mumbai.
- Hundreds in Algeria.
- Hundreds in Kenya.

Heavy losses
- From dozens to hundreds killed, and hundreds wounded, in each of the three cases.
- Some of the dead were foreign citizens from a variety of countries.

Summary

The way in which the Nairobi mall attack was carried out aligned with al Qaeda's new policy, proclaimed by Ayman al Zawahiri on 13 September 2013, against attacking non-western states unless the regime was part of "the American forces". Al Zawahiri called upon supporters to ensure that chosen targets were western-affiliated and to take measures to avoid Muslim casualties, while recommending taking "the citizens of the countries that are participating in the invasion of Muslim countries as hostages so that our prisoners may be freed in exchange".[22]

The modern urban arena offers a multitude of high-profile, publicity-rich potential targets, and effective protection of all is near impossible. So what lessons can be learned for the future? I would suggest three:

- Better and more efficient intelligence prior to an attack and during the phase of crisis management.
- Qualified counter-terrorism units capable of fast responses. Kenyan, Algerian, and Indian authorities waited too long before taking definitive action and allowed the sieges to stretch out over three or four days. If they were dealing with a "normal" hostage situation, that may have made sense, but future terrorists should not be allowed to work their evil deeds for so long.
- Better coordination between different agencies and services involved in the crisis management phase.

An attack of this type keeps the terror organization in the news, extracting maximum publicity value, and there is evidence that other militant groups become motivated to adopt similar tactics. Terror organizations continue to threaten their adversaries, already traumatized by previous tragedies, by declaring that similar attacks will follow. It is imperative now to prepare an effective response to further, inevitable, attacks of this nature.

NOTES

1. "Incompetence and Politicking in Zamboanga", *The Manila Times*, 15 September 2013.
2. Floyd Whaley, "Philippine Fighters Surrender After Capturing Police Chief", *The New York Times*, 17 September 2013.
3. "Philippines: Mistreatment, Hostage-Taking in Zamboanga", *Human Rights Watch* (HRW), 19 September 2013.
4. Whaley, "Philippine Fighters Surrender", *New York Times*, 17 September 2013.
5. "Philippines: Mistreatment, Hostage-taking", *HRW*, 19 September 2013.
6. "Nairobi Westgate Mall Massacre And Siege Is Now Officially Over – A News Roundup", *War News Updates*, 25 September 2013.
7. Jeffrey Gettleman, Nicholas Kulish, and Eric Schmitt, "Before Kenya Attack, Rehearsals and Planting of Machine Guns", *The New York Times*, 24 September 2013.
8. Alex Marquardt, "U.S. Agents Already Sifting Rubble of Kenya Mall Attack", *ABC News*, 25 September 2013.
9. *Ibid*.
10. Michael Martinez, "Kenya Terror Timeline: Four Deadly Days of a Store-to-Store Siege", *CNN*, 24 September 2013.
11. Gettleman, Kulish, and Schmitt, "Before Kenya Attack", *New York Times*, 24 September 2013.
12. Martinez, "Kenya Terror Timeline", *CNN*, 24 September 2013.
13. *Ibid*.
14. "Nairobi Westgate Mall Massacre", *War News Updates*, 25 September 2013.

15 Tom McCarthy and Shiv Malik, "Kenya Mall Siege: Security Forces 'Continue to Secure' Site", *The Guardian*, 23 September 2013.
16 Martinez, "Kenya Terror Timeline", *CNN*, 24 September 2013.
17 Gettleman, Kulish, and Schmitt, "Before Kenya Attack", *New York Times*, 24 September 2013.
18 "Kenyan Forces Scour Mall for Siege Survivors", *al Jazeera*, 25 September 2013.
19 *Ibid.*
20 Hamza Mohamed, "Somalia Intervention Cited for Mall Assault", *al Jazeera*, 24 September 2013.
21 Gettleman, Kulish, and Schmitt, "Before Kenya Attack", *New York Times*, 24 September 2013.
22 Paul Cruickshank and Tim Lister, "Al-Shabaab Breaks New Ground with Complex Nairobi Attack", *CNN*, 23 September 2013.

Select Bibliography

Alvanou, Maria. *Hamas and Hizbullah Kidnappings: The Political and Strategic Implications.* Milan: Italian Team for Security, Terroristic Issues and Managing Emergencies (ITSTIME), July 2006.
Antokol, Norman and Mayer Nudell. *No One A Neutral: Political Hostage-Taking in the Modern World.* Medina, OH: Alpha Publications of Ohio, 1990.
Bakhash, Shaul. *The Reign of the Ayatollahs: Iran and the Islamic Revolution.* New York: Basic Books, 1986.
Bergen, Peter L. *Holy War Inc.: Inside the Secret World of Osama Bin Laden.* London: Weidenfeld and Nicolson, 2001.
Bodansky, Yossef. *Bin Laden: The Man Who Declared War on America.* New York: Forum, 1999.
Bowden, Mark. *Guests of the Ayatollah: The First Battle in America's War with Militant Islam.* New York: Atlantic Monthly Press, 2006.
Burgin, Maskit, Ariel Merari, and Anat Kurz. *Foreign Hostages in Lebanon.* Issue 25 of JCSS Memorandum. Tel Aviv: Jaffee Center for Strategic Studies, Tel Aviv University, 1988.
Carter, Michael E. *Islamic Terrorism in Southeast Asia: An Effects-Based U.S. Regional Strategy against Jemaah Islamiyah and Abu Sayyaf.* School of Advanced Military Studies, United States Army Command and General Staff College, Fort Leavenworth, Kansas, AY 04–05, May 2004. United States: BiblioScholar, 2012.
Chubin, Shahram. *Iran and Its Neighbors: The Impact of the Gulf War.* London: Centre for Security and Conflict Studies, 1987.
Cline, Ray S. and Yonah Alexander. *Terrorism as a State-sponsored Covert Warfare.* Fairfax, VA: Hero Books, 1986.
Crenshaw, Martha. *Terrorism, Legitimacy and Power.* Middletown, CT: Wesleyan University, 1983.
Doval, Ajit. "Islamic Terrorism in South Asia and India's Strategic Response". In *Oxford Papers: Policing.* Volume 1, Issue 1. Oxford: Oxford University Press, 2007, pp. 63–69.
Edelist, Ran and Ilan Kfir. *Ron Arad: The Riddle.* Tel Aviv: Yediot Aharonot, 2000.
Ganor, Boaz. *The Labyrinth of Countering Terror: Tools for Decision Making.* Herzliya: Mifalot Publishing, 2005.
Haqqani, Husain. "The Ideologies of South Asian Jihadi Groups". In *Current Trends in Islamist Ideology.* Indianapolis, IN: Hudson Institute, 2005, pp. 12–26.

Harel, A. and A. Issacharoff. *34 Days: Israel, Hezbollah and the War in Lebanon.* New York: Palgrave Macmillan, 2008.

Kfir, Ilan (ed). *The "Irangate" Affair: The Tower Committee Report.* Tel Aviv: Modan Publishing, 1989.

Kramer, Martin S. *The Moral Logic of Hizballah.* Volume 101 of Occasional Papers. Tel Aviv: The Dayan Center for Middle Eastern and African Studies, The Shiloah Institute, Tel Aviv University, 1987.

Kurz, Anat, Maskit Burgin, and David Tal. *Islamic Terror and Israel.* Tel Aviv: Papyrus Press, 1993.

Lacey, Robert. *The Kingdom: Arabia and the House of Sa'ud.* New York: Avon Books, 1981.

Luttwak, Edward. *Strategy: The Logic of War and Peace.* Cambridge, MA: Harvard University Press, 2001.

Mondale, Walter. *The Good Fight: A Life in Liberal Politics.* New York: Simon and Schuster, 2010.

Netanyahu, Binyamin. *Terror: How Can the West Win?* Tel Aviv: Sifriat Ma'ariv, 1987.

Rabasa, Angel, Robert D. Blackwill, Peter Chalk, Kim Cragin, C. Christine Fair, Brian A. Jackson, Brian Michael Jenkins, Seth G. Jones, Nathaniel Shestak, Ashley J. Tellis. *The Lessons of Mumbai.* Santa Monica, CA: The RAND Corporation, 2009 (PDF).

Ranstorp, Magnus. *Hizballah in Lebanon: The Politics of the Western Hostage Crisis.* New York: St. Martin's Press, 1997.

Schaefer, Robert W. *The Insurgency in Chechnya and the North Caucasus: From Gazavat to Jihad.* Santa Barbara, CA: Praeger, 2010.

Schmid, Alex and Albert Jongman. *Political Terrorism: A New Guide To Actors, Authors, Concepts, Data Bases, Theories, and Literature.* New Brunswick: Transaction Publishers, 2005.

Shay, Shaul. *The Axis of Evil: Iran, the Hizballah and Palestinian Terror.* New Brunswick: Transaction Publishers, 2005.

——. *The Red Sea Terror Triangle: Sudan, Somalia, Yemen, and Islamic Terror.* New Brunswick: Transaction Publishers, 2011.

——. *Islamic Terror Abductions in the Middle East.* Brighton: Sussex Academic Press, 2008.

Tankel, Stephen. "Lashkar-e-Taiba: Past Operations and Future Prospects". In *National Security Studies Program Policy Paper.* Washington, DC: New America Foundation, April 2011, pp. 1–4.

Trofimov, Yaroslav. *The Siege of Mecca: The Uprising at Islam's Holiest Shrine.* New York: Anchor Books, 2007.

Wilkinson, Paul. *Terrorism and the Liberal State.* London: Macmillan Education Ltd., 1997.

Zonis, Marvin and Daniel Brumberg. "Khomeini, The Islamic Republic of Iran and the Arab World". In *Harvard Middle East Papers.* Issue 5. Cambridge, MA: Harvard University Press, 1987, p. 34.

Index

Aballes, Cosme, 211
Abd al Rahman, Fuad, 196
Abdal, Thaier Saad, 150
Abdel Nasser, Gamal. *See* Nasser, Abdel Gamal
Abdel Rahman, Omar, 205, 223
Abdel Wadoud, Abu Musab. *See* Droukdal, Abdelmalek
abduction
  arenas, 9, 13, 274–275, 282
  as a criminal act, 8, 15–16
  as an act of war, 15–16
  classification, 9, 11–12, 18
  conclusion of, 15, 19
  counter-abduction, 272
  definition of, 7
  financial aspects, 22, 31–32, 143, 148, 203, 215, 248
  for ransom, 7–8, 15, 22, 31–32, 36, 78, 87, 93–94, 102, 114, 125, 142–143, 148, 159, 181, 186, 191, 202–203, 207, 211, 215, 235, 249, 274
  goals of, 7–10, 12–15, 31, 67, 72, 215, 220, 228, 274, 281
  mass, 257, 259, 276
  model for the conduct of, 14
  modus operandi, 8–10, 14, 16, 22, 58, 229, 281
  negotiation, 8–15, 19, 25–26, 28, 31, 34, 40–42, 51, 59–63, 67–68, 70–73, 75–76, 78–79, 82, 86, 88, 93, 95, 97–98, 103–104, 111, 113–114, 129, 142, 146–148, 203, 216, 222, 227, 230, 237–238, 244, 258, 260–262, 266, 270, 276, 281
  of groups, 7–8, 24, 104, 144, 174, 185–186, 194–195, 217
  stages of, 14–15, 24–26
  state intervention in, 17–18, 29, 40, 80

  targets of, 24, 31, 34, 36, 38, 61, 65, 80–81, 84, 135, 144, 151, 168, 191–192, 248–249, 281–282
  timing of, 12, 34, 90
  war of, 196
  "waves" of, 275
Abdulkhadzhiev, Aslambek, 259
Abdullah, King. *See* Saud, Abdullah bin Abdulaziz bin
Abdullah, King, II. *See* Hussein, Abdullah ibn al, II
Abu al Yazid, Mustafa, 22
Abu Bakr al Siddiq Brigade, 144
Abu Ghraib, 171
Abu Hamza. *See* Masri, Abu Hamza al
Abu Ibrahim, Mustapha. *See* Sahraoui, Nabil
Abu Iyad. *See* Khalaf, Salah Mesbah
Abu Mohammad, Saleh, 218–219
Abu Nidal. *See* Banna, Sabri Khalil al
Abu Qatada. *See* Othman, Omar Mahmoud
Abu Sabaya. *See* Tilao, Aldam
Abu Sayyaf Group (ASG), 201–212
Abu Zeid, Abdelhamid, 224, 228
Abyan, 182, 189
Adam, Udi, 66
Aden, 175, 182. *See also* Gulf of Aden
Aden-Abyan Islamic Army, 180, 182–183
Adham, Amran, 92
Afghanistan, 28–30, 53, 102–108, 110, 112, 114–115, 118–121, 125, 128–129, 154, 168–169, 179–180, 186, 202, 216, 219, 221, 237, 274
  "Afghan alumni", 263
  Independent Election Commission (IEC), 103
  International Chamber of Commerce (AICC), 102

Afghanistan *(continued)*
  National Directorate of Security (NDS), 102
Africa, 214, 219–220, 225, 227, 238, 249, 280
  East, 119, 180, 247, 274, 281
  Horn of, 238, 248
  Maghreb, 214–215, 230, 274
  North, 28–30, 196, 215, 227
  Sahel, 215, 218, 228–231, 274 (*see also* Sahara)
  South Africa, 2, 210, 247, 280
  West, 29–30
African–American, 38, 40
African Union, 236–237
  Mission in Somalia (AMISOM), 241
Ağca, Mehmet Ali, 169
Agosti, Livia Leu, 50
Ahajan, Hatib, 209
Ahmadi, Qari Yousef, 103, 112
Ahmadinejad, Mahmoud, 35, 43, 47–48, 51–52, 54
Ahmar, Ali Mohsen al, 183
Ahmed Awa, 49
Ahmed, Sharif Sheikh, 236
Aioun, 218
Air Africa, 94
aircraft, 9, 17, 24, 41, 51, 100n46
  antiaircraft, 60
  cargo, 41
  carrier, 89, 248
  drone, 49, 175, 221, 226, 240
  fighter, 49, 58, 60–61
  helicopter, 41, 43, 60, 64, 73, 84, 109, 133, 167, 170, 173, 207, 222, 238, 241, 243, 260, 268, 277
  hijack, 17–24, 38, 84, 89–92, 94, 128–129, 256, 271
  passenger, 11, 87, 89
airport, 24, 44, 52, 84–85, 94, 128–129, 148, 192, 198, 206, 222
al Anbar, 144
al Azhar, 209
al Dawa, 83
al Hiyam, 63
al Itihaad al Islamiyah (AIAI), 250
al Jamaah al Islamiyah al Musallaha. *See* Armed Islamic Group

al Jamaah as Salafiyyah lid Dawah wal-Qital. *See* Salafist Group for Preaching and Combat
al Malahem, 175
al Minhad, 129
al Muhajiroun, 228
al Mulathameen, 223–224, 228
al Qaeda, 29–32, 114, 119–121, 124–126, 143, 151–152, 154–155, 171–172, 174–176, 180, 186–188, 198, 237–238, 270, 275, 281–282
  finance, 21–22, 32
  in Iraq (AQI), 31, 143–144, 170, 229
  in Pakistan, 22, 115, 117–119
  in Somalia (al Shabaab), 31, 236–246, 250, 277–281
  in the Arabian Peninsula (AQAP), 31, 162, 170, 175, 185–187, 249
  in the Islamic Maghreb (AQIM), 31, 214–221, 223–224, 228–231, 238, 281
  in the Philippines, 203
  in Saudi Arabia, 22, 188
  in Yemen, 174–175, 182, 186, 188
  maritime strategy, 248–251
  of Jihad in the Land of the Two Rivers, 144
  prisoners, 28, 150, 170, 175, 180
  training manual, 22, 28
al Qa'im, 144
al Quds. *See* Iran: Revolutionary Guards
"al Quds Brigade", 172
al Shabaab al Mujahideen. *See* al Qaeda: in Somalia
al Tawhid wal Jihad. *See* Group of Monotheism and Jihad
Alani, Mustafa, 143
Alawi, Yusuf bin, 51
Aldakheel, Bandar and Faisal, 171
Aleppo, 197
Algeria, 22, 41, 84, 86, 91–92, 111, 154, 184, 214–218, 222–231, 238, 270, 274, 281–283
Algiers, 22, 215, 225
Allex, Denis, 236–238
Almeda, Wilde, 210
Alsaykhan, Rakan, 171

Alsheikh, Rahamim, 58, 60, 71, 73, 75, 98
Amal, 58, 61–62, 76, 81, 90
Amane, Abu Yahya, 228
ambassador
   Algerian, 218
   Arab, 147
   Egyptian, 147
   German, 94
   Iranian, 72
   Mauritanian, 218
   Pakistani, 114, 124
   Somali, 241
   Swiss, 50–51
   US, 38, 122
America. *See* United States
American Airlines, 115
Amman, 194
Amnesty International, 154, 195–196
amputation, 154. *See also* decapitation
Amritsar, 128
Anderamboukane festival, 217
Ankara, 256
Ansar al Sharia. *See* Supporters of Sharia Law
Ansar al Sunna. *See* Assembly of the Helpers of Sunna
anti-terrorism, 131, 220
Antiterrorism Act, 41
Antsaria, 58
Aquino, Benigno S., III, 208, 276
Arab, 109, 117, 147, 154–155, 170, 194–195, 198, 202, 217, 249, 270–271
   Arab–Israel conflict, 34–35
   Arabism, 159
   fighters (see *mujahideen*)
   government, 147
   hostages, 59, 158
   Israeli, 70
   League, 69
   prisoners, 75, 77
   states, 37, 77, 128, 134, 144, 153, 191, 210
   world, 58, 65, 143
Arab Petroleum Investments Corporation (APICorp), 171–172
"Arab Spring", 187, 191, 198, 228–229
Arabian Sea, 130, 249–250

Arad, Jumadali, 206
Arad, Ron, 58, 60–62, 71–73, 75–76, 98
Arafat, Yasser, 83
Aramaic, 152
Areva, 219–220
Arlit, 219
Armed Islamic Group (GIA), 214, 238
Armstrong, Eugene, 146, 155
Army of Jhangvi. *See* Lashkar-e-Jhangvi
Army of Muhammad. *See* Jaish-e-Mohammed
Army of the Guardians of the Islamic Revolution. *See* Iran: Revolutionary Guards
Army of the Pure. *See* Pakistan: Lashkar-e-Taiba
Asadullah National Task Force (ANTF), 209
Asayib Ahl al Haq. *See* League of the Righteous
Asia, 102, 115, 203–204, 247
Assad, Bashar al, 54, 191–194, 196–198
Assad, Hafez al, 86, 90
Assembly of the Helpers of Sunna, 144
Assyria, 152
Ataq, 184
Athens, 84, 89
Atlit, 90
Atyani, Baker, 208–209
Aubriere, Marc, 236
Aushev, Ruslan, 267, 270
Australia, 28, 182–183, 204, 207
Austria, 51, 183, 188–189, 215–216
Autonomous Region in Muslim Mindanao (ARMM), 202, 276
Avitan, Adi, 58, 64
Avraham, Binyamin, 58, 64
Avrazya, 261
Awa, Muhammad Salim al, 155
Aweys, Hassan Dahir, 236
Awoonor, Kofi, 280
"axis of evil", 33
Azaz, 197
Azdi, Abu Sufyan al. *See* Shihri, Said Ali Jabir al Khathim al
Azhar, Maulana Masood, 129
Azizuddin, Tariq, 114

Bab al Mandab, 247, 249
Babar, Khalid, 122
Babylonia, 152
Badakhshan, 110
Badr, Izz al Din, 196
Baghdad, 43–44, 46, 49, 142, 144–145, 147–153
  Sadr City, 44–45, 149
Baghdadi, Abu Omar al Qurashi al, 150
Bagram, 106, 112, 120
  "Grey Lady" of, 120–121
Bahktiar, Shahpour, 38
Bahrain, 45
Baidoa, 241
Balala, Najib, 243
Balkans, 154–155
Balochistan, 115, 118, 125
Balochistan Liberation United Front, 115
Baluchi, Ammar al, 120
Bamako, 218
Bangalore, 131
Bangkok, 84
Bangladesh, 168
Bangsamoro, 209, 276
Banisadr, Abolhassan, 40
Bank of America, 168
Banna, Sabri Khalil al, 81
Barak, Ehud, 64–65
Barangay Bulanting, 211
Barangay Rio Hondo, 276
Barayev, Arbi and Movsar, 262
Barcelona Acció Solidària, 218
Barqawi, Isam Mohammad Tahir al, 169–170
Barre, Mohammed Siad, 235
Barsukov, Mikhail, 260
Basayev, Shamil, 23, 255–259, 264, 267, 269–271
Basilan, 202, 206, 208, 210–212, 276
Basra, 44, 47
Battar, al, 22
Bates Treaty, 201
Bauer, Shane, 49–52, 54
Baumel, Zecharia, 98
Bayona, Armando, 211
Bazargan, Mehdi, 38–39
Bearer of the Sword. *See* Abu Sayyaf Group

Beckett, Margaret, 47–48
Bedouin, 30, 162–163
Beirut, 61, 68, 73–74, 81, 83–84, 86, 88, 90, 94, 155, 197–198
Beit Jabil, 59
Bekaa Valley, 198
Belgium, 131
Belmokhtar, Mokhtar, 271, 223–225, 228
Benalia, Yacine, 270
Benedict, XVI, 151
Berg, Nicholas, 155
Bergdahl, Bowe Robert, 105–108, 121
Berlin, 37
Berlusconi, Silvio, 219
Berri, Nabih, 61–62
Beslan, 11, 257, 264, 269–270
Bhutto, Zulfikar Ali, 165
Bigley, Kenneth, 145–146
Black Flags, 144
Black September, 12
Blechschmidt, Rudolf, 113
Bolshevik, 254. *See also* Communism
Bonn, 95
Borneo, 209, 276
Bosnia, 25, 119, 154
Boston, 119
Boucheneb, Mohamed Lamine, 222
Boumerdassi, Oussama al, 216
Bouralha, Kamel Rabat, 270
Bouteflika, Abdelaziz, 231
Britain. *See* United Kingdom
Brown, Gordon, 217
Brunei, 47
Brzezinski, Zbigniew, 167
Buckley, William, 85–86, 88
Budyonnovsk, 257
Bulani, Jawad al, 152
Bulgaria, 155
Bulo Marer, 237–238
Burkina Faso, 216, 218
Burnham, Gracia and Martin, 205–206, 211
Burundi, 237
Bush, George W., 1, 29, 33, 43–44, 46, 203, 256, 266

Cagayan de Tawi-Tawi, 210–211, 276
Calipari, Nicola, 148

Cama hospital, 130
Camatte, Pierre, 218, 228
Cameron, David, 242
Camp Julien, 108
Canada, 40, 184, 216–217, 224–225, 279–280
Cape of Good Hope, 247
Care International, 246
Carr, Bob, 207
Carr, Camilla, 255
Carter, Jimmy, 39–42, 53, 167–169
Catholic. *See* Christian: Catholic
Caucasus, 254, 257, 269
Central Intelligence Agency (CIA), 86, 88, 116–117, 120, 123–124, 146, 226
Chabad House, 133, 281
Chad, 216
Chaffei, Abdallah, 216
Chaldean. *See* Christian: Chaldean
Chandler, Paul and Rachel, 240, 242
Charkh, 108, 110
Charles de Gaulle airport, 85
Chatrapati Shivaji, 130
Chavez, Ernan, 211
Chechnya, 22–23, 119, 154, 254–264, 267, 270–271, 274
   Republic of Ichkeria, 254, 267
   terrorism, 11, 22–23, 215, 256–264, 270–271, 281
   war, 254–260, 264
Cheh, Camilia, 151
Chernomyrdin, Viktor, 258–260
Chicago, 136–137
China, 43, 125, 132, 204, 207, 212, 280
Chirac, Jacques, 63, 82, 92
Chirazi, Mohsen, 44
Christian, 29, 51, 72, 143, 151–153, 171, 173–174, 202, 211, 217, 274
   Anglican, 152, 182
   apostle, 152, 155
   Armenian Orthodox, 152
   Catholic, 151–152, 211
   Chaldean, 152
   Coptic, 151
   Christ, Jesus, 48, 155, 158, 214
   Christmas Day, 106, 119
   Christmas Eve, 182
   Church of England, 87, 93
   Church of Rome, 151
   Egyptian Church, 152
   Greek Orthodox, 152
   Presbyterian, 104
Church of Our Lady of Salvation, 150–152
Church of the Nativity, 274
CIA. *See* Central Intelligence Agency
Cicala, Nicola Sergio, 218–219
Cicippio, Joseph, 75, 88
Clark, Ramsey, 39
Clemente, Jacinto, 211
Clinton, Hillary, 52, 124, 204
coalition, 1, 43–44, 48, 98, 105, 107, 109, 142–149, 154–155, 180, 183, 191, 240, 250
Coballes, Noel, 207
Colaba, 133
Cole, USS. *See* USS *Cole*
"Colonel Orstkhoyev". *See* Khuchbarov, Ruslan Tagirovich
Combined Task Force 150 (CTF-150), 250
Commonwealth of Independent States (CIS), 267
Communism, 166
Communist Party of the Philippines (CPP), 201. *See also* New Peoples Army
Community of the Impoverished. *See* Jamaat-ul-Fuqra
Compaoré, Blaise, 216
Constantine, Wafa, 151
convert
   to Christianity, 217
   to Islam, 149, 151, 205, 210, 218, 280
convoy, 24, 59, 84, 91, 110, 148, 182, 194, 214, 238, 250, 260
Cordes, Rudolph, 94–95
counter-terrorism, 23, 29, 89, 122, 127, 180, 203, 218, 243, 250, 283
Creswell, Jason, 46
Cuba, 116, 180
crusade, 31, 169, 172, 210, 219–220, 237, 249
Cruz, Angelo de, 146
Cumbers, Simon, 170

Cyprus, 51, 84

Dacquer, Sonny, 211
Dadaab, 245–246
Dagestan, 254–256, 258, 260–261
Dakar Rally, 216
Damascus, 61, 72, 85, 90, 92, 95, 97, 192–193, 196–197
Dargo, 258
Davis, Raymond, 123–124
Davutoğlu, Ahmet, 192
Dawlat al Iraq al Islamiyyah. *See* "Islamic State of Iraq"
decapitation, 142–146, 153–155, 274. *See also* amputation
Dedieu, Marie, 243–244
Dehere, Abdul Rahman, 240
Deir ez-Zor, 196
Delhi, 128–129, 133
Delory, Vincent, 221
democracy, 1–2, 35, 82, 127
Denmark, 136
Dichter, Avi, 69
Din, Mustafa Badr al and Saada Badr al, 83–84
dinar, 229
Dirani, Mustafa, 58, 61–62, 72, 76–77
Direction Générale de la Sécurité Extérieure (DGSE), 237
Djibouti, 244, 249
Dodge, David, 81
Dol, Thierry, 221
Dos Palmas, 205–206, 210
Droukdal, Abdelmalek, 214–215, 228
Dubai, 29, 59, 84, 128–129, 143, 174
Dubrovka theater, 262
Dudayev, Dzhokhar, 254–255, 260–261
Dulaimi, Azhar al, 149
Dyer, Edwin, 217–218, 228
Dzasokhov, Aleksander, 266, 270

economic, 4, 30–31, 43, 93, 97, 101, 143, 187, 215, 225, 231, 246, 281
  conflict economy, 102
  cooperation, 6, 124
  "Economic Jihad", 251
  global, 247–248, 251
  local, 187, 220, 235, 281
  recession, 201–202
  sabotage, 245
  sanctions, 6, 22, 40–41, 47, 249
Egypt, 41, 69, 144, 147, 150–152, 155, 159, 163, 166, 169, 172, 179, 184, 225
Egyptian Church. *See* Christian: Egyptian Church
Elysée, 111
"Embassy War", 92
Engel, Richard, 195
English. *See* United Kingdom
English language, 7, 106, 109, 111, 119, 270, 277
Entebbe, 78
Euphrates River, 142
Euro, 31
Europe, 22, 32, 89–90, 97, 102, 132, 165, 188, 214–218, 229–231, 247, 254
European Union (EU), 188, 230
Evin, 52
explosive, 8–9, 24, 43, 62–64, 67, 72, 94, 112, 130, 135, 142, 164, 173, 182, 203, 222–223, 227, 249, 257, 262–268, 274, 277, 279

Fadlallah, Muhammad Hussein, 59, 72, 75, 81, 83, 93–94
Faisal, Saud al, 69, 163
Faisal, Turki al, 175
Faithful Resistance, 58, 62, 72, 76
Fallahian, Ali, 37
Fallon, Scott, 46
Fallujah, 145
Fallujah Squadron, 170
Farah, 112–113
Farahi, Abdul Khaliq, 103
Farouq, Omar al, 248
Farrall, Leah, 28
Fatah, 83
Fattal, Joshua, 49–52, 54
FBI. *See* Federal Bureau of Investigation
Federal Bureau of Investigation (FBI), 119–121, 136, 146
Feldman, Zvi, 98
Féret, Marc, 221
Fillon, François, 230, 244

Index 293

finance, 29, 44–45, 130, 148, 174, 187, 248, 251. *See also* economic
aid, 5, 18, 23
demands, 229
institutions, 21, 33, 255
international, 22, 117
self-, 31, 215
of terror, 22, 32, 36, 120, 126, 135, 180, 203, 224, 241, 251
Fini, Gianfranco, 148
Fink, Yosef, 58, 60, 71, 73, 75, 98
Finland, 188–189, 210, 279
Finsbury Park Mosque, 270
Fowler, Robert, 216
France, 22, 29–30, 34, 38, 53, 63, 80–84, 91–93, 105, 110–111, 125, 147, 155, 166, 181–182, 184–186, 194, 204, 210, 215–216, 218–224, 226–228, 230–231, 235–238, 243–246, 249–250, 274, 279–280, 282
Frattini, Franco, 219
Free Syrian Army (FSA), 191–194, 198
al Baraa brigade, 192
Frouzanda, Minojahar, 44

G-7 conference, 259
G-8 conference, 69
Gaddafi, Muammar (father of S), 204, 216, 229
Gaddafi, Saif al Islam (son of M), 216
Galashki, 271
Gamez, Alicia, 218
Ganor, Boaz, 3
Gao, 219, 223
Gardner, Frank, 45, 170
gas, 26, 119, 125, 184, 220, 222–228, 231, 261, 281
facility, 222–228
noxious, 262–263, 266, 280
Gaza, 67, 69
Gemayel, Amine, 69
Geneva Convention, 17, 62, 158, 192
Georgia, 254
Germaneau, Michel, 219, 230
Germany, 37, 41, 76, 80, 93–95, 107, 174, 181, 185, 215, 254
hostages, 94–95, 110, 113, 173–174, 181, 183–185, 204, 210, 215–217, 224
Mikonos restaurant, 37
West, 36
Ghailam, Mohssin, 182
Ghazni, 120
Ghesquière, Hervé, 110–111
Gilani, Daood Sayed. *See* Headley, David
Gilani, Mubarak Ali, 115–116
Gilani, Yousaf Raza, 122–124
Gillard, Julia, 207
Golan Heights, 194
Goldwasser, Ehud, 59, 67, 70
Gordji, Wahid, 92
Gorelov, V. V., 193
Grand Imam of al Azhar. *See* Tayeb, Ahmed al
Grand Mosque, 162–164, 166–167, 274
Green Brigades, 144
"Green Zone", 142
Gregg, Herbert, 255
Group of Monotheism and Jihad, 144
Groupe d'Intervention de la Gendarmerie Nationale, 166
Grozny, 254–255, 257
Gruenwald, Anita, 174
Guantanamo Bay, 28, 106, 108, 116–117, 120, 180
Guay, Louis, 216
guillotine, 155
Gul, Samer, 108
Gulf of Aden, 235, 247–250
Gulf of Oman, 250
Gulf, Persian. *See* Persian Gulf
Gulf state, 21, 52
Gulf war, 97
Guran, 271. *See also* Kurdish
Gurazhev, Sultan, 264
Guy, Golan, 63
Gyeong-ja, Kim, 104

Haddad, Fadi Jamil, 191
Hadi, Abdrabuh Mansur, 188
Hadramawt, 179, 185
Hague, William, 226, 242
Hague Convention, 17
Haji, Mohamed Yusuf, 246
Halima, Atsam, 159

Hamadi, Abbas Ali and Muhammad Ali, 94–95
Hamas, 69, 75, 77
Hamid, Mustafa. *See* Masri, Abu Walid al
Hammadou, Yahia Abu Amar Abid. *See* Abu Zeid, Abdelhamid
Hammond, Philip, 226
Hapilon, Isnilon, 206
Haq, Zia-ul-, 119, 165
Haqqani group, 105, 107–108
Haqqani, Husain, 124
Haqqani, Jalaluddin, 105
Hariri, Ali Muhammad, 94
Harkat-ul-Mujahideen, 117, 128–129
Harper, Stephen, 216
Hassan, Abu al, 182–183
Hassoun, Abdessattar, 193
Hattab, Hassan, 214
Headley, David, 136
Helmand, 110
Hensley, Jack, 146, 155
Hentschel, Anna and Lydia, 173
Hermon. *See* Mount Hermon
Higgins, William, 73–75, 85, 90–91, 97
Hiin Dawa'o, 241
hijack, 79, 94
 of aircraft, 11, 17–18, 21–22, 24, 38, 84–85, 89–90, 94, 96, 100n46, 117, 128–129, 180, 256
 of buses, 79, 197
 of ships, 17, 130, 240, 247, 249–250, 261
 of transportation, 8–11
 of vehicles, 172
Hindu, 134, 168, 173
Hizb al Islam, 236, 240
Hizballah, 8, 27, 38, 46, 58–62, 64–77, 81–89, 91, 93–98, 149, 192, 195–198
 abductions, 28, 58–59, 64–67, 80–85, 88, 93–94
 and America, 86–87
 and Hamas, 69, 77
 and Iran, 33, 37–38, 43, 58–59, 62, 72, 75–76, 79, 83–85, 91, 93–94, 97, 198
 and Israel, 96–97
 political leaders, 59, 68, 72, 75–79,

81, 83, 90, 94–95, 98, 192, 197
 "Shurat al Jihad", 88
 Special Security Agency (SSA), 38, 77, 84–87, 89–90
HMS *Cornwall*, 47
Hollande, François, 238
Holtzberg, Gavriel and Rivka, 133
Homs, 193
Hoogendoorn, Jan, 184
Horn of Africa, 238, 248
Houthi, 185
Hudaydah, 188
human rights, 194, 210, 257
Human Rights Watch (HRW), 69, 152
Humanitarian Relief Foundation (IHH), 193
Hussain, Altaf, 121
Hussein, Abdullah ibn al, II, 69, 267
Hussein, Saddam, 45, 98, 143, 147, 153
Hyderabad, 168
Hyung-kyu, Bae, 104

ibn Baaz, Abdel Aziz, 163, 166
Iliya, Itamar, 62–63
Imam's Disciples, 38
In-Amenas, 222, 229, 231, 281
India, 24, 115–117, 126–130, 132–136, 168, 173, 184, 240, 250, 274, 279–280, 282–283
 Kashmir, 22, 116–117, 126–129, 134–135
 National Security Guard (NSG), 132–134
 Naxalite-Maoist insurgency, 126
 Rapid Action Force, 132
 response to terrorism, 127
Indian Airlines, 117, 128
Indian Ocean, 235, 250
Indira Gandhi airport, 128
Indonesia, 104, 203, 248
Ingushetia, 254, 264, 267, 270–271
international, 5, 9, 32–33, 38, 54, 132, 147, 189, 225, 227, 231, 237, 244, 251
 community, 1, 9, 40, 74, 105, 116, 251, 278
 Court of Justice, 40
 diplomacy, 40, 97

forces, 102, 113, 248
incident, 18
law, 6, 17, 70, 106, 114, 158
media, 23
organizations, 8, 114, 158, 180, 194, 246
relations, 17, 40, 87, 101, 127, 157, 184, 209, 231
sanctions, 6, 9, 22, 235, 275
terrorism, 1, 4–5, 33, 37–40, 96, 204, 208, 270
trade, 132, 248, 251
zone, 17
International Committee of the Red Cross (ICRC), 61–63, 69–70, 189, 206, 211
International Federation of the Muslim *ulema*, 155, 157–159
International Maritime Bureau (IMB), 247
International Red Cross. *See* International Committee of the Red Cross
International Security Assistance Force (ISAF), 103, 110
Ipil, 202, 207, 212
Iran, 19, 33, 35–37, 39–43, 45–53, 62, 69, 71–72, 75–76, 81, 83–90, 92–98, 117, 125, 149, 152, 167–168, 179, 191–195, 197–198
  exiles, 34
  foreign policy, 34, 53, 77, 82, 95, 97
  Iraq policy, 44
  judiciary, 49–54
  leadership, 33–40, 44, 47, 49, 51–52, 54, 84, 90, 192
  Ministry of Intelligence and Security (MIS), 37
  moderates, 34–37, 89
  nuclear program, 47, 53
  president, 47–48, 52, 97
  prime minister, 38–39
  radicals, 35–37, 39, 89
  revolution, 38–39, 43, 53
  Revolutionary Guards (IRG), 39, 41, 43–47, 62, 191–192, 195
  shah (*see* Pehlavi, Reza)
  sponsor of terrorism, 19, 33–36, 38, 43, 45, 47, 53, 58, 80, 82, 90–91, 275
  Supreme Council for Intelligence Matters (SCIM), 37
Iran–Iraq war, 34, 41, 81, 87–88, 97
"Irangate" affair, 85–87, 90
Iraq, 28, 34, 43–44, 46–51, 81–82, 93, 95, 107, 142–148, 150–153, 155–160, 162, 166, 171, 179, 183, 214, 217, 219, 274
  Christians in, 152–153
  coalition forces, 31, 43–45, 49, 54, 142–143, 146–147, 153, 155, 157–159, 274
  "death triangle", 145
  government, 43, 45, 147–148
  insurgency, 31, 45, 53, 142–144, 162, 170, 229
  invasion of Kuwait, 97–98
  militants, 43, 142, 146, 153–157, 186
  military, 46
  prime minister, 151
  Provincial Joint Coordination Center (PJCC), 149
  security services, 146, 149–152
Irbil, 44
Ireland, 211
Irish Republican Army (IRA), 2
Islam, 26, 33, 35, 37–39, 48, 53, 72, 75, 78, 81, 102, 106, 114, 119, 121–122, 127, 133–134, 151, 154–159, 163, 167, 169, 180, 193, 202, 208–209, 214, 218–220, 223, 227, 236, 249–250, 255
  fatwa, 37, 164
  "Golden Age", 154
  Hadith, 78
  Mahdi, 144, 163–165, 169
  radicals, 39, 62, 115, 136, 154–155, 162, 179–180, 182, 184, 187, 195, 203, 209, 214, 220, 223–225, 227–228, 235–237, 240, 245, 250, 256, 272
  Ramadan, 50, 123
  revolution, 33, 38–39, 43, 47, 50, 53, 72
  sharia, 157–158, 182

Islam *(continued)*
  terror organizations, 8–9, 62, 74, 78, 83, 116, 121, 126, 130, 136, 142–144, 150–155, 170, 179, 185, 201, 208, 214–215, 217, 229, 235–236, 238–240, 244, 250–251, 263, 274, 276, 278, 281
  world, 21, 77, 168
Islamabad, 116–118, 124–125, 167
Islambouli, Khalid, 169
Islamic Army, 144, 180, 182–183
Islamic Army of Iraq, 144
Islamic Congregation, 201
Islamic Courts, 239, 250
Islamic Jihad. *See* Hizballah: Special Security Agency
Islamic Party. *See* Jamaat-e-Islami
Islamic revolution. *See* Islam: revolution. *See also* Iran: revolution
"Islamic State of Iraq", 150–152
Islamic Union. *See* al Itihaad al Islamiyah
Israel, 11, 19, 29, 36–38, 58–82, 84–86, 89–90, 96–98, 133–134, 147, 153, 168, 194, 274, 281
  air force (IAF), 58, 60, 65, 71
  Arabs, 70
  defense force (IDF), 58–60, 63–67, 69–71, 73, 76, 78–79, 91, 98
  General Security Service (GSS), 63
  government, 68–71, 80
  Ground Operations Command (GOC), 66,
  hostages, 58–60, 67, 75–78
  Israel–Arab conflict, 34–35
  navy, 60–62
  POWs, 59, 73, 77, 98
  president, 63
  prime minister, 63–64, 68, 79, 89
  release of prisoners, 62–63, 70, 76, 89–90, 96
Israr, Muhammad, 123–124
Istanbul, 256
Italy, 113, 147–148, 151, 173, 184, 193, 206, 211, 218–219, 224, 228
ITERATE Project, 5

Jaafari, Ibrahim al, 147
Jaar, 189
Jacobsen, David, 86–87
Jafari, Mohammed, 44
jail. *See* prison
Jaish al Mahdi. *See* Mahdi Army
Jaish-e-Mohammed, 22–23, 116
Jamaah Islamiyah (JI). *See* Islamic Congregation
Jamaat Ansar al Sunna. *See* Assembly of the Helpers of Sunna
Jamaat-e-Islami, 122. *See also* Hizb al Islam
Jamaat-ud-Dawa (JuD), 134. *See also* Lashkar-e-Taiba
Jamaat-ul-Fuqra, 115
James, Jon, 255
Jamla, 194
Jammu, 126–127, 134
Jammu Kashmir Liberation Front, 128
Jane's Intelligence Review, 179, 250
Janjalani, Abdurajik Abubakar and Khadaffy, 202
Janszen, Heleen, 184
Japan, 107, 184, 227
  Red Army, 25
Jeddah, 162–163
Jehovah's Witness, 211
Jenco, Lawrence Martin, 87
Jerusalem, 74
Jerusalem force. *See* Iran: Revolutionary Guards
Jesus. *See* Christian: Christ, Jesus
Jesus Miracle Crusade (JMC), 210
Jewish, 23, 70, 77–78, 115, 130, 133–134, 154, 169, 249, 281. *See also* Zionist
Ji-na, Kim, 104
Jibsheet, 72–73
jihad, 22, 25, 28, 31–32, 105, 121–122, 126, 134, 144–145, 153, 156–158, 162, 179–180, 186, 191, 198, 202, 214–217, 224–225, 228–229, 249–251
  Islamic Jihad (*see* Hizballah: Special Security Agency)
  global, 143, 180, 198, 249, 275
  maritime, 249
John Paul, II, 169

Johnson, Paul Marshall, Jr., 155, 170–171
Jolo, 204–205, 209–211
Jongman, Albert, 3
Jordan, 69, 144, 152, 170, 194, 208, 216–217, 267
José Maria Torres Memorial Hospital, 211
Jubeir, Adel al, 171
Judaism. *See* Jewish
Judeh, Nasser, 194
Juppé, Alain, 221

Kabardino-Balkaria, 257, 271
Kabouree, Philomen, 218–219
Kabul, 102–104, 106, 108, 110–113, 128
Kadyrov, Akhmed, 256
Kadyrov, Ramzan A., 257
Kahale, Famau, 239
Kaleva, Atte and Leila, 189
Kamel, Muhammad Mustafa, 182
Kamptner, Tomas, 95
Kandahar, 104, 110, 112–113, 129
Kapisa, 110–111
Karachi, 84, 115–117, 119–121, 130
Karbala, 149
   Provincial Joint Coordination Center (PJCC), 44, 149
Karim, Fazal, 117
Karrada, 150
Karzai, Hamid, 111, 113–114
Kasab, Mohammed Ajmal, 134–135
Kashmir. *See* India: Kashmir
Kathmandu, 128
Katsfi, Juad, 73
Katz, Yehuda, 98
Kayes, 219
Kenya, 180, 189, 235, 239–246
Kenyatta, Uhuru, 277, 280
Kerry, John, 123
Kesayev Report, 268
Kfar Kaser, 76
Kfar Kunin, 59
Kfar Suseh, 85
KGB. *See* USSR: Committee for State Security
Khadkhutcha, 115
Khalaf, Salah Mesbah, 83

Khalid ibn al Walid Brigades, 144
Khalidi, Abdullah al, 175–176
Khalil, Hussein, 69
Khamenei, Sayyid Ali, 54
Khan, Amjad Mohammed and Muhammad Ahmed, 119
Khan, Chaudhery, 137
Khan, Ismail, 130–131
Khan, Majid, 119
Khatami, Mohammad, 35
Khazali, Laith and Qais, 44–46, 149. *See also* League of the Righteous
Khobar, 171–172
Khodov, Vladimir, 272
Khomeini, Ruhollah, 35–43, 72, 81, 87, 92, 97, 167–168
Khrushchev, Nikita, 254
Khuchbarov, Ruslan Tagirovich, 271
Khurikau, 264
Khyber Pakhtunkhwa, 125
Khyber Pass, 114
kidnap. *See* abduction
Kismayo, 237, 240–241
Kiunga, 241
Kiwayu, 239
Kizlyar, 260–261
Kizlyar–Pervomayskoye, 259
Kochneva, Anhar, 193–194
Kololo, Ali Babitu, 239
Koran, 78, 154, 156–159, 169, 208–209. *See also* Islam
Korea, 155
   South, 103–104, 113, 153–154, 174, 184, 280
Kouchner, Bernard, 236–237
Kremlin. *See* Russia: Kremlin
Kuarkin, Yosef, 63
Khuchbarov, Ruslan Tagirovich, 265, 271
Kulayev, Nur-Pashi, 271–272
Kulikov, Anatoly, 260
Kunar, 121
Kunduz, 110
Kurdistan, 44
Kurdish, 37, 44, 49, 152, 155
Kuwait, 34, 38, 80, 84, 95, 97–98, 101, 168, 198

Lacaba, Mary Jane, 211

Laden, Osama bin, 21, 28–30, 32, 85, 105, 114, 124–125, 179–180, 182, 202, 214, 237, 249
Lahore, 117, 123–124, 128–130
Lamitan, 210–211
Lamu, 239–240, 244, 246
Larnaca, 84
Larribe, Daniel, 221
Larribe, Françoise, 220
Larussi, Osman, 270
Lashkar-e-Jhangvi, 117
Lashkar-e-Taiba. *See* Pakistan: Lashkar-e-Taiba
Latakia, 193
League of the Righteous, 44–46
Lebanon, 33–35, 37–38, 46, 58–80, 82–83, 85, 87, 89–92, 94–98, 107, 195–198, 272. *See also* Hizballah. *See also* United Nations: Interim Force In Lebanon (UNIFIL)
  first Lebanon war, 72, 83, 98
  government, 63, 66, 68–70, 196–197
  hostages, 19, 38, 80–81, 85, 87–88, 92–97, 111, 197
  second Lebanon war, 70, 74
  South Lebanese Army (SLA), 59–60, 96
Leggett, Christopher Ervin, 217
Legrand, Pierre, 221
Lehrner, Carl, 181
Lenku, Joseph Ole, 279
Leocour, Antoine de, 221
Leopold café, 130
Lewthwaite, Samantha, 280–281
Libi, Abu Yahya al, 120–121
Libya, 89, 168, 202, 204, 216, 223, 225, 229, 282
Lima, 25
Limburg, 251
Lions of al Tawhid, 196
Livni, Tzipi, 69
Logar, 108–110
  Joint Coordination Center (LJCC), 109
London, 47, 155, 182, 270, 280
Loralai, 117–118
Lunsmann, Gerfa Yeatts, 212
Lupah Sug, 209. *See also* Sulu

Luttwak, Edward, 6–7
Luzon, 201

Maadushiya, 61
Maareb, 181
Macapagal-Arroyo, Gloria, 204–205, 210–211
MacLachlan, Alec, 46
Madagascar, 30, 219–220
Madobe, Ahmed, 240
Maghreb. *See* Africa: Maghreb
Maharashtra, 115, 135
Mahdi. *See* Islam: Mahdi
Mahdi Army, 144
"Major Iqbal". *See* Khan, Chaudhery
Makrum, Rashid, 95
Malaysia, 202, 204–205, 209–210
Maleh, Haitham al, 192
Mali, 215–219, 221–231, 238, 274, 282
Malik, Rehman, 123, 125
Malik, Ustadz Habier, 209
Maliki, Nouri al, 151
Manasseh, 188
Manba al Jihad, 107
Manda, 243, 245
Mandera, 235
Manila, 203, 205–206, 208
Manila Times, 209–210. *See also* Romero, Reghis, II
Mansoora, 122
Mansour, 152
Maqdisi, Abu Mohammed al. *See* Barqawi, Isam Mohammad Tahir al
Marib, 184, 188
Markowitz, David, 65
Martyrs of Yarmouk, 194
Mashhad, 84, 197
"Masked Brigade". *See* al Mulathameen
Maskhadov, Aslan, 255, 262, 267, 270
Masri, Abu Hamza al, 182–183
Masri, Abu Walid al, 28–29
Mastrogiacomo, Daniele, 113
Maupin, Keith "Matt", 148
Mauritania, 215–219, 225, 228–231
Mazgaon, 130
McCain, John, 124
McMenemy, Alan, 46

McNeley, Justin, 108–109
Mecca, 21, 162–163, 166–169, 274
Meckfessel, Shon, 49
Médecins Sans Frontières (MSF), 245
Medina, 163, 256
Mediterranean, 229
Mehmanparast, Ramin, 46
Ménaka, 218
Mercy International Relief Agency, 119
metro, 257
Metro cinema, 130
Metulla, 65–66
Miami, 115
Middle East, 36, 54, 70, 175, 196, 203, 270
Mihdhar, Khalid al, 180
Mikonos. *See* Germany: Mikonos restaurant
Mindanao, 201–203, 206, 208, 211, 276
Miqdad, Hassan Salim al and Hatem al, 197–198
Mir-Gholikhan, Shahrzad, 51
missionary, 104, 205, 211, 255
Misuari, Nur, 276
Mitterand, François, 82, 226
Model Town, 123
Mofaz, Shaul, 69
Mogadishu, 236–237, 240–241, 246
Mohammed, Khalid Sheikh, 29, 117, 120
Mohamud, Hassan Sheikh, 280
Mohtashami-Pour, Ali Akbar, 72, 74
Mokhefi, Mansouria, 227
Mondale, Walter F., 42
Moore, Peter, 44–46
Moro Islamic Liberation Front (MILF), 201–203, 211, 276
Moro National Liberation Front (MNLF), 201–203, 209, 276–277
Moscow, 11, 23, 255–257, 262–263, 266, 269, 271
mosque, 119, 158, 162–167, 260, 270, 274
Mottaki, Manouchehr, 46
Mount Dov, 58, 64–66. *See also* Shebaa Farms
Mount Hermon, 64

Muaskar Ras Kamboni. *See* Ras Kamboni Brigade
Mubarak, Hosni, 69
Muhammad, Prophet. *See* Prophet Muhammad
Muhammad's Army. *See* Jaish-e-Mohammed
Muhsini, Ghulam Mustafa, 110
Mujahid, Zabihullah, 106–107, 109
mujahideen, 22–23, 25, 28, 106, 112, 126, 151–152, 170, 216, 218, 220–221, 249, 271, 280
Mujahideen-e-Khalq, 92
Mukhajar, Muhammad, 93
Mukherjee, Pranab, 135
Mullen, Mike, 109
Mumbai, 115, 129–136, 281–282
Muqrin, Abdul Aziz al, 22, 170–171
Muraniya, Imad Fayez (son of M), 38, 83–85, 89, 98
Muraniya, Jihad (son of M), 83
Muraniya, Muhammad (father of I and J), 83
Murshi, Ustadz Ibrahim, 209
Musawi, Abbas al, 59, 76, 83–84
Musawi, Hassan, 84
Musawi, Hussein, 75, 81, 95
Muscat, 128
Musharraf, Pervez, 116, 134
Muslim. *See* Islam
Muslim Brotherhood (MB), 163
Muttahida Qaumi Mahaz, 121
Muttahida Qaumi Movement. *See* Muttahida Qaumi Mahaz
Muzaffarabad, 129

Nairobi, 119, 239–240, 242, 246, 277–278, 280–282
Najadi, Abu Ammar al, 152
Najaf, 147, 149
Najd, 162–163
Nakash, Anis, 93
Nalchik, 257
Nariman House, 130–131, 133
Nashiri, Abdel Rahim al, 248
Nasr Aflou, 228
Nasrallah, Hadi (son of Hassan), 63, 78
Nasrallah, Hassan (father of Hadi), 63–69, 78, 83, 85, 192, 197

Nasser, Gamal Abdel, 163, 166
Nasser, Nassim, 67
National Movement for the Land of the Two Rivers. *See* al Qaeda: of Jihad in the Land of Two Rivers
National Movement for the Restoration of Pakistani Sovereignty, 116
NATO. *See* North Atlantic Treaty Organization
Naxalite-Maoist. *See* India: Naxalite-Maoist insurgency
NBC News, 52, 195. *See also* Engel, Richard
Nepal, 24, 128, 144, 155
Netanyahu, Binyamin, 63, 79, 95
New Delhi, 134
New Peoples Army (NPA), 201. *See also* Communist Party of the Philippines
New York, 39, 52, 54
New York Times, 110, 167
Newlove, Jarod, 108–110
Niamey, 221, 230
Niger, 30, 216–217, 219–221, 224–225, 228–231, 238
Nigeria, 28, 216, 221–222
9/11, 1, 7, 21–22, 29, 120, 129, 132, 134, 180, 183, 240, 256, 263
Nir, Amiram, 89
Nobel Prize for Peace, 91
Norgrove, Linda, 121
North, Oliver, 89
North Atlantic Treaty Organization (NATO), 107–110, 113
North Ossetia-Alania, 11, 264, 266, 268–272
North Waziristan. *See* Waziristan: North
Northwest Frontier, 130
Notter, Andreas, 211
Nouakchott, 217
nuclear, 47, 53, 135, 219–221. *See also* uranium
Nur, Mohammed Ali, 241

Obama, Barack, 29, 44, 50, 52–54, 204
Obeid, Abdel Karim, 71–78, 82, 91, 97
Obeidi, Abdul Qader al, 150
Oberoi Trident hotel, 130, 132
Och, Olivier David, 117
Olmert, Ehud, 68
Oman, 50–52, 128, 167, 183, 186, 188–189, 247
Omar, Mohammed, 249
Omar, Mullah. *See* Omar, Mohammed
operations
 "Black Tornado", 134
 "Change Direction", 69 (*see also* "Fair Pay")
 "Eagle Claw", 40
 "Electric Pipe", 60
 "Fair Pay", 68–69 (*see also* "Change Direction")
 "Freedom for Samir al Quntar", 67
 "Poplar's Whistle", 62
 "Purging for Peace", 209
 "Truthful Promise", 67
Oppressed on Earth, 74–75, 91
Oreña-Drilon, Ces, 211
Osani, Ivy, 205
Osman, Mohammad, 121
Osoud al Tawhid. *See* Lions of al Tawhid
Otaibi, Juhayman ibn Muhamad Sayf al, 162–166, 169
Othman, Omar Mahmoud, 217,

Pagadian, 207, 211
Pakistan, 22, 28, 103, 105, 107, 110, 113–126, 128–134, 136–137, 155, 165–168, 274, 282
 Inter-Services Intelligence (ISI), 115, 117, 120, 126, 130, 135–136
 Lashkar-e-Taiba (LeT), 130, 134–136
 Taliban (TTP), 117–118, 121, 125, 281
 tribal areas, 21
Paktika, 105
Palace of Culture. *See* Dubrovka theater
Palawan, 205, 210, 276
Palestine, 12, 29, 35–36, 64, 70, 74–78, 81–83, 152, 169, 179, 193, 214. *See also* Fatah. *See also* Hamas

Palestine Liberation Front (PLF), 70.
  See also Popular Front for the
  Liberation of Palestine
Palestine Liberation Organization
  (PLO), 83
Pan Am, 168
Pandanan, 204, 210
Para, Abderrazak al. See Saifi, Amari
Parad, Albader, 206
Paris, 85, 92, 111, 115, 230
Party of God. See Hizballah
Pascual, Roque, 218
Pashtun, 21, 118
Patikul, 206, 209
Patterson, Anne, 122
Pearl, Daniel, 23, 115–117, 155
Pehlavi, Reza, 38–41, 51, 53, 92–93
Pentagon, 21, 224, 226
People's Mujahideen of Iran. See
  Mujahideen-e-Khalq
Peres, Shimon, 69
Peretz, Amir, 68–69
Peri, Yaakov, 63
Persia, 152
Persian Gulf, 46–47, 166–167, 169
Peru, 25, 205
Peshawar, 103, 124
Petraeus, David, 45
Philippines, 22, 28, 146, 167, 184,
  194, 201–212, 274, 276–277
pilgrim, 21, 151, 164–165, 169, 192,
  197
piracy, 235, 239–242, 244–251
PLO. See Palestine Liberation
  Organization
Poland, 125
pope, 72, 151–152, 169. See also
  Vatican
Popular Front for the Liberation of
  Palestine, 11
prison, 46, 51–54, 62–64, 67, 72, 90,
  94, 98, 104, 106, 112–113, 116,
  121–122, 136, 145, 163, 171,
  174, 185, 206, 223, 272, 274
  escape from, 112–113, 169
prisoner, 28–30, 38, 50–51, 53,
  60–63, 67–68, 70–73, 75–78,
  80–82, 89–90, 94–96, 98,
  104–108, 112–114, 120,
  122–123, 126, 129, 143, 145,
  150, 152, 163–164, 166, 170,
  174–175, 180, 184, 192–193,
  195, 216, 218–219, 223, 236,
  247, 254, 257, 259, 282
  exchange, 10, 28, 51, 59, 62–64,
    67, 73, 77, 90, 106, 113, 119,
    129, 191, 193, 195, 218
  Islamic treatment of, 78, 156, 159
  prisoner of war (POW), 17, 59, 98
Prophet Muhammad, 75, 136, 154,
  156, 158, 192
Prouteau, Christian, 226
Psedakh, 264
Puerto Princesa, 205
Pune, 135
Punjab, 117, 125
Putin, Vladimir, 255–256, 262–263,
  266–270

Qadeer, Mohammad Hashim, 117
Qahtani, Muhammad bin Abdallah al,
  163, 165. See also Islam: Mahdi
Qaradawi, Yusuf al, 155–157, 159
Qasser Shiereen, 45
Qassir, Hayla al, 29, 174
Qatar, 108, 188, 192–193, 198, 220
Qatin, Raphael, 150
Qom, 51, 72
Quetta, 115, 117, 125
Quntar, Samir al, 67–70
Qutb, Muhammad and Sayyid, 163

Raad, Razah, 92
Rabin, Yitzhak, 73, 78
Raduyev, Salman, 260–261
Rafsanjani, Ali Akbar Hashemi, 35, 90,
  97
Rage, Ali Mahmoud, 238, 279
Raja Sansi airport, 128
Rajah Sulaiman Islamic Movement
  (RSIM), 201
Rajar, 65–66
Rajavi, Massoud, 92
Rana, Tahawwur, 136
RAND Corporation, 5
Ras Kamboni, 241
Ras Kamboni Brigade, 240–241
Ras Kitau, 243
Raz, Tubi, 63
Reagan, Ronald, 41–42, 53, 89

Red Cross. *See* International Committee of the Red Cross
Red Sea, 247
Reed, Frank, 88
Regev, Eldad, 59, 67, 70
Rehman, Wali-ur-, 118
Reid, Richard, 115
Reiss, Clotilde, 53
republic, 33, 38, 48, 58, 102, 114, 126, 134, 142, 179, 191, 196, 201, 221, 235, 239, 254–255, 257, 260, 267, 272
Repubblika, La, 147–148
Republican, 2, 41–42, 166
reward, 7, 23, 105, 109, 206, 230
Riyadh, 85, 162–163, 170–171, 174–175, 188
Riyadus-Salikhin Reconnaissance and Sabotage Battalion, 264, 269
rocket, 43, 60, 65–66, 68, 70–71, 182, 187, 260, 264, 277
rocket-propelled, 60, 113, 172, 248
Rodwell, Warren Richard, 207–208
Rohde, David, 110
Roman, 152, 155
Rome, 84, 89, 94, 147, 151, 219
Romero, Reghis, II, 210–211
Roshal, Leonid, 270
Rushdie, Salman, 35, 37
Russia, 23, 61, 191–194, 215, 250, 254–261, 264–272, 274, 281. *See also* USSR
   Duma, 258–259
   Federal Security Service (FSB), 258, 260, 266
   forces, 255–258, 260–270
   first Russian–Chechen war, 257, 259
   government, 193, 257–259, 262–263, 266, 268–271
   Kremlin, 256–257, 259, 264, 269
   Ministry of Internal Affairs (MVD), 258, 266
   premier, 254–255, 258
   president, 255, 258, 264
   Special Purpose Mobile Unit (OMON), 266

Saada, 174, 184

Sabah, 210, 276
Sabah, Jaber al, 84
Saberi, Roxana, 53
Sabieh, Wasim, 150
Sadat, Anwar, 169
Sadr, Mohammed Sadeq al (father of Muqtada), 44–45
Sadr, Mousa al, 89
Sadr, Muqtada al (son of MS), 44–45, 144
"Sadr Brigades", 89
Sadr City. *See* Baghdad: Sadr City
Sadr movement, 44
Sadulayev, Abdul Halim, 269
Saemmul Presbyterian Church, 104
Sahara, 215–216, 222, 224, 229–230. *See also* Africa: Sahel
Sahel. *See* Africa: Sahel
Sahhaf, Yehye, 68
Sahraoui, Nabil, 214
Said, Qaboos bin, 186, 189
Saifi, Amari, 215–216
Saint Paul, 155
Saint Peter's Church, 211
Saint Peter's Square, 151, 169
Saint Petersburg, 269
Saint Thomas, 152
Saint Xavier's college, 130
Saitoti, George, 246
Sakalahul, al Rasheed, 208
Salafi, 163, 214, 228. *See also* Suna
Salafist Group for Preaching and Combat (GSPC), 214–215, 238. *See also* al Qaeda: in the Islamic Maghreb
Saleh, Ali Abdullah, 181, 183, 185, 187–188
Saleh, Amrullah, 102
Salehi, Ali Akbar, 50, 193
Salim, Hasan, 152
Samal Island, 210
Samoha, Shahar, 153
Sana'a, 174, 180–181, 184–185, 188
sanctions. *See* economic: sanctions
Sangay, 209
Sarkozy, Nicolas, 30, 111, 218, 220–222, 230, 236–238
Sarposa, 112–113
SAS. *See* United Kingdom: Special Air Service

Saud, Abdullah bin Abdulaziz bin, 170–171, 175
Saud, Sultan bin Abdulaziz al, 165
Saudi Arabia, 21–22, 28–29, 85, 91–92, 154–155, 162–172, 174–176, 179–180, 186, 188, 198, 202, 215, 217, 256, 270, 274
    Administration for Scientific Research and Legal Rulings, 166
    Council of Senior Scholars, 166
    government, 69, 162–166, 169–171, 173–175
    Grand Mufti, 166
    National Guard, 163–166, 170–171, 173, 175
    oil industry, 171
    royal family, 29, 164–166, 170–171, 174–175, 179
Sayeed, Mufti Mohammad and Rubaiya, 128
Sayun, 185–186
SBS. *See* United Kingdom: Special Boat Service
Schilling, Jeffrey, 205, 210
Schmid, Alex, 3
Schmidt, Alfred, 94–95
School Number One, 264–265. *See also* Beslan
second Lebanon war. *See* Lebanon: second Lebanon war
sectarianism, 191
security zone, 60, 73
Seeb airport, 128
Seif, Mahmoud, 51
Sellal, Abdelmalek, 222, 225
Seong-min, Shim, 104
Serbia, 154
Serra, Monserrat, 245
Sgrena, Giuliana, 147–148
Shabwah, 184
Shadaa, 174
Shafii, Masoud, 50
Shah of Iran. *See* Pehlavi, Reza
Shalit, Gilad, 67, 69
sharia. *See* Islam: sharia
Sharif, Ihab al, 147
Sharif, Nawaz, 122
Shatt al Arab, 46

Shebaa Farms, 67
Shebam, 185
Shehri, Saeed al, 29, 174
Sheikh, Ahmed Omar Saeed, 116–117, 129
Shia, 34, 36, 43–44, 54, 61, 73, 76–77, 79–81, 83–84, 89–90, 94–96, 98, 142, 149, 167, 192, 197–198
    in Iraq, 45, 144, 149
    in Lebanon, 61, 73, 89–90, 92, 197–198
    in Saudi Arabia, 166, 174
    Valiat Fakia, 37
Shihri, Said Ali Jabir al Khathim al, 249
Shiite. *See* Shia
Shiraz, 53
"shoe bomber". *See* Reid, Richard
Shourd, Sarah, 49–51
Shueiba, 84
"Shurat al Jihad". *See* Hizballah: "Shurat al Jihad"
Siddiqui, Aafia (sister of F), 118–123, 125–126, 223
Siddiqui, Fauzia (sister of A), 120
Sindh, 125
Singapore, 136
Singh, V. P., 131
Siniora, Fouad, 69
Sipadan, 204–205, 209–210
Site Intelligence Group, 106
Sitio Arco, 211
SLA. *See* Lebanon: South Lebanon Army
sniper, 24, 43, 66, 164–165, 197, 223, 277
Snor, Dan, 146
Sobero, Guillermo, 205–206
Solecki, John, 115, 125
Soleimani, Qasem, 43
Somali Islamic Courts. *See* Islamic Courts
Somalia, 28, 31, 107, 214, 235–251, 277–280, 282. *See also* al Qaeda: in Somalia
South Africa, 2, 210, 247, 280
South Korea. *See* Korea: South
South Lebanon Army. *See* Lebanon: South Lebanon Army

South Waziristan. *See* Waziristan: South
Sovetskoye, 261
Soviet Union. *See* USSR
Spain, 154, 201, 218, 224, 228, 245
Special Security Agency. *See* Hizballah: Special Security Agency
Spindelegger, Michael, 189
Stalin, Joseph, 254, 269
Status of Forces Agreement, 46
Stavropol Krai, 257, 259
Stepashin, Sergei, 259
Student Movement of Pakistan. *See* Pakistan: Taliban
Stumpp, Rita, 174
Sturbig, Heinrich, 95
Sudan, 166, 239
Sued, Omar, 58, 64
suicide attack, 36, 84, 227, 248, 251, 263, 274, 281
suicide bomber, 36, 38, 112, 135, 150, 162, 229, 256–257, 263, 280
Sultan, Prince. *See* Saud, Sultan bin Abdelaziz al
Sulu, 201, 203–204, 206, 208, 276
Sulu Sea, 206
Sum-il, Kim, 153–154
Suna, 77, 117, 142, 145, 149, 209, 214
Sunni. *See* Suna
Supporters of Sharia Law, 182
Suri, Abu Musab al, 248
Swahili, 277
Swindlehurst, Jason, 46
Switzerland, 36, 50–51, 94, 117–118, 125, 188–189, 206, 211, 215–217, 224
Syria, 36, 48, 54, 59, 61, 64, 69–70, 85–86, 90, 95, 97, 144, 152, 184, 191–199, 202, 216. *See also* Free Syrian Army
  National Coalition for Syrian Revolutionary and Opposition Forces, 191
  Syrian National Council (SNC), 196–197

Taghavi, Reza, 53

Taj Mahal Palace & Tower hotel, 130–132, 134
Talaat, Hussein, 94
Talaia al Salafiya, 228
Talania, Randelle, 212
Taliban. *See* Pakistan: Taliban
Taluqan, 110
Tamanrasset, 230
Tannenbaum, Elhanan, 59, 76
Tanzania, 180
Tanzim Qa'idat al Jihad fi Bilal al Rafidayn. *See* al Qaeda: of Jihad in the Land of the Two Rivers
Taponier, Stéphane, 110–111
Tariq ibn Ziyad Brigade (TIZB), 228
Tatarstan, 255, 271
Tawhid wal Jihad, al, 144–145
Tawi-Tawi. *See* Cagayan de Tawi-Tawi
Tayeb, Ahmed al, 209
Tebbutt, David and Judith, 239–242
Tehran, 38–42, 44, 47–48, 50–53, 84, 92, 167, 191–192
Tehrik-i-Taliban. *See* Pakistan: Taliban
terror, 2–4, 6–9, 12–19, 30–34, 36–37, 44, 60, 63, 65–67, 70, 73, 75, 77–82, 84–85, 90, 92–95, 98, 105, 107, 114–116, 121, 126–129, 131, 134–136, 142–146, 148, 150–155, 162, 170–175, 179–180, 182–183, 188, 201, 203–204, 208–209, 214, 216–218, 221–223, 227–231, 235–240, 244–245, 247, 249–251, 256–267, 269–272, 274–275, 277–283
  defining, 1–4, 15, 17, 75, 275
  analytical definition, 1, 3
  counter-terror, 23, 28, 89, 122, 127, 131, 180, 203, 220, 238, 250, 272, 283
  finance, 21, 31, 114, 148, 230
  goals of, 2, 4–5, 10, 34, 77, 80, 83, 127, 142, 155, 274–275, 281
  international, 1, 4–5, 8, 34, 37–38, 96, 127, 180, 223, 249
  normative definition, 1–3
  state-supported, 1, 4–6, 17–19, 33, 35, 37, 41, 43, 80, 85, 88, 90, 96, 158, 179–180, 275
  targets of, 3–4, 18, 36, 38, 80, 152

techniques, 2, 8, 10–11, 31, 34, 80, 155, 247, 263, 274, 281–282
theoretical model, 8, 281
training manuals, 22, 28
war on, 1, 28–29, 31, 87–89, 126, 134, 180, 183, 203, 227, 230, 238, 250, 256, 280
Thani, Hamad bin Jassim bin Jabr al, 192
Thiebaut, Blanca, 245
Tigantourine. *See* In-Amenas
Tigris River, 152
Tilao, Aldam, 203, 210–211
Tillabéri, 217
Titay, 212
Togo, 30, 219–220
torture, 15, 17, 29, 86, 111, 115, 120, 143, 145, 170–171, 191, 195, 198
Touré, Amadou Toumani, 218
Toure, Paul, 92
tourist, 24, 182–183, 186–187, 204, 215, 224, 243–244, 246, 256, 281
   western, 48–49, 117, 125, 181, 183–184, 205, 209, 215, 217, 229, 239
   eastern, 184, 217
   industry, 31, 187, 215, 245, 281
Tower Committee, 87–88, 96
Tracey, Edward, 88
Trans World Airlines (TWA), 84–85, 89–90, 94, 96
Triangle Génération Humanitaire, 185
Tribhuvan airport, 128
Trustee Council of the International Federation of the Muslim *ulema*, 155, 157–159. See also *ulema*
TTP. *See* Pakistan: Taliban
Tuareg, 216–217, 228
Tuburan, 210
Tufeili, Subhi, 83
Tunisia, 216, 225, 228–229
Tuomioja, Erkki, 189
Turkey, 144, 152, 168–169, 192–193, 198, 261
Turki, Hassan, 240
Turney, Faye, 48
Tyre, 83, 90

Uganda, 237
Ukraine, 193–194
ulema, 29, 164, 174. *See also* Trustee Council of the International Federation of the Muslim *ulema*
Ullah, Roland, 205, 210
Union of Soviet Socialist Republics. *See* USSR
United Arab Emirates (UAE), 128
"United Federated States of Bangsamoro Republik", 276
United Kingdom (UK), 2, 35, 44–48, 87, 93–94, 110, 116, 119–121, 134, 145–146, 155, 173, 179, 182–185, 212, 217–218, 223–224, 226–228, 230, 239–243, 246, 255, 270, 274, 279–280
   Foreign Affairs Select Committee, 48
   Ministry of Defence (MoD), 48
   Royal Navy, 46, 241
   Special Air Service (SAS), 241
   Special Boat Service (SBS), 242
United Nations (UN), 25, 53–54, 66, 74, 91, 97–98, 115, 129, 157, 184, 194, 198, 215, 240, 245–246
   Disengagement Observer Force (UNDOF), 194
   General Assembly, 52, 54, 231
   High Commission for Refugees (UNHCR), 115, 125
   Interim Force In Lebanon (UNIFIL), 69–70, 90–91
   resolutions, 40, 47, 69, 71
   Security Council, 40, 47, 69, 71, 194, 250, 266
   special envoy, 81, 216, 280
United States (US), 1, 4, 21, 28–32, 38–48, 50–54, 74–75, 80–91, 93–94, 96–98, 106–108, 110, 115–116, 118–126, 134, 136–137, 142, 146–149, 152, 157, 159–160, 165, 167–170, 174, 180, 182–183, 194, 201, 203–206, 209–210, 215–216, 223, 225–226, 230, 236, 240, 247–248, 250–251, 256, 274, 278–279

United States *(continued)*
  administration, 33, 38–39, 43, 53, 82, 84, 86, 88–89, 98, 107, 109, 118, 120–123, 126, 146, 167, 170, 180, 203–205, 226, 230, 279
  ambassador *(see* ambassador: US)
  congress, 41, 86, 122, 124
  embassies, 46, 84, 94, 119, 122, 124, 162, 167–168, 174, 180, 205 *(see also* Tehran: American embassy in)
  hostages, 28, 38, 42, 48–54, 74–75, 80–81, 85–89, 91, 93–94, 96, 105–110, 115–116, 121–125, 136, 146, 149, 155, 159, 167, 170, 182, 205–206, 210–212, 217, 225, 255, 279
  military, 22, 31, 43–46, 49–50, 54, 75, 84, 89, 105–107, 110, 120–121, 142, 145, 148–150, 157, 159, 165, 167, 173, 175, 201–203, 225–226, 250, 282
  president, 1, 29, 33, 39–42, 44, 50, 52–54, 89, 167–169, 204, 256, 266
  senate, 123–124
uranium, 220. *See also* nuclear
USS *Cole*, 171, 180, 248, 251
USSR, 87, 97, 168–169, 179, 202, 216, 254–255, 267, 272
  Committee for State Security (KGB), 272
Ustinov, Dmitriy, 168

Vagni, Eugenio, 211
Valiat Fakia. *See* Shia: *Valiat Fakia*
Vance, Cyrus R., 41, 168
Vatican, 72, 151–152. *See also* pope
Velayati, Ali Akbar, 74
Verbruggen, Patrick, 186
video, 22, 31, 46, 48, 85, 91, 105–107, 111, 119, 124, 142, 144–148, 153–154, 170–171, 175, 191–194, 196–197, 207, 214, 220–221, 236–237, 255, 267
Vietnam, 106–107
Vilalta, Albert, 218

Visayas, 201
Vladikavkaz, 269
Wachsman, Nachshon, 75, 77
Wahhabi, 163, 166. *See also* Islam
Waite, Terry, 91, 97
Wall Street Journal, 115–116. *See also* Pearl, Daniel
Washington, 46, 50–53, 106, 116, 125, 134, 167–168, 171, 201, 203–204, 206. *See also* United States
Waziristan
  North, 119
  South, 21, 118
Weinstein, Warren, 123–124
Weir, Benjamin, 87
Weizmann, Ezer, 63
Werley, Eric, 94
western, 21, 31, 37–38, 79, 82, 85, 95, 97–98, 127, 136, 153–154, 162, 179, 182, 195–196, 228, 230–231, 235, 246, 248, 251, 282
  anti-, 215
  countries, 28, 31, 81–82, 84, 88, 96–97, 144, 215, 226–227, 230, 278
  culture, 35
  democracy, 1, 35, 82
  government, 98, 227, 270
  hostages, 19, 21, 28, 31–32, 38, 59, 81, 84–85, 87, 94–98, 103, 116–117, 174, 180, 187–188, 203, 209, 224, 242, 275
  imperialism, 81
  security services, 162, 250, 280
  world, 1, 118, 155
Westerwelle, Guido, 185
Westgate mall, 277–278, 280–282
Wetangula, Moses, 244
White House, 29, 43, 106. *See also* United States
Widmer, Daniela, 117
Wilkinson, Paul, 5
Winograd Commission, 70
World Trade Center, 21, 204–205
World War II, 82, 134, 254

Yap, Ediborah, 206
Yassin, Ahmad, 77

Yeltsin, Boris, 255, 258–259, 261
Yemen, 29, 69, 166, 174–175,
    179–189, 247, 249, 251, 274
  abductions in, 23, 28, 173, 181,
    183–186, 188
  government, 174, 179–181,
    183–188
  North, 179
  South, 166, 179
Yerin, Viktor, 259
Yildirim, Bülent, 193
Young-sun, Eom, 174
Yousef, Ramzi, 204–205
Yousuf Khiel, 110
Yunis, Awaz, 98

Zadran, Sangreen, 107
Zakayev, Akhmed, 270
Zamboanga City, 211–212, 276–277
Zamboanga Sibugay, 207
Zandak, 258
Zargar, Mushtaq Ahmed, 129
Zarit, 59, 64, 67
Zarqawi, Abu Musab al, 144–147,
    154, 170
Zawahiri, Ayman al, 121, 214, 249,
    282
Zawi, Hamid Dawud Mohamed Khalil
    al. *See* Baghdadi, Abu Omar al
    Qurashi al
Zaynab, Sayyidah, 192
Zeeiter, 198
Zhob, 118
Zindani, Abdul Majid al, 180
Zionist, 74, 82, 85, 159, 172. *See also*
    Jewish
Zurich, 94
Zyazikov, Murat, 270